PERL
P O W E R !

The Comprehensive Guide

John P. Flynt, Ph.D.

THOMSON

COURSE TECHNOLOGY

Professional ■ Technical ■ Reference

ISBN: 1-59863-161-6

Library of Congress Catalog Card Number: 2006920362

Printed in the United States of America

06 07 08 09 10 PH 10 9 8 7 6 5 4 3 2 1

THOMSON

COURSE TECHNOLOGY

Professional ■ Technical ■ Reference

Thomson Course Technology PTR, a division of Thomson Learning Inc.
25 Thomson Place
Boston, MA 02210
http://www.courseptr.com

Publisher and General Manager, Thomson Course Technology PTR:
Stacy L. Hiquet

Associate Director of Marketing:
Sarah O'Donnell

Manager of Editorial Services:
Heather Talbot

Marketing Manager:
Mark Hughes

Senior Acquisitions Editor:
Todd Jensen

Marketing Coordinator:
Jordan Casey

Project Editor:
Jenny Davidson

Technical Reviewer:
Robert Johnson

PTR Editorial Services Coordinator:
Elizabeth Furbish

Interior Layout Tech:
Digital Publishing Solutions

Cover Designer:
Mike Tanamachi

Indexer:
Kelly D. Henthorne

Proofreader:
Gene Redding

This book is dedicated to its readers.

} Acknowledgments

Thanks to Adrian Flynt, who developed some of the art for the book. To Brent Jones for being a helpful friend. To Rob Johnson for reading the manuscript for its technical content. To Stacy Hiquet for the referral. To Todd Jensen for making the writing of the book possible. To Jenny Davidson for watching over the schedule and making it happen. To Emi Smith for allowing me to work on books simultaneously. To Kevin Claver for perspectives.

As always, thank you Marcia for your faith, trust, guidance, and support. Amy, thank you for everything.

} About the Author

John P. Flynt, Ph.D., works in the software development industry, has taught at colleges and universities, and has authored courses and curricula for several college-level game development programs. His academic background includes work in information technology, the social sciences, and the humanities. Among his works are *In the Mind of a Game, Simulation and Event Modeling for Game Developers* (with co-author Ben Vinson), and *Software Engineering for Game Developers*. John lives in the foothills near Boulder, Colorado.

TABLE OF } Contents

CHAPTER 1   Perl Basics 1

    Having Fun 1

    Power and Perl 2

    The Community 4

    The Other End of the Galaxy 5

    Derivations 5

    Getting It 6

    Perl Scalars, Arrays, Hashes, Handles 8

    Source Books 9

CHAPTER 2   Getting Started 11

    Accessing and Installing Perl 11

        First Time Installation 14

        Testing Your ActivePerl Installation 16

        Perl Files 18

    Getting Started with an Editor 20

    Obtaining the DzSoft Perl Editor 22

    First View of the Perl Editor 25

        HTML Output 26

        Text Output and the DOS Window 27

        Saving Files 28

    Conclusion 29

CHAPTER 3   Scalars and Strings 31

    Preliminary Work 31

The print( ) Function 32

Fundamental Programming Syntax 34

Scalars and Strings 39

Making Scalars 40

Scalars as Stored and Printed 43

Strings and More Strings 44

Concatenation and Printing Scalars 45

Multiplying String Output 47

Relational Operators for Strings 48

Evaluating Relationships 49

Testing with Scalars 50

Increment Operations on Strings 53

The q( ) and qq( ) Functions 54

Blocks 55

Blocks and print 55

Blocks and Variables 56

Conclusion 57

CHAPTER 4   Print Functions 59

How Functions Work 59

Basic Call and Return Operations 59

Variations on Call and Return 60

Changing the Cases of Strings 62

Case with First Characters 62

Case with Entire Strings 63

Obtaining the Length of a String 64

Hidden Characters and Strings 65

Hidden Characters in Strings 66

Eliminating Characters 68

Command Line Interactions 72

Indexes of Characters 74

An Algorithm for Searching 75

Implementing the Algorithm 76

Searching from the End of a String 78

Extracting and Replacing Strings 79

Extracting Substrings with substr( ) 79

Simplifying Extraction and Replacement 82

Joining Strings 84

Using Manual Concatenation 85

Using the join( ) Function to Concatenate Strings ... 86

Creating the Notification with the join( ) Function 87

Variations with Joining 89

Replacing Join with a Block 91

Conclusion 93

CHAPTER 5   Scalars and Formatting 95

Scalars, Functions, and Numbers 95

Defined and Undefined Scalars 97

Operations with Numbers 100

Numbers and Built-In Functions 102

Standard Presentation Using the print( ) Function 103

Random Numbers and Integers 105

Rational Operations 107

Using printf( ) 109

Conversion Specifiers 110

Conversion from Strings and Space 113

Formatting and Precision 113

Controlling Precision 114

Creating a Table 115

Variations 117

Using sprintf( ) 121

Reworking the Table 122

Conclusion 126

CHAPTER 6   Array Fundamentals 127

Basics of Arrays 127

    Adding Elements 128

    Problems with Initialization 132

Concatenation and Iteration 135

Accessing Elements in Arrays 138

More on Implicit Assignment 140

Array Slicing 141

Swapping 142

Using qw( ) to Populate Arrays 143

Splicing 144

    Basic Splice 144

    Splice with a Range or a Selected Set 146

    Remove a Range of Elements 148

    Remove Elements to the End of the Array 149

    Inserting with No Deletions 150

Conclusion 152

CHAPTER 7   Arrays and Data Containers 153

Reverse Elements in an Array 153

Sorting Array Elements 155

Sorting Number Arrays 157

Splitting Strings into Array Elements 158

Joining Elements from an Array 159

Extracting Elements from the Front of an Array 160

Inserting Elements into the Front of an Array 162

Removing Elements from the End of an Array 164

Adding Elements to the End of an Array 166

Uses of Dynamic Arrays 168

Controlling Shuttles with Stacks 169

Using a Stack as an Accumulator 170

Tracking Customers with a Queue 174

Conclusion 178

CHAPTER 8   Hashes 179

Basics of Hashes 179

Identifying and Initializing Hashes 181

Order of Initialization 183

Variations on Initialization 184

Accessing Hash Elements 185

Using the keys( ) Function 188

Using the values( ) Function 190

Using the pop( ) Function 192

Reversing Keys and Values 195

Using the shift( ) Function 198

Working each( ) to Retrieve Keys and Values 200

Conclusion 202

CHAPTER 9   Extending Hash Applications 205

Checking for Existence 205

Determining if Elements Are Defined 208

Ascertaining the Number of Key-Value Pairs 211

Slicing Hashes 213

Converting a String into a Hash 216

Deleting Elements 218

Converting a Hash into a String 220

Reversing Keys and Values 223

Conclusion 225

CHAPTER 10   Control Structures 227

Expressions and Statements 227

Control Statements 229

Program Flow 229

Flow and Sequence 230

    Goto Problems 231

    Functional Ordering 233

    Sequence and Incremental Operations 235

Relational and Logical Operators 237

Flow and Selection 240

    Selection Using the if Control Statement 241

    The unless Structure 244

    The if...else Selection Structure 246

    The if...elsif...else Statement 248

Conclusion 252

CHAPTER 11 Control Structures and Applications 255

Flow as Repetition 255

Repetition and the for Statement 257

Exiting for Loops Using last 260

Infinite for Loops with Controls 262

The while Statement 270

The do...while Statement 273

The until Statement 275

The do...until Statement 277

The foreach Control Statement 280

Using a Block with last and redo 282

Using continue with while, last, and next 285

Mineral Luck Using while and Selection Statements 288

    Losing with 7 292

    Winning with 12 293

    Using each to Count Word Occurrences 294

Conclusion 296

CHAPTER 12 Functions 297

Abstraction and Functional Decomposition 297

    Functional Abstraction in Programs 299

Identifying Functional Subroutines 301

Basic Program Organization for Functions 302

Functions with No Arguments 303

    The Basics of Calling and Defining a Function 307

    More Functions and Scope Specifics 308

Functions That Accept Arguments 309

Passing an Array and Efficiency Measures 313

Passing a Hash as an Argument 316

Functions That Return Values 319

    The Explicit Use of return 322

    The Implicit Use of return 323

Contexts and Returning Arrays and Hashes 324

Conclusion 328

CHAPTER 13 References 331

References in General 331

Creating References 334

    Using the ref( ) Function 336

    Dereferencing References 338

    Accessing Items in References to Arrays 340

    Accessing Hash Keys and Values 342

Passing Hash References to a Function 344

Passing Arrays to a Function 347

References to Functions 349

Anonymous Array References as Data Containers 352

    Anonymous Hash References as Data Containers 356

Returning References 358

Conclusion 361

CHAPTER 14 File IO 363

  Input/Output Streams 363

    Handles 364

    Basic IO Interactions 364

  Basic Open, Print, and Close Activities 364

  Reading Data from a File 368

    Basic Reading and Formatting 369

    The Use of die and warn 372

  Functions Relating to IO 374

    Variations on the open( ) Function 375

    The tell( ) Function 375

    The seek( ) and getc( ) Functions 378

    The read( ) Function 383

    The pack( ) Function 386

    Accessing Fixed Length Records 390

  Conclusion 392

CHAPTER 15 Regular Expressions 395

  General Notions 395

  Overview 396

    Statement Formulations and Matches 396

    Identifiers 397

    Match Variations 399

    Exactness 399

    Matching with Arrays or Lists 400

  Substituting 401

    Global Changes 401

    Exactness 402

    Fundamental Ranges 402

    Numbers and Identifiers 403

  Substitution and Matching with the System Variable 403

  Translation 404

❁ ❁ ❁

Reversing Strings 404

Translating a Range 405

    Substitution and Translation 405

    Substitution and Encryption 406

Escape Sequences and Limiters 406

    ASCII Characters 408

    The Caret (^) 408

    The Dollar Sign ($) 408

    Using a Sequence of Items 409

    Use of the Braces (Multiplier) and the Period 409

    The Comma (Multiplier) as a Range Setting 410

    The Asterisk (*) 410

    The Plus Sign (+) 411

    The Question Mark (?) 412

Ways of Extending Expressions 412

    Using Character Classes—Square Braces [] 412

    A Series in a Class 413

    Use of Multiple Periods 413

    Overcoming Case Problems 413

    Searching for Numbers 414

    Using the Caret for Negation 414

    Excluding a Range of Characters 415

Special Characters and Other Operations 415

    Matching Digits 415

    Matching Non-Digits 416

    Using Groups—( ) 416

    Sentences Containing Specific Terms 417

Conclusion 417

Index 419

About This Book

This book provides you with an essential view of programming with Perl. Its chapters are based on Perl classes the author has taught over several years and includes over 160 sample programs. This book is suitable for beginning and intermediate programmers who seek a learning and reference resource on Perl.

Who Should Read This Book

If you are a beginner, this book provides you with a tutorial that you can work from as soon as you get it home. The first chapters allow you to approach Perl as a total beginner. Later chapters tend to fold in the lessons provided in earlier chapters. All chapters offer complete programs to demonstrate the topics discussed. You can access the source code through the book's website (www.courseptr.com/downloads). The programs are ready to run, and line-by-line commentary in the programs and in the book allows you to understand the logic and syntax behind them.

For intermediate programmers seeking a deeper knowledge of Perl, the discussions the book offers provide an easy way to become conversant in Perl. Topics are laid out in traditional categories that allow you to use the book purely as a reference source. The book provides certain advantages over other books because it offers programs that tell or follow stories (or use cases). At the same time, efforts have been made to present verbose samples that emphasize language features in isolation. The code contains extensive commentary, and the book covers the code on a line-by-line basis whenever possible and supplements the commentary in the code files.

The Topics

The chapters concentrate on making programming fun. They provide a friendly programming context in which you can acquire a fundamental knowledge of Perl without developing dependencies on modules.

Chapter 2 concentrates on getting up you up and running with the Perl interpreter and the DzSoft Perl Editor. You acquire the editor from the DzSoft site and the interpreter from the ActiveState site. No cost is involved unless you want to pay the nominal registration fees or buy the software. Installation requires less than half an hour. You can go right to work from there. It is assumed that you are working on a PC and that your PC is networked.

Chapters 3 and 4 focus on using the scalar data type and the functions associated with it. A variety of programs are included that enable you to experiment with the syntax. Work is divided between text and numbers.

Chapter 5 investigates formatting and data display. By exploring different printing functions Perl makes available to you, you acquire a strong sense of how simple tools provide many options.

Chapter 6 focuses specifically on Perl arrays and the functions associated with them. Chapter 7 takes the discussion of arrays into the context of data containers. The topics covered include making use of Perl arrays to create stacks and queues.

Chapter 8 investigates the use of hashes and functions associated with hashes. Working from the fundamentals of using hashes into more advanced topics, Chapter 9 concerns developing applications that incorporate hashes.

In Chapter 10, you explore sequence and selection statements as they relate to Perl. In addition to investigating the basic statements, you see their many applications and are able to draw from the sample programs a sense of how Perl furnishes you control mechanisms that are easy and flexible to use.

Chapter 11 further expands on the topics Chapter 10 covers, allowing you to explore the use of repetiton controls in a number of contexts.

Chapter 12 concentrates on the behaviors of functions in Perl. You work extensively with the use of the argument array and passing arguments to functions and returning values.

In Chapter 13, you examine how to enhance your options in the use of functions by passing arguments as references. In this way, you can pass several arrays or hashes simultaneously and combine into reference structures any combination of data you choose. You likewise explore the use of references to functions.

Chapter 14 focuses on file IO. In addition to learning about handles and the functions associated with IO processes, you put to work the knowledge acquired in previous chapters to create data structures for reading, writing, and presenting data.

Chapter 15 offers you a view of the use of regular expressions in Perl. You investigate matching expressions, substitution expressions, and translations. The chapter provides a multitude of examples that you can work with as you further your knowledge of regular expressions.

The Programs That Accompany This Book

You must install the Perl interpreter before you can work with the programs this book includes. Flip to Chapter 2 and follow the instructions. You'll be up and running in half an hour, more or less. I suggest that you install the DzSoft Perl Editor, also, but if you use another editor, that's fine.

Obtaining the Code for the Book

It is important to have on hand the source code for the book if you want to fully benefit from the discussion the book offers of Perl programming. To obtain the code, access www.courseptr.com/downloads and enter the title of the book.

Identifying Files

Copy the programs that accompany this book from the www.courseptr.com/downloads site to the hard drive of your computer. You'll find them in chapter folders. They are all named in a standard way:

```
ListingNN_nn.pl
```

Within a file and the book, you see:

```
#ListingNN_nn
```

NN refers to the chapter, and nn refers to position of the program in a chapter. So Listng12_03 is the third program in Chapter 12. In most cases, you can click on the file in Windows to see it execute.

Comments

Within the program, I do not use line numbers to talk about the code. You probably know this story. You write a program and pass it around. People do this and that with the program when you are not looking, and before you know it, your line 38 is their line 45, and you tell them to do something that messes up their code.

For this reason, you'll see numbered comments in each file. There are never more than seven per program. They always take the following form:

```
#1 This is a comment
```

In the explanations the text provides, the commentary refers you to the comment: "At comment #1 in Listing09_04, you …."

The book includes over 160 programs available through the website. They are programs that my students liked when they took classes from me on Perl, so I'm assuming you'll enjoy them, too. They are all intended to provoke you into finding better, more interesting ways of doing things.

The Flash Phenomenon

After installing the Perl interpreter, you should be able to click on the programs in Windows and see them execute. If it so happens that you encounter a program that flashes and disappears, there's probably nothing wrong with it (not to start with, anyway). The problem is that it executes too quickly. You need to pause the program.

Your options are along the following lines:

* Install the DzSoft Perl Editor, open the file, and then press Shift + F9.
* Open the DOS window and drag and drop the file from Windows Explorer into the DOS window. Press Enter and watch the file execute.
* Or do a little preliminary programming. To follow this route, open the flashing file in Notepad and insert one of the following lines at the end of the file:

```
<STDIN>;
system('pause');
$AnyChar = <STDIN>;
<>
```

Just one is enough. Save and close the file. Then click on it in Windows Explorer.

In most cases, you find a diamond operator at the end of the file (<>). If the file flashes, open it in your editor and check to verify that the operator is at the end of the file. If it's not there, put it in.

I have made a strong effort to place a diamond operator at the end of every file, but … well, you get the point.

To get the most out of the experience, install the DzSoft Perl Editor. Chapter 2 provides you with all the information you need in this respect.

Armchair Programming

As an inveterate armchair programmer, I have tried to set up the chapters so that three things happen:

* Each program is introduced in a way that gives you a story about what it does and what you can learn if you study it.

* You find the complete program with many notes. Each program provides numbered commentaries.

* In the passages following each program, you find line-by-line explanations of the programs, together with screenshots that show you the program's output.

Before you settle into a routine, take a minute to skim one of the chapters to see how this approach works. It is somewhat literary in nature, but I have used it over the years and have read plenty of books that employ the same approach. The difference is that you find a short introduction preceding the program, the program, and then a long explication or discussion following the program (along with the snapshots of the output). Then, if that's not enough, you see what it looks like when it executes.

And Thanks

By the way, thanks for having an interest in Perl and picking up this book. I wish you the best with your efforts to learn Perl.

1 } Perl Basics

This chapter provides an introduction to this book, with a little information on the history of Perl and its general features as a programming language. It provides you with a few observations relating to the purpose of this book and how it can contribute to your work with Perl. Among the topics dealt with are the following:

* Perl is a language that you can easily learn.
* You can acquire the Perl interpreter on an open, freely available basis.
* The Perl development community is immense.
* The language features of Perl could occasion a lifetime of learning.
* If you want to learn Perl, work with it on the most essential level; then go from there.

Having Fun

The inventor of Perl is a linguist/programmer named Larry Wall, and a point of his philosophy as a developer is that if you do not have fun programming, then something is wrong.

This is one of the most wonderful statements ever made by a world-class programmer and goes against the standard wisdom of any number of programming efforts and programming languages. Many languages are anything but fun. Many programming efforts seem to have as their ground rule a dictate that anyone involved shall be reduced to a slave-like condition and subjected to endless hours of harsh, unremitting labor, involving the resolution of itty-bitty programming language details.

Perl can provide one of the most pleasant programming experiences to be found anywhere. This book is based, in any event, on this assumption. It focuses on the bare details of the Perl programming language with the hope that you will take what it offers and then proceed to deepen your knowledge from there.

If you gain an understanding of the basics, then you are equipped to take your explorations as far into the universe as you want to. The basics allow you to deal with the strange metaphorical planets, solar systems, and galaxies that characterize any number of modular approaches to Perl, and if it so happens that you want to do your own explorations, well …

Figure 1.1
Planning for exploration.

This book originated in my efforts as a teacher at a trade college. I taught one course after another on Perl. How many such courses there are at the college level is hard to say, but whatever the case, over time I learned that the students in the class were delighted when they discovered programming through Perl. On thing I learned as a teacher was that the people in the classes (and they constituted a fairly diverse group) enjoyed the essentials most. They tended to express dissatisfaction when I approached Perl as a module-driven language.

It could have been the teacher, of course.

Power and Perl

Many programmers regard Perl as a powerful and useful programming language because it offers modules. This is a most tenable position, and I fully accept it. At the same time, trying to acquire a knowledge of Perl through modules proves difficult. Perl modules can be black holes (to extend a metaphor). It is easy to lose sight of the essentials even while you are trying to learn the essentials. Allow me to name a few items that can easily come into play in your efforts to learn Perl:

- ❋ The practice of imposing strict requirements for data definitions, which force you to broaden your vocabulary by learning that personal pronouns like "my" and "our" lead hidden lives.

- ❋ Discovery of thousands of functions and an armada of modules that you can bring to bear on any number of programming problems, many of which never occur to you until you discover through an obscure webpage that a module has been developed to address the problem.

- ❋ Spending hours on the Internet searching for information on an obscure module because someone said that is has already been done and you would be stupid even to think about doing it again.

- ❋ Making any given function (method) call in at least six different ways, so that if you consider the functions even a smattering of modules provide and multiply them by the number of ways you can use them, you suddenly have to start using exponents when you talk about the number of things you might do in a given day of programming.

- ❋ Encountering situations in which you learn what it is to program with few words and even go so far as to participate in competitions that challenge you to write programs that contain no words at all.

- ❋ Become absorbed by the notion that Perl is a language designed only to write CGI programs.

- ❋ Decide that you should use only modules to do anything, especially when it comes to creating webpages.

- ❋ Feel that if you cannot do it with the Apache webserver, then it should not be done at all, especially with Perl.

- ❋ Regard database connectivity as essential to programming with Perl, especially with respect to MySQL.

The preceding list provides a set of topics on which good books have been written. The list could be considerably lengthened. As it stands, however, if you are trying to learn a programming language rather than a category of applied programming, the foregoing list proves as much a bane as boon. The problem lies in the bewildering complexity of Perl as used by its maestros, in contrast with its essential grace and simplicity as a resource for beginning programmers.

The simplicity and grace of Perl allow you to start writing interesting programs after only a few hours of exposure. If you concentrate on the language itself and put aside the thousands of exotic uses people have made of it (at least for a while), you can learn how to work with it in fundamental ways. You gain a sound understanding of its essential features. Then you go on to colonize planets.

The Community

The Perl programming community extends around the Earth and possibly into distant parts of the galaxy. As you can see in Table 1.1, surveys reveal that over a million people program using Perl. The widespread use of Perl as a programming language dates from the mid-1990s, and Perl is almost always associated with the spread of the Internet. Where the Internet goes, Perl goes.

It could be the other way, also. There are plenty of reasons for this. Perl is an interpreted language, and the Perl interpreter has been ported to Windows and Unix/Linux operating systems, spreading in its use in much the same way that the Internet has spread.

Figure 1.2
The community.

If you write a program in Perl that executes on the Windows operating system, you can move it fairly easily to Unix or Linux. This is called portability. In addition to portability, Perl appeals to many people because you can acquire it free of charge, install it in a few minutes, and start composing programs with it almost immediately.

To a certain extent, the same can be said of other programming languages, especially Java, but with Java you face the task of learning how to work with object-oriented programs and the Java class libraries. As you'll discover in Chapter 2, none of this is necessary with Perl. You can download the ActivePerl interpreter and begin programming in a few minutes. Writing your first Perl program requires one line (maybe two) of code.

Further, you can compose Perl programs using vi, Notepad, or any other word processor that allows you to save your files as ASCII text. You don't have to worry about packages or byte code compilation. You just type it, save the file, and then run it. Life is good.

The Other End of the Galaxy

Perl is a fairly friendly language to program with if you are interested in learning how to program. It does not enforce restrictive data-typing requirements. The four fundamental data categories you work with in this book (scalars, arrays, hashes, and handles) are represented in a reference table that allows you to convert one to the other with relative ease. This means that if you don't like your data in one form, you can change it to another with what usually amounts to a single function call. That is about as friendly as a language can get.

As mentioned before, however, while Perl is friendly, it also has what might be viewed as possessing a dark side. The dark side has two faces:

❋ As mentioned previously, over the years, advanced Perl developers have created an armada of modules. The modules offer functions. The functions are often mysterious. The documentation grows voluminously, accumulating on the web in every country and dozens of languages. Neophyte Perl programmers dig into these modules and their accompanying documentation, create programs that they think they understand but ultimately do not, and sometimes end up saying that they regret that they ever endangered their website, programming class, or sanity by engaging in such a dangerous activity.

❋ The syntactic flexibility of Perl allows clever programmers to write arcane programs that rival the work of master cryptographers. Out in the more remote regions of the galaxy there are possibly new religions being founded on such programs. Closer to home, however, people who have to maintain such programs resent them and say harsh things about them. In slightly different terms, when programmers write programs that others cannot understand and maintain, the cost of the program increases over time. The cost is both in the money companies must spend on maintaining programs and the stress those who work to maintain such programs endure.

Well…such things can be said about any programming language, but in many ways the stories you hear about Perl result because it is, after all, a vastly democratic language and so exposes itself to all sorts of abuse.

Derivations

Perl provides a set of functions that allows you to easily begin working with its primary categories of data. You can sort or reverse the items in an array, for example, and if you want to use a hash, you do not have to resort to extraordinary construction operations to add keys and values to it or to access them afterward. And along simpler lines, if you create a character and want to make it a number, you can.

Such ease of use in many ways presents an enigma when you consider that Perl possesses the look and feel of the C programming language. The C programming language is something like the ancient Greek of the Unix world (or the programming word as a whole). As wonderful as it might have been for many of us twenty-five or so years ago to begin programming with C, the story is now different. C was austere and unforgiving, and that was that.

On the other hand, Perl owes much to the scripting languages in the UNIX world. It provides many features that allow you to readily interact with operating systems as a system administrator. It provides you with regular expressions. It appeals to a fairly essentialist view of how to interact with a computer. (Old salts call this being close to the hardware.)

Still, Perl tends to be to a great extent what its user/developer community has made it. One way that the community continuously shapes Perl involves the use of modules. Modules extend Perl into thousands of special applications. In fact, some books teach Perl as an extension of one or another module rather than a programming language that makes use of modules.

As has already been mentioned, however, learning Perl through modules is probably not the best idea. At least, that is the perspective I take. When pushed to defend my position, I usually recount a story that involves a student who once brought me a fantastic book on Perl modules. It showed you how to build websites. It was great! Just access these modules and go to work.

No explanations of the basics accompanied the book.

Further, use of the modules assumed that you had installed them. To install them, you had to know where to find them. To find them, you had to obtain the right versions of them. Likewise, it was necessary to access a server…and a database.

The student reported that the learning experience was beneficial, generally, for he learned that he was ignorant of many things, but since he could not get any of the code in the book to work, he said he was not having fun.

I'll admit that as much as I enjoy solving problems, the venture did not sound fun. In the end, he said a very strange thing: "I think I need to learn the language first."

Getting It

Among other companies and organizations, ActiveState and O'Reilly have emerged as leading support centers for Perl. Likewise Perl is often associated with the Apache Server, and you can discover quite a bit about Perl modules by visiting the Apache Software Foundation site. The perl.org site provides you with information on Perl libraries and many pages of documentation and source code. The O'Reilly site provides extensive resources, along with books by Larry

Wall and his close associates. CPAN is what might be viewed as the core non-commercial site for Perl. You can download an interpreter from CPAN in addition to modules and documentation.

The easiest way to get started with Perl if you work with a PC running Windows is to obtain your Perl interpreter from ActiveState. As for databases, MySQL is one option. Perl modules exist for many databases.

Chapter 2 provides more information on these topics. The current version of Perl is 5.8. Over the past decade, Perl has tended to grow steadily but slowly, so you do not face extraordinary changes from one version to the next. What version 6 will offer remains to be seen. Table 1.1 provides discussion of a few topics that might prove useful if you seek to extend your knowledge of Perl.

Table 1.1   Expanding Perl Horizons

Topic	Discussion
Larry Wall	Perl's creation dates back to 1987. That is largely concurrent with the emergence of the Internet. Larry Wall did not start out as a programmer. He's a linguist by training. His website is http://www.wall.org/~larry/.
CPAN	This is an acronym for Comprehensive Perl Archive Network. This is a core site for Perl. Access it at: http://cpan.perl.org.
ActiveState	http://aspn.activestate.com/ASPN/Downloads/ActivePerl. This is where you go in Chapter 2 to obtain the current version of Perl.
O'Reilly	Access O'Reilly at http://www.perl.com. The orientation is toward Unix and Linux system administrators and programmers, but that also represents the majority of Perl users.
MySQL	You can access the site at http://dev.mysql.com/downloads.
Apache	You can access the Apache Software Foundation at www.apache.org. For Perl, click on the Perl menu item. This provides you with access to mod_perl.
http://www.perl.org/	Visit this site and look at the Perl Directory. Get a sense of the resources available to you if you are learning Perl.
Prevalence	Perl is the most popular web programming language. Over a million people program with Perl. That is approximately one Perl programmer for every resident of Hyderabad, Pakistan or Donetsk, Ukraine.
Editors	Chapter 2 provides more information. For DzSoft, you can go to http://www.dzsoft.com.

Topic	Discussion
Groups and Lists	Go to http://lists.cpan.org/ and inspect the list there to get a sense of the resources available to you. There are hundreds of Perl user groups spread around the world. K, Q, U, and Z are the only letters not represented on the CPAN list as of this writing.
State of the Onion	It is probably important to gain some sense of why Perl is sometimes referred to as a postmodern programming language. See http://www.itconversations.com/shows/detail656.html.
Documentation	Any number of sites support Perl documentation. You can download it from http://perldoc.perl.org. The CPAN site links you to perldoc.org.

Perl Scalars, Arrays, Hashes, Handles

The heading of this section summarizes everything. That's what this book is about. You might add a few other terms on such things as data structures, references, file IO, and programming methodologies. But if you get these four terms, you have the essence.

Perl is sometimes called a *contextually typed language*. This means, in essence, that when you define and use a given identifier, the meaning of the identifier depends on how you use it. (In one respect, you might say that programming in Perl is a lot like life in general.)

As a contextually typed language, Perl differs from languages like C, C++, or Java. When you program using those languages, how you define an identifier to a great extent determines the contexts in which you can use it.

To repeat the topic heading, Perl has four types of variables (or as you'll read most often in this book, *identifiers*): scalars, arrays, hashes, and handles. You initially designate these type identifiers using type specifiers. The specifiers are as follows:

* **Dollar sign.** Put your money where you scalar is. Example: `$ScalarName`
* **Business "at" sign.** Perl offers you an array of names, just like the Internet. Example: `@ArrayName`
* **Percent sign.** Example: `%HashName`
* **The diamond operator.** Handle identifiers are often capitalized. Example: `<STDIN>`

Scalars, arrays, hashes, and handles each afford you a set of functions that allow you to perform your work. Likewise, you find that certain control statements, such as `foreach` and `each`, allow you to work readily with one type of data rather than another.

References are also an important part of basic Perl, as are regular expressions. Using references, you can extend the powers of arrays and hashes in enormous ways. You can also create arrays of functions.

As for regular expressions (regexes), this book includes a chapter on them because Perl allows you to readily use them in the contexts provided by common programming problems. If you use them, you can accomplish more than you would otherwise using far fewer lines of code. One chapter on regexes is in many ways an unfair treatment of the topic, for regexes form an enormous asset for programmers throughout the programming and system administration communities. Likewise, what you learn using regexes in Perl carries over to work in other languages, for in general, the form and use of such expressions tend to be uniform across many languages. With Perl you enjoy the advantage of being able to join regular expressions with a flexible programming language that enables you to use them in a number of sophisticated ways.

Source Books

There are many books that are always good to have around if you find that you like Perl. Here is a short list:

Christiansen, Tom and Torkington, Nathan. *Perl Cookbook*. Cambridge: O'Reilly & Associates, 1998.

Deitel, H. M., Deitel, P. J., Nieto, T. R., McPhie, D. C. *Perl, How to Program*. Upper Saddle River, N.J.: Prentice-Hall, 2001.

Schwartz, Randal L. and Christiansen, Tom. Foreword by Larry Wall. *Learning Perl*. Cambridge: O'Reilly & Associates, 1997.

Wall, Larry, Schwartz, Randal L., Christiansen, Tom. *Programming Perl*. Cambridge: O'Reilly & Associates, 1996.

2 } Getting Started

In this chapter, you'll download and install the interpreter for Perl and an editor you can use to develop Perl programs with relative ease. The Perl interpreter you'll employ is ActivePerl. As mentioned in Chapter 1, ActiveState provides a version of Perl you easily can install on a variety of operating systems. In this chapter, the emphasis is on the Windows version. After installing ActivePerl, you first test it by developing a Perl program using Windows Notepad. Run this file from the DOS command line or from a Windows directory. After testing your installation, you then download and install the DzSoft Perl Editor. You can obtain a demonstration copy of the editor that takes care of most of your needs for this book. However, if you elect to purchase a license, the fee is relatively modest compared to many software packages. Following the installation of the editor, run a demonstration program to see output to both a browser and a command line. This chapter covers the following topics, among others:

* Accessing the ActiveState site and obtaining ActivePerl
* Installing ActivePerl
* Writing a basic Perl program using Notepad
* Accessing the DzSoft site and downloading the Perl Editor
* Installing the DzSoft Perl Editor
* Running a program so it executes in both the browser and text modes

Accessing and Installing Perl

As mentioned in Chapter 1, you can obtain the latest Perl interpreter from the ActiveState Programming Network (ASPN). This is the easiest way to directly access the current version of Perl (as of this writing, version 5.8.7). The URL is http://aspn.activestate.com/ASPN/Downloads/ActivePerl/. When you access the ASPN download site, the latest Perl interpreter appears on the left of the page at the top. Click it to begin the download. (See Figure 2.1.)

Figure 2.1
Access the ActiveState site to download ActivePerl.

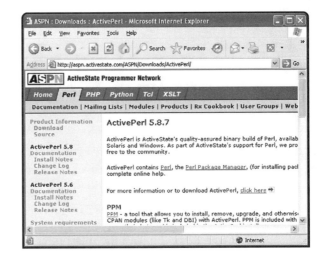

Take a moment to register. (See Figure 2.2.) Click Next.

Figure 2.2
Registration does not obligate you to pay anything.

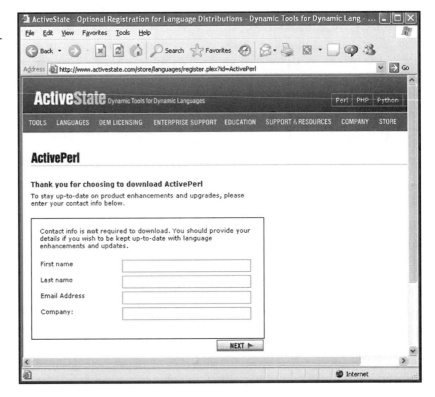

A page appears that thanks you for registering. Click Continue To Download.

As shown in Figure 2.3, the site displays the current versions of the ActivePerl installation package. To download the Windows version of ActivePerl, click the link for MSI under Windows. This provides a standard installation package that automatically configures your system to use Perl.

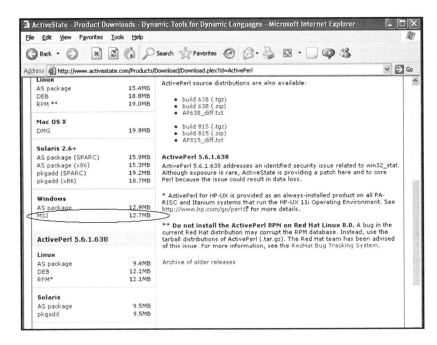

Figure 2.3
Select the MSI version for easy Windows installation.

As Figure 2.4 illustrates, when the Save As dialog appears, click Save. Save the ActivePerl

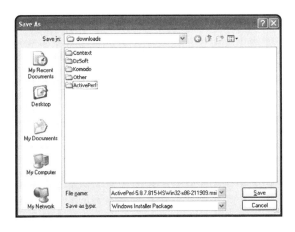

Figure 2.4
Create conspicuous download directories.

installation executable to a directory you create in a conspicuous place on your C: drive. (The directory created for the two downloads in this chapter is C:\downloads directory.)

Click Close on the Download Complete dialog.

As is the case later on in this chapter when you download and install the DzSoft Perl Editor, you do nothing special when you install ActivePerl. Use the Windows Start > Control Panel option. Select Add or Remove Programs. Click Add New Programs. Click CD or Floppy and the Next button. Click the Browse button and select the directory in which you have placed the ActivePerl installation executable. You must set the Files of Type field to All Files to see the ActivePerl installation executable (for example ActivePerl-5.8.7.815-MSWin32-x86-211909.msi). You then select the ActivePerl executable and click Open. The Run Installation Program dialog appears, and you click Finish.

You'll then see a security warning. The publisher as of this writing is identified as "unknown," but you can still safely install the program. Click Run. The standard Windows installer for ActivePerl will appear. The first message that appears explains that the installer is determining whether adequate disk space exists on your computer for the installation. (See Figure 2.5.)

Figure 2.5
The installation checks for adequate disk space.

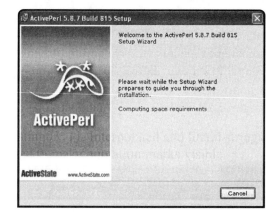

First Time Installation

If the installer determines your computer possesses adequate disk space, the installation dialog automatically refreshes, and you can then continue with the installation. If this is the first time you have installed ActivePerl, you'll see a dialog that confirms the installation (see Figure 2.6). Click Next.

In the next dialog, you'll see the license agreement. Click the radio button to confirm that you accept the terms of the license. Click Next.

Figure 2.6
The wizard asks you to
confirm the installation.

As Figure 2.7 illustrates, the dialog you see after the license dialog offers some installation options. Accept all the defaults. PPM stands for Perl Package Manager. The documentation and examples do not represent a heavy drain on resources, and they are worth having on hand during your programming efforts. Click Next.

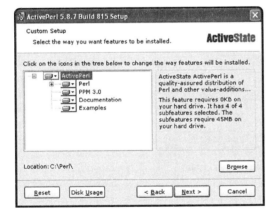

Figure 2.7
Allow the installation
package to place all the
default material on your
computer.

The Choose Setup Options dialog contains important options. Leave the two default boxes checked. The boxes add Perl to your path variable and create a Perl file extension association. (The file type is *.pl.) If either of these operations is not completed, your installation will not end in complete success. Click Next.

In the Ready to Install dialog, click Install. You then see a series of dialogs that show progress bars for the installation. When the installation completes, you'll see a final dialog. If you are new to Perl, deselect Display the Release Notes. Then click Finish.

Testing Your ActivePerl Installation

Even if this chapter provides instructions that allow you to use the DzSoft Perl Editor to conduct your Perl programming activities, it remains that being able to work with Perl programs at the command prompt is essential.

Toward this end, to access the command prompt, begin on your Windows desktop with the Start menu. Select Start > All Programs > Accessories > Command Prompt. Figure 2.8 maps the path to Command Prompt from the Windows Start menu.

Figure 2.8
From the Start menu locate the command prompt.

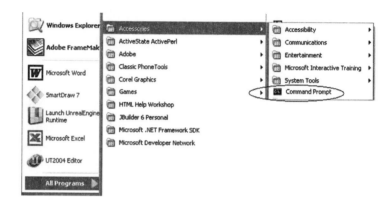

After you locate Command Prompt in the Windows menu system, create a shortcut and place it on your Windows desktop. As shown in Figure 2.9, to create a shortcut, right-click Command Prompt and then select Send To and Desktop (create shortcut).

Figure 2.9
Create a shortcut and place it on your desktop.

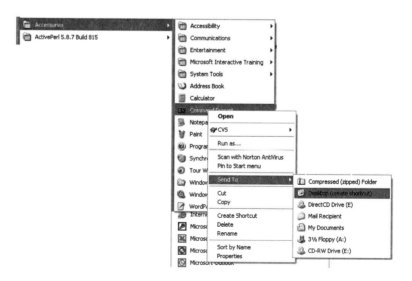

❄ Customizing the Prompt Window

To make your work with the command prompt easier, set up the command prompt window so that the background is white and the text is black. To accomplish this, open the command prompt window. Right-click on the top bar of the window and select the Properties option from the drop-down menu. You'll see the Properties dialog, as Figure 2.10 illustrates.

Click the Colors tab. Then click the Screen Background radio button and set the value as shown in Figure 2.10 (255, 255, 255). To set the background color values, click the white box in the color palette. To set the text, click the Screen Text radio button and set all of the values to zero (0, 0, 0) by clicking the black box in the color palette. When you finish setting the background and text colors, click OK. When the OK dialog appears, click the radio button that corresponds to "Modify shortcut that started this window." Click OK once again.

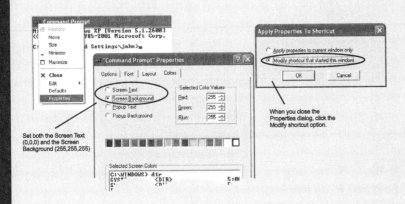

Figure 2.10
Set the properties of the DOS command prompt window so that you have dark text and a light background.

Given that you have set up the DOS command prompt window with a light background and dark font, you'll see something along the lines of Figure 2.11. This window is now available to you on your desktop when you need to interact with the operating system.

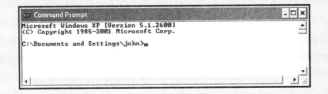

Figure 2.11
The command prompt is available through a DOS window.

Perl Files

Using either DOS commands or the Windows options, create a directory at the root of your primary drive (C:). Call it MyPerlPrograms.

Use Notepad to create a file called HelloWorld. To create the file, save it with a *.pl extension. To save the file with a *.pl extension, select All Files for the Save As Type field. See Figure 2.12.

Figure 2.12
Perl files have a *.pl file type.

After saving your file, type the following lines exactly as shown. Include a blank line after the first line. Save and close your file when you finish.

```
print "Hello World!\n";
$AnyChar = <STDIN>;
```

Figure 2.13 shows the lines as typed in the text area of Notepad.

Figure 2.13
Test your installation.

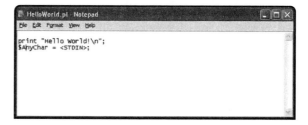

The line with `print` tells the program to print Hello World! to the command line. The second line is a rather cumbersome way to tell the program not to exit until you press the Enter key.

If you are adept at DOS, you can now navigate to the MyPerlPrograms directory and type the name of your file. Figure 2.14 illustrates how you type the name of the file. The *.pl extension invokes the Perl interpreter. The file executes as shown in Figure 2.14.

Figure 2.14
The Hello World Perl program executes at the command prompt.

Alternatively, open Windows and navigate to your MyPerlPrograms directory. You'll see your file represented with an icon for the Perl interpreter. Figure 2.15 illustrates the situation. Double-click the name of the file.

Figure 2.15
Click on the Perl program in your Windows directory.

A command prompt window opens as the file executes. See Figure 2.16. Press Enter to exit the program.

Figure 2.16
A command prompt window opens, and the Perl program executes.

❋ If your files flash and disappear when you click on them in Windows Explorer, it is usually for one of two reasons. One is that they contain code problems. This problem must be dealt with in due course. On the other hand, the problem might be simply that they contain no code that causes the execution of the file to pause long enough to allow you to see it. To remedy this situation, open the Perl file with Notepad (or your editor) and type the following line right at the end of the file:

```
$AnyChar = <STDIN>;
```

You can also type only the following:

```
<>
```

This accomplishes the same thing as the longer statement.

This lines causes the execution of the file to pause until you press the Enter key. They create no problems in a Perl file you are not displaying as a webpage.

❄ File Type Associations

With reference to Figure 2.15, if you do not see the icon, then Windows has not associated the *.pl extension with your Perl file. To correct this situation, Select Start > Control Panel > Folder Options. Click the File Types tab. Scroll to the PL extension and click on it. Then click Change and select Perl Command Line Interpreter, as illustrated in Figure 2.17.

Figure 2.17
Associate the file type, if
necessary.

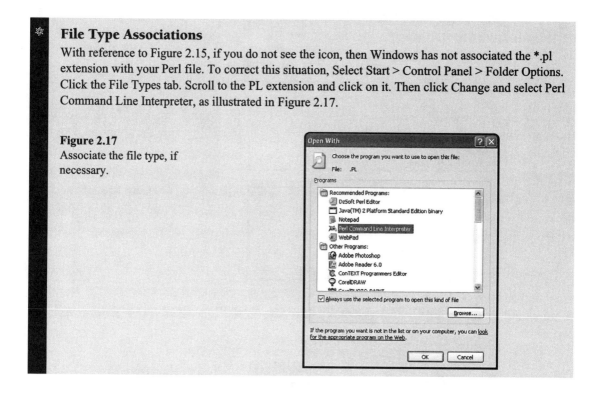

Getting Started with an Editor

Several editors that make it possible for you to create programs with Perl easily are currently available. Some are free. Others are available for less than $50 (US). Table 2.1 provides a short list of some of the best editors. Generally, if you want to get started quickly, the DzSoft Perl Editor provides a suitable option, and that is the one chosen for this book. On the other hand, if you want a very powerful editor designed to work with ActiveState Perl, then Komodo makes the greatest sense. Generally, editors are a matter of personal preference. You can even edit Perl in Windows Notepad or vi and go from there. (If you are curious about WinVi, the URL to download it is http://www.winvi.de/en/download.html.)

Table 2.1 Perl Editors

Editor	Discussion
Komodo	Currently available as release 3.5.2. You can obtain the demonstration version and after approximately a month invest in a personal or professional edition. This editor is the product of ActiveState, which offers a number of editors for such languages as PHP, Python, Tcl, and Ruby. The editor is certainly among the best on the market if you want to make use of ActiveState's extensive Perl resources. On the other hand, this editor requires, like Eclipse, a great deal of startup work to get used to it. (The site is http://www.activestate.com.)
Eclipse	You can obtain Eclipse for free. This is an extensive development environment used by many developers who work with Java-based applications. Eclipse offers a Perl extension. The extension proves difficult to configure if you are not an experienced programmer. Additionally, you must download and install the runtime for Java. Generally, if you want to invest quite a bit of time in learning how to use a free development tool, Eclipse is an option. It is a very powerful and interesting editor with a wide variety of capabilities. (The site is http://www.eclipse.org.)
ConTEXT	This is an editor you can obtain as freeware. If you feel inclined, you can make a voluntary contribution to the development effort. ConTEXT is a basic, efficient, lightweight editor that you can use with a number of languages. To set it up for specific use with Perl, you download a supplementary file that allows it to parse Perl for keywords. You must configure it to compile files and provide you with the output you want. To make it so that the editor can operate with Perl files, you associate function keys with the Perl executable. This is all fairly easy to accomplish, but it can be painful for beginners. (The site is http://www.context.cx.)
DzSoft Perl Editor	This is the editor used in this book. Its advantages are its ease of use and the fact that it provides you with a built-in browser output window and other features that help you develop Perl programs. Among other things, it has a built-in browser, so you can immediately go to work developing Perl programs that create webpages. Also, you can either compile your programs to the DzSoft text or

Editor	Discussion
	browser areas or opt for a DOS command line (you press F9 or Shift + F9.) As soon as you install it, you are ready to go; you do not need to perform any configuration work. If you do not want to buy it, the number of lines it allows you to edit is limited. (The site is http://www.dzsoft.com.)

Obtaining the DzSoft Perl Editor

As Table 2.1 indicates, the internet address of DzSoft is http://www.dzsoft.com. Figure 2.18 illustrates the home page for DzSoft with a view of the DzSoft Perl Editor. Click the Perl Editor link.

Figure 2.18
DzSoft lists the Perl Editor among other selections.

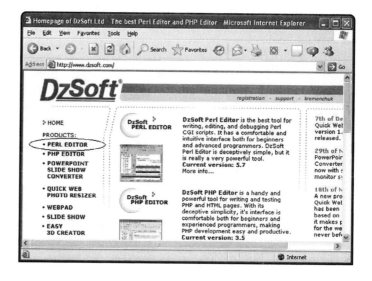

In the page that describes the Perl Editor (see Figure 2.19), click on the Click Here to Download link. The download dialog immediately appears. Click the Save option and save the executable to your local drive.

Generally, it is best to save the installation executable to your local drive. Figure 2.20 illustrates a folder set up as c:\executables\DzSoft. Create such a folder and save the executable (currently, the version is dzperl57.exe) to it.

DzSoft provides half off prices if you are a student, so you might want to keep this in mind if you are in that category. Otherwise, you see the price posted. When you buy your license, DzSoft sends it to you in an e-mail. As a precaution, save a copy of the license to the directory in which you store the installation executable. Figure 2.21 illustrates a saved file with the license and the DzSoft installation file.

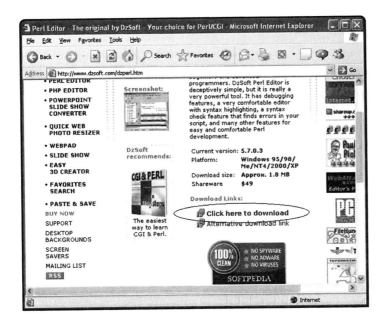

Figure 2.19
The Click Here to Download link immediately starts the download.

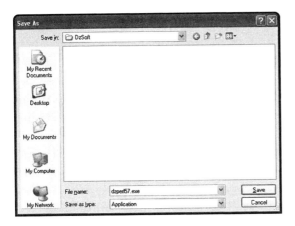

Figure 2.20
Save the installation executable in case problems occur.

Figure 2.21
If you purchase DzSoft's Perl Editor, you receive a key in an e-mail, which you can save to a text file and then cut and paste into the license window.

There are only a few points of interest about the installation of DzSoft. These are covered in the steps that follow.

To begin the installation, use the Windows Start > Control Panel option. Select Add or Remove Programs. Click Add New Programs. Click CD or Floppy and the Next button. Click the Browse button and select the directory in which you have placed the DzSoft installation executable for the Perl Editor. You must set the Files of Type field to *All Files* to see the DzSoft installation executable. Then select the DzSoft executable and click Open. The Run Installation Program dialog appears. Click Finish.

You'll then see a security warning. The publisher, DzSoft, is identified. You can safely install the program. Click Run. As Figure 2.22 illustrates, you'll then see the standard installer for DzSoft.

Figure 2.22
DzSoft is ready to install.

After that you see the license dialog. Click the radio button and Next to show you agree with the terms of the license.

Use the default directory DzSoft provides (see Figure 2.23). Click Next.

In Select Start Menu folder, allow DzSoft to create a shortcut for you using the default name (DzSoft Perl Editor). Click Next.

In the Select Additional Tasks dialog, leave the first two options as they are. (See Figure 2.24.) Still, if you do not want a desktop icon or a Quick Launch icon (this appears in the tray of your desktop), you can certainly deselect these options.

One important point! Deselect the option for Associate with Perl Files. You can always associate the *.pl extension with DzSoft, but for now do not do so. It is best if you allow the *.pl extension to invoke the Perl interpreter rather than DzSoft. Click Next.

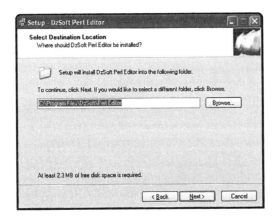

Figure 2.23
Accept the default
directory.

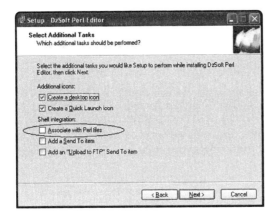

Figure 2.24
Deselect the box for Associate with Perl Files.

In the Ready to Install dialog, you'll see the files and directories to be created. Click Install.
You'll see a window with a progress bar, and then the final dialog appears. Leave the Launch
DzSoft Perl Editor item checked and click Finish.

First View of the Perl Editor

As Figure 2.25 illustrates, your first view of the DzSoft Perl Editor provides you with a Perl file
that is ready to be run. Notice the Edit and Run tabs on the left and the Perl program in the edit
area on the left.

As you can see from Figure 2.25, the first message you see creates an HTML document. The
document consists of three lines. The first line is called the "bang" line. This identifies the
directory in which the Perl interpreter resides. A blank line follows. Then you'll see two lines
that begin with `print`. In each line, the Perl code consists of the word `print`, double quotation

Figure 2.25
By default, you'll see a Perl
program that prints an
HTML message.

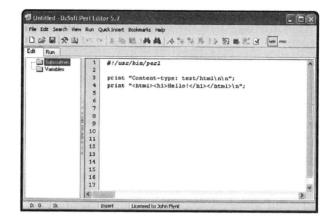

marks, and a semicolon at the end of the line. Inside the double quotation marks on each line
are HTML messages. When these messages appear in a browser, you see standard HTML.

HTML Output

To execute the file, select Run > Quick Run from the top menu. Alternatively, press F9.

As illustrated in Figure 2.26, the window changes immediately. You see As Text and In Browser
tab options. By default, the display shows the In Browser tab, so in the case of the program
DzSoft provides, you see the printed HTML line as it might appear in a standard browser.

> If your DzSoft Perl Editor window differs from what you see in the screenshots in this chapter,
> select View > Status Bar or View >Toggle Code Explorer. To eliminate line numbers, select View >
> Options > Editor and deselect both Show Line Numbers and Show Line Numbers on Gutter.
>
> Also, when you use you DzSoft Perl Editor, use Shift + F9 to execute the files in this book. They are
> developed for command line interaction. When you press F9 alone, you invoke the interpreter for web
> content, and some of the programs are not designed to display in this mode.

To gain a sense of how easy it is to edit your code, click the Edit tab. Then change the Perl file
so it reads as follows. (Do not save your work for now. When you finish, click the Run tab. Then
click In Browser.)

```
#!/usr/bin/perl

print "Content-type: text/html\n\n";
print "<html><h1>Hello</h1>\n";
print "<h1>World!</h1></html>\n";
```

26
❄ ❄ ❄

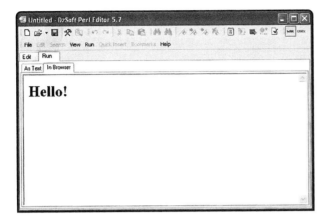

Figure 2.26
DzSoft parses your file to allow you to check the syntax of your program and to show HTML output.

Figure 2.27 illustrates the code as changed in the edit area.

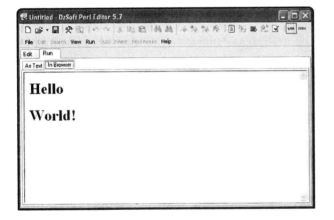

Figure 2.27
Click the In Browser tab to view web content.

Text Output and the DOS Window

Now that you have had a chance to look at how the DzSoft Perl Editor handles HTML, click on the As Text tab. The As Text tab allows to see the output as it appears at the command line (most of the programs you write in this book during the first several chapters involve the command line rather than the browser). Figure 2.28 shows you the result.

In the course of this book, you'll work both from the text view and the browser view as you work with your Perl code. For the programs in this text, execute them by pressing Shift + F9. This approach does not display your programs in the DzSoft Text area but instead allows you

Figure 2.28
You see the text output as it might appear if processed at the command prompt of the operating system.

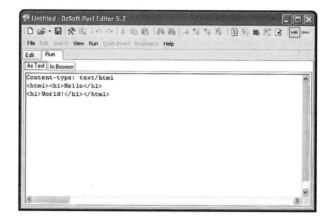

to see them in a separate DOS window. When you execute the programs in the DOS window, you put yourself in a much better position to work with the programs outside of any given editing environment. To close the programs, you press Return. This returns you directly to the DzSoft Editor, and you can make changes as needed.

Saving Files

To save a file, select File > Save. Navigate to MyPerlPrograms. Save the file you have modified as HelloWorld01. You'll see files with the *.pl file. This is the extension for Perl files. (See Figure 2.29.)

Figure 2.29
You'll see the file type as Perl Files (the *.pl extension).

Conclusion

This chapter has helped you to acquire and install the ActivePerl interpreter and the DzSoft Perl Editor. Given these two items, you are now ready to develop Perl programs. When you work with Perl, you do not need a specific editor, of course. You can work with a command prompt and a generic application like Notepad. Using an editor designed to parse Perl makes your work much easier than it would be otherwise, however. The programs in this book have been developed using the DzSoft Perl Editor.

Perl files have a *.pl extension, and as long as this extension is associated with the Perl interpreter, you can readily execute Perl files at the command line. When you install an editor, you should refrain from associating the Perl extension with your editor. Instead, associate the *.pl extension with the Perl interpreter. In the installation processes this chapter documents, the ActivePerl installer installs the Perl interpreter in the Perl directory. When you associate the *.pl extension with the interpreter, you can use the command prompt or the Windows directory to directly execute the Perl programs you create.

3 } Scalars and Strings

This chapter introduces you to scalars, primarily as used to program with strings. A scalar variable is a variable in which you can store a single value. A single value can be a number or a string. If the scalar stores a string, it can constitute a fairly vast amount of information. When you deal with strings, Perl allows you to use either interpolated strings or character strings. One of the best ways to experiment with strings involves performing output to your computer system using the `print()` function. In addition to exploring the basics of outputting strings, it is also important to become acquainted with operations relating to strings. Among these operations are concatenation, comparison, incrementing, and the use of blocks to store large bodies of text. This chapter takes you through a variety of topics and programs that help you to understand Perl strings. Among the topics covered are the following:

- ✳ What makes a string a scalar
- ✳ How strings can be interpolated
- ✳ How strings can be read as characters
- ✳ How to print strings
- ✳ How to put strings together
- ✳ Using operators to manipulate and compare strings

Preliminary Work

The best way to learn a programming language often involves typing sample programs, studying them, and modifying them. Toward this end, this section allows you to work with the `print()` function and also offers a few essential points about Perl that furnish you with learning tools you can use throughout this book.

The print() Function

The most important functions you use as a beginning programmer in any language usually involve writing messages from your programs and reading messages into your programs. Such functions concern input and output (shortened to IO). When you want to write messages from your program in Perl, you use the `print()` function. To use this function in its simplest form, you type the word `print` and follow it in single or double quotes with whatever you want to write to an output device. Consider the following code sample:

```
#Listing03_01
#the print function
print "\nHere are some data about Mt. Everest: ";
print "\nClimber: Edmund Hillary, ";
print "\nClimber: Tenzing Norgay.";
```

Figure 3.1 illustrates the appearance of the output of this program as displayed in the DzSoft Perl Editor.

Figure 3.1

The `print()` function writes text to the output device.

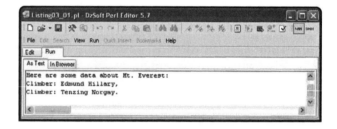

The word `print` represents a function call. Much more is presented later on concerning functions. For now, note only that after the word `print` you see text placed in double quotation marks. This defines the text as an *interpolated* string. You use opening and closing quotation marks. You end the line with a semicolon, which is a terminating mark for a program *statement*. As is explained at greater length later on, at the beginning of each line, the \n forces the text to appear on a new line when it is printed to the output device.

Code Composition Strategies with the Editor

If you use an unregistered version of the EzSoft Perl Editor, you can still work with the programming examples in this book. EzSoft limits the length of the programs you can work with if you do not purchase a license. Otherwise, your use remains unrestricted.

To work with the program examples in this book, access the chapter folders in the *Perl Power!* code directory. The programs are arranged on a chapter-by-chapter basis. You can find the examples for this chapter in Chapter03. Each program is numbered sequentially and begins with the word "Listing." Listing03_02.pl is an example of a file for this chapter.

An effective way to learn a programming language involves typing programs and then modifying them to see how they work. It is suggested, in any event, that you use this approach with this book. If you run into problems, you can always open and compile the samples.

When you develop a program, use an *iterative* and *incremental* approach to adding code to your program. Accordingly, start with a program of only a few lines of code. Compile these few lines to see whether they work. If they work, add a few more lines. The action of adding a few lines at a time involves incremental building of your program. The iterative part is the repeated testing by compiling.

If your code results in an error, and you are working with the DzSoft Perl Editor, you'll see an error report in a text area that opens automatically. In some cases, if you can click the line in the message window that reports the error, the editor positions the cursor on either the line that contains the error or one in close proximity to it. On the other hand, the error can also be serious enough that the editor cannot help you. In this case, try working from a single line. You can comment out all but one line if you must and work from there.

Figure 3.2 provides a standard starter set of lines for the programs you compose using the EzSoft Perl Editor. (You can use the editor to automatically generate this code whenever you start a new file.) At the top of the text area is a set of two lines that make it so that you can use F9 to toggle between compiling and editing without error messages. Later on, when you become comfortable with command line compilation, you might decide to leave these lines out.

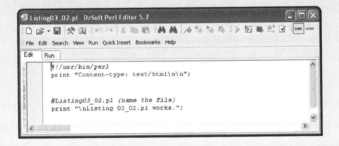

Figure 3.2
Start with the standard
bank and content-type
lines and then type only a
couple of lines of code.

The print() function that prints the "Listing…" message serves as a "sanity check." It reports whether the most rudimentary form of your program compiles. Press F9. If you see the starter line displayed, work forward from there. Figure 3.3 illustrates the output of Listing03_02.

The editor provides some automated code generation macros. For example, to insert the content-type line, position the cursor on a blank line and select Quick Insert > Content-Type from the main menu. You can also press Ctrl and zero (Ctrl + 0). As mentioned previously, if you work with DzSoft for a while, you can learn how to modify the macros to suit your tastes and practices.

You can certainly proceed on whatever basis brings you contentment, but generally, consider resisting the urge to type an entire page of code prior to trying to compile even a line of it. If you type many lines and then try to compile, you are likely to face a long list of errors, and you deprive yourself of the positive feedback an interpreter (or compiler) can provide when you work in an incremental, iterative way.

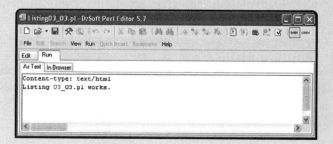

Figure 3.3
Press F9 to compile; if you meet with success, add a few more lines.

To preserve space, in most of the code examples presented in this book, you do not see the bang and content-type lines. These lines remain in many of the programs that you download from the book's Internet site.

Fundamental Programming Syntax

Among the most elementary items of syntax you use when programming with Perl are those you use to create comments, make statements, force new lines, and escape from regular program interpretation so that you can display special characters. This section reviews these items.

Comments Using

The pound sign (#) provides a way that you can tell the Perl interpreter to skip over notes you include in a program. Such notes are referred to as *comments*. Comments are not part of the code. Any line that begins with a pound sign is considered a comment.

The interpreter reads from left to right. For this reason, if you want to make it so that the interpreter does not read a line of text you have included in your program, you type the pound sign as the first character at which you want the interpreter to stop reading. From that point on, until the interpreter reaches the end-of-line character, it does not try to interpret anything you have typed as Perl code. Consider the following sample of code:

```
#Listing03_04
#Comments proceeded to the end-of-line character
#You press Enter to insert an EOL character
print "\nListing03_04.pl works."; #Comments can follow code
print "\nReady to add lines!";
```

The first three lines of Listing03_04.pl provide standard comments. Each line begins with a pound sign. On the fourth line, beginning "Comments can …," you see a comment to the right of the program statement. Such a comment creates no problem. The interpreter knows not to read it. If you were to reverse the position of the comment and the statement, however, the interpreter would immediately have a problem. You must place the comment on a separate line or, if on the same line, after your program statements. Figure 3.4 illustrates the output of Listing03_04.

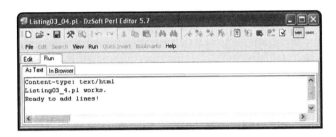

Figure 3.4
Comments to the left of code do not create problems.

How to Make a Statement

The semicolon (;) indicates that the interpreter should read the words to the left of the semicolon as a complete unit. A complete unit is a *statement*. The shortest statement you can make in Perl consists of a semicolon. Consider the following sample of code:

```
#Listing03_05
print "\nListing03_05.pl works.";    #Comments can follow code
print "\nReady to add lines!";
;;;
;
;
print "\nReady to add more lines!";
```

The first two lines of Listing03_05 provide standard statements. For example, interpolated strings (strings within double quotation marks) follow the print() function. The next three lines provide only semicolons. On the third line, you see three semicolons in a row. On the following two lines, one semicolon occupies each line. For the final line, you see a standard statement beginning with the print() function.

The interpreter reads the semicolons as statements even if they do nothing more than cause the interpreter to continue on the next statement. As Figure 3.5 illustrates, the semicolons cause no extra line spaces to appear in the program output.

Figure 3.5
Semicolons alone consti-
tute statements but pro-
duce no visible change.

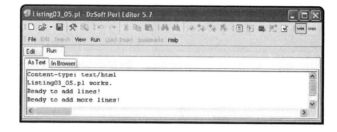

Leaving Out Semicolons

If you delete one of the semicolons following a statement, you can create an interpreter error. Consider the following code sample:

```
#Listing03_06
#Missing semicolons result in interpreter error messages
# To correct the problem, add a semicolon on each line
# right after the closing quotation marks
print "\nListing03_06.pl works."    #1 semicolon left off
print "\nReady to add lines!"     #2 semicolon left off
;;;
;
;
print "\nReady to add more lines!";
```

The lines identified in the comments as #1 and #2 lack semicolons. When you submit your code to the interpreter, you might see a message along the following lines:

```
syntax error at Listing03_06.pl line 8, near "print"
Execution of Listing03_06.pl aborted due to compilation errors
```

The Perl interpreter might not object every time you forget to type a semicolon. Consider the lines identified with the #2 comment in Listing03_06. The first semicolon on the following line (the line of three semicolons) replaces the missing semicolon. In such a situation, the interpreter does not object. However, if you leave out the semicolon for #1, the interpreter invariably objects.

Multiple Statements on One Line

You saw in the previous example a succession of semicolons (statements) on one line. What applies to statements consisting of one semicolon applies to statements consisting of full expressions. Consider the following code sample:

```
#Listing03_07.pl
#Multiple statements on one line
print "\nListing03_07.pl works.";                    #single statement
print "\nMultiple statements on one line.";          #single statement
#Mutliple statements on one line follow
;;;
print "\nReady to add more lines!"; print "\nAnd more lines...";!";
```

Figure 3.6 illustrates the output. Notice that the interpreter reads the statements on the final line without problems. The output appears on separate lines because the \n forces the string following it onto a new line.

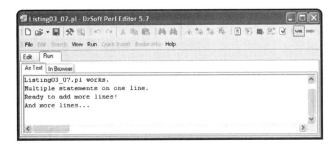

Figure 3.6
Successive statements on a single line cause no errors.

❋ Although composing code with several statements on one line creates no syntax errors, consider that many experienced programmers regard this as poor programming style. Experienced programmers often insist that you should place no more than one statement on each line of code.

Escape Sequences

In most of the code samples shown so far, the quoted text used with the print() function begins with a slash character followed by an "n" character (\n). This combination of characters causes a line return to be inserted into the output of the print() function. The slash can be used with several other characters as well. The slash and the character that accompanies it are together called an *escape sequence*. An escape sequence escapes the normal execution of your program. It makes it so that the Perl interpreter interprets a character like any other text character rather than trying to process it as a language feature. To see how this works, consider the following code sample:

```
#Listing03_08.pl
#Different uses of the escape sequence
```

```perl
print "\nListing03_08.pl works.";
print "\nEscape characters:";
print "\nNew\nNew\nNew";
print "\nHe said, \"That's new.\"";
print "\nShe said \'vlap\' twice.";
print "\nThe bill was \$25.00.\b\b";
print "\nHere's a \uv\la\ur\li\ue\ld word.";
print "\nThe lines read: \nLife teaches \n\t\tof time \n\tand sorrow.";
```

Figure 3.7 illustrates the appearance of the command line output after the use of the escape sequences in Listing03_08.

Figure 3.7
Escape sequences allow you to format interpolated strings.

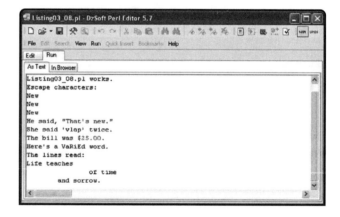

As Figure 3.7 illustrates, using a slash and double quotes (\ ") displays double quotes. A slash with a single quote (\ ') shows a single quote. A slash with a u (\u) forces the character that follows to uppercase. In each instance, the escape sequence allows you to perform a formatting procedure or some other type of operation that the characters on the keyboard do not alone allow you to perform. Table 3.1 provides a summary and discussion of escape sequences.

Table 3.1   Escape Sequences

Sequence	Discussion
\n	Forces a new line.
\t	Forces a tab. What you see depends on the tab setting of your display.
\$	Creates a dollar sign. Otherwise, the next term is read as a scalar.
\\	Allows you to show a backslash. Otherwise, the next character is likely to be read as a part of an escape sequence.

Sequence	Discussion
*	Allows you to show an asterisk.
\"	Allows you to show double quotation marks within quotation marks that create an interpolated string. Otherwise, the quotation marks end the string and in all likelihood cause an error.
\@	Allows you to show the "at" sign.
\b	Forces a backspace.
\u	Sets the character that follows to uppercase.
\U	Sets all of the characters that follow to uppercase.
\l	Sets the character that follows to lowercase.
\L	Sets all of the characters that follow to lowercase.
\'	Same as with double quotes, except here you deal with a literal string.

Scalars and Strings

When you write programs in Perl, you deal with categories of data rather than data types. As mentioned in Chapter 1, these data categories fall under the headings of *scalar*, *hash*, *array*, and *handle*. Of these four categories of data, the most basic has to do with identifiers that pertain to isolated or individualized strings and numbers. In Perl, such individualized strings and numbers fall under the heading of scalar values. Figure 3.8 abstractly illustrates the way that you can visualize the different forms of scalar values. (Figure 3.9 provides a concrete version of scalars.)

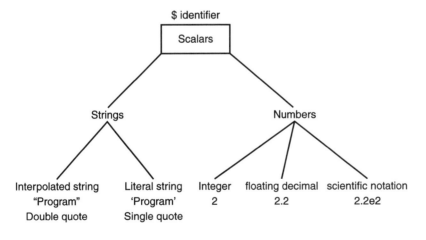

Figure 3.8
Scalar values in Perl consist of strings and numbers.

As Figure 3.8 illustrates, when you program with Perl, you identify scalars with a currency sign ($). Any value that you store as a scalar exists as a single retrievable value, even if it is a collection of words (a sentence or longer unit of composition). When you store text in a scalar, you store it as an *interpolated string* or as a *literal string*. An interpolated string allows you to place variables in the string and retrieve values from the variables. A literal string makes it so that you see exactly what you include in the string, regardless of how you use it.

When you store a number, such as 2 or 2.2 in a scalar, the value 2 is known as an *integer*, a whole number. The value 2.2 is known as a rational or real number or *floating decimal*. With Perl you can assign interpolated strings, literal strings, integers, and floating decimals to scalars.

Making Scalars

Consider the scalars that Figure 3.9 illustrates. The name of each scalar consists of a word known as an *identifier* combined with a dollar sign ($) that precedes each identifier. The dollar sign itself is called a *type identifier*. When you prefix the type identifier to the identifier, you create a *scalar identifier* (sometimes called a *scalar variable*).

An equals sign (=) then follows each scalar variable. The equal sign is know as an *assignment operator*. The assignment operator assigns a single value to each of the scalar variables. When the assignment operator assigns the value on its right side to the scalar on its left side, it converts the value so that the scalar knows how to store it.

Figure 3.9
Perl scalars hold numerical and textual (string) values.

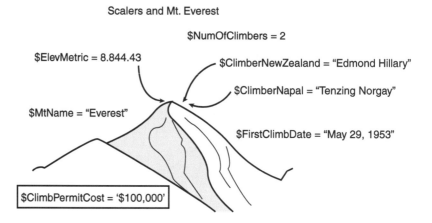

Scalers and Mt. Everest

$NumOfClimbers = 2

$ElevMetric = 8.844.43

$ClimberNewZealand = "Edmond Hillary"

$ClimberNapal = "Tenzing Norgay"

$MtName = "Everest"

$FirstClimbDate = "May 29, 1953"

$ClimbPermitCost = '$100,000'

Table 3.2 provides brief discussions of the scalar variables Figure 3.9 illustrates. In each instance, it's important to remember that the assignment operator allows you to assign different types of numbers or strings to scalar identifiers. In later sections of this chapter, you'll see that other operators allow you to retrieve the values and work with them according to their status as strings or numbers.

Table 3.2   Scalar Variables

Scalar Variable	Discussion
`$ElevMetric = 8.844.43`	The value stored consists of a rational or real number, also known as a floating decimal. The short term for such a number is *float*. In other programming languages, a number that takes an extremely large value is usually labeled as a *double*. Perl allows you to control numbers in several ways (as becomes evident later in this book with the use of *conversion specification*), but generally, when you assign a number to a scalar identifier, Perl takes care of storing the number. An integer is stored as an integer, and a floating decimal as a floating decimal.
`$ClimberNewZealand = "Edmund Hillary"`	The value stored in this case consists of two words and a space between the words. You can refer to the words together with the space as a *string*. In some instances, a string that contains a space might present a problem, but with Perl, the key to understanding a string is *interpolation*. Perl interpolates a group of characters you put between double quotation marks as a string. The blank space is stored the same way as any other character.
`$ClimberNapal = "Tenzing Norgay"`	As with the first string, the second consists of two words and a space enclosed by double quotation marks. This, then, is another interpolated string.
`$ClimbPermitCost='$100,000'`	Notice that a dollar sign ($) precedes the number 100,000, and the number contains a comma. This is not a

Scalar Variable	Discussion
	number, then; it is a string. It is not an interpreted string, however; it is a *literal string*. The single quotation marks make the number into a literal string. The string stores a set of characters precisely as you have typed them. For this reason, the use of the dollar sign as a part of the string does not cause the interpreter to try to read the expression $100,000 as a scalar. The dollar sign is read literally as a dollar sign. Such a string is called either a *literal string* or a *character string*. Perl allows you use letters and number to create the names of scalars and other identifiers. Among the rules that apply to naming identifiers is that you cannot start them with numbers. For example, $1aaa is not a permissible identifier name.
$FirstClimbDate="May 29, 1953"	Here you have a combination of a word and two numbers, along with a comma. The double quotation marks cause the expression to be read as a single string. It is an *interpolated* string.
$MtName="Everest"	The assignment of a single word to a single scalar value creates the most generally recognized version of a string. It is an interpolated string. To add to the discussion concerning $100,000, Perl is *case sensitive*, so $FirstName and $firstname are different identifier names.

Scalar Variable	Discussion
$NumOfClimbers = 2	The number 2 is an *integer*. If you wanted to speak about the number of days required for a given climb, you might use a rational number, or float, such as 2.2. (Note that more than two climbers were involved in the expedition in 1953.)

Scalars as Stored and Printed

Given the scalar values in Table 3.1, you can create a program that prints the values to your command prompt (or the output area of DzSoft's Perl Editor). Listing03_09 provides the complete program. As Listing03_09 shows, when you employ scalar variables inside double quotations, the interpreter reads the value stored in the scalar variable. This is one of the distinguishing criteria of interpolated strings.

```
#Listing03_09
#set up a series of scalar variables
$ClimberNewZealand = "Edmund Hillary"; #interpolated string
$ElevMetric = 8844.43;                 #floating decimal
$ClimberNapal = "Tenzing Norgay";      #interpolated string
$FirstClimbDate="May 29, 1953";        #interpolated string
$MtName="Everest";                     #interpolated string
$ClimbPermitCost='$100,000';           #character string


#print functions for the scalars
#Interpolated strings allow you to retrieve the values
#the scalars store
print "\nHere are some data about Mt. $MtName:\n";
print "\nClimber: $ClimberNewZealand";
print "\nClimber: $ClimberNapal";
print "\nDate of first climb: $FirstClimbDate";
print "\nHeight of Mt. $MtName: $ElevMetric";
print "\nApprox climbing permit cost: $ClimbPermitCost";
```

Figure 3.10 illustrates the output of Listing03_09.

Figure 3.10
Scalars placed in interpolated strings display facts about Everest.

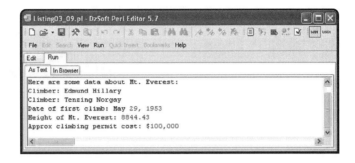

Strings and More Strings

To review a bit, if you enclose text in double quotes, you create an interpolated string. If you enclose text in single quotes, you create a character (or literal) string. An interpolated string allows you to retrieve values from variables. A literal string does not. Consider the lines of code shown in Listing03_10:

```
#Listing03_10.pl
$MtName="Everest";                       #interpolated string
$ClimberNewZealand = "Edmund Hillary"; #interpolated string
$ClimberNapal = "Tenzing Norgay";        #interpolated string


print "\nHere are some data about Mt. $MtName:\n";
print '\nClimber: $ClimberNewZealand'; #literal string output
print "\nClimber: $ClimberNapal";        #interpolated string output
```

Figure 3.11 illustrates the output of Listing03_10.

Figure 3.11
The output of Listing03_10.

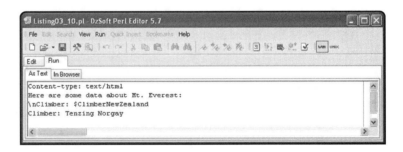

As Figure 3.11 illustrates, when a string supports variables, you can place a scalar value in a string. If you employ the `print()` function, the Perl interpreter reads the quoted part of the string, and when it comes to the variable it retrieves the value stored in it and prints it as part of the output. The line beginning `"\nClimber"` represents a literal (single quotes) string. For this reason, you see exactly what you place within the single quotes. Interpolated and literal strings together give you great prerogatives. Among other things, you can proceed to construct strings from strings and perform a variety of string manipulations. You can create strings that store commands. The following sections examine several such activities.

❊ **String Cheese Talk**

You can consider an interpolated string to be, in at least one respect, a scalar identifier that contains other scalar identifiers. On the other hand, a literal string consists of a group of literal characters.

Consider these three statements:

```
$CheeseA = "cheddar";                    #1 Interpolated
$CheeseTalkA = 'He likes $CheeseA.';     #2 Literal
$CheeseTalkB = "He likes $CheeseA.";     #3 Interpolated
```

The first statement (#1) assigns a set of *interpolated* characters (a string) to a scalar identifier, `$CheeseA`. When you print the scalar, you see the string:

```
cheddar
```

The second statement (#2) assigns a set of *literal* characters to a scalar identifier (`$CheeseTalkA`). The single quotation marks make the string literal. If you print this scalar, the string you see is, literally, what you see:

```
He likes $CheeseA.
```

The third statement assigns an interpolated string that consists of a set of characters *and* a scalar identifier (`$CheeseA`) to yet another scalar identifier (`$CheeseTalkB`). In this case, the resulting string allows you to see the value the scalar identifier stores:

```
He likes cheddar.
```

Concatenation and Printing Scalars

The concatenation operator in Perl is the period (.). When you join one string with another using a period, you concatenate them. You can concatenate interpolated and literal strings. When you concatenate two strings, you can assign the result to a third string. Listing03_11 provides an example of several forms of concatenation. In addition, notice that if you store a string in an identifier, you can use the `print()` function to print a string without enclosing the identifier in quotation marks.

```
#Listing03_11
#Uses of concatenation
```

```
#Concatenate interpolated strings
#and assign them to a scalar variable
$WordString = "\"There is a blessing in this gentle breeze,\"";
$AuthorString= "wrote Wallace Stevens. ";

#Concatenate an interpolated escape sequence and two scalar variables...
$WordString = $WordString . "\n" . $AuthorString;

print "\n" . "$WordString";

#A character string allows you to literally reproduce
#text as set up with white spaces
#Assign the character string to a scalar
$StanzaWords =
    'In summer at least some things,
        such as breezes, can be
            gentle, and this is probably
                what the poet referred to...';

#concatenated scalar variables - no quotation marks used with the scalars.
print "\nConcatenated scalar variables:\n";
print $WordString . $StanzaWords;
```

Figure 3.12 illustrates the output of Listing03_11. Interpolated and literal strings can be combined, and escape sequences can be used to make quotation marks visible.

Figure 3.12
Concatenation provides a
way to achieve a number of
textual effects.

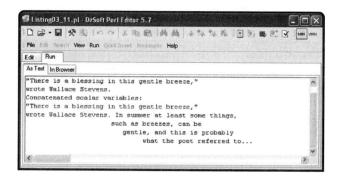

Multiplying String Output

Operators cause identifiers to act on each other. You use them to create relations among identifiers. In Perl, since scalars are numbers or strings, there are also two sets of operators. For numbers, many of the operators are those that you are familiar with through mathematics. However, with respect to strings, you use a set of operators that differ from those that mathematics provides. If they are the same, you find in many instances that when you use them, you might not be able to easily predict the result. Consider for instance what a *multiplication operator* (x) means when applied to strings. Perl sports such an operator. It allows you to duplicate and concatenate a string with itself. Listing03_12 illustrates two approaches to such concatenation.

```
#Listing03_12
#"Multiplying" and concatenating a string


#Use of a standard arithmetic operator
#Copies and concatenates an interpolated string three times
#Then assigns the result to a scalar variable

$MultipliedString = "\nDo it!" × 3;
print "$MultipliedString";


#Another approach using the same general notion
#but this time preceding the scalar variable
#with the multiplication expression

$TextSource = "Done that!";
#With a little variation
$SpacePlace = "...";


print "\n" . $SpacePlace × 1 . "$TextSource\n";
print $SpacePlace × 2 . "$TextSource\n";
print $SpacePlace × 3 . "$TextSource\n";
```

In Listing03_12, you combine the operator and the scalar that contains the three dots ($SpacePlace × 3) into an *expression*. You then concatenate the expression to the scalar that contains the text source. However, you place the scalar containing the text source in quotes to combine it with an escape sequence. Figure 3.13 illustrates the output of Listing03_12.

Figure 3.13
Using string multiplication allows you to enhance the effects of basic concatenation.

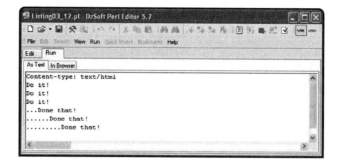

Relational Operators for Strings

The concatenation operator is one of several operators that apply to strings. Another type of operator is a *relational operator*. Relational operators allow you to compare items to each other. One form of string comparison involves discovering whether one string is alphabetically prior to (less than) another or comparatively the same as (equal to) another. Table 3.3 provides a discussion of the relational operator and a few other operators that apply to strings.

Table 3.3   Operators for Strings

Operator	Discussion
eq	One string is equal to another. This applies with letters, words, or longer units of text. The equality is exact, not relative to length.
ne	One string is not equal to another. This applies with letters, words, or longer units of text.
lt	One string occupies an alphabetical position that is less than another. "Another" is less than "Brother."
gt	One string occupies an alphabetical position that is greater than another. "Brother" is greater than "Another."
ge	One string is the same as or alphabetically greater than another. "Another" is equal to itself, but not greater than itself. The test would render a true finding.
le	One string is the same as or alphabetically less than another. "Another" is equal to itself, but not less than itself. The test would render a true finding.
++	This is a unary operator. Suffixed to a scalar, it causes the last letter of the scalar to change so that it increases one place in the alphabet. If the letter is "z", then it shifts back to the beginning of the alphabet and moves to "a."
comma (,)	Allows you to append strings to each other.

Evaluating Relationships

In most cases, when you evaluate a relationship between two strings, you use selection. Selection statements (also known as selection control structures) receive extensive discussion later in this book, but it does not hurt to introduce one such statement (the `if` statement) at this point to illustrate how to work with relational operators.

Consider what happens if you want to determine if two items are equal to each other. You can use an `if` selection statement. An `if` selection statement sets up an expression that can be interpreted more or less as follows: *if* the relation I describe between *A* and *B* is *true*, *then* do something. The selection involves selecting an action to perform based on the truth of a given relationship. The relationship usually involves determining whether *A* and *B* are equal to, less than, greater than, or not equal to each other.

Selection and Equality (eq)

As Listing03_13 shows, to create an `if` selection statement, you type the word `if` and a set of parentheses that enclose the relation you want to test. The relation usually consists of the terms you want to test related by a relational operator (in this case `eq`). You then create a statement inside curly braces following the selection statement. The statement you place inside the curly braces tells the interpreter what to do if the result of the selection test (the test inside the parentheses) is true.

```
#Listing03_13
#Generic selection statements using eq with strings
if("Chicago" eq "Chicago")
{
    print "\nStatement 1 (\"\"): Chicago to Chicago, okay.";
}
    if('Chicago' eq 'Miami')
{
    print "\nStatement 2: Chicago to Miami, okay.";
}
if('Chicago' eq 'Chicago')
{
    print "\nStatement 3 (\'\'): Chicago to Chicago, okay.";
}
if('Chicago' eq "Chicago")
{
    print "\nStatement 4 (\'\'): Chicago to Chicago, okay.";
}
```

In Listing03_13, string constants are used in the selection statements. In Statement 1, the tested strings are interpolated. In Statements 2 and 3 the strings are literal. As the interpreter enters each `if` statement, it encounters the strings to be compared and a relational operator (`eq`).

This type of operator is called a *binary operator*. It is binary because it relates two (bi) terms. The interpreter tests the items presented according to the logic the relational operator establishes. If the relationship is true, then the interpreter goes on to process statements inside of the curly braces. If the relationship is false, then the interpreter skips over the statements inside the curly braces and goes on with the remainder of the program.

As Figure 3.14 illustrates, Statements 1 and 3 turn out to be true (Chicago equals Chicago). Again, while Statement 1 involves an interpolated string and Statement 3 involves a literal (character) string, the selection statements find the strings equal. On the other hand, with Statement 2, involving Chicago and Miami, the interpreter finds the test false and so skips the statement inside the curly braces.

Notice, however, Statement 4. It involves a selection statement that evaluates a literal and an interpreted string. As Figure 3.14 illustrates, these, too, prove equal. They prove equal because the interpolated string and the literal string represent different forms of the same data.

Figure 3.14
The `eq` relational operator renders three true results.

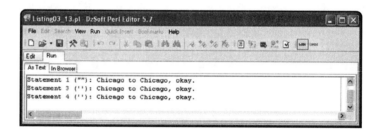

Testing with Scalars

Selection statements that work with interpolated and character strings also work when you assign the strings to scalar identifiers. Consider Listing03_14:

```
#Listing03_14
#Selection using scalars
#Assign interpolated and character strings to scalars
$CityA = "Chicago";
$CityB = 'Chicago';
$CityC = "Miami";

#interpolated strings tested
if($CityA eq $CityA)
```

```
{
    print "\nStatement 1 (\"\"): Chicago to Chicago, okay.";
}
#interpolated strings tested
if($CityA eq "Chicago")
{
    print "\nStatement 2: \$Chicago to \"Chicago\", okay.";
}
#literal strings tested
if($CityB eq $CityB )
{
    print "\nStatement 3 (\'\'): Chicago to Chicago, okay.";
}
#interpolated string tested against a character string
if($CityA eq $CityB )
{
    print "\nStatement 4 (\"\'): Chicago to Chicago, okay.";
}
```

Listing03_14 reworks the previous listing to substitute scalar for *constant* string values. A constant string is one that you see between quotes (literal or interpolated). In most of the examples so far, you have typed constant strings and assigned them to scalars.

Statement 1 tests a scalar against a scalar, and the strings tested are interpolated. Statement 2 tests a scalar to which an interpolated string has been assigned against an interpolated (constant) string. Statement 3 tests scalars to which you have assigned character strings. Statement 4 tests two scalars: one containing a character string, the other containing an interpolated string.

Selection and ne

Testing for equality using eq provides the most reliable approach to comparing two items, but circumstances often require that you compare items to determine whether it is true that they are *not* equal. To accomplish this, you employ the ne operator. As Listing03_15 shows, if two operands related by the ne operator are not equal, then the statement tested is true.

```
#Listing03_15
#Testing for lack of equality
$CityA = "Chicago";
$CityC = "Miami";
```

```
#a "not equals" statement tested
if($CityA ne $CityC)
{
    print "\nStatement true; cities not equal.";
}
```

Selection and lt and gt

You can use the less than (lt) and greater than (gt) relational operators to create complex programs that perform operations like sorting and ordering. Here, it is enough to demonstrate that they work with strings, as is shown in Listing03_16:

```
#Listing03_16
#Testing for greater than or less than relationships
$CityA = "Chicago";
$CityC = "Miami";

#selection test to discover one value alphabetically greater than the other
if($CityC gt $CityA)
{
    print "\nMiami comes later in an alphabetical list than Chicago.";
}

#selection test for one value alphabetically less than the other
if($CityA lt $CityC)
{
    print "\nChicago is earlier in an alphabetical list than Miami.";
}
```

Listing03_16 provides two selection statements, and both involve ordering Chicago and Miami so that when compared in selection statements using lt and gt, the results prove true. The first selection statement tests whether Chicago occurs in an alphabetical list prior to Miami. The second selection statement tests whether Miami occurs in an alphabetical list later than Chicago. In both cases, the selection statements result in true evaluations, so the interpreter processes the statements between the curly braces. Figure 3.15 illustrates the output of the two selection statements.

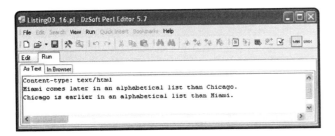

Figure 3.15
Greater than (gt) and less than (lt) operators establish alphabetical ordering.

Increment Operations on Strings

The *unary increment operator* can be used on strings. A unary operator is an operator that involves only one term. It does not relate two terms, as does a binary operator. Instead, it operates directly on one term. In this case, the unary operator is an *increment operator* (++). The increment operator for Perl strings causes the value of the character that is last in the string to increase by one whenever the interpreter processes a statement involving the increment operator. When a character increases by one, it become the next "greater" letter in the alphabet. An "a" becomes a "b." In Listing03_17 the "x" offers a way to illustrate that the increment operator affects only the last character of a string.

```
#Listing03_17
#Testing the unary operator with strings
$SmallA = "a";
$LargeA = "xA";

#create an alphabet with a unary operator

print"\n 1. " . $SmallA . "\t" . $LargeA;
print"\n 2. " . $SmallA++ . "\t" . $LargeA++;
print"\n 3. " . $SmallA++ . "\t" . $LargeA++;
print"\n 4. " . $SmallA++ . "\t" . $LargeA++;
print"\n 5. " . $SmallA++ . "\t" . $LargeA++;
print"\n 6. " . $SmallA++ . "\t" . $LargeA++;
```

Figure 3.16 illustrates the output of Listing03_17. When you first use the operator, you do not see any change (1) because the line that prints the string includes no increment operator. In the first increment line (2), you see no change because the increment operator in this example increments the value only after the statement in which it occurs has been executed. The value you see for line 2 actually shows the value as it exists prior to being incremented. For line 3, you see the value changed by the previous line.

Figure 3.16
The increment operator increases the value of the final letter in the string to which it is applied.

The q() and qq() Functions

Although the next chapter deals extensively with functions you can apply to strings, two functions work in ways that closely resemble double and single quotation marks. These are the q() and qq() functions. The names of the functions abbreviate single and double *quotations*. In general, in fact, you can picture these functions as performing the work of double and single quotation marks. Instead of the quotation marks, however, you employ the functions.

When you use the functions, you place whatever you want to translate into a string between the opening and closing parentheses that follow the names of the functions. Listing03_18 provides examples of basic uses of the two functions:

```
#Listing03_18
#q() and qq()
#set up a scalar for testing in the functions
$TestValue = "Hello";


#q() gives you a character string, so you see what you type
$CharacterQ = q($TestValue, it is good to see you.);
print "\nq(): " . $CharacterQ;


#qa() gives you an interpolated string,
#so you have some options with embedded identifiers
$CharacterQQ = qq($TestValue, it is good to see you.);
print "\nqq(): " . $CharacterQQ;
```

When you insert the scalar value ($TestValue) into the q() function, as Figure 3.17 illustrates, you see only the identifier's name, not the value the identifier stores. This demonstrates that the q() function creates a character string. On the other hand, when you insert the scalar identifier into the qq() function along with some text, the interpreter extracts the string from the identifier. This demonstrates that the qq() function creates an interpolated string.

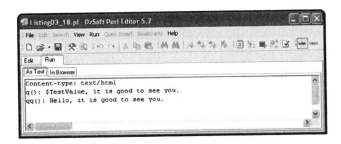

Figure 3.17
The q() and qq() functions create literal and interpolated strings.

Blocks

A block is a portion of a program that you create using beginning and end block labels. Each block has one label. The label consists of a word you choose. You type the beginning label at the beginning of the block you want to designate. You type the end label at the end of the block you want to designate. With the addition of a little syntax to make things official, this is all that is involved in creating a block.

You can assign blocks of text to scalars and in this way use Perl to manage fairly large bodies of information. When you use blocks, you cannot include variables inside the blocks. If you want to use a variable in association with a block, you can store the block and then associate it with a variable. The following section provides an example of this type of activity.

Blocks and print

As already mentioned, you designate a block using a block label. The label can consist of any word you choose so long as it is not a keyword. To designate the beginning of the block, you prefix a shift operator (<<) to the first use of the block label. Then you follow with whatever text you want to type. When you finish typing your text, you again type the label. The second time you type the label, you must place it snug against the right margin of your text editing area. Listing03_19 shows a basic approach to setting up a block. In this example, when you create the block, you also print it.

```
#Listing03_19
#Creating blocks
#Print the block to show its creation
print <<NOTES;
    Thank you for contacting us.
    A service representative will
    contact you within 24 hours.
NOTES
```

Figure 3.18 illustrates the block from Listing03_19 as displayed as output.

Figure 3.18
The block is displayed with
a `print` command.

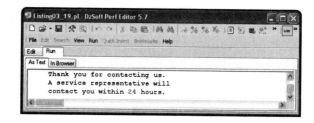

Blocks and Variables

Printing blocks can prove a useful way to handle large bodies of text immediately, but an equally beneficial use of blocks involves assigning them to scalar identifiers. You can assign blocks to scalar variables and then use the identifiers later. Parentheses enclose the assignment statement. Listing03_20 shows a basic approach to storing a block in a scalar variable and then printing the block afterward.

```
#Listing03_20
#Blocks assigned to and used with variables

#Variable to be combined with block
$TestValue = "Mr. Blue";

($BlockVariable = <<NOTES);
    Thank you for contacting us.
    A service representative will
    contact you within 24 hours.
NOTES

#Concatenating a value with the block
print "\n \n" . " $TestValue,\n" . $BlockVariable;
```

Figure 3.19 illustrates the block displayed as output.

Figure 3.19
A block makes printing the
notification convenient.

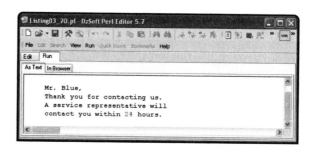

Conclusion

In this chapter, you have explored how to use scalar variables. The focus of your work has been scalar variables with relation to interpolated and character strings. Although scalar values in Perl involve both numbers and strings, many programmers view Perl as a language that is ideal for processing text. Your work with strings in this chapter is a concession to this viewpoint.

The strings you work with encompass interpolated and character stings. You create interpolated strings using double quotation marks. An interpolated string allows you to extract the value from a variable when you create or display the string. You create character stings using single quotation marks. A character string preserves everything you include in it exactly as you have typed it, including the names of variables. It does not allow you to extract the value from a variable as you create it.

To work with strings, you examined uses of the `print()` function. The `print()` function provides a primary tool for learning how to program. It allows you to write output to a selected device.

In addition to the `print()` function and strings, you explored escape sequences, which provide ways of performing such actions as forcing line returns and inserting special characters, such as dollar signs. After examining escape sequences, you experimented with string concatenation. Concatenation allows you to combine the text stored in variables or to deal with literal text and assign it to variables.

Beyond concatenation, you dealt with operators that apply specifically to strings. To explore how operators work, you briefly experimented with simple selection statements. Given the grounding you gained from selection statements, you were able to examine such operators as the `eq`, `gt`, `lt`, and `ne` operators. All of these are binary operators. You also examined a single unary operator, the increment operator. This allows you to increase the alphabetical value of a letter at the end of a string. As a final sally in this chapter, you explored the `q()` and `qq()` functions and the use of labeled text blocks. Work with these functions sets the stage for the next chapter, which extensively investigates the use of functions relating to strings.

4 } Print Functions

While many of the functions Perl offers originate in modules that accompany the Perl interpreter, it is best to begin your work with the built-in Perl functions. Toward this end, this chapter introduces functions, function arguments, and the returned values of functions. Among key functions that most Perl programmers learn first are the `uc()`, `ucfirst()`, `chomp()`, `chop()`, `length()`, `substr()`, and `join()` functions, and these and other functions receive attention in this chapter. As you go, you work with the functions through a number of elementary programming exercises. The topics this chapter addresses include the following:

- ❉ Functions applied to scalars
- ❉ How arguments and return values apply to functions
- ❉ Using functions to change the cases of characters
- ❉ Hidden characters and truncating strings
- ❉ Command line input and Perl programs
- ❉ Manipulating strings in a variety of ways

How Functions Work

Although a great deal more remains to be said about functions in chapters to come, a few preliminary points can be made in this chapter to ensure that you understand the use of the built-in Perl functions as they relate to strings.

Basic Call and Return Operations

As Figure 4.1 illustrates, in the standard presentation and use of functions, the name of the function directly precedes a set of parentheses that enclose an *argument that you pass to the function*. When you type the name of a function, the interpreter processes the arguments. When you use a built-in function, you do not see the code that performs this work. (After all, the function is built into Perl. In later chapters, you see how you can build your own functions.) After the

Figure 4.1
Function calls can accommodate arguments and return values.

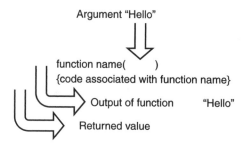

interpreter processes the argument using the code associated with the function, it frequently *returns* a value. Some functions accept many arguments, but most are restricted to one return value. Sometimes the returned value consists of an altered form of the argument you have passed to the function. At other times the returned value consists of an integer (usually 0 or 1) that reports whether the function has successfully completed its operation. In the case of the print() function, you see the argument(s) you have passed to it rendered to the appropriate output device (usually either the monitor or a file).

 In this book, to distinguish function names from the names of other things, parentheses are appended to function names. Example: print().

Variations on Call and Return

Perl can sometimes prove confusing because it requires you to use no strict syntax conventions when you call functions. For example, if you program with a language like C, C++, or Java, you use a standard form of function call. This standard form always involves the name of the function, parentheses, and inside the parentheses the argument you submit to the function. With Perl, you can employ this form of calling functions, and throughout this book you are encouraged to do so, but in many instances, particularly respecting the print() function, you often see function calls as represented in Listing04_01.

```
#Listing04_01
#Perl functions allow you to use parentheses
#to enclose arguments (standard form, recommended):

$ArgumentForFunction = "\nHello";
print "\n#1";
#1 Standard function form
print ("$ArgumentForFunction");
```

```
#Standard approach to a cascading set of function calls
print (uc($ArgumentForFunction));

print "\n#2";
#2 Using quotes instead of parentheses
print "$ArgumentForFunction";
#This form causes no compiler errors
#But the uc() function is read as part of the text
print "\nUnintended result:\n";
print "uc($ArgumentForFunction)" ;

print "\n#3";
#3 Using nothing at all
print $ArgumentForFunction;

#Cascading function calls with no parentheses or quotations
print uc $ArgumentForFunction;
```

Comment #1 in Listing04_01 shows what might be viewed as the most explicit and accepted approach to calling a function. This form of calling functions involves enclosing the arguments to the function in parentheses. The advantage of this form of function call is that it makes clear to the reader of your code precisely what you have submitted to the function as an argument. (Figure 4.2 illustrates the output of Listing04_01.)

In the lines that comment #1 introduces, you also see a function within a function. The uc() function converts the contents of a string from lower- to uppercase. In this context, the uc() function also uses parentheses. You pass an argument to it, and when you employ the parentheses with the function, it is easy to discern that you are passing an argument to the uc() function and then, in turn, feeding the returned value of the uc() function to the print() function. Such an approach to using functions is often referred to as *cascading* functions.

At comment #2 in Listing04_01, you see that it is possible (as has been shown repeatedly in the previous chapters) that you can follow the print() function with its argument in quotes. This approach to using the print() function proves acceptable in many contexts, but in this case, if you place the uc() inside the quotes, the interpreter reads the uc() function as part of the text. (See the output in Figure 4.2.)

In the lines comment #3 identifies, you see a form of code that programmers often find irritating to work with if they have little experience with Perl. Here, neither parentheses nor quotes appear to distinguish the functions and their arguments. You see only one function name, another function name, and then a scalar. The interpreter processes the combination without problems. Still, the readability of the code is questionable.

Figure 4.2
You can use different forms of syntax with functions and achieve the same results.

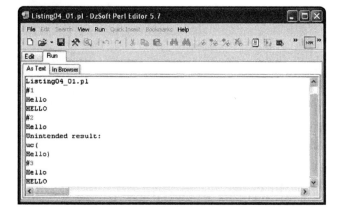

Changing the Cases of Strings

As the use of the uc() function in the previous section indicated, Perl offers you functions that allow you to change the case of characters in strings. Some of the functions affect only the starting characters of a string. Others allow you to change all the characters in a string. This section provides a review of these functions.

Case with First Characters

If you want to change the first character of a string to upper- or lowercase, you can do so through the ucfirst() and lcfirst() functions. Consider Listing04_02:

```
#Listing04_02
#Changing the cases of first letters in strings
#The first letter of the writer's name remains lowercase
$NameToChange = "herman Melville";
print "\nPrior to capitalization: " . $NameToChange;


#Assign the scalar back to itself
$NameToChange = ucfirst($NameToChange);
print "\nAfter capitalization: " . $NameToChange;


#Change the first letter back to lowercase
$NameToChange = lcfirst($NameToChange);
print "\nRestored to original: " . $NameToChange;
```

In Listing04_02, you first assign a string containing the name of the author of *Moby-Dick* to a scalar, $NameToChange. You employ the `print()` function to print the string to the output area. Then you employ the `ucfirst()` function to change the first character of the string to uppercase. The function capitalizes the small "h" of the original string. To make the change effective, you must assign the string back to itself. Afterward, you restore the first character of the string to the lowercase by using the `lcfirst()` function. Figure 4.3 illustrates the output of Listing04_02.

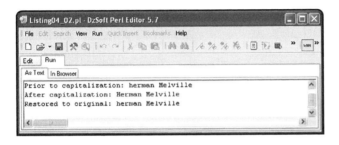

Figure 4.3
The `ucfirst()` and `lcfirst()` functions convert first characters of strings to lower- or upper-case.

Case with Entire Strings

You use the `uc()` function to convert all the characters of a string to uppercase characters. You use the `lc()` function to change entire strings to lowercase characters. Listing04_03 demonstrates the use of the `uc()` and `lc()` functions:

```
#Listing04_03
#Changing the cases of first letters in strings

#The writer's name begins as lowercase
$NameToChange = "william wordsworth";
print "\nPrior to capitalization: " . $NameToChange;

#Assign the scalar back to itself
#Convert to all capital letters
$NameToChange = uc($NameToChange);
print "\nAfter capitalization: " . $NameToChange;

#Change the string back to lowercase
$NameToChange = lc($NameToChange);
print "\nRestored to original: " . $NameToChange;
```

In Listing04_03, you first assign the name of the poet to a scalar, $NameToChange. You then pass the scalar as an argument to the uc() function, which converts the string containing the poet's name to uppercase. Notice that, as before, to make the conversion effective, you must assign the string back to itself. The lc() function converts the string to lowercase. Again, you must assign the string back to itself to make the conversion effective. Figure 4.4 illustrates the output of Listing04_03.

Figure 4.4
The uc() and lc() functions convert all characters in a string to upper- or lowercase.

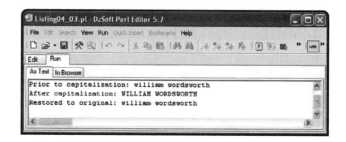

Obtaining the Length of a String

To obtain the length of a string, you employ the Perl length() function. Like the uc() and print() functions, the length() function requires a string for an argument. Unlike these functions, it returns a value that is not itself a string. The value that it returns is an integer that indicates the number of characters in the string. Listing04_04 illustrates some uses of the length() function:

```
#Listing04_04
#Use the length() function

#1 Basic string
#characters in the first line: 22
#characters in the second line: 40
#white spaces are counted as characters
($PreludeLines = <<WORDW);
I should learn to love
The end of life and everything we know.
WORDW

#2.Print the lines
print("\n". "$PreludeLines" . "\n");
```

```
#3.Obtain the length and store the value in a scalar
$CharLength = length($PreludeLines);
#Then show the results
print "\nThe number of characters in the lines," .
    " \nincluding blank spaces " .
    "(from Wordsworth's \"Prelude\")is $CharLength.";


#4.You can also just print the return value
print "\nAgain, the length: ". length($PreludeLines);
```

The lines accompanying comment #1 in Listing04_04 create a block consisting of two lines from William Wordsworth's "The Prelude." Preceding the creation of the block, the comments show counts of the characters, including the blank spaces, that each line contains. You store the lines in a scalar, $PreludeLines. The code affiliated with comment #2 prints these lines.

In the lines trailing comment #3, you call the length() function and provide $PreludeLines to it as its argument. The function obtains the number of characters in the lines, including white spaces, and returns this value to the scalar $CharLength. Having obtained the character length of the lines, you then print a concatenated string that interpolates the value stored in $CharLength.

At comment #4, you call the print() function to print the return value of length(). Figure 4.5 shows you the output of Listing04_04.

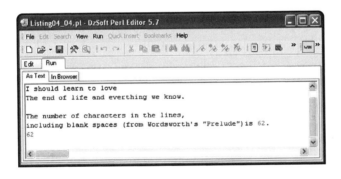

Figure 4.5
Use the length() function to obtain string lengths with white spaces.

Hidden Characters and Strings

It often happens that when you process a string, a newline character concludes the string. Such characters are not visible and can create problems if you want to compare strings with each other. The eq operator, for instance, does not find a string containing a newline character equal to another that lacks a newline character even if all the characters other than the newline characters are the same in the two strings.

Hidden Characters in Strings

Figure 4.6 illustrates two lines from the poetry of W. H. Auden. The first set of lines contains hidden characters. The second set contains no such characters.

Figure 4.6
Lines from W. H. Auden's "Fish in the Unruffled Lakes" shows extra characters.

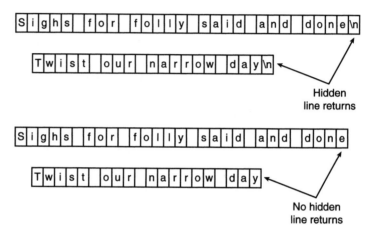

Comparison of the two lines illustrated in Figure 4.6 results in the wrong outcome if you are examining the lines only on the basis of whether the two sets of text you see are equal. Consider Listing04_05:

```
#Listing04_05
#1 Set up lines with and without hidden newline characters
$CoupletALineA= "Sighs for folly said and done\n";
$CoupletALineB= "Twist our narrow days\n";
#without
$CoupletBLineA= "Sighs for folly said and done";
$CoupletBLineB= "Twist our narrow days";

#2 Print to show visual equality but different lengths
print("\nA-A: ". $CoupletALineA . "\n");
print("\nA-B: ". $CoupletALineB . "\n");
print length($CoupletALineA);
```

```
print("\nA-A: ". $CoupletBLineA . "\n");
print("\nA-B: ". $CoupletBLineB . "\n");
print length($CoupletBLineA);

#3 Compare the lines to show the interpreter
#considers them to be different
if($CoupletALineA eq $CoupletBLineA)
{
    #Does not print since equal operator returns false
    print "\nLines are the same."
}

if($CoupletALineA ne $CoupletBLineA)
{
    #Prints since the not equal operator returns true
    print "\nLines are not the same."
}
```

At comment #1 in Listing04_05, you establish two sets of strings. You attach newline characters to the first set but leave them off the second set. Then you assign the two sets of strings to scalars. In the lines associated with comment #2, you print the two couplets to show their visible resemblance, but you also employ the length() function to evaluate their lengths. Appearances indicate the lines equal each other, but from the returned values of the length() function you see that hidden characters leave them unequal. In the lines comment #3 identifies, you conduct a test using selection statements and the eq and ne operators. Figure 4.7 shows you the results. The selection statements indicate that the interpreter finds the strings unequal.

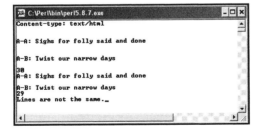

Figure 4.7
Unseen characters render
the strings unequal.

Eliminating Characters

Perl provides the chomp() and chop() functions to eliminate characters from the ends of strings. The chomp() function receives the greatest use since it eliminates newline characters and removes no characters other than the newline character.

Using the chomp() Function

The chomp() function directly addresses the problem illustrated in Figure 4.7, in which the interpreter finds two strings that visibly possess the same characters to be unequal. The lack of equality results from hidden characters attached at the ends of lines. Listing04_06 illustrates the use of the chomp() function:

```
#Listing04_06
#1 Set up lines with and without hidden end-of-line characters
$CoupletALineA= "Sighs for folly said and done\n";
$CoupletALineB= "Twist our narrow days\n";


#Use Chomp to remove the hidden end-of-line characters
print "\nWith hidden EOL:" . chomp($CoupletALineA);
print "\nWith hidden EOL:" . chomp($CoupletALineB);


#without
$CoupletBLineA= "Sighs for folly said and done";
$CoupletBLineB= "Twist our narrow days";


print "\nWithout hidden EOL:" . chomp($CoupletBLineA);
print "\nWithout hidden EOL:" . chomp($CoupletBLineB);


#2 Print to show visual equality but different lengths
print("\nA-A: ". $CoupletALineA . "\n");
print("\nA-B: ". $CoupletALineB . "\n");
print length($CoupletALineA);


print("\nA-A: ". $CoupletBLineA . "\n");
print("\nA-B: ". $CoupletBLineB . "\n");
print length($CoupletBLineA);


#3 Compare the lines to show the interpreter
#considers them to be different
```

```
if($CoupletALineA eq $CoupletBLineA)
{
    #Does not print since equal operator returns false
    print "\nLines are the same."
}


if($CoupletALineA ne $CoupletBLineA)
{
    #Does since the not equal operator returns true
    print "\nLines are not the same."
}
```

Listing04_06 is the same as Listing04_05, with the exception of the two lines that contain the chomp() function. Calls to this function appear in the lines associated with comment #1. Figure 4.8 shows the change in the output. Now, rather than finding the two sets of lines unequal, the interpreter finds them equal. The lengths of the lines are now the same. They are visibly and invisibly equal.

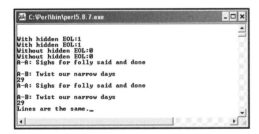

Figure 4.8
The interpreter now finds the lines to be equal.

In addition to removing hidden characters, the chomp() function returns value. The return value is 1 if the chomp() function finds that the string you have provided contains a hidden newline character. The return value is 0 if the chomp() function finds that the string you have provided as an argument contains no hidden newline character. In the lines accompanying comment #1, Listing04_07 shows you the return values of the chomp() function.

```
#Listing04_07

#1 Set up lines with and without hidden end of line characters
$CoupletALineA= "Sighs for folly said and done\n";
$CoupletALineB= "Twist our narrow days\n";
```

```
#Use Chomp to remove the hidden end-of-line characters
print "\nReturn value with hidden EOL:" . chomp($CoupletALineA);
print "\nReturn value with hidden EOL:" . chomp($CoupletALineB);

#without
$CoupletBLineA= "Sighs for folly said and done";
$CoupletBLineB= "Twist our narrow days";

print "\nReturn value without hidden EOL:" . chomp($CoupletBLineA);
print "\nReturn value hidden EOL:" . chomp($CoupletBLineB);

#2 Print to show visual equality but different lengths
print("\nA-A: ". $CoupletALineA . "\n");
print("\nA-B: ". $CoupletALineB . "\n");
print length($CoupletALineA);

print("\nA-A: ". $CoupletBLineA . "\n");
print("\nA-B: ". $CoupletBLineB . "\n");
print length($CoupletBLineA);

#3 Compare the lines to show the interpreter
#considers them to be different
if($CoupletALineA eq $CoupletBLineA)
{
    #Does not print since equal operator returns false
    print "\nLines are the same."
}

if($CoupletALineA ne $CoupletBLineA)
{
    #Does since the not equal operator returns true
    print "\nLines are not the same."
}
```

Figure 4.9 illustrates the output of Listing04_07. In addition to showing the returned values, you see from the reports rendered for the number of characters in the string that if you apply the chomp() function to a string after you have used it to delete a newline character, it does not truncate the string.

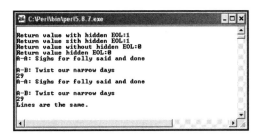

Figure 4.9
The return values of the chomp() function confirm whether a newline character exists.

Using the chop() Function

The chop() function allows you to remove a character from the end of a string. It continues to remove characters from a string every time you call it. In this respect, it differs from the chomp() function, which removes only the newline character. Listing04_08 provides an example of how this works:

```
#Listing04_08


#1 Set up a few lines from Hart Crane's
#"For the Marriage of Faustus and Helen"
# Simultaneously print the lines to show the lines
print (<<HCRANE);
    The mind has shown itself at times
    Too much the baked and labeled dough
    Divided by accepted multitudes.
HCRANE
#2 Assign the last line to a separate string
#Add a newline character
$LastLine = "Divided by accepted multitudes.\n";


#3 Employ the chop() function to show the string being truncated
print "\n 0 No action taken: $LastLine";
print "\nLength before actions: " . length($LastLine);
$ChopReport = chop($LastLine);
#show no return value
print "\n No return value:" . $ChopReport;
print "\n 1 EOL removed: $LastLine";
```

```
print "\nLength after the first action: " . length($LastLine);
chop($LastLine);
print "\n Now the characters...:\n";
print "\n 2 $LastLine";
chop($LastLine);
print "\n 3 $LastLine";
chop($LastLine);
print "\n 4 $LastLine";
```

Comment #1 in Listing04_08 introduces a passage from a poem by Hart Crane. In the lines trailing comment #2, you assign the last line of the passage assigned to a scalar, $LastLine. Notice that you attach a newline character to the string. At comment #3, the truncation operations involving the chop() function begin. You call the print() function to show that the chop() function provides no return value. At the same time, it removes the hidden character. Then, in subsequent calls to chop(), you continue truncating the string. Figure 4.10 shows the output Listing04_08 produces.

Figure 4.10

The chop() function removes a character each time you call it.

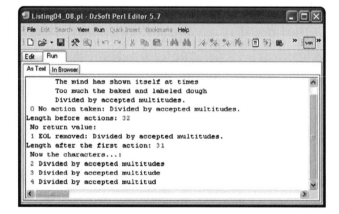

Command Line Interactions

While many of the programs you write using Perl are not likely to involve command line interaction, it remains worthwhile to know how to work with the command line so that you can test your programs. Listing04_09 provides a basic example of a program that supports user interactions.

```
#Listing04_09
#Respond to a command prompt
print "Type your name and press Return: ";
```

```
#1 Prompt for information from the user
$NameTyped = <STDIN>;
print "\nYour name: " . $NameTyped;
```

You can write programs to run at the command line without including the first two lines of Listing04_09, but it does not hurt to include them for form's sake. In the lines associated with comment #1, you type a linc that includes a handle (<STDIN>). A handle allows you to enter information. In this instance, the information you enter is stored in a scalar ($NameTyped). You then use the print() function to display the information.

Handles are dealt with more extensively in a later chapter, but for now note that the expression <STDIN> represents a convention. If the program line included only a less than sign (<) and a greater than sign (>), with no handle identifier (STDIN), the interpreter would find no fault with the program, and you would still be able to enter input as prompted.

To run the program, you can type it and execute at the DOS prompt as you do any other Perl program. If you run the program from the DzSoft Perl Editor, select Run > Run in command prompt or press Shift + F9. Then at the prompt as instructed, type your name and press Return. The program displays your name. If you press Return a second time, the program exits. Figure 4.11 illustrates the program's execution. (See the sidebar for setting up a session that has a light background and dark font.)

Figure 4.11
The program prompts you for your name and then echoes your input.

You then see the DOS window illustrated at the bottom of Figure 4.12. Having set the color scheme for the DOS window once, in future instances of your use of the window, you see the white background and the dark text. You can easily change the color scheme to meet personal preferences by repeating the actions shown in Figure 4.12.

Figure 4.12
Alter the colors for ease of proofing.

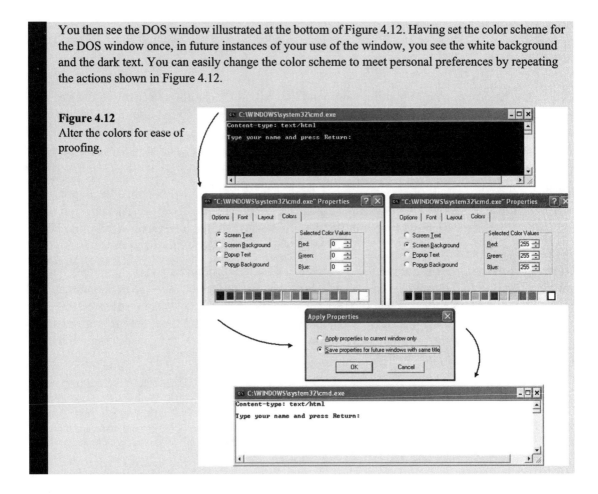

Indexes of Characters

The index() function returns the starting position of a string within a string. The index() function derives its name from the *index* of an *array*. As Figure 4.13 illustrates, an array is analogous to a bureau of drawers. You can identify a drawer by its number. A string is an array of characters, so you can identify each of its characters by its index number. Array indexes begin at 0.

To use the index() function, you provide it with three arguments. The first argument is the string for which you want to search. This can be a scalar or a literal string. The second argument is the target string—the string you want to search. The final argument is the *offset*. The offset indicates the position in the target string you want to designate as the starting point of your search. You identify this position with an integer that identifies an index in the target string. The

Bureau	Array
drawer 0	index 0
drawer 1	index 1
drawer 2	index 2
drawer 3	index 3
drawer 4	index 4

Figure 4.13
An array has indexes just
as a bureau has drawers.

offset identifies a position relative to the starting index of the string, and the starting index of a string is always the zero (0) index. As Figure 4.14 illustrates, the `index()` function searches by default from the beginning (0 index) of the target string. When the `index()` function finds the string it is looking for, it returns the position in the target string that marks the beginning of the string you are looking for.

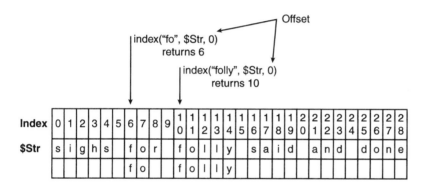

Figure 4.14
The `index()` function searches from the starting index you indicate and finds the first occurrence of the search string you provide.

An Algorithm for Searching

The arguments you supply to the `index()` function reflect the logic of an algorithm you can use to conduct searches of extensive bodies of text to find repeated occurrences of a given string. When you search through a text for the occurrence of a given string, you begin at the start of the text. You move through the text until you find the string you are looking for. As mentioned previously, when you find the string you are looking for, you report the index of the text at which the string you are looking for has its beginning.

Suppose more than one instance of the search string exists in the text. The solution to this problem involves resuming the search with a new start (offset) position. To continue your search, you use the reported starting location of the string you have found and add one to it. You then feed this new starting position to another call to the `index()` function. Figure 4.15 illustrates how this works.

Figure 4.15

The index() function reflects the fundamentals of search algorithms.

1. Search for the first occurrence of search term.
2. Return the index.
3. Set the offset equal to previously returned index plus 1.

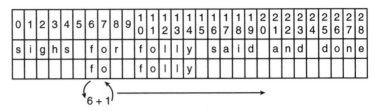

4. Resume the search for next occurrence of search term.

Implementing the Algorithm

Given the search algorithm laid out in the previous section, Listing04_10 uses the index() function to search for two occurrences of a term. In a later chapter, using a repetition control structure, you improve on this program to allow it to find many occurrences of a given string in a target text.

```
#Listing04_10
#Search a string using the index() function


#1 Show users the string that is the target
print ($TargetString= <<TARGET);
Sighs for folly said and done
Twist our narrow days
TARGET


#2. Initialize a scalar to hold the search string
$SearchString = "";
print "\nType the string \"fo\" to begin a search: " . $SearchString;


#3. Collect input from the user
$SearchString = <STDIN>;


#4. Important! Truncate the string to eliminate the newline character
chomp($SearchString);
print "\nSearch begun for \"" . $SearchString . "\"...";
```

```
#5. Use the index function to begin the search from index 0
# Return the index to a scalar and report the position to the user
$IndexLocation = index($TargetString , $SearchString, 0);
print "\nString found at index " . $IndexLocation . "...";


#6. Increment by one and continue the search
$IndexLocation = $IndexLocation + 1;
$IndexLocation = index($TargetString, $SearchString , $IndexLocation);
print "\nString found at index " . $IndexLocation . "...\n";
```

In the lines that comments #1 through #3 designate, you set up a text sample to display to the program user. You initialize a scalar ($SearchString) in which to store user input and then collect input. In the lines trailing comment #4, you call the chomp() function to remove the newline character from the string you type to use as the basis of your search.

The chomp() function is necessary because you add a newline character to the string you type when you press Enter. If you do not remove the newline character, the search does not prove effective unless it so happens that the text you have designated as your target happens to have a string in it that corresponds to the one you type containing the newline character. This is not very likely.

At comment #5 of Listing04_10, you begin the first search using the index() function. Your first argument to the index() function furnishes the target string ($TargetString). Your second argument provides the string ($SearchString) you want to find. The final argument identifies the offset, or starting index (0). You return the result to $IndexLocation and report it to the user using the print() function.

Following the first increment of the search, you proceed with another (see comment #6). To proceed with the search, you add 1 to the returned value residing in $IndexLocation. You use this incremented value as the third argument in the index() function and once again call the function. Figure 4.16 shows the execution of the program with user interaction. The search returns findings at indexes 6 and 10.

Figure 4.16
User input allows you to conduct a search using the index() function.

Searching from the End of a String

If you have worked with the index() function, you can easily work with the rindex()
function. The rindex() function differs from the index() function only because it begins
its search from the end of the string rather than from the beginning. Using such a function at
times proves an important way of increasing the efficiency of search operations. Listing04_11
provides an example of how to use the rindex() function.

```
#Listing04_11
#Search a string using the rindex() function

#1 Show users the string that is the target
print ($TargetString= <<TARGET);
Sighs for folly said and done
Twist our narrow days
TARGET


#Use the length() function
#to initialize a scalar to hold the length of the string
#Report the length
$TargetStringLength = length($TargetString);
print "\nLength of string: " . $TargetStringLength;


#2. Initialize a scalar to hold the search string
$SearchString = "";
print "\nType the string \"fo\" to begin a search: ";


#3. Collect input from the user
$SearchString = <STDIN>;


#4. Important! Truncate the string to eliminate the newline character
chomp($SearchString);
print "\nSearch begun for \"" . $SearchString . "\"...";


#5. Use the index function to begin the search from the end of the string
# Return the index to a scalar and report the position to the user
$IndexLocation = rindex($TargetString , $SearchString, $TargetStringLength);
print "\nString found at index " . $IndexLocation . "...";
```

```
#6. Subtract 1 from the returned index
$IndexLocation = $IndexLocation - 1;
$IndexLocation = rindex($TargetString, $SearchString , $IndexLocation);
print "\nString found at index " . $IndexLocation . "...\n";
```

The primary way in which the use of the `rindex()` function differs from the `index()` function involves identifying the length of the function you want to use for your search. At comment #1, you use the `length()` function to discover the length of the target string. The length of the target string constitutes the starting point of the search the `rindex()` function conducts. The string's length marks the final index.

At comment #5, you initiate the search. The first call to `rindex()` starts at the last index of the target text and moves toward the beginning (the zero index) of the target text. When the `rindex()` function finds the first occurrence of the string you are looking for, it returns the index position in the target string that corresponds to the start of the string you are looking for. To make it so that the search can continue, you subtract 1 from the returned index value. You feed this value to the third argument of the next call to the `rindex()` function. The function can then continue to move toward the zero index of the target text. Figure 4.17 illustrates the output of Listing04_11. Notice that the index value decreases with each iteration of the search (from 10 to 6).

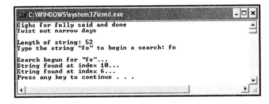

Figure 4.17
The `rindex()` function allows you to search from the end of the string.

Extracting and Replacing Strings

Perl provides a function called `substr()` that allows you to either extract a substring from a given target string or replace a substring in a given target string with another substring. The operation the function performs depends on the number of arguments you provide to the function. With three arguments, you can extract a substring. With four arguments, you can replace a substring. The next few sections elaborate on these themes.

Extracting Substrings with substr()

If you supply three arguments to the `substr()` function, you can extract a substring from a target string. The first argument you supply to the `substr()` function consists of the target string. The second consists of an offset from the zero index. This establishes the starting point of the substring you want to extract. The third argument supplies the length of a string you want to extract. To extract a string from a block of text, the program you develop requires a few operations, as follows:

* Divide the source string so it consists of two parts.
* The first part extends from the beginning of the source string to the index of the substring you want to extract.
* The second part extends from the end of the string you want to extract to the end of the source string.
* Extract the two parts and then rejoin them to re-create the source string without the extracted substring.

Listing04_12 accomplishes these operations.

```
#Listing04_12
#extract a substring using three arguments with substr()

#1 Create a target string from W. B. Yeats' "The Choice"
print ($TargetString= <<TARGET);
The intellect of man is forced to choose
Perfection of the life, or of the work,
And if it take the second must refuse
A heavenly mansion, raging in the dark.
TARGET
print "\n------\n";
$TargetStringLength = length($TargetString);
print "\nTargetStringLength: " . $TargetStringLength;


#2. Create a string to be extracted
$StringToExtract = "heavenly";
print "\nString to be removed: " . $StringToExtract;


#3 Use the index function to find the index of the substring.
$IndexOfSubstring = index($TargetString, $StringToExtract, 0);
print "\nIndex of string: " . $IndexOfSubstring;


#4 Use the length function to establish the length of the
```

```
# substring to be extracted
$LengthOfSubstring = length($StringToExtract);
print "\nLength of string: " . $LengthOfSubstring;
$LengthFromIndex = $TargetStringLength - $IndexOfSubstring;
print "\nLength of target after index: " . $LengthFromIndex;
print "\n------\n";

#5. Extract the last part of the string
$EndOfString = substr($TargetString,
     $IndexOfSubstring + $LengthOfSubstring, #start pos
     $LengthFromIndex - $LengthOfSubstring); #num of chars
print "\nLast part of string: \n". $EndOfString . "\n";
print "\n------\n";

#6. Extract the first part of the string
$BeginningOfString = substr($TargetString,
     0,
     $IndexOfSubstring);
print "\nFirst part of string: \n". $BeginningOfString . "\n";
print "\n------\n";

# Removing "heavenly" leaves two white spaces. Only one is needed.
chop($BeginningOfString);

#7. Concatenate the new string and print
print "\nNew String: \n". $BeginningOfString . $EndOfString . "\n";
```

The lines associated with comments #1 and #2 allow you to set up two scalars to contain the text to be used as a target ($TargetString) and the text to be extracted ($StringToExtract). To have on hand values to use for the third argument of the substr() function, you use the length() function to obtain the lengths of these two strings.

At comments #3 and #4 you call the index() function to find the index position in the target string of the start of the expression you are searching for.

The lines comments #5 and #6 indicate allow you to determine the starting positions and lengths of the two parts of the target string that precede and follow the string you want to extract. In the first call to the substr() function, you extract the trailing part of the target text ($EndOfString). For the first argument of this call to the function, you furnish the source

❋ ❋ ❋

string ($TargetString). For the second argument, you add the value of the starting index of the substring to the length of the substring. For the third argument, you determine how many characters lie between the end of the substring and the end of the target string.

At comment #6 you use the substr() function to extract the text that precedes the substring. In this call, you furnish the source string ($TargetString) for the first argument. For the second argument, you establish the zero (0) index as the starting point of the extraction. For the final argument, you insert the starting index of the substring ($IndexOfSubstring). You store the result of the extraction to $BeginningOfString.

Your final bit of work involves using the chop() function to remove the extra space that remains with the removal of a single word from the target text. Figure 4.18 illustrates the output of Listing04_12.

Figure 4.18
You can use the substr() function with three arguments to extract a word from text.

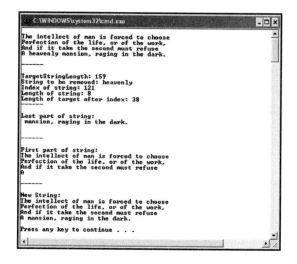

Simplifying Extraction and Replacement

The version of the substr() function that allows you to use four arguments rather than three removes the necessity of dividing the source text into two parts prior to extracting or inserting a substring. Listing04_13 provides a program that uses the four-argument version of the substr() function:

```
#Listing04_13
#extract a substring using four arguments with substr()


#1 Create a target string from W. B. Yeats' "The Choice"
```

```perl
print ($TargetString= <<TARGET);
The intellect of man is forced to choose
Perfection of the life, or of the work,
And if it take the second must refuse
A heavenly mansion, raging in the dark.
TARGET
print "\n------\n";

#2. Create a string to be extracted
$StringToExtract = "heavenly";
print "\nString to be removed: " . $StringToExtract;

#3 Use the index function to find the index of the substring.
$IndexOfSubstring = index($TargetString, $StringToExtract, 0);
print "\nIndex of string: " . $IndexOfSubstring;

#4 Use the length function to establish the length of the
# substring to be extracted
$LengthOfSubstring = length($StringToExtract);
print "\nLength of string: " . $LengthOfSubstring;

#5. Extract/Replace the substring
substr($TargetString,
    $IndexOfSubstring,
    $LengthOfSubstring + 1,
    " ");
print "\nNew String: \n". $TargetString . "\n";
```

The lines that comments #1 and #2 in Listing04_13 indicate set up the source text and the substring to be extracted. At comment #3 you employ the index() function to determine the starting index of the substring to be extracted. The lines that comment #4 designates obtain the starting index of the substring using the index() function.

Given the starting index and length of the substring you want to extract, you proceed at comment #5 to employ the substr() function using four arguments to extract the substring. For the first argument, you provide a scalar with the target text. For the second argument, you provide the starting index of the substring. For the third argument, you furnish the length of the substring. With the final argument, you present the text to be substituted. In this case, since the goal is to extract a substring, you provide an empty string (" "). Figure 4.19 illustrates the output of Listing04_13. The word "heavenly" has been removed.

Figure 4.19
Four arguments for the `substr()` function substantially reduces the complexity of the program.

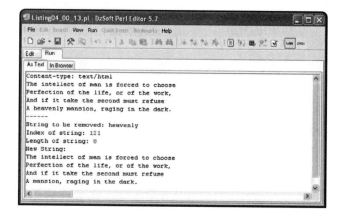

Joining Strings

When you employ the concatenation operator, you can create a single string from two or more constituent strings. To accomplish this, you assign the concatenated result to a scalar you designate to store the concatenated result. To push this theme to an applied context, consider a situation in which you want to create a greeting that involves several scalar data items. See Figure 4.20.

Figure 4.20
A shipping notice contains text and scalar data items.

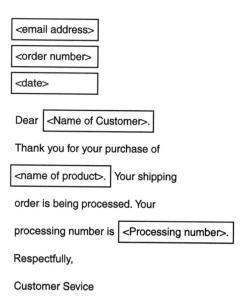

Using Manual Concatenation

To set up a program that might generate the notice that Figure 4.20 displays, you can make use of a concatenation operator. Listing04_14 provides a program that uses a series of concatenations to create a string that might be sent over the Internet to a customer.

```
#Listing04_14
#Setting up a memo of concatenated strings

#1 Simulation of a record in a database
$NameOfCustomer = "Abe Washington";
$NameOfProduct = "Razor Might Version 4";
$CustomerEMailAddress = 'abeWash@my.com'; #single quotes for @ operator
$OrderNumber = "ASGM000456A7";
$ProcessingNumber = "GH09824AA345-202029";
$Date = "12//12//06";
$PurchaseShipmentNotification = "";

#2 A standard shipment notification form
# A single scalar stores the text for the message,
# including the values from the scalar variables embedded in it
$PurchaseShipmentNotification = "\n \n " .
$CustomerEMailAddress . "\n \n " .
$OrderNumber . "\n \n " .
$Date . "\n \n " .
"Dear " . $NameOfCustomer . ",\n \n " .
"Thank you for your purchase of \n \n " .
$NameOfProduct . ". Your shipping \n \n " .
"order is being processed. Your \n \n " .
"processing number is " . $ProcessingNumber . ".\n \n " .
"Respectfully, \n \n " .
"Customer Service" . "\n \n ";

#3 Use the single scalar variable to print an e-mail (HTML) message
print $PurchaseShipmentNotification;
```

At comment #1 in Listing04_14 you simulate what might be a record taken from a database. To put the information to work, you must concatenate it with text of the message. To hold the resulting message, you declare a scalar called $PurchaseShipmentNotification.

The lines comment #2 identifies create the contents to be assigned to $PurchaseShip-mentNotification. To create the string, you code one line after another of concatenated literal strings and scalar values. To format the text, you add new line escape characters.

The call to the print() function that trails comment #3 allows you to display the concatenated string at the prompt. A few HTML tags might be added to the string to make the text appear as a formatted webpage. As it is, the text displays in double-spaced lines at the command prompt. Figure 4.21 illustrates the output of Listing04_14.

Figure 4.21
Concatenation of literal text values and values stored in scalars allows you to create a single string scalar.

Using the join() Function to Concatenate Strings

You can use the join() function as an alternative approach to creating the notification shown in Figure 4.21. The join() function joins two or more items into a string. When it joins these items, it uses a *delimiter*, which is any character or text you provide.

To accomplish its work, the join() function requires two arguments. The first of two arguments furnishes the delimiter. The second argument is a list of items you want to join. The delimiter can be any character or set of characters (including white spaces) that you want to use between the items in your list. The items in the list can be literal values or variables. You use parentheses (sometimes referred to as the list function of Perl) to enclose the items you want to join. Listing04_15 uses the list function to join (or concatenate) two scalar values and a literal string into a comma-delimited list.

```
#Listing04_15
#Using join to create a concatenated string
#1 Simulation of a record in a database
$CustomerEMailAddress = 'abeWash@my.com';
$Date = "12/12/06";
$PurchaseShipmentNotification = "";
$NL = "\n"; #Create a scalar substitute for the escape sequence
```

```
#2 Create a comma-delimited string
$PurchaseShipmentNotification =
    join(", ", (
        $CustomerEMailAddress,
        "Abe Washington", #literal string
        $Date));
print "\nCustomer Notice: " .
            $PurchaseShipmentNotification . $NL;
```

In the lines trailing #1 in Listing04_15, you use the same scalars used before in Listing04_14. You add a scalar to hold the escape sequence for a new line. Then at comment #2 you call the join() function. The first argument consists of a string. In this case the string contains a comma followed by a space.

The second argument provides a list of items enclosed in parentheses. Within the parentheses, you use two of the scalars defined previously. For purposes of demonstration, you add one literal string holding a name. To join the items into a single string, you assign the result of the join() function (the return value) to a scalar, $PurchaseShipmentNotification. You then print the contents of the scalar. Figure 4.22 illustrates the output of Listing04_15.

Figure 4.22
The join() function creates a string consisting of items you enumerate between parentheses.

Creating the Notification with the join() Function

Given the discussion that the previous section provides, you can make use of the join() function as an alternative approach to creating the customer notification shown in Figure 4.21. Listing04_16 shows how this can happen.

```
#Listing04_16
#Using join to create a concatenated string

#1 Simulation of a record in a database
$NameOfCustomer = "Abe Washington";
$NameOfProduct = "Razor Might Version 4";
$CustomerEMailAddress = 'abeWash@my.com'; #single quotes for @ operator
$OrderNumber = "ASGM000456A7";
```

```
$ProcessingNumber = "GH09824AA345-202029";
$Date = "12/12/06";
$PurchaseShipmentNotification = "";
$NL = "\n "; #Create a scalar new line


#2 A standard shipment notification form
#The entire report is created through arguments
# to one call to the join function
$PurchaseShipmentNotification =
    join("", (                                        $NL,
        $CustomerEMailAddress,                        $NL,
        $OrderNumber,                                 $NL,
        $Date,                                        $NL,
        "Dear ", $NameOfCustomer,                     $NL,
        "Thank you for your purchase of",             $NL,
        $NameOfProduct, ". Your shipping ",           $NL,
        "order is being processed. Your ",            $NL,
        "processing number is",
        $ProcessingNumber,                            $NL,
        "Respectfully," ,                             $NL,
        "Customer Service",                           $NL));
print "\nCustomer Notification",                      $NL
          . $PurchaseShipmentNotification .           $NL;
```

In the lines associated with comment #1 in Listing04_16, you set up the same set of scalar variables you set up previously (in Listing04_14). In this case, you make one addition, the declaration of a scalar to hold the escape sequence for a new line. At comment #2, you proceed to create the string that holds the text of the message ($PurchaseShipmentNotification).

The first argument of the join() function consists of an empty string. You employ an empty string as the first argument because you need no delimiter between the items you concatenate. You then proceed in the second argument to set up a table to attend to the contents of your notification. Any number of approaches might be used to set up the notification. Placing the contents on the left side and the new line scalar variable on the right allows you to more easily discern the items in the report and its layout.

Figure 4.23 illustrates the output of Listing04_16. The output appears nearly the same as that of Listing04_14. The difference is that the items appear singly spaced. To make them double-spaced, you can alter the value assigned to $NL in Listing04_16 so that it consists of two new line escape sequences \n \n.

Figure 4.23
The join() function allows you to concatenate elements to create a customer notification.

❊ Take a few moments to compare Listing04_16 to Listing04_14. Which is easier to read? What advantages might one have over the other? Does white space contribute to readability? What advantage is to be gained from assigning formatting strings such as the escape sequence to scalar identifiers?

Variations with Joining

You can vary the use of the join() function to accomplish many types of operations. All of the variations dealt with in this section involve only two items in the list argument of the join() function. In Listing04_17 you examine the following activities:

❊ **Insert one string between two others.** You accomplish this by using the string you want to insert as the first argument of the join() function. In the list that constitutes the second argument, you use the two items between which you want to insert the string. See comment #1.

❊ **Join a string that changes to one that does not.** For example, "He said...." You then add what he said. You accomplish this by inserting the added text in the first argument of the join() function. Then, in the second argument, you provide a list that consists of an empty string and then a string containing the text you want to add after "He said." See comment #2.

❊ **Reverse the order of two strings.** This activity constitutes nothing more than a further innovation on the previous one. You accomplish this by leaving either the first or second item in the joined list empty. You start by assigning a given string to the first argument of the join() function. Then, you provide a two-item list. If you want to put another string before your given string, you assign it to the first position in the two-item list. For the second item, you supply an empty string. If you want to put another string after your given string, you assign it to the second position in the two-item list. For the first item, you supply an empty string. See comment #3.

Here's the code for Listing04_17:

```
#Listing04_17

#Three variations with the join() function

$TextA = "he laughed "; #expressions
$TextB = "he cried ";
$TextC = "he said ";
$TextD = "after that";

$TextE = "often "; #adverbs
$TextF = "bitterly ";
$TextG = "seldom ";

$NL = " \n"; #scalars for escapes
$TB = " \t";
$NLTB = $NL . $TB;

#1 Insert one term between two others
# Make a sentence ... /little/bitterly/seldom ...
print $NL . "#1 One item inserted between two others:";
$NewString = join($TextF, (ucfirst($TextA), $TextD));
print ($NLTB . $NewString);
$NewString = join($TextG, (ucfirst($TextA), $TextD));
print ($NLTB . $NewString);
$NewString = join($TextE, (ucfirst($TextA), $TextD));
print ($NLTB . $NewString . $NL);

#2 Use an empty string to join a varying string
# to a default. TextH is the default (He said)
# You can insert TextA or TextB or any quote
print $NL . "#2 Join a varying string with a default (\"he said\"): ";
$NewString = join(ucfirst($TextC), ("" , $TextA));
print ($NLTB . $NewString);
```

```
$NewString = join(ucfirst($TextC), ("", $TextB));
print ($NLTB . $NewString . $NL);

#3 You can reverse the order of two strings
# To accomplish this, you alter the position of the
# empty string in the two-item list
print $NL . "#3 Reverse the order of two strings: ";
$NewString = join($TextC, (ucfirst($TextA), "" ));
print ($NLTB . $NewString);
$NewString = join(ucfirst($TextC), ("", $TextA, ));
print ($NLTB . $NewString . $NL);
```

Figure 4.24 illustrates the output of Listing04_17.

Figure 4.24
Several variations on the use of the `join()` function exist.

Replacing Join with a Block

The `join()` function allows you to exert extensive control over how you position identifiers in a program so that you can easily maintain the program. At the same time, Perl blocks allow you to create bodies of text that merge variable and literal information in a fairly convenient way. Listing04_18 reworks an earlier program (Listing04_16) to create a memo using a block with embedded identifiers. The advantage of this approach is that you more directly see the resulting text. The disadvantage is that you embed the identifiers in the text and possibly create a situation in which maintaining the program can prove difficult.

```
#Listing04_18
#Alternative to join - blocks with embedded identifiers
#1 Simulation of a record in a database
$NameOfCustomer = "Abe Washington";
$NameOfProduct = "Razor Might Version 4";
$CustomerEMailAddress = 'abeWash@my.com'; #single quotes for @ operator
$OrderNumber = "ASGM000456A7";
$ProcessingNumber = "GH09824AA345-202029";
```

```
$Date = "12/12/06";
$PurchaseShipmentNotification = "";

#2 A standard shipment notification form
#The entire report created with a block
$NL = "\n"; #Create a new line to accommodate the double space
# Start the block
($PurchaseShipmentNotification=<<CUSTOMERNOTICE);

$CustomerEMailAddress
$OrderNumber
$Date

Dear, $NameOfCustomer,

Thank you for your purchase of
$NameOfProduct. Your shipping
order is being processed. Your
processing number is $ProcessingNumber,
Respectfully,

Customer Service
CUSTOMERNOTICE
#End the block

print "$NL Customer Notification: $NL ".
    " $PurchaseShipmentNotification $NL" ;
```

At comment #1, you set up a few identifiers to simulate data you might have received from a database. You also provide a data. The data is likely to be a value the system generates, but it might end up stored in the database, also.

In the lines comment #2 identifies, you set up a block of text that incorporates the information the identifiers provide. To create the block, you enclose the name of a scalar identifier and the name of the block in parentheses. To define and assign the block, you combine an assignment operator with two less than operators (<<). Together these are known as a *shift* operator. You then type the memo as you want it to appear, inserting the identifiers. Given the definition of the memo text, you then call the `print()` function to print it. Figure 4.25 illustrates the memo as it appears when you print it.

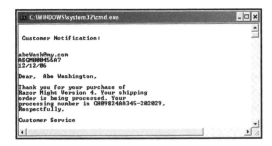

Figure 4.25
A block allows you to format a memo that incorporates information identifiers provide.

Conclusion

In this chapter, you have investigated how to use functions related to strings. To begin with, you explored some of the ideas associated with function arguments and return values. From there, you moved on to explore several programs that allowed you to familiarize yourself with how you call functions. Given a grounding in the use of functions, you then proceeded to explore some of Perl's most frequently used built-in functions. Among these functions are those that attend to capitalization, obtaining the lengths of string, extracting and inserting substrings, and concatenation.

Learning how to using built-in functions provides you with the grounding you require to write sophisticated programs. Likewise, familiarity with the built-in functions proves a good way to equip yourself to write customized functions.

In this chapter, a number of poetical works were cited. The works cited are as follows:

Auden, W. H. "Twelve Songs." *Collected Shorter Poems 1927-1957*. New York: Random House, 1964.

Crane, Hart. "For the Marriage of Faustus and Helen." *The Complete Poems and Selected Letters and Prose of Hart Crane*. Ed. Brom Weber. New York: Doubleday & Company, Inc., 1966.

Wordsworth, William. "The Prelude," 1799, 1805, 1850. Ed. Jonathan Wordsworth, et al. London: W. W. Norton and Company, 1979.

Yeats, W. B. "The Choice." *Norton Anthology of Modern Poetry*. Ed. Richard Ellman and Robert O'Clair. London: W. W. Norton and Company, 1973.

5 } Scalars and Formatting

A set of functions accompanies each category of data in Perl. The most extensive set of such functions concerns the scalar data category. Of these functions, most manipulate strings, but several also deal with numbers. Still others deal with both strings and numbers. In the previous chapter, you investigated the use of several functions associated exclusively with strings. In this chapter, you extend your investigation to include numbers. After investigating scalar numbers and their associated functions and operations, you are in an excellent position to examine how you can use the print functions (`print()`, `printf()`, and `sprintf()`) to effect different formatting operations. The `sprintf()` function proves to be an ideal tool for casting number types, formatting decimal numbers, setting up table columns, and using generic formatting specifiers. Among topics addressed in this chapter are the following:

❋ Distinguishing defined from undefined identifiers
❋ Operators that pertain to numbers
❋ Specification of number types
❋ The `printf()` and `sprintf()` functions
❋ Creating generic formatting identifiers in Perl
❋ Formatting output for tables

Scalars, Functions, and Numbers

Perl poses certain dangers with respect to using numbers. The dangers arise because, if you use a string as a number in a mathematical expression, the Perl interpreter processes the string as though it were a number. It processes the string as a number because it automatically reads the string as a number when you employ the string in association with a numeric operator. Consider Listing05_01:

```
#Listing05_01
#Dangerous use of strings as numbers

#1 Initialize scalars
#Scalars as strings
$FirstValue = "Hello";
$SecondValue = "World";
#Scalars as numbers
$ThirdValue = 0;
$FourthValue = 10;
$FifthValue = 6;
#Other
$NL = "\n";

#2 Add two numbers and assign the sum to a third
$ThirdValue = $FourthValue + $FifthValue;
print $NL . " The sum of two numbers, $FourthValue and $FifthValue, is "
                                    . $ThirdValue . ".$NL";

#3 Add two strings and assign the sum to a third
$ThirdValue = 0;
$ThirdValue = $FirstValue + $SecondValue;
#print $NL . "The sum of the two strings is ". $ThirdValue;
print $NL . " The sum of the strings, \"$FirstValue\" " .
            " and \"SecondValue\", is " . $ThirdValue . ",$NL";

#4 Add a string and number and assign the sum to a third
$ThirdValue = 0;
$ThirdValue = $FirstValue + $FourthValue;
#print $NL . "The sum of the two strings is " . $ThirdValue;
print $NL ." The sum of the strings \"$FirstValue\" " .
            " and \"$FourthValue\" is " . $ThirdValue . ".$NL";

#5 Multiply number by a string and assign the product to a third
$ThirdValue = 0;
$ThirdValue = $FirstValue * $FourthValue;
```

```
print $NL . " The product of the strings \"$FirstValue\" ".
          " and \"$FourthValue\" is ". $ThirdValue . ",$NL";
```

Figure 5.1 illustrates the output of Listing05_01. The lines associated with comment #1 in Listing05_01 create two sets of scalar values. The first set consists of strings. The second set consists of numbers. You then proceed to the lines affiliated with comment #2. Those lines add two of the scalars you have initialized as numbers and assign the sum to a third. No problem characterizes such an operation.

At comment #3, the situation proves exceptional but nevertheless presents an acceptable logic. Perl can automatically assess the value of a string as zero (0), regardless of length or other characteristics. Consequently, when you add two strings and assign the result to a scalar that you have initialized as a number, the result can be zero. If you see a zero in a situation in which you expect to see the concatenated expression "Hello World," you can easily enough assess that you might have inadvertently used a math operator such as the plus sign (+) when you meant to employ the concatenation operator (.).

For the lines trailing comments #4 and #5, the situation becomes problematic. Such a situation arises because the flawed result might not be easy to discern in the flow of a large program. The zero the string generates when used mathematically combines with a legitimate value. The scalar integer value of 10 is added to a zero (the value of the string) and results in 10. Nothing seems to be amiss. When the program contains only two numbers, it might be easy enough to discern the problem, but suppose these two items appear among dozens of items in an invoice? The customer is likely to receive a free item while the merchant suffers a loss of revenues.

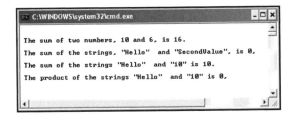

Figure 5.1
Mixing strings and numbers can yield problematic results.

Defined and Undefined Scalars

Perl provides the `defined()` and `undef()` functions to allow you to reset identifiers and to determine whether you have assigned values to identifiers. While these functions do not help directly when you must determine whether you have accidentally assigned a string to an identifier you intended to use for a numeric variable, they can at least help you avoid situations in which your calculations go afoul because you have not initialized an identifier. They can also help you ensure that if you are going to use them to control the logic of your program (for example in a for or while loop), they do not cause your loops to repeat too many or too few times (see Chapters 10 and 11).

As a reminder, an *identifier* is a word you use as the name of a variable. Generally, programmers say that they *declare* a variable when they type the identifier. When you assign a value to a variable, you *initialize* it. Some programmers refer to this as *defining* the variable.

The Perl interpreter regards an identifier to which you have assigned a value as *defined*. It recognizes an identifier to which you have not assigned a value as *undefined*. The defined() function does not change the value in your identifier; rather, it evaluates your identifier. If it determines that you have defined the identifier, it returns true (1). If it finds that you have not defined the identifier, it returns false (0). In contrast to the defined() function, the undef() function does change the value of your identifier, for it strips the identifier of its definition. Listing05_02 examines some of the uses you can make of the defined() and undef() functions.

> When you use the undef() function, you make it so that you can safely reuse identifiers. If you are unsure of whether you might have assigned a string to an identifier and now want to use an identifier as a number, undef() ensures that you can remove the definition of the identifier as a string and make a fresh start with a number.

```
#Listing05_02
#use of define() and undef()

#1 Defining some scalars
#Scalars as strings
$FirstValue = "Hello";
#An undefined scalar
$SecondValue;
#A defined numeric scalar
$ThirdValue = 10;
#Other
$NL = "\n";

#2 Use defined to detect defined identifiers
```

```
if(defined($FirstValue)){
    print $NL . '$FirstValue '
                    . "(1.1) initialized with " . $FirstValue;
}
if(defined($SecondValue)){
    print $NL . '$SecondValue '
                    . "(1.2) initialized with " . $SecondValue;
}
if(defined($ThirdValue)){
    print $NL . '$ThirdValue '
                    . "(1.3) initialized with " . $ThirdValue;
}


#3 Undefine the identifier and then test it using the defined function

undef($FirstValue);

if(defined($FirstValue)){
    print $NL . '$FirstValue '
                    . "(2.1) initialized with " . $FirstValue;
}

#4 apply the NOT operator to defined: if NOT defined

if(!defined($FirstValue)){
    print $NL . '$FirstValue ' . "(3.1) is not defined";
}

if(!defined($SecondtValue)){
    print $NL . '$SecondValue ' . "(3.2) is not defined" . $NL;
}
```

Figure 5.1 illustrates the output of Listing05_02. The lines in Listing05_02 identified by comment #1 provide numerical, string, and undefined identifiers. Given the declarations of these identifiers, comment #2 employs the defined() function to test the status of the definitions. As Figure 5.2 shows, the calls to the defined() function in the selection statements return true (1) for only two of the identifiers. These are the two identifiers ($FirstValue and

$ThirdValue) to which you assigned values. Figure 5.2 illustrates the output as items 1.1 and 1.3.

The lines at comment #3 call the undef() function to remove the definition you have given the identifier $FirstValue. Given this operation, the defined() function in the selection statement returns false. In Figure 5.2, you see no message printed for item 2.1. This proves somewhat unhelpful if you are trying to debug code. The code associated with the final comment, comment #4, provides an alternative. You use the negation of the defined() function (!) to allow the selection statement to print a message that confirms that the identifiers $FirstValue and $SecondValue have not been defined. The output, as shown in items 3.1 and 3.2 of Listing05_02, tells the story.

Figure 5.2

Use the undef() and defined() functions to establish legitimate values.

Operations with Numbers

When you perform operations on numbers in Perl, the operators you employ differ from the operators that apply to strings. For example, you employ eq to test for the equality of strings, but you employ double equal signs (==) to perform a similar operation with numbers. Generally, the numeric operators that Perl provides resemble those of other programming languages (such as C or C++). Table 5.1 provides a summary of operators that the Perl interpreter allows you to use.

The operators for both strings and numbers are characterized by how they can be associated (*associativity*) and what *precedence* they have with relation to each other. Precedence has to do with the order in which the interpreter performs operations. The operators listed in Table 5.1 appear in a top-down scheme of precedence. At the top are the parentheses, which stand as what might be viewed as the super operators of operators, for they allow you to arbitrarily enforce the precedence of almost any operation you want to perform.

As Figure 5.3 illustrates, associativity involves how the interpreter reads an expression. In some cases, it reads *left to right*. In other cases it reads *right to left*. In still other cases, associativity does not apply. Left-to-right associations characterize all the arithmetic operators. If you add the variables a and b ($a + b$), the interpreter reads b, reads the addition operator, and then reads a. On the other hand, with the assignment operator (=), the association is from right to left. When you assign the sum of a and b to an identifier named c ($c = a + b$), the interpreter attends first to the addition ($a + b$), then to the assignment operator (=), and then to the target identifier (c), which lies on the left side of the assignment operator.

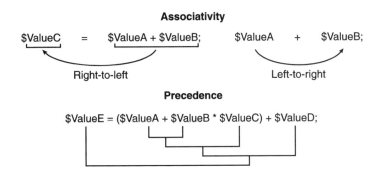

Figure 5.3
Associativity and precedence characterize numerical (and other) operators.

Table 5.1 Numerical Operators

Category	Operators	Description
Grouping	( )	Ensures that you can control how operations impact each other. Parentheses allow you to group operations visually if you lack certainty about the precedence of operators. The interpreter associates items in parentheses from left to right.
Unary	++$c $c++ --$d $d--	Allows you to successively increment or decrement a value. Unary operators immediately affect variables, so next to the parentheses, they have the highest precedence of any operator. Since unary operators involve only one operand (identifier), there is no associativity.
Arithmetic	* / % + -	Standard arithmetic operators. Multiplication and division have higher precedence than the modulus (remainder) operator, and these three operators in turn have higher precedence than addition and subtraction. All math operations are associated on a left-to-right basis.
Relational	> < >= <=	Allows you to evaluate the relations that pertain between values. After you increment, decrement, or perform arithmetic operations, you conduct relational evaluations. Since relational operators do not involve combinations of values, they have no associativity.
Equality	== !=	Boolean operations require you to evaluate expressions according to equality or lack of equality. Equality and inequality have no associativity.

Category	Operators	Description
Assignment	=	You assign the results of operations after performing them, so it makes sense that the assignment operator has relatively low precedence. Assignment always proceeds according to a right-to-left association. On the left of the assignment operator you create an expression and then assign it to the value on the right of the assignment operator.
Augmentation	+= -= *= /= *= **=	Allows you to augment a variable and assign the result of the augmentation back to the variable. The double asterisks (**) relates to powers (exponents). These operators have slightly lower precedent than the lone assignment operator. If you lined up three values, two related by the assignment operator and two by one of the augmentation operators, the assignment would occur prior to the augmentation. Augmentation proceeds according to right-to-left associativity. You create an expression on the right side of the augmentation operator, and the interpreter assigns the result to the value on the left.

Numbers and Built-In Functions

As with string operations, life becomes particularly interesting when you begin using Perl's built-in functions to perform operations that only painstaking hours of labor would allow you to perform if you were to work from scratch with the basic operators and create your own functions. Although programmers often report that it does not provide an ideal language for mathematical programming (C is generally viewed as the best of all languages in this respect), Perl makes use of the C math library and provides a good set of math functions. Table 5.2 lists some of these functions.

Table 5.2 Perl Math Functions

Function	Discussion
abs()	Returns the absolute value of the number you supply.
atan2()	Returns the arctangent of the value you supply. The return value is in the range of pi to –pi (in radians).

Function	Discussion
cos()	Returns the cosine of the argument you supply. The return value is in radians.
exp()	Returns *e* to the power of the argument you supply. To raise a number to a power, use the double asterisks (`number ** 3`).
hex()	Returns the decimal value of a hexadecimal number.
int()	If you have a decimal number, this function returns the integer part of the number.
log()	Returns the natural logarithm of a number.
sin()	Returns the sine of the argument you supply. The return value is in radians.
sqrt()	Returns the square root of the number you supply to it.
square()	Returns the square of the number you supply to it.
oct()	Returns the decimal value of an octal number.
ord()	If you supply a character (in single quotes `'c'`) to this number, it returns the ASCII value of the character.
rand()	Returns a rational number greater than or equal to 0 and less than 1 (0.1, 0.2, and so on). However, if you supply an integer argument to the rand() function, it generates an integer that is greater than or equal to 0 and less than the number you supply. To deal with most situations, programmers use a tactic called shifting. To shift the return of rand() so that you get randomly generated values of 1, 2, 3, 4, and 5, you use an expression along the following lines: `1 + int(rand(5))`.
sin()	Returns the sine of the number you supply. The value returned is in radians.
srand()	To make it so that you get different results each time you call the rand() function, you help it out by seeding a different starting value into the formula the rand() function uses. To accomplish this, you use the srand() (for "seed" random) function.
time()	The number of seconds since January 1, 1970. There are 3,600 seconds in an hour, so the numbers tend to be large.

Standard Presentation Using the print() Function

To gain a sense of some of the basic alternatives that exist for you as you formulate numeric expressions in Perl, consider Listing05_03. This program provides a set of numeric identifiers and a display of the values the identifiers store. The program provides a starting point for experimentation in the use of formatting, conversion, printing, and other Perl capabilities.

```
#Listing05_03
#Scalars initialized to numbers
# Integers
```

```
$PlRadiusOfEarth = 6357;
$EqRadiusOfEarth = 6378;
#rational number - floating decimal values
$EarthToSun = 149597870.7;
# Scientific notation
$EarthToMoon = 3.84401e6;
$AgeOfSolarSystem = 4.6e9;
# Raising 10 to the ninth power
$AgeOfKnownUniverse = 16.5 * (10 ** 9);
# Large integers
$SpeedOfLight = 299792458; #meters per second


#2 Print the values
print "\nPolar radius of earth: " .
            " $PlRadiusOfEarth kilometers.";
print "\nEquatorial radius of earth: " .
            " $EqRadiusOfEarth kilometers.";
print "\nThe distance to the sun from earth: " .
            " $EarthToSun kilometers.";
print "\nThe distance to the earth to the moon: " .
            " $EarthToMoon kilometers.";
print "\nThe age of the solar system: " .
            " $AgeOfSolarSystem years.";
print "\nThe age of the known universe: " .
            " $AgeOfKnownUniverse years.";
print "\nThe known universe: " .
            " $RatioOfSStoKU times older than the solar system.";
print "\nThe speed of light: " .
            " $SpeedOfLight meters per second.";
```

In Listing05_03, you create a scalar, $PlRadiusOfEarth, to represent the polar radius of Earth in kilometers as an integer (6357). An integer ($EqRadiusOfEarth) also accommodates the equatorial radius of Earth (6378). Figure 5.4 illustrates the output of Listing05_03.

Next, you create a scalar identifier ($EarthToSun) to accommodate a rational (floating decimal) number that represents the distance to the sun in kilometers (149597870.7). You need no type identifiers. Assignment creates the number as named.

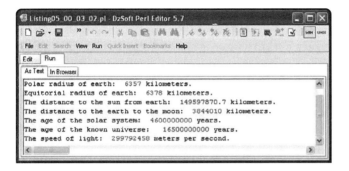

Figure 5.4
Different types of numbers result from your definition and operations.

In the next two declarations, you define variables using scientific notation. The e raises the base to a given power of 10. For distance to the moon ($EarthToMoon), you create a rational number with a precision of 5 places and then raise the power of 10 to 6 (3.84401e6). To jump into the dimension of time ($AgeOfSolarSystem), given an estimation that the solar system is 4.6 billion years old, you create a rational number with a precision of just one place but raise the power of 10 to 9 (4.6e9).

Perl provides different ways to deal with powers. To simply raise a number to any power, you employ double asterisks (**). To define an identifier for the age of the known universe ($AgeOfKnownUniverse), you can vary from the use of scientific notation employing e and use a more literal approach. Rather than coding the definition as 16.5e9, in this example, you employ the expression 16.5 * (10 ** 9).

In the final declaration, you experiment with a relatively large integer ($SpeedOfLight), which represents the meters per second that light travels (299792458). If you type a particularly large integer value (one that exceeds 14 characters), Perl automatically begins to present your output in scientific notation with a large rational component.

Random Numbers and Integers

In Table 5.1, the integer is important enough that a numeric function addresses the need of programmers to create integers. To exercise the int() function in a slightly complicated context, consider the use of the int() function in relation to the rand() function. The int() function removes the decimal portion of a number. The rand() function generates a random number:

```
#Listing05_04
#int() used to make a random number an integer
#A random number less than 6 and equal to or greater than 0
$RandomNumber = 1 + rand(6);
print "\nRandom number without integer status:\n"  . $RandomNumber;
print "\nRandom number converted to an integer:\n" . int($RandomNumber);
```

In Listing05_04, to use the int () function, you insert the rational number you want to convert to an integer. In this instance, the number ($RandomNumber) possesses a decimal precision of 14. If you are working with a dice game, such precision is not likely to be very useful. The int () function truncates the number for you. The output is as follows:

```
Random number without integer status:
4.77630615234375
Random number converted to an integer:
4
Press a key to continue...
```

Range Problems and the rand() Function

To generate the random number shown in Listing05_04, you use the rand () function. By default, the return value of this function is a rational number in a range that is zero or greater and less than a whole number value of the digit you use as an argument. As Figure 5.5 illustrates, a problem results when you consider that a die has 6 dots. If you use an argument of 6 for the rand () function, the largest value the rand () function can generate is 5.99999999999999. This not quite 6. Likewise, a die has 1 to 6 dots; no face is blank. Such inconsistencies constitute a *range* problem.

Figure 5.5
Truncate and shift the randomly generated number.

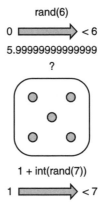

rand(6)

0 ⟹ < 6
5.99999999999999

?

1 + int(rand(7))

1 ⟹ < 7

To solve the range problem, you *shift* the returned value of rand () function by one. Given the truncation that the int () function performs, if you add one to the value the rand () function generates and set the argument of rand () to 7, you then acquire numbers in the range of 1 to 6.

Gargantuan Integers

Consider again the use of the int () function. In this case, the problem is that you want to do something like name the number of photons bombarding a rooftop on a sunny day. Listing05_05 does not accurately name this number, but it provides an example of the number of digits likely to be involved.

```
#Listing05_05
$LargeNumber = 393939393933838;
print "\nLarge: " . int($LargeNumber);
$GargantuanNumber = 393939393933838393383930383938309303830303830303039389;
print "\nGargantuan: " . int($GargantuanNumber);
```

Rather than reporting with the second number that you have exceeded the limits of the integer range available to you as you have counted your photons, the Perl interpreter simply transforms the integer into a rational number presented in scientific notation. The output is as follows:

```
Large: 393939393933838
Gargantuan: 3.93939393933838e+051
```

The Perl interpreter creates a rational number with a decimal precision of 14, lops off any digits you might have exceeding that limit, and generates the scientifically noted number you see.

Rational Operations

When you combine numbers, the Perl interpreter follows the logic of *type promotion*. Type promotion stipulates that if you combine two numbers of different types, the resulting value is of (or cast to) the type that provides the greatest storage ability. For example, an integer requires relatively little storage space. A float requires more than an integer. If you combine an integer and a float, the result is a float. Perl does not work in this way on a visible level because it does not require strict type designation for the identifiers you create. Still, when you work with numbers, Perl tends to maintain a logic of type promotion as you combine different values. Listing05_06 provides examples of what happens with the declaration and combination differed identifiers.

```
#Listing05_06
#1 Use of decimals, scientific notation, and integers
#1 Initialize identifiers
$LightYear = 9.6 * (10 ** 12);        #kilometers
$DToProximaCentauri = 4.26;           #light years
$FarthestGalaxy = 15 * (1.0e9);       #light years
$MilkyWayDiameter = 1000000;          #light years
$MilkyWayThickness = 1000;            #light years
$StarsInMilkyWay = 1.0 * (10 ** 11);
$PI = 3.1415926;
```

```
#2 Display value
#Interpolated string
print "\nA lightYear is $LightYear kilometers.";
#Isolated variable
print "\nDistance to Proxima Centauri:" . $DToProximaCentauri . " lys.";
print "\nThe distance to the farthest Galaxy: $FarthestGalaxy lys.";
print "\nThe diameter of the Milky Way: $MilkyWayDiameter lys.";
print "\nThe thickness of the Milky Way: $MilkyWayThickness lys.";
print "\nThe number of stars in the Milky Way: $StarsInMilkyWay.\n\n";
print "Value of PI: $PI";


#3 Perform a calculation
#V = (4 Pi/3)r^3
#Calculate the volume of the universe if it were a sphere
#extending to Proxima Centauri

print "\n \nPerform a calculation: V = (4 Pi/3)r^3.\n";
print '((4 * $PI) / 3) * (($DToProximaCentauri/2) ** 3)' . "\n ";
$VolumeToProxima = ((4 * $PI) / 3) * (($DToProximaCentauri/2) ** 3);


#4 Print using default
print "\nVolume of sphere " .
"(in cubic light years)\n" .
"extending to Proxima Centauri:" . $VolumeToProxima . ".\n\n";


#5 Preliminary view: Print using the sprintf() function
print "\nVolume of sphere " .
"(in cubic light years)\n" .
"extending to Proxima Centauri:" . sprintf("%e", $VolumeToProxima) . ".\n\n";
```

The lines trailing comment #1 in Listing05_06 provide you with a number of different data definitions. All of the definitions involve scalars, but the expressions that initialize the identifiers involve a variety of number types. You define the identifier $LightYear using a combination of a rational number (9.6), a multiplication operator, and an exponential operator (**) that creates 10 to the power of 12. As Figure 5.6 illustrates, the result is an integer. The same procedure characterizes your definition of the identifier $DtoProximaCentauri, but this time you assign a simple rational number (4.26).

For the definition of the identifier $FarthestGalaxy, you employ an integer, 15, a multiplication operator, and in parentheses, an expression that translates as "1.0 times 10 to the ninth power" (1.0e9). The identifiers that establish the diameter and thickness of the Milky Way galaxy ($MilkyWayDiameter, $MilkyWayThickness) both involve integers. For the number of stars in the Milky Way, you employ the same approach you employed for describing the number of meters in a light year. As for the designation of pi, you employ a rational number (3.1415926) that provides an approximation.

The lines of code associated with comment #2 furnish a set of printing operations. To print the values, notice that whether you concatenate or interpolate values makes no difference in the appearance of the output.

The lines trailing comment #3 set up a formula for calculating the volume of space that is described if the sun is designed as the center of a sphere that extends as far as Proxima Centauri. The way you implement a given formula depends largely on how much you use the implicit associativity and precedence of the language with which you are programming. In this instance, the code implements the formula as explicitly as possible using parentheses.

Only one feature in Listing05_06 might prove a surprise (see comment #5). This involves the use of the sprintf() function to force the output of the program to appear in scientific notation. The next section addresses how to accomplish this feat.

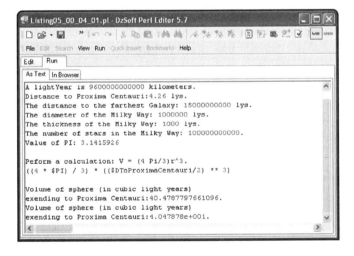

Figure 5.6
The display of values tends to follow the logic of type promotion.

Using printf()

As becomes evident in Figure 5.6, you can use a function similar to the print() function to format the output of your programs. The function you use in Listing05_06 is called sprintf(). The "f" designates formatting. The "s" designates string. To understand how to use `sprintf()`, you can first master the features of `printf()`. Both functions represent different and more powerful versions of the `print()` function.

Formatting encompasses a variety of activities. For example, you can use `printf()` to *cast* your data in different ways. Casting might involve making a number appear as a letter, or you can make a letter appear as a number. You can transform an integer into a float or a float into an integer. You can also control strings so that they are of uniform length, allowing you to create columns in a table. Figure 5.7 illustrates the main features of the `printf()` function.

Figure 5.7
Type specifiers allow you
to convert and format data.

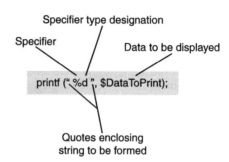

If you have worked with the C programming language, you recognize the `printf()` function as a familiar, powerful entity. The Perl interpreter incorporates most of the features of the `printf()` function from the C programming language. As Figure 5.7 illustrates, two sets of arguments characterize the `printf()` function. The first consists of information you provide inside quotation marks. The other consists of data that you provide in the form of identifiers. A comma separates the two sets of arguments.

Conversion Specifiers

To use the `printf()` function, you employ one or more output specifiers to format the data you want to print. A specifier both designates the location in the output string at which you want to locate data and identifies the type and other characteristics of the data. As for the arguments pertaining to the data you provide to the `printf()` function, you can use as many identifiers or literal strings or values as you want, so long as you include a specifier inside the quotes to cover each value you introduce. Consider the examples in Listing05_07.

```
#Listing05_07
#1 Use of decimals, scientific notation, and display

#1 Initialize identifiers
$LightYear = 9.6 * (10 ** 12); #kilometers
$DToProximaCentauri = 4.26; #light years
```

```
$FarthestGalaxy = 15 * (1.0e9); #light years
$MilkyWayDiameter = 1000000; #light years
$MilkyWayThickness = 1000; #light years
$StarsInMilkyWay = 1.0 * (10 ** 11);
$LY = "lys.";


#2 Display values with specifiers and variables
#Interpolated string (s), scientific notation (e), rational number (f)
printf("%s %e %s" , "\nA light year is", $LightYear, "kilometers.");
printf("%s %f %s" , "\nor...", $LightYear, "kilometers.");


#Multiple arguments, literal sting, rational number (float), string scalar
printf("%s%f %s", "\nDistance to Proxima Centauri: ",
                  $DToProximaCentauri, $LY);
printf("%s%f %s", "\nDistance to the farthest Galaxy: ",
                  $FarthestGalaxy, $LY);
#3 Use of integer specifier (d)
printf("%s%d %s", "\nDiameter of the Milky Way: " ,
                  $MilkyWayDiameter, $LY);
printf("%s%d %s", "\nThickness of the Milky Way: ",
                  $MilkyWayThickness, $LY);
#No space, three sting (s) specifiers
printf("%s%s%s", "\nNumber of stars in the Milky Way ",
                  $StarsInMilkyWay, ".\n\n");


#The output appears spaced according to the spacing of the
#format specifiers
```

At comment #1 in Listing05_07, you define the same set of identifiers you worked with in Listing05_06. You add an identifier ($LY) to hold an abbreviation for "light years" and a period. At comment #2, you begin calling the printf() function to display the information stored in the identifiers you have defined at the beginning of the program. Figure 5.8 illustrates the output.

In the lines that accompany comment #2, the first call to the printf() function involves the use of two specifiers, %s and %e. The %s specifier sets up a string. The %e specifier sets up a value displayed in scientific notation (9.600000e+012). The string specifier serves to display a literal string: "\nA light year...". The %e specifier serves to convert an expression to power notation. The expression uses double asterisks to raise a decimal number to a power of 10. In the second call to printf(), as Figure 5.8 shows, you see the same value displayed as a floating decimal (9600000000000.000000). The %f specifier accomplishes this conversion. After the first two calls to the printf() functions, two others follow that involve the use of the %f specifiers.

Figure 5.8
The printf() function allows you to display data as strings and floating decimals.

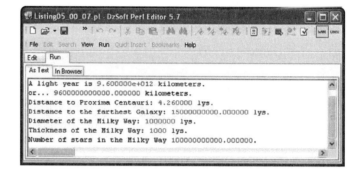

Trailing comment #3 you see lines in which another specifier appears. This is the %d specifier, which renders an integer. This specifier can be used in this place because the numbers involved are relatively small (at least in astronomical realms). If you were to substitute a %d for the %f in some of the calls to printf() involving large numbers, the result would be a negative one (-1), meaning that the specifier cannot handle the size of the number you have designated. The %d specifier renders a number without a decimal point.

Generally, specifiers convert arguments to different display formats. The specifiers you use in Listing05_07 constitute a subset of the total set available to you. Table 5.3 provides a list of your options.

Table 5.3 Conversion Specifiers for Printing

Specifier	Description
%d	Integer value (signed).
%I	Integer value (signed).
%u	Integer value (unsigned).
%c	Single character.
%o	Displays an unsigned octal. You see 0x prefixed to the number.
%u	Unsigned decimal integer.
%x %X	Unsigned hexadecimal. Case is determined by case.
%e	Floating point or exponential.
%f	Floating point value.

Specifier	Description
%g %G	Floating point for f or exponential if e or E.
%c	Converts a number to a character. The number corresponds to the ASCII value of the character. For example, "a" results from the following: `printf("%c", 97);`.
%s	Displays a string. You can convert a number to a string using this specifier.
%%	Produces a percent sign.

When you place the specifiers between quotes, the space you allow between them makes a difference. In the last call to the `printf()` function in Listing05_07, you place no spaces between the %s specifiers. The absence of the space in the quoted specifiers closes the space between the period and the data represented by the $StarsInMilkyWay identifier. In the previous examples, you add space to allow for the space between the data and the abbreviation for light years.

Conversion from Strings and Space

One other action to note under comment #3 involves the use of the %s specifier to reformat, or convert, a number to a string. For convenience, here again are the lines:

```
#No space, just a period - and note string formatting
printf("%s%s%s", "\nNumber of stars in the Milky Way ",
    $StarsInMilkyWay, ".\n\n");
```

You can convert a number to a string using the `printf()` function. You can also convert a string to a number. Consider the following short program:

```
#Listing05_08
#conversion of string to number
print "\nConvert String: ";
printf("%f", "45");
#Output
#Convert String: 45.000000
```

The output that Listing05_08 produces shows trailing zeros. The string contains only the two characters representing the number. This indicates that the string is now a floating decimal. (See the next section for how to control the number of zeros.)

Formatting and Precision

In Figure 5.8, the presentation of the numbers for the farthest galaxy and other data items proves disconcerting due to the prolixity of trailing zeros. For example, for the farthest galaxy, you see:

```
Distance to the farthest Galaxy: 15000000000.000000 lys.
```

To remedy the situation, you can employ precision specifiers in addition to conversion specifiers to control the number of decimal places. Table 5.4 discusses some of the precision specifiers you can use. (Likewise, refer to Figure 5.9.)

Table 5.4 Formatting Flags for Printing

Flag	Discussion*
%**fw**.dpcs	**fw** designates the field width of the data you are displaying. This is an integer value.
%fw.**dp**cs	**dp** designates the decimal precision you are displaying. This is an integer value.
-%fw.dpcs	The minus sign (–) indicates that you want to left justify the content of the field you have created. The default is right justification (which you indicate by leaving the position blank).
+%fw.dpcs	The plus sign (+) indicates that you want to prefix a sign to the value. If the value is negative, then you see a minus sign. If the value is positive, then you see a plus sign.
' '%fw.dpcs	Use one or more blank spaces (' ') to create blank spaces. If you leave a blank space, you see a space before positive values.
%#x.dpcs	Use a pound sign (#) if you want to display 0x before hexadecimal or 0 before octal values. (The expression printf("%#x", 344335) gives you 0x5410f.)
0%fw.dpcs	A zero (0). This pads the whole field with zeros, so if the field were 5 characters wide and right justified, then you would see 00032 for 32.

*Note that **cs** designates the conversion specifiers (s, f, I, d, and so on) as presented in Table 5.3.

Controlling Precision

When you use the precision control flags of the printf() function, you combine the conversion specifiers with the precision flags to format both the data you are printing and the field in which the data appears. As Table 5.4 reveals, in addition to setting the width of the field, the precision flags allow you to determine the justification of the data in the field. If you apply a minus sign, you can align the data to the left. Otherwise, the data remains aligned to the right. In addition to the width and alignment, you can control the number of decimal places. Assigning decimal places involves using a period to append a number to the field specifier. This number establishes how many decimal places you want to maintain. Figure 5.9 illustrates the essential layout of the specifiers and flags.

In Figure 5.9, you see that printf() function is employed to create three columns. The three columns display a line of text, a number, and then an abbreviation for kilometers. To format the fields (or columns in a table), you combine specifiers and flags. For the first field, the minus sign (–) indicates the column should be justified to the left. You set this column to be 36 characters wide. The s indicates the field is to be a string. With the next file, you specify that it is to

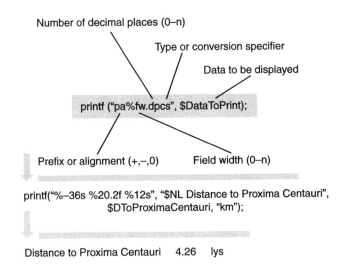

Figure 5.9
Specifiers and flags allow you to control the appearance of the text.

Distance to Proxima Centauri   4.26   lys

be 30 characters wide and is to have a decimal precision of two digits. It is to hold a floating value (f). The third field is set up, like the first, as a string. It is 12 characters wide and is by default justified to the right.

Creating a Table

Listing05_09 puts the formatting specifiers you have examined in previous sections to work to create a table.

```
#Listing05_09
# Creating a table using specifiers and flags

#1 Definitions of identifiers
$PlRadiusOfEarth = 6357; #kilometers
$EqRadiusOfEarth = 6378; #kilometers
$EarthToMoon = 3.84401e6; #kilometers
$EarthToSun = 149597870.7; #kilometers
$AgeOfSolarSystem = 4.6e9; #years
$AgeOfKnownUniverse = 16.5 * (10 ** 9); #years
$SpeedOfLight = 299792458; #meters per second
$LightYear = 9.6 * (10 ** 12); #kilometers
$DToProximaCentauri = 4.26; #light years
$FarthestGalaxy = 15 * (1.0e9); #light years
$MilkyWayDiameter = 1000000; #light years
```

```
$MilkyWayThickness = 1000; #light years
$StarsInMilkyWay = 1.0 * (10 ** 11);
$KmspeedOfLight = $SpeedOfLight/1000; #kilometers
$RatioOfSSStoKU = $AgeOfKnownUniverse/$AgeOfSolarSystem;
$LY = "lys"; #light years
$KM = "km"; #kilometers
$EY = "years"; #years
$NL = "\n";


#2 Construction of a table
print "$NL $NL $NL";
print("$NL---------------------Astronomy Data Table".
               "------------------------");
printf("%-36s %20d %12s", $NL . "Equatorial radius of earth",
                $EqRadiusOfEarth, $KM);
printf("%-36s %20d %12s", $NL . "Polar radius of earth",
                $PlRadiusOfEarth, $KM);
printf("%-36s %20d %12s", $NL . "Distance of Earth to Sun",
                $EarthToSun, $KM);
printf("%-36s %20d %12s", $NL . "Distance of Earth to Moon",
                $EarthToMoon, $KM);
printf("%-36s %20.0f %12s", $NL . "Age of the Earth/Solar System",
                $AgeOfSolarSystem, $EY);
printf("%-36s %20.0f %12s", $NL . "Age of the known universe",
                $AgeOfKnownUniverse, $EY);
printf("%-36s %20.2f %12s", $NL . "Ratio of earth / universe age",
                $RatioOfSSStoKU, "");
printf("%-36s %20.0f %12s", $NL . "Speed of light",
                $SpeedOfLight, "m sec");
printf("%-36s %20.2f %12s", $NL . "Speed of light",
                $KmspeedOfLight, "$KM"." per s");
printf("%-36s %20.2e %12s", $NL . "Light year (si)" ,
                $LightYear, $KM );
printf("%-36s %20.2f %12s", $NL . "Light year",
                $LightYear, $KM);
printf("%-36s %20.2f %12s", $NL . "Distance to Proxima Centauri",
                $DToProximaCentauri, $LY);
```

```
printf("%-36s %20.0f %12s", $NL . "Distance to the farthest Galaxy",
                    $FarthestGalaxy, $LY);
printf("%-36s %20.0f %12s", $NL . "Diameter of the Milky Way" ,
                    $MilkyWayDiameter, $LY);
printf("%-36s %20.0f %12s", $NL . "Thickness of the Milky Way",
                    $MilkyWayThickness, $LY);
printf("%-36s %20.0f %12s", $NL . "Number of stars in the Milky Way",
                    $StarsInMilkyWay, "$LY");
print "$NL $NL $NL";
```

The code accompanying comment #1 in Listing05_09 defines a set of values for the table. With the code associated with comment #2, you begin working through the list of data to create the table using the printf() function. In each use of the printf() function you create three columns. The first column presents a string. For the string, you concatenate a scalar identifier containing a new line escape sequence with literal strings that introduce the astronomical data the table presents. Each use of the print() function creates a row in your table.

You set the field width for the first column of the table to be 36 characters wide, justified to the left, and of the string type. In this respect, all the rows are the same. You make the third column of the table consist of fields 12 characters wide and of the string type. You allow the default right justification to apply to these fields.

The middle or second column of the table sports three types of fields. The fields are all 20 characters wide, but in some cases they display decimal values. In other cases, they display float values. In one field you use the e specifier to force the number to display in scientific notation. This value pertains to the speed of light in kilometers. To show a comparison between scientific notation and a standard decimal number, you also use the f formatting specifier.

Figure 5.10 illustrates the appearance of the table. The conversion specifiers for the data you employ in the table considerably improve the appearance of the data over previous displays. The numbers show no decimal places when it does not seem reasonable to display them. On the other hand, they can be shown (in the instance of the distance to Proxima Centauri) when the decimal places make sense.

Variations

Listing05_10 provides a few examples of common formatting operations. As previous sections have emphasized, you can use a minus sign to left justify a column. You can employ such capabilities in combination with type specifiers to create specific results, such as fillers. Such techniques can come in handy for creating headers. You can also prefix a zero to a specifier to fill a column with zeros. You might use this formatting procedure to generate inventory or other

Figure 5.10
Specifiers and flags allow
you to create table
columns.

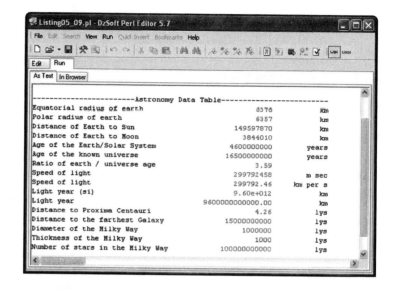

numbers that must possess a uniform number of characters. Appending a plus sign to a number
is at times handy, also.

```perl
#Listing05_10
# Variations
$PlRadiusOfEarth = 6357; #kilometers
$NL = "\n";
#1. #Prefixing a minus sign aligns the field to the left.
# No minus sign renders right justification.
printf ("%-1s %-10s %1s", "1|", "="x10, "|1");
print $NL;
#2. Append a period after the field width specifier and
# define the number of visible decimal places
# The field width is 9; the decimal places is 3
printf ("|%9.3f|", 123.1234567);
print $NL;
#3. Prefix a plus sign to show the sign
printf "%-20s %+15.2f","Polar radius of earth (km)", $PlRadiusOfEarth;
```

Figure 5.11 illustrates the output of Listing05_10.

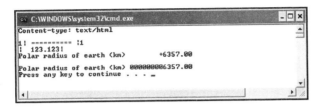

Figure 5.11
Some variations on for-
matting can come in
handy.

Investigating ASCII Conversions

Figure 5.12 provides a truncated version of a table displaying ASCII codes. ASCII stands for American Standard Code for Information Interchange, and you can find such tables on the Internet (www.lookuptables.com, for example). The ASCII code for a given character is its numerical representation. As Figure 5.12 indicates, 060 represents the less than (<) character, while 062 represents the greater than (>) character.

Decimal	Octal	Hex	Char	Decimal	Octal	Hex	Char
035	043	023	#	035	043	023	#
036	044	024	$	036	044	024	$
037	045	025	%	037	045	025	%
038	046	026	&	038	046	026	&
048	060	030	0	048	060	030	0
049	061	031	1	049	061	031	1
050	062	032	2	050	062	032	2
060	074	03C	<	060	074	03C	<
062	076	03E	>	062	076	03E	>
063	077	03F	?	063	077	03F	?
064	100	040	@	064	100	040	@
065	101	041	A	065	101	041	A
066	102	042	B	066	102	042	B
067	103	043	C	067	103	043	C
088	130	058	X	088	130	058	X
089	131	059	Y	089	131	059	Y
090	132	05A	Z	090	132	05A	Z
097	141	061	a	097	141	061	a
098	142	062	b	098	142	062	b
099	143	063	c	099	143	063	c
120	170	078	x	120	170	078	x
121	171	079	y	121	171	079	y
122	172	07A	z	122	172	07A	z
123	173	07B	{	123	173	07B	{
124	174	07C			124	174	07C		
125	175	07D	}	125	175	07D	}

Figure 5.12
A table of ASCII values allows you to see the numeric face of characters.

Listing05_11 provides examples of some of the operations you can perform to manipulate data using the ASCII designations.

```
#Listing05_11
#convert ASCII, hexadecimal, and octal values
```

```
$NL = "\n ";
#Decimal Octal Hex Character
#60 074 03C <
062 076 03E >
# 1. Print the character that a given ASCII value designates
printf("$NL The character for %d is %c", 60, 60);
printf("$NL The character for %d is %c", 62, 62);

#2 Use hex() to return the decimal value of a hexadecimal
printf($NL x 2 . "An ASCII value of %d renders an %c", 60, 60);
print("$NL Hex: 03C");
#convert to decimal
$HEXA = hex("03C");
printf("$NL The character is %c", $HEXA);

#3 Use oct() to return the decimal value of an octal
printf($NL x 2 . "An ASCII value of %d renders an %c", 60, 60);
print("$NL Octal: 074");
#convert to decimal
$OCTA = oct("074");
printf("$NL The character is %c", $OCTA);

#4 Use ord() to extract the ASCII value from a character
print($NL x 2 . "$NL For \'<\' ord() returns " . ord('<'));
printf("$NL The number for \'%s\' is %d", 'c', ord('<'));
```

At comment #1 in Listing05_11, you employ the printf() function to display a literal number and to convert a number using the c specifier to a character. At the start of the program, columns from an ASCII table allow you to view a few numerical values of characters. When you use the c specifier (%c), you convert an integer value to a character. You can convert numbers between 0 and 255 using this approach. As Figure 5.13 illustrates, Listing05_11 converts 60 to < and 62 to >.

The lines trailing comments #2 and #3 venture into exploring hexadecimal and octal values. To employ such values, you use the hex() and oct() functions. Both of these functions return decimal values.

In the code affiliated with comment #4, you make use of the ord() function to convert a character to a number. This is the reverse of the action you perform with the c specifier.

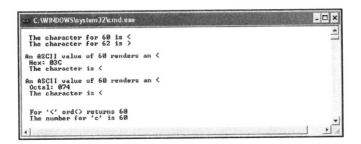

Figure 5.13
Use the print functions to
convert all types of data.

Using sprintf()

Given your mastery of the `printf()` function, you are ready to use the `sprintf()` function.
The `sprintf()` function differs from the `printf()` function because it generates a return
value that represents the arguments you submit to it converted (or formatted) according to your
specifications. You can use it to convert a number to a string or a string to a number. When you
employ it to create a string, the `sprintf()` function forms everything you submit as an argument to it, together with the changes you effect using specifiers and tags, into a single tidy
string. Given this capability, it proves a powerful vehicle for refining the work of creating tables
or in other ways formulating data for presentation. Listing05_12 provides a simple example of
how you can use the `sprintf()` function to create a table.

```
#Listing05_12
#1 Define the data for the table
$PlRadiusOfEarth = 6357;
$EqRadiusOfEarth = 6378;

#2 Create formatting variables
$COLSTRF = '%-40s %15.2f';
$NL = " \n";
#3 Use the sprintf() function to create table rows
$RowA = sprintf("$COLSTRF",
    "Polar radius of earth (km)",
    $PlRadiusOfEarth);
$RowB = sprintf("$COLSTRF",
    "Equatorial radius of earth (km)",
    $EqRadiusOfEarth);
# Use join to form the string table and print the table
$AstroTable = join("$NL", $RowA, $RowB , $NL );
print $AstroTable;
```

After defining the values of two identifiers at the start of Listing05_12, you then proceed at comment #2 to set up two scalars to hold formatting strings for use as arguments in the printf() function. This approach to formatting substantially reduces the complexity of arguments and provides a particularly effective approach to escaping the need to repeatedly code and debug formatting tags and specifiers. If you assign the specifiers as characters (using single quotes), the sprintf() and other functions can read them without errors.

Following the creation of the formatting scalars in the lines trailing comment #3, you create two rows for a table using the sprintf() function. When you create these rows, you assign the resulting strings to scalars ($RowA and $RowB). This work completed, you then use the join() function (explained in Chapter 4) to create a single scalar ($AstroTable) that contains the information for rows. When you employ the join() function, the first argument delimits the table you create using the $NL identifier, which stores a new line escape sequence. This work accomplished, you call the print() function to print the table. The scalar $AstroTable is the sole argument. Figure 5.14 illustrates the output of Listing05_12.

Figure 5.14

Use of the sprintf() function allows you to create the rows of a table in a componential manner.

```
C:\WINDOWS\system32\cmd.exe                                    _ □ ×
Polar radius of earth (km)                        6357.00
Equatorial radius of earth (km)                   6378.00
```

Reworking the Table

When you use the sprintf() function in conjunction with formatting identifiers and concatenation, calling the join() function allows you to create a table that features a great deal of formatting detail and yet requires a minimum of redundant detail work—far less, in any event, than has been necessary in some of the previous coding efforts shown in this book. Listing05_13 represents a number of such labor-saving devices.

```
#Listing05_13
#1 Define the data for the table
$PlRadiusOfEarth = 6357;
$PRoEText = "Polar radius of earth (km)";
$EqRadiusOfEarth = 6378;
$ERoEText = "Equatorial radius of earth (km)";
$EarthToMoon = 3.84401e6;
$EtMText = "Distance from Earth to Moon(km)";
$EarthToSun = 149597870.7;
$EtSText = "Distance from Earth to Sun (km)";
```

```
$AgeOfSolarSystem = 4.6e9;
$AoSSText = "Age of the solar system (years)";
$AgeOfKnownUniverse = 16.5 * (10 ** 9);
$AoKUText = "Age of the known universe (years)";
$SpeedOfLight = 299792458; #meters per second
$SoLMSText = "Speed of light m/s";
$KmspeedOfLight = $SpeedOfLight/1000;
$SoLKSText = "Speed of light km/s";
$RatioOfSStoKU = $AgeOfKnownUniverse/$AgeOfSolarSystem;
$REtoUText = "Ratio of earth to universe age";


#2 Define the formatting elements for the table
$NL = "\n ";
$DC = "="; #character for top and bottom lines of table
$SC = "-"; #character to divide rows of table


$TW = 55; #Table width
$COLAW = '%-40s'; #Col A Width
$COLBW = '%15'; #Col B Width
$PREC2 = '.2'; #Decimal Precision


#Define table lines
$DL = sprintf( "$COLAW", $NL . $DC x $TW); #top and bottom lines
$SL = sprintf( "%s", $NL . $SC x $TW); #row division lines


#Define column title and headings
$TableTitleText = 'Astronomical Data Table';
$COLAHEAD = "Item";
$COLBHEAD = "Measurement";


#columns Col A Co B Prec type and
$COLSTRSTR = $COLAW . $COLBW . 's'; #format column string
$COLSTRF = $COLAW . $COLBW . $PREC2 . 'f'; #format column float
$COLSTRE = $COLAW . $COLBW . $PREC2 . 'e'; #format column scientific notation


#Title
$TableTitle = sprintf( "%s", $DC x int(($TW - length($TableTitleText))/2) .
```

```
    $TableTitleText .
    $DC x int(($TW - length($TableTitleText))/2));
#3 Create the table rows
$RowZ = sprintf "%s", $NL . $TableTitle;
$RowE = sprintf "$COLSTRSTR",
    $NL . $COLAHEAD, $COLBHEAD;
$RowA = sprintf "$COLSTRF",
    $NL . $PRoEText,
    $PlRadiusOfEarth;
$RowB = sprintf "$COLSTRF",
    $NL . $ERoEText,
    $EqRadiusOfEarth;
$RowC = sprintf "$COLSTRE",
    $NL . $EtSText,
    $EarthToSun;
$RowD = sprintf "$COLSTRF",
    $NL . $EtMText,
    $EarthToMoon;
$RowF = sprintf "$COLSTRF",
    $NL . $AoSSText,
    $AgeOfSolarSystem;
$RowG = sprintf "$COLSTRF",
    $NL . $AoKUText,
    $AgeOfKnownUniverse;
$RowH = sprintf "$COLSTRF",
    $NL . $REtoUText,
    $RatioOfSStoKU;
$RowI = sprintf "$COLSTRF",
    $NL . $SoLMSText,
    $SpeedOfLight;
$RowJ = sprintf "$COLSTRF",
    $NL . $SoLKSText, $
    KmspeedOfLight;
#4 Create the table
$AstroTable = join("", ($DL, $RowZ,
    $DL, $RowE, $DL,
    $RowA, $SL,
```

```
        $RowB,  $SL,
        $RowC,  $SL,
        $RowD,  $SL,
        $RowF,  $SL,
        $RowG,  $SL,
        $RowH,  $SL,
        $RowI,  $SL,
        $RowJ,
        $DL));

#Print the table
print $AstroTable;
```

In the lines trailing comments #1 and #2 in Listing05_13, you define the data and formatting information that the program uses. After you complete this code, you write no code that cannot be used in a fairly generic way. The goal of this approach to defining formatting for the table involves removing as much detail as possible from the work of constructing the table (an activity that begins with the code associated with comment #3). When you employ scalars to store formatting information, you can, for example, change the width or content of any field of the table, altering only the identifiers you set up in the sections designated by comments #1 and #2. Such isolation of tasks characterizes many programming efforts.

In the code accompanying comment #3, you make use of the identifiers created earlier in the program and no longer use literal text strings, tags, or formatting specifiers. Instead, you make use of the generic components defined in the line associated with comments #1 and #2. Likewise, notice the "Perlism" of leaving the parentheses out of the calls to sprintf(). This practice is probably more common than use of parentheses, but it remains that leaving the parentheses out constitutes (in this context) a programming idiosyncrasy. Ultimately, how easily you can read and maintain your code should determine whether you employ parentheses.

Figure 5.15 illustrates the output of Listing05_13. The lines of code trailing comment #1 serve as what you might view as a set of data retrieved from a database.

In the section of Listing05_13 affiliated with comment #4, you construct the table. The construction of the table might be reduced much further than it is. Use of the row identifiers allows you to see how to construct the table and affords you the chance to add or subtract rows with relative ease. To eliminate a row, just comment it out.

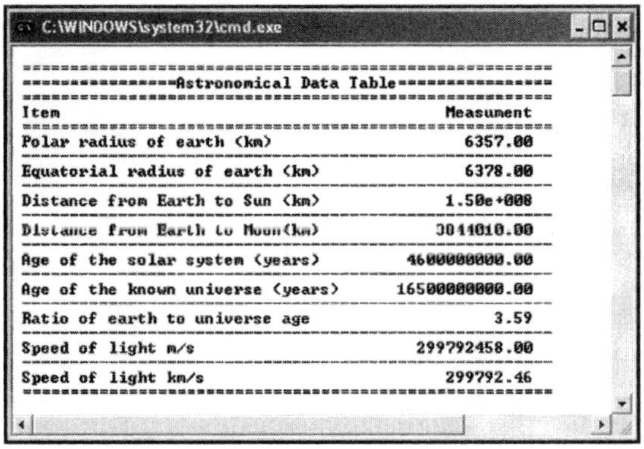

Figure 5.15
Formatting your table be-
comes a matter or tweaking
custom formatting tags.

Conclusion

In this chapter, you investigated different approaches to determining whether a given identifier has been defined. Use of the defined() and undef() functions proved helpful in this respect. After examining some of the issues that using numeric values entails, you created some programs involving defining numeric data and included in them functions Perl offers for processing numeric data. Among these function are the int(), ord(), rand(), and hex() functions. The functions that prove most beneficial in working with numbers are the printf() and sprintf() functions.

The printf() function allows you to format information using type specifiers and precision flags. Using the printf() function, you place yourself in a position to create precisely formatted tabular data. In this chapter the focus has remained on command line output, but it should be clear that all the work you perform learning how to use the formatting capabilities of the printing functions can be carried into work with HTML, XML, and other Internet development areas.

All the formatting tricks you learn for printf() apply to sprintf(). With sprint(), you acquire the ability to change one type of data into another. You can use it to change a string into a number or a number into a string. In addition to data conversion, one great advantage it offers you involves creating modular programs. In such programs you isolate complexity and create data displays that you can change with relatively little effort.

6 } Array Fundamentals

This chapter provides you with an introduction to Perl arrays. A Perl array is more of a container than it is a fundamental array. It expands automatically. It allows you to employ a number of functions associated with it to perform such actions as inserting and extracting elements. In this chapter, you focus primarily on issues concerning initializing arrays and working with a few basic functions relating to them. Among the topics this chapter addresses:

- ❋ Getting used to the scalar and implicit forms of Perl arrays
- ❋ Exploring a few definition issues
- ❋ Combining smaller arrays to form larger arrays
- ❋ Changing the order of elements in an array
- ❋ Using specialized functions to add lists of items to arrays
- ❋ Swapping, slicing, and splicing arrays

Basics of Arrays

An array consists of a sequence of items stored sequentially in your computer's memory. An array is analogous to a set of drawers. Each drawer is an element. You can know each element in the array according to its *index*. The indexes of arrays start at zero.

As Figure 6.1 illustrates, Perl arrays possess two forms. One form is known as the *literal* or *scalar* form of the array. You can recognize this form of the array because it looks like a scalar identifier with a suffix that consists of square braces containing a number. The other form is known as the *implicit* form of the array. The implicit form of an array consists of an identifier prefixed with the business "at" sign (@).

Figure 6.1
Arrays have scalar and
implicit forms.

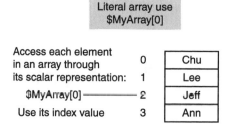

As this chapter and the next explore fairly extensively, when you employ the scalar form of the array, you access its element using the indexes of the elements. On the other hand, to work with the implicit form of the array, you use any of a fairly large group of functions Perl provides specifically for use with arrays. Figure 6.1 illustrates one such function, sort(), which allows you to alphabetically or numerically organize the elements in an array.

Adding Elements

Arrays expand dynamically. For this reason, you do not need to declare them or initialize them in any way other than the use you make of them when you first declare and define them. To add elements to an array, you can take two basic approaches. From one approach, you can add an element to an array by using the scalar ($) form and naming the index to which you want to assign a value. From the other approach, you can employ what is known as the *list function* to assign new elements to the implicit (@) form of the array. Some programmers refer to the @ as the *implicit* form of the array. Listing06_01 provides several examples of how you can define, retrieve, and print elements in arrays.

```
#Listing06_01
#Array definitions

$NL = "\n";
#1 Add items using the scalar form of the array
$NewArray[0] = "Fields ";
$NewArray[1] = "of ";
$NewArray[2] = "Green ";


#2 Print as a scalar or interpolated value
print "$NL Array element identified by index 1: "
                            . $NewArray[1] . "$NL";
```

```
print "$NL Array element identified by index 1: $NewArray[1] $NL";

#3 Use the list operation to add elements to an array
@SomeArrayA = (@SomeArrayA, "Little");
@SomeArrayA = (@SomeArrayA, "things", "always" );
@SomeArrayA = (@SomeArrayA, "matter", "in ", "the", "end");

#4 Interpolate an array to see all the values in it
print "$NL Elements after list add: " . "@SomeArrayA";

#5 Arrays accept any combination of data
@MixedArray = (32,all,22,44.7,32,34.5,numbers);
print "\n";
print "$NL Mixed array: @MixedArray";

#6 Retrieving values for printing
print "$NL Mixed array [0]: ". $MixedArray[0];
print "$NL Mixed array [1]: ". $MixedArray[1];
print "$NL Mixed array [2]: ". $MixedArray[2];
print "$NL Mixed array [3]: ". $MixedArray[3];

#7 Extracting values into a numeric context
$AddedValues = $MixedArray[0] + $MixedArray[3];
print "$NL Added Value " . $AddedValues . $NL ;
```

Assigning Values to Arrays

As the lines associated with comment #1 in Listing06_01 reveal, to add an element to an array, you can employ the $ form of the array and assign an item to a specific index. You can designate any index. The array expands to accommodate your assigned value:

```
$NewArray[0] = "Fields ";
$NewArray[1] = "of ";
$NewArray[2] = "Green ";
```

As is evident at comment #3 in Listing06_01, to add elements to the @ identifier of the array, you can use the list function. The list function, as mentioned previously, involves two parentheses. You can name the items in the list by separating them with commas. To add one element at a time to an array, place the array and the element you want to add within the parentheses. The array occupies the first position. Here is the code from Listing06_01:

```
@SomeArrayA = (@SomeArrayA, "Little");
@SomeArrayA = (@SomeArrayA, "things", "always" );
@SomeArrayA = (@SomeArrayA, "matter", "in ", "the", "end");
```

In each case, you assign the array back to itself as you populate it. No element is lost through the repeated list assignment operations.

With both the scalar and implicit (@) identifiers, when you assign values to arrays, you do not need to worry about data types. You can assign both numbers and strings. Certainly, in many respects, as with the creation of undefined value through arbitrary assignments, mixing array values can create problems. However, it remains that Perl arrays have no strict data types, so you can add whatever elements you want. Consider the following use of the list operator from Listing06_01:

```
@MixedArray = (32,all,22,44.7,32,34.5, numbers);
```

Each element is associated with an index. You can retrieve the value from the array using the index. The value the element possesses when you retrieve it from the array depends on how you use it. If you do not use the value in a specific way, it is displayed as a string value. Here are the values that display when you employ the print() function to print the interpolated elements:

```
Mixed array: 32 all 22 44.7 32 34.5 numbers
```

Retrieving and Printing Values

To retrieve a value using the scalar identifier, you employ the index of the value you want to retrieve. As shown in the lines associated with comment #2 in Listing06_01, you can concatenate it with an interpolated string or print it as a scalar value. For the item just assigned to index 1, you use the following statements:

```
print "$NL Array element identified by index 1: "
                                . $NewArray[1] . "$NL";
print "$NL Array element identified by index 1: $NewArray[1] $NL";
```

As Figure 6.2 illustrates, when the interpreter processes this statement, you see the following output for both statements:

```
Array element identified by index 1: of
```

In a the previous list assignment, 32 was assigned to the 0 index. The word all was assigned to the 1 index. As you add them to your array, the values you add are assigned the next available index. To retrieve values for display, you can use the print() command and the index form of the array:

```
print "$NL Mixed array [0]: ". $MixedArray[0];
print "$NL Mixed array [1]: ". $MixedArray[1];
```

The output is as follows:

```
Mixed array [0]: 32
Mixed array [1]: all
```

To print all of the elements in an array, you use the `print()` function in conjunction with double quotes (or the `qq()` function). The contents of the array display at the terminal. Consider the following statement:

```
print "$NL Elements after list add: " . "@SomeArrayA";
```

Given that you have populated `@SomeArrayA` as previously shown, you see the following output:

```
Elements after list add: Little things always matter in the end
```

Context and Retrieval

When you retrieve a value from an array, the operations you use on it determine what it means. If you want to retrieve a value from an array as a number, for example, you can extract it by assigning it to a scalar identifier that you then use as a number. You can also extract a value from an array as part of a math operation. As Figure 6.2 illustrates, here is an example of an extraction that results in the conversion of the numbers in arrays to scalars suitable for an addition operation:

```
$AddedValues = $MixedArray[0] + $MixedArray[3];
```

Using the `print()` function to print the resulting value, you see the following output:

```
Added Value 76.7
```

Figure 6.2 illustrates the output of Listing06_01.

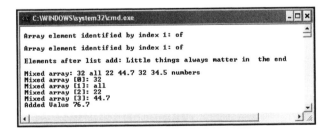

Figure 6.2
Use determines the form items assume when you retrieve them from an array.

Problems with Initialization

Implicit declaration of an array identifier does not initialize an array with values. The same can be said of defining an array in the scalar form. If you do not assign values to an array, the elements of the array remain undefined. To explore how this is so, consider the lines associated with comment #1 in Listing06_02, in which you declare an implicit (@ImplicitArray) and an array using the scalar ($NewArray[2]) syntax.

```
#Listing06_02
#Array definition issues
$NL = "\n";
#1 Declare identifiers
@ImplicitArray; #Array as array
$NewArray[20]; # Array as a scalar


#2 Test for definition
$LenA = @NewArray;
print "$NL Non-initialized array length of \$NewArray[20]: " . $LenA;
$LenA = @ ImplicitArray;
print "$NL Non-initialized array length of \@ImplicitArray: " . $LenA;


#3 Arbitrary definitions more or less successful
$NewArray[15] = 40;
$LenA = scalar(@NewArray);
print "$NL 3.A Initialized (\@) array length: " . $LenA;
$NewArray[20] = 40;
$LenA = scalar(@NewArray);
print "$NL 3.A Initialized (\@) array length: " . $LenA;
print "$NL 3.A Elements in the array: @NewArray";
print "$NL 3.A Value at 15: $NewArray[15]";
print "$NL 3.A Value at 20: $NewArray[20]";
print "$NL";
if(defined ($NewArray[15])){
    print "$NL 3.B Value DEFINED for 15.";
}
if(!defined($NewArray[15])){
    print "$NL 3.B Value NOT DEFINED for 15.";
}
```

```
if(defined ($NewArray[18])){
    print "$NL 3.B Value DEFINED for 18.";
}
if(!defined($NewArray[18])){
    print "$NL 3.B Value NOT DEFINED for 18.";
}
if(defined ($NewArray[20])){
    print "$NL 3.B Value DEFINED for 20.";
}
if(!defined($NewArray[20])){
    print "$NL 3.B NOT DEFINED for 20.";
}
print "$NL";

#4 Initializating each element
$LENGTH = 20;
#implicit using list
@NewArrayA = (1 .. $LENGTH);
#Scalar using a for statement
for($Itr = 0; $Itr< $LENGTH; $Itr++){
    $NewArrayB[$Itr] = 0;
}
#Explorations
$LenA = scalar(@NewArrayA);
$LenB = scalar(@NewArrayB);

print "$NL 3.C Initialized (\@NewArrayA) array length: " . $LenA;
print "$NL 3.C Initialized (\$NewArrayB) array length: " . $LenB;
print "$NL";
print "$NL 3.C \@NewArrayA value at 15: $NewArrayA[15]";
print "$NL 3.C \$NewArrayB value at 15: $NewArrayB[15]";
print "$NL";
print "$NL 3.C All values \@NewArrayA: \n @NewArrayA";
print "$NL 3.C All values \$NewArrayB: \n @NewArrayB";
print "$NL";
```

```
#Test for definition
print "$NL"." Tests for definitions. index number : [D - defined, U -
undefined]";
print "$NL Array A: $NL";
for($Itr = 0; $Itr< $LENGTH; $Itr++){
    if(defined ($NewArrayA[$Itr])){
        print " $Itr:D ";
        if($Itr==10){print "$NL";}
    }
    if(!defined($NewArrayA[Itr])){
        print " $Itr:U ";
    }
}
print "$NL Array B: $NL";
for($Itr = 0; $Itr< $LENGTH; $Itr++){
    if(defined ($NewArrayB[$Itr])){
        print " $Itr:D ";
        if($Itr==10){print "$NL";}
    }
    if(!defined($NewArrayB[Itr])){
        print " $Itr:U ";
    }
}
print "$NL $NL";
```

At comment #1 in Listing06_02, you might conclude that the value of 20 creates 20 indexes for the array and initializes them, say, to zero. This does not happen. A couple of approaches to seeing how the values have not been defined are open to you. One is to employ the approach that comment #2 identifies. Such an approach tests for the length. As Figure 6.3 shows, the lengths are zero, even if you have used an index value of 20 for one of the arrays.

At comment #3, you again test for lengths. In this case, you test for the length and the contents of the arrays. Notice that when you assign the value of 40 to index 15, the length becomes 16 (the indexing begins at 0). When you assign the value to the index of 20, the length becomes 21. You then use the implicit form of the array in an interpolated string and show that the string contains two 40s. The distribution of the two numbers across the screen indicates that the interpreter is reading the contents of the array. What the space means, however, remains unclear.

To see that the space indicates undefined elements, you implement a series of if statements that use the defined() function. You select index values of 15, 18, and 20 to test. As Figure 6.3 shows, while the array supposedly contains 20 elements, the value of index 18 remains undefined.

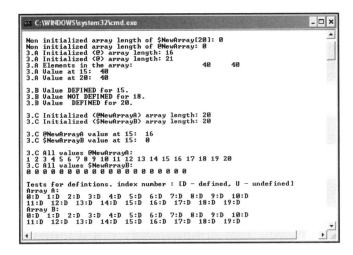

Figure 6.3
Definitions of array elements can remove confusion.

Comment #4 in Listing06_02 provides a few examples of how you can assign values to arrays in comprehensive ways. You can use either the implicit or the explicit form. To define the elements of the implicit form of an array, use the list function. In this instance, employ the dot operators to iterate through a sequence of numbers ranging from 0 to 20 ($LENGTH). To assign values to the indexes of the scalar form of the array, you employ a for statement and iterate through the indexes from 0 to 20, assigning 0 to each element. In both cases, as the first lines of 3.C in Figure 6.3 reveal, the arrays show lengths of 20.

You also print values from the two arrays. In both cases, the output reveals that values are stored in the elements of the array. You see a value of 15 for the array implicitly initialized, and you see a value of 0 for the array you initialized using its scalar form. You can then also display the contents of the two arrays and see that values have been assigned to each index. Finally, you can also subject the two arrays to tests that involve iterating through all their elements using the defined() function to verify their definitions. In this way, you see that values reside at each index for the two arrays.

Concatenation and Iteration

You can assign one array to another, and you can concatenate lists. In the previous section, you used the list function to add individual scalar items to an array. You can also use the list function to concatenate an array with one or more other arrays. Listing06_03 illustrates several such operations.

```
#Listing06_03
#1 List initialization
@StateArrayA = ("New York" , "Texas" , "California");
print "\n First list: @StateArrayA";


#2 Assignment of one list to another
@StateArrayB = @StateArrayA;
print "\n" . ' Printed as @StateArrayB: ' . "@StateArrayB";


#3 Two arrays can be concatenated using the list function.
@StateArrayC = ("Delaware", "Vermont", "Maine");
print "\n Create a third array: @StateArrayC ";


#4 concatenated arrays
@StateArrayD = (@StateArrayA, @StateArrayC);
print "\n Concatenate A and C to form array D: \n @StateArrayD";


$DLength = @StateArrayD;
print "\n Length of array D: $DLength \n";


#5 Access elements for iterative display
print "\n Ways to iterate through the elements in an array \n";
print "\n Use a for loop for the \$ identifier of array D: ";
for($Itr = 0; $Itr < $DLength; $Itr++){
    print "\n " . $Itr . ". $StateArrayD[$Itr]";
}


print "\n Use a foreach loop for the @ identifier of array D: ";
$Itr = 0;
foreach $State (@StateArrayD){
    print "\n " . $Itr++ . ". $State";
}
```

At comment #1 in Listing06_03, you initialize @StateArrayA using a list. In the lines trailing comment #2, you assign @StateArrayA to $StateArrayB and then print

$StateArrayB by making it a part of an interpolated string. With the lines trailing comment #3, you create a third array, $StateArrayC, and then at #4, you use a concatenation procedure involving a list to form the elements of @StateArrayA and @StateArrayC into yet another array, @StateArrayD. You then extract the length of the array from the @ identifier and print the result. As Figure 6.4 illustrates, the @StateArrayD contains six elements.

When you iterate through the elements in an array, you move from one element to the next, from beginning to end, in a way that allows you to operate on each element individually if you choose. You can iterate through the elements in an array individually in a number of ways. Two common ways involve the for and the foreach *repetition* controls.

In the lines that comment #5 identifies, you first use a for repetition statement to access the element in the scalar form of the array ($StateArrayD[ ]). To accomplish this, you create an iterator ($Itr) and make use of the $DLength identifier to which you have assigned the length of @StateArrayD. The iterator allows you to visit each element in the array. As the output shown in Figure 6.4 illustrates, the indexes corresponding to the elements range from 0 to 5.

After accessing the elements in the scalar ($) form of the identifier, you proceed to investigate using the foreach statement to visit each element in the @ form of the identifier. In essence, the foreach statement makes use of the list function in much the same way that concatenation procedures associated with comments #2 and #3 made use of it. The foreach statement moves from one element to the next in the array until it reaches the last element in the array. Each time it reaches a new array item, it transfers it to the $State scalar, and this in turn you print. Figure 6.4 illustrates the output of both the for and foreach approaches to iteration you employ in Listing06_03.

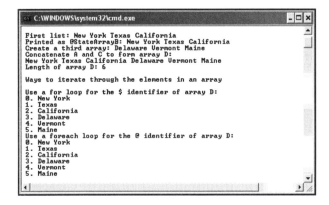

Figure 6.4
You can copy, concatenate, and iterate through the elements in an array with relative ease.

Accessing Elements in Arrays

You can access individual elements in an array using the `for` and `foreach` statements, and you can then make use of functions associated with scalars to make decisions about and effect transformations of the elements in the arrays. Listing06_04 creates arrays of the names of nations and concatenates the lists into a master array. It then selects elements for a final list on the basis of the second letter in their spelling.

```
#Listing06_04
#1 Initialize two lists
 @NationArrayB = (@NationArrayB, "Bangladesh");
 @NationArrayB = (@NationArrayB, "Barbados");
 @NationArrayB = (@NationArrayB, "Belarus");
 @NationArrayB = (@NationArrayB, "Belgium", "Belize", "Benin");
 print "\n A: @NationArrayB";

 @NationArrayL = (@NationArrayL, "Laos", "Latvia",
                                 "Lebanon", "Lesotho" ,
                                 "Liberia" , "Libya");
 print "\n B: @NationArrayL";

 #2 Concatenate the two nation lists
@NationArrayAll = (@NationArrayB, @NationArrayL);

# 3 show the second letter in each nation's name
print "\n Nations from the \'L\' list with second e\'s\n ";
foreach $Nation (@NationArrayAll){
        $Letter = substr($Nation, 1, 1);
             print "$Letter ";
}

# 4 Create a list of nation names with \'e\' as the second character
print "\n Take L\'s with second e\'s and move them to the E list: \n";
foreach $Nation (@NationArrayAll){
     $Letter = substr($Nation, 1, 1); #Get the letter at index 1
     #Select on the basis of the letter
     if("e" eq $Letter){                #if the second letter is \'e\'
         print "\n $Letter";
```

```
        print "\n Adding $Nation . . . ";
        #Capitalize the letter
        substr($Nation, 1, 1, "E"); #capitalize the second letter
        #Add the changed spelling to the new array
        @NationArrayWithE = (@NationArrayWithE, $Nation);
    }
}
print "\n E: @NationArrayWithE";
```

In the lines associated with comment #1, you create two arrays containing the names of nations. One list contains the names of nations that begin with the letter "B." The other array contains the names of nations that begin with the letter "L." To add items to the arrays, you repeatedly make use of the list function to add scalars to the two arrays. At comment #2, you then concatenate the two basic arrays, again employing the list function. The resulting array (@NationArrayAll) contains all of the nations.

With the lines trailing comment #3, you create a foreach statement and visit each element in the @NationArrayAll array. As you iterate through the array, you place the elements in a scalar ($Nation) and then submit this scalar to the substr() function to discover the identity of the letter that occupies its second index. This letter you assign to a scalar ($Letter).

At comment #4, you repeat the basic activities performed in association with comment #3, but this time you employ a selection statement to filter the names of nations based on the second letter of their spellings. Additionally, you supply the substr() function with the scalar containing the nation's name ($Nation) to capitalize the second letter. After capitalizing the second letter, you then employ the list function to add the name of the nation to yet another array, @NationArrayWithE. The finale arrives when you print this final list. Figure 6.5 illustrates the output of Listing06_04.

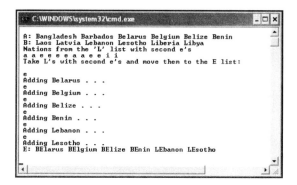

Figure 6.5
Selection of elements from arrays allows you to examine and transform them.

More on Implicit Assignment

The list function combined with the dot operators allows you to initialize arrays in a number of ways. Listing06_05 explores a few of the approaches.

```
#Listing06_05
#1 Numbers
@ArrayNum = (1..8);
print "\n ArrayE: @ArrayNum \n";


#2. Letters
@ArrayLet = ('f'..'m');
print "\n ArrayE: @ArrayLet \n";
#3. Expressions
@ArrayExpr = ('ab' .. 'am');
print "\n ArrayE: @ArrayExpr \n\n";


#5 Inventory and other numbers
@InventoryNumbers = (A0001111 .. A0009999);


print "\n A few numbers from the inventory list: \n";
for($Itr = 0; $Itr < 10; $Itr++){
    print "\n " . $Itr . ". $InventoryNumbers[$Itr]";
}
```

The use of the list function in Listing06_05 illustrates numbers, letters, and expressions. As Figure 6.6 shows, you can create an extensive list of sequential numbers and then print them using a `for` statement. To access the inventory numbers, you can access the elements with a procedure similar to the one used in Listing06_05.

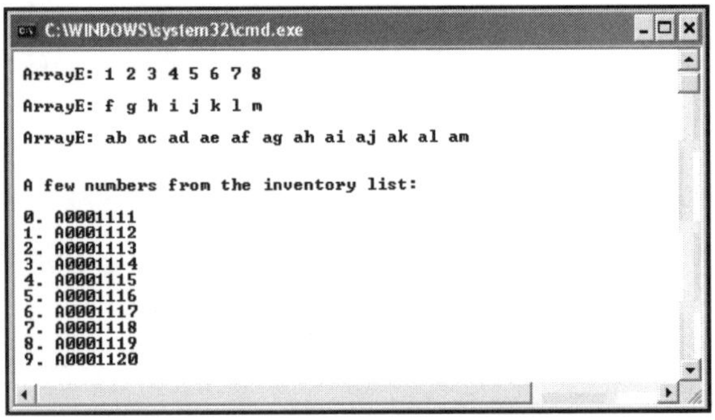

Figure 6.6
The list function provides several ways to initialize arrays.

Array Slicing

Slicing allows you to replace designated elements in an array using either scalar values or other arrays. When you employ the slice operation, you use the implicit (@) form of the array, but you combine this with the square brackets. You can slice as many elements as you choose. As Listing06_06 shows, you can do this with a combination of the list and the array context:

```
#Listing06_06
#1 Define an array
@CanadianCities = ("Amos" , "Barrie" , "Battleford" ,
                   "Beauport", "Bonavista");
print "\n Original list:\n @CanadianCities";


#2 Slice in scalars -- two slices
@CanadianCities[1, 2] = ("Chicoutimie", "Estevan");
print "\n Slice at indexes 1 and 2:\n @CanadianCities";
@CanadianCitiesA = ("Saskatoon", "Moose Jaw");
#slice in three elements
@CanadianCities[0, 2, 3] = ("Gagnon", "Perce", "Gaspe");
print "\n Splice at indexes 0, 2 and 3:\n @CanadianCities";


#3 Slice in elements of an array
print "\n Alternate array:\n @CanadianCitiesA";
@CanadianCities[3] = (@CanadianCitiesA);
print "\n Splice of alternate list at index 3 :\n @CanadianCities";
```

At comment #1, you set up an initial array of Canadian cities. Then, with the lines comment #2 identifies, you conduct slices. The first slice involves replacement of the elements at indexes 1 and 2. The second slice involves the replacement of the elements at indexes 0, 2, and 3. Both of these slices involve scalar substitutions. You employ string constants to replace elements in @CanadianCities on the basis of index position.

In the lines that comment #3 identifies, you slice an array into the original array. The slicing begins at index 3. Figure 6.7 illustrates the result of the slicing in Listing06_06.

Figure 6.7
Replace indexed elements
with literal strings.

Swapping

When you swap elements in an array, you improvise on the basic routine afforded by slicing. To effect a swap, you reassign an array to itself, and as you do so you employ indexes to define how you want to reorganize (or swap) the elements. Listing06_07 explores a basic swapping scenario:

```
#Listing06_07
#1 Create an array
@CanadianCities = ("Amos" , "Barrie" , "Battleford" ,
                   "Beauport", "Bonavista");

$Itr = 0;
print "\n Original order:\n ";
foreach $City (@CanadianCities){
    print "\n ". $Itr++ . ". $City";
}


#2 Use swapping to rearrange the elements
@CanadianCities[0,3,2,1] = @CanadianCities[4,1,2,3];


#print results of swapping
$Itr = 0;
print "\n\n Rearranged order: \n";
foreach $City (@CanadianCities){
    print "\n ". $Itr++ . ". $City";
}
```

At comment #1, you set up an array of Canadian cities and then print the array with an iterator so that you can see the order. Then at comment #2, you set up a swapping routine. The routine involves using the implicit (@) form of the array and multiple indexes between brackets to indicate the elements you want to swap. To make the swap, you assign the array back to itself.

The order you indicate to the left of the assignment operator supplants the order to the right. Figure 6.8 shows you the outcome of the swapping operations of Listing06_07.

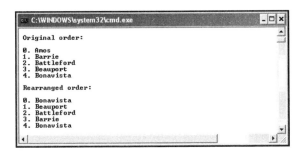

Figure 6.8
Swapping using indexes to change the order of elements.

Using qw() to Populate Arrays

The qw() function allows you to insert items into an array one at a time, to create separate array elements. To distinguish the elements, you provide them as literal text and separate them with spaces. Listing06_08 illustrates some of the uses you can make of the qw() function.

```
#Listing06_08

#1 Define an array of cities in India
@CitiesInIndia = qw(Hyderabad Imphal
                    Behra'Dun, New'Delhi,
                    Indore Jodhpur
                    Merest Nagpur
                    Raipur);
# 2 Explicit use of scalar
$Length = scalar(@CitiesInIndia);
print "\n Number of cities: $Length.";

#print
foreach $City (@CitiesInIndia){
    print "\n $City";
}
```

The lines trailing comment #1 create an array of cities in India. Use of the apostrophe is a work-around for the qw() function. This makes it so that the function recognizes the cities consisting of two names as single elements. To populate the array, you employ its @ identifier. After creating the array, in the lines associated with comment #2, you then use a function not named previously.

This is the `scalar()` function, which can be used to obtain the number of elements in an array. The `scalar()` function takes as its argument the @ form of the array and renders the same result that you obtain if you implicitly assign the @ array identifier to a scalar. It has the advantage of making the purpose of the statement clearer to the reader of your code. Figure 6.9 illustrates the output of Listing06_08.

Figure 6.9
You can populate a list using a space-delineated list.

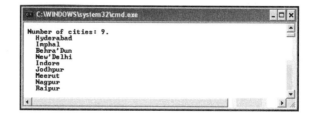

```
C:\WINDOWS\system32\cmd.exe
Number of cities: 9.
    Hyderabad
    Imphal
    Behra'Dun
    New'Delhi
    Indore
    Jodhpur
    Meerut
    Nagpur
    Raipur
```

Splicing

Splicing differs from slicing. Splicing involves taking elements from one array and placing them in another array. You overwrite the elements in the destination array.

Basic Splice

To perform a basic splice, you work with four arguments, as shown in Figure 6.10. The first argument identifies the destination array. The second argument indicates the position in the destination array after which you want to splice elements. The third argument identifies the number of elements placed in the destination array from the source array.

Figure 6.10
Splicing allows you to insert elements from one array into another.

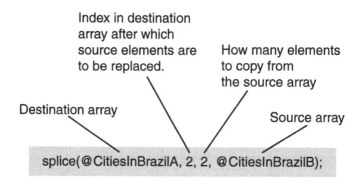

Index in destination array after which source elements are to be replaced.

How many elements to copy from the source array

Destination array

Source array

splice(@CitiesInBrazilA, 2, 2, @CitiesInBrazilB);

Listing06_12 explores a simple scenario in which you replace three elements in the destination array. You start at the element following the second element.

```
#Listing06_12
#1 Set up arrays
```

```
@CitiesInBrazilA = qw( Aracaju Brasilia Canoas Itabuna Manaus);
@CitiesInBrazilB = qw( Salvador Teresina Natal Curitiba);


$Itr = 1;
print "\n Brazilian city group A: \n";
foreach $City (@CitiesInBrazilA){
    print "\n " . $Itr++ . ". $City";
}


$Itr = 1;
print "\n\n Brazilian city group B: \n";
    foreach $City (@CitiesInBrazilB){
        print "\n " . $Itr++ . ". $City";
}


#2 Two elements
#array to copy to, starting position, number of elements deleted, source array
print "\n\n Elements from B spliced into A; 2 deleted, following 2 in A: ";
print "\n " . 'Syntax splice (@CitiesInBrazilA, 2 , 2 , @CitiesInBrazilB);';
splice(@CitiesInBrazilA, 2, 2, @CitiesInBrazilB);


$Itr = 1;
foreach $City (@CitiesInBrazilA){
    print "\n " . $Itr++ . ". $City";
}
```

The lines accompanying comment #1 set up two arrays, @CitiesInBrazilA and @CitiesInBrazilB. The first consists of six city names, the second of four. Then you use for statements to iterate through the elements in the array. Following the definition and display of the arrays containing the cities, in the lines associated with comment #2, you call the splice() function to transfer the elements from @CitiesInBrazilB to @CitiesInBrazilA. Figure 6.11 illustrates the effects of the splice() operation.

As the lines trailing comment #2 reveal, the first argument to the splice() function is the destination array, @CitiesInBrazilA. Following the designation of the destination array, you then name the position after which you want to begin replacing elements. In this case, this element is the second, "Brasilia." You then designate the number of elements in the destination

Figure 6.11
One version of splicing
allows you to selectively
replace elements.

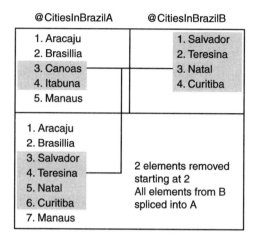

array that you want to delete when you splice elements from the source array into it. In this case, you remove two elements (Canoas and Itabuna). Finally, you name the source array. The `splice()` operation selects all the elements from the source array beginning with index 0 and inserts them into the destination array. Figure 6.12 illustrates the output of Listing06_12.

Figure 6.12
Use splice with four arguments to replace elements.

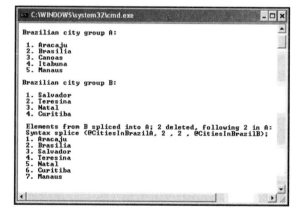

Splice with a Range or a Selected Set

You can employ the splice function so that you can designate the specific elements or range of elements you want to appropriate from the source array. In this way, you can pick just those elements you want to designate as the replacement elements for the destination array. Listing06_13 uses the arrays of cities from the previous example to fine-tune the `splice()` function.

```
#Listing06_13
#1 Set up arrays
@CitiesInBrazilA = qw( Aracaju Brasilia Canoas Itabuna Manaus);
@CitiesInBrazilB = qw( Salvador Teresina Natal Curitiba);

$Itr = 1;
print "\n Brazilian city group A: \n";
foreach $City (@CitiesInBrazilA){
    print "\n " . $Itr++ . ". $City";
}

$Itr = 1;
print "\n\n Brazilian city group B: \n";
 foreach $City (@CitiesInBrazilB){
    print "\n " . $Itr++ . ". $City";
}

#2 Two elements
#array to copy to, starting position, number of elements, source array
print "\n\n" . 'splice (@CitiesInBrazilA, 2, 2, @CitiesInBrazilA[1, 3]);';
print "\nElements at indexes 1 and 3 from B" .
      " spliced into A after position 2: \n";
#Starts at the second element, inserts the array at pos 4,
#removes one element - pos 3.
splice (@CitiesInBrazilA, 2, 2, @CitiesInBrazilB[1, 3]);

$Itr = 1;
foreach $City (@CitiesInBrazilA){
    print "\n " . $Itr++ . ". $City";
}
```

Figure 6.13 illustrates the output of Listing06_13. As the lines trailing comment Listing06_13 illustrate, this time you inset an array in which you designate the specific indexes of the items you want to select from the source array. To accomplish this, you use a slice operation. Since you identify the elements using their indexes, item 1 is Teresina and item 3 is Curitiba.

Figure 6.13
Use the slice operation with the `splice()` function to replace selected elements.

Remove a Range of Elements

Splice can be used to remove a range of elements from an array. In this version of the splice function, you employ only three argument. These arguments designate the array on which you want to perform operations, the position in the array after which you want to remove elements, and the number of elements you want to remove. Listing06_14 revisits one of the arrays of cities from the previous examples.

```
#Listing06_14
#1 Set up arrays
@CitiesInBrazilA = qw( Aracaju Brasilia Canoas Itabuna Manaus);
$Itr = 1;
print "\n Brazilian city group A: \n";
foreach $City (@CitiesInBrazilA){
    print "\n " . $Itr++ . ". $City";
}


#2 Remove two elements
# Identify the array, the starting position, number of elements
print "\n\n" . 'splice (@CitiesInBrazilA, 2, 2);';
print "\nRemove two elements following position 2: \n";
#extract two elements after element two
splice (@CitiesInBrazilA, 2, 2);
#view the result
$Itr = 1;
foreach $City (@CitiesInBrazilA){
    print "\n " . $Itr++ . ". $City";
}
```

As the lines at comment #2 illustrate, to eliminate the third and fourth elements of the array, you first supply the name of the array (@CitiesInBrazilA) and the element after which you want to delete elements (2). You then name the number of elements you want to delete (2). Figure 6.14 shows you the result of this operation.

Figure 6.14
Use three arguments with the splice() function to remove elements.

Remove Elements to the End of the Array

You can also employ the splice() function to remove elements from the end of an array. To accomplish this, you use a form of the splice() function that involves only two arguments. Listing06_15 explores this activity.

```
#Listing06_15
#1 Set up an array
@CitiesInBrazilA = qw( Aracaju Brasilia Canoas Itabuna Manaus);
$Itr = 1;
print "\n Brazilian city group A: \n";
foreach $City (@CitiesInBrazilA){
    print "\n " . $Itr++ . ". $City";
}


#2 Remove all elements except the first three
# Identify the array, the starting position, number of elements
print "\n\n" . 'splice (@CitiesInBrazilA, 3)';
print "\nRemove all elements except the first three: \n";
splice (@CitiesInBrazilA, 3);
#show the result
$Itr = 1;
foreach $City (@CitiesInBrazilA){
    print "\n " . $Itr++ . ". $City";
}
```

In the lines accompanying comment #3, you supply two arguments to the splice() function. The first argument identifies the array you want to truncate. The second argument identifies the number of elements you want to retain after the truncation. Figure 6.15 shows you the results of the splicing operation performed in Listing06_15.

Figure 6.15
Use two arguments with the splice() function to delete end elements.

Inserting with No Deletions

As you might have suspected following the variations of uses to which you have put the splice() function so far, you can also splice elements from a source array into a destination array without deleting any elements from the destination array. To accomplish this, you employ a form of the splice() function that requires four arguments, but you set the third argument, which designates the number of elements to be replaced, to zero. To control the range of elements you introduce into the destination array, you use the slice operation. Listing06_16 delves into this activity.

```
#Listing06_16
#1 Set up arrays
@CitiesInBrazilA = qw( Aracaju Brasilia Canoas Itabuna Manaus);
@CitiesInBrazilB = qw( Salvador Teresina Natal Curitiba);
$Itr = 1;
print "\n Brazilian city group A: \n";
foreach $City (@CitiesInBrazilA){
    print "\n " . $Itr++ . ". $City";
}


$Itr = 1;
print "\n\n Brazilian city group B: \n";
 foreach $City (@CitiesInBrazilB){
    print "\n " . $Itr++ . ". $City";
}
```

```
#2 Two elements added to the destination array
#array to copy to, starting position, number of elements, source array
print "\n\n" . 'splice(@CitiesInBrazilA, 2, 0, @CitiesInBrazilB[1, 3])';
print "\nInsert elements at indexes 1 and 3 from array B" .
      "\n into array A after position 2: \n";
#the third argument is zero
splice(@CitiesInBrazilA, 2, 0, @CitiesInBrazilB[1, 3]);
$Itr = 1;
foreach $City (@CitiesInBrazilA){
    print "\n " . $Itr++ . ". $City";
}
```

As the lines accompanying comment #2 show, you supply four arguments to the splice()
function. The first names the destination array. The second designates the position after which
you want to insert elements. The third you set to zero (0) to indicate that you do not want any
elements replaced. The last argument provides a list of scalars, an array, or a sliced array that
designates the elements you want to insert into the destination array. In this case, the slice operation designates the elements at indexes 1 and 3 of the source array (@CitiesInBrazilB
[1, 3]). Figure 6.16 illustrates how the splicing operation inserts elements into the destination
array from the source array.

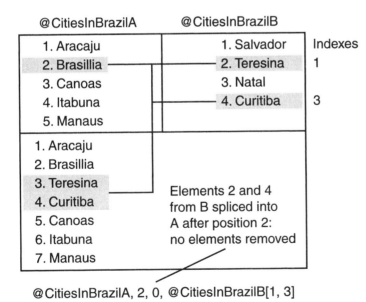

Figure 6.16
You can use the splice operation to insert elements
into the target array.

Figure 6.17 illustrates the output of Listing06_16.

Figure 6.17
You can use the
`splice()` function to
insert without deletion.

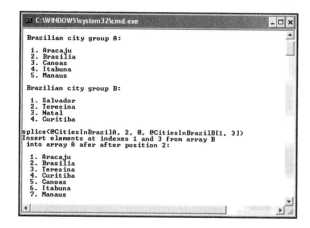

Conclusion

In this chapter, you have explored a few fundamental aspects of arrays in Perl. The array that Perl provides automatically expands as you add elements to it. It has two forms: the scalar form and the implicit form. To use the implicit form of the array, you use a variety of functions.

A key issue you encounter when using Perl arrays concerns initialization. While you can create Perl arrays of almost any length by assigning an element to an index of the array, you do not in this way define all of the elements in the array to which you have not explicitly assigned values. To remedy this situation, you can employ the list function or a `for` statement to define definitions.

You can concatenate lists in a variety of ways. In this chapter, you have explored how you can employ the list function to selectively or comprehensively combine arrays. By using the slicing operation (a combination of the implicit form of the array with the square brackets), you can swap and replace elements. By using the `splice()` function, you can effect any number of changes, including swapping, adding, and eliminating elements.

7 } Arrays and Data Containers

In this chapter you'll explore a variety of functions associated with the implicit form of the array. Such functions as `reverse()`, `sort()`, `split()`, and `join()` allow you to easily increase the number of problems you can solve using Perl arrays. Along with the built-in operations, this chapter also explores how the array that Perl provides is in essence a flexible container. You can use it as a traditional dynamic array, or through such functions as the `push()`, `pop()`, `shift()`, and `unshift()` functions you can transform it into data containers. Among the containers you investigate are stacks and queues. Toward this objective and others, the topics in this chapter include the following:

- ❋ How to reverse the order of elements in an array
- ❋ Using the `join()` function with arrays
- ❋ Adding and extracting elements from the front of an array
- ❋ Adding and extracting elements from the end of an array
- ❋ Using the array as a stack
- ❋ Using the array as a queue

Reverse Elements in an Array

One basic function associated with arrays allows you to reverse their contents. This is the `reverse()` function. If you have a sorted list that goes from 1 to 10 or "a" to "z," then when the `reverse()` function does its work, you see as a result a list that goes from 10 to 1 and "z" to "a." The `reverse()` function itself does sort the contents of an array; it works with the items as it finds them. When you reverse the elements of an array, you must assign the array back to itself for the reversal to take effect. Listing07_01 explores how to reverse an alphabetical list of Japanese cities.

```
#Listing07_01
#1 Set up an array of Japanese cities
@CitiesJapan = qw( Akita Chiba Fukui Funabashi Hofu Mito Ngano);

$Itr = 1;
print "\n Japanese cities: \n";
foreach $City (@CitiesJapan){
    print "\n " . $Itr++ . ". $City";
}


#2 Reverse the elements
print "\n\n" . '@CitiesJapan = reverse(@CitiesJapan);';
print "\nReverse the elements in the array: \n";

@CitiesJapan = reverse(@CitiesJapan);

$Itr = 1;
foreach $City (@CitiesJapan){
    print "\n " . $Itr++ . ". $City";
}
```

In the lines associated with comment #1 in Listing07_01, you set up an alphabetical array of cities in Japan. Given this list, you then proceed in the lines that comment #2 identifies to call the reverse() function. The sole argument you supply to the function consists of the array you want to reverse (@CitiesJapan). To reverse the array, you assign it back to itself. Then, when you print the array using a for statement, you see the elements have been positioned in the array in reverse order. Figure 7.1 illustrates work of the reverse() function in Listing07_01.

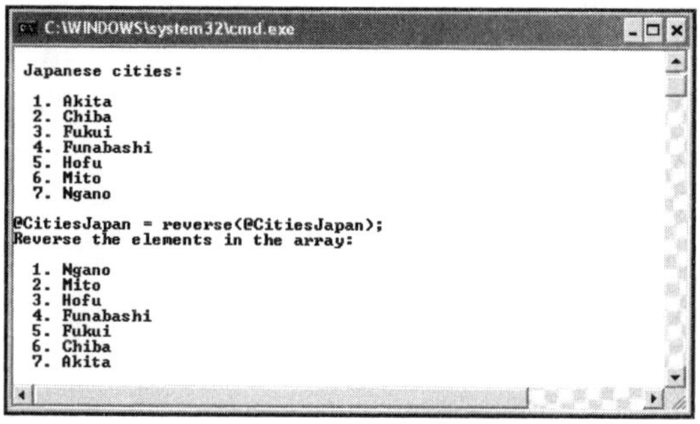

Figure 7.1
The reverse() function reverses items alphabetically or numerically.

Sorting Array Elements

You use the sort () function to alphabetically or numerically sort items. The sorting process orders the elements in your array in ascending order. For this reason, the sort () function places capitalized words before words that are not capitalized. The sort () function also works with numbers. Generally, when using the sort () function, if you combine letters and numbers, the results you encounter can vary. The reason for this becomes clear in the next few programs. As a starter, the sort () function evaluates words according to the ASCII values of the letters. When you sort words, then, you can always rely on it to perform its work in good form, for ASCII values fall between 0 and 255. When you deal with very large numbers, however, you need to augment the sort () function with a supplemental operation (see the next section). Generally, serial numbers or other such items, which consist of alphanumeric elements, create no problem. Listing07_02 explores the sort () function as applied to capitalized and lowercase versions of the names of Japanese cities.

```
#Listing07_02
#1 Set up an array of Japanese cities
@CitiesJapan = (@CitiesJapan, qw(Fukui Hofu Funabashi Ngano));
@CitiesJapan = (@CitiesJapan, ("mito", "chiba", "akita"));
@CitiesJapan = (@CitiesJapan, qw( Mito Chiba Akita));

$Itr = 1;
print "\n Japanese cities: \n";
foreach $City (@CitiesJapan){
    print "\n " . $Itr++ . ". $City";
}
#2 Reverse the elements
print "\n\n" . '@CitiesJapan = reverse(@CitiesJapan);';
print "\Sort elements in the array: \n";
@CitiesJapan = sort(@CitiesJapan);

$Itr = 1;
foreach $City (@CitiesJapan){
    print "\n " . $Itr++ . ". $City";
}
```

At comment #1 you employ three concatenation operations to create a mixed array of the names of Japanese cities. Some of the names appear without capitalization. At comment #2, you submit the array to the sort() function. As Figure 7.2 reveals, the sort() function sorts words so that capitalized words come before words that are not capitalized.

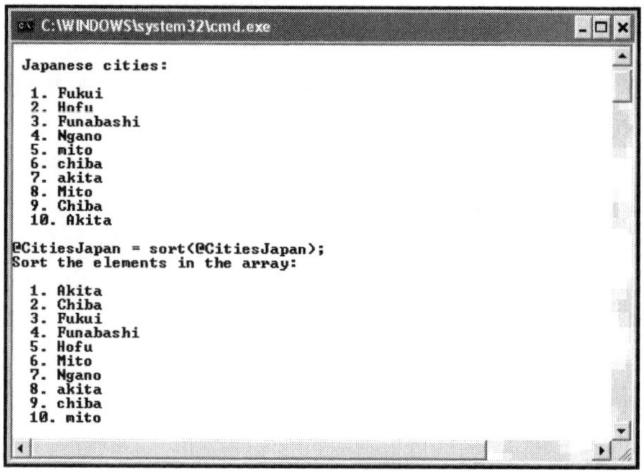

Figure 7.2

The sort() function gives capitalized alphabetical precedence over words that are not capitalized.

```
C:\WINDOWS\system32\cmd.exe

Japanese cities:

1. Fukui
2. Hofu
3. Funabashi
4. Ngano
5. mito
6. chiba
7. akita
8. Mito
9. Chiba
10. Akita

@CitiesJapan = sort(@CitiesJapan);
Sort the elements in the array:

1. Akita
2. Chiba
3. Fukui
4. Funabashi
5. Hofu
6. Mito
7. Ngano
8. akita
9. chiba
10. mito
```

You can achieve consistency in your sorting procedures if you first iterate through the array and force all the terms to either capitalized or lowercase versions. The code that accomplishes this task is as follows:

```
#Listing07_02_02
print "\n\n Japanese cities sorted: \n";
$Itr = 1;
foreach $City (@CitiesJapan){
# print "\n " . $Itr++ . ". $City";
    @CitiesJapanCaps = (@CitiesJapanCaps, ucfirst($City));
}
$Itr = 1;
@CitiesJapanCaps = sort(@CitiesJapanCaps);
$Itr = 1;
foreach $City (@CitiesJapanCaps){
    print "\n " . $Itr++ . ". $City";
}
```

When you use the basic form of sort(), you can depend on the success of the operation when you deal with words. The reason is that the sorting algorithm can handle the values it processes. When you move to numbers, however, the sort() function alone tends to give out, so the result you see will be only partially sorted. To solve this problem, you employ an augmented form of the sort() function for numbers, which the next section covers.

156

Sorting Number Arrays

The basic `sort()` function does not work with numbers. It works only with words or strings. To work with numbers, you require a numerical version of the `sort()` function. This is the `sort{$a < = > $b}()` function. The syntax of this function includes the approximation operator. This operator allows the function to process numerical values not encountered in the range of values alphabetical sorting involves. Listing07_02_03 provides a basic example of how to use the `sort{$a < = > $b}()` function. It takes as its sole argument an array containing numerical values.

```
#Listing07_02_03

#1 Set up an array
@Numbers = qw(256 76 284 12 35 85 9.4 3.1 5.2);

$Itr = 1;
print "\n Numbers unsorted: \n";
foreach $Num (@Numbers){
    print " $Num ";
}

print "\n\n Numbers sorted: \n";
$Itr = 1;
@Numbers = sort{$a <=> $b}(@Numbers);
#To invert the order, use reverse(@Numbers);
$Itr = 1;
foreach $Num (@Numbers){
    print " $Num ";
}
```

Here's the output of Listing07_02_03:

```
Numbers unsorted:
256 76 284 12 35 85 9.4 3.1 5.2
Numbers sorted:
3.1 5.2 9.4 12 35 76 85 256 284
```

Splitting Strings into Array Elements

The split() function allows you to break a string in which the elements are in some way consistently separated (by commas, spaces, periods, and so on) into elements of an array. To split a string in this way, the split() function requires two arguments. The first argument designates the punctuation or element to be used to segment the items in the source string into elements. The second string consists of the scalar string source. Listing07_03 explores the use of the split() function to separate a string containing the names of the countries bordering Hungary into an array.

```
#Listing07_03
#1 create a string
print "\n\nUsing split with a string of countries bordering Hungary: \n";
$HungaryBorderCountries = "Slovakia, Austria, Slovenia, Croatia, " .
                          "Yugoslavia, Romania, Ukraine";
print "\n\n" . $HungaryBorderCountries;
#2 Use the split function; break at commas with space
print "\n\nAfter split and sort:";
@BorderArray = split(", ", $HungaryBorderCountries);
#3 sort after array is formed
@BorderArray = sort(@BorderArray);
$Itr = 1;
foreach $Country(@BorderArray)
{
print "\n". $Itr++ . ". \t$Country";
}
```

The lines accompanying comment #1 create a string that consists of the names of nations bordering Hungary. After printing this string, you proceed with the lines trailing comment #2 to split the string. To split the string, you designate the first argument of the split() function as a comma followed by a space. For the second argument, you supply the name of the string holding the names ($HungaryBorderCountries). To receive the elements the split() function creates, you assign the returned values of the split() function an array (@BorderArray).

In the lines associated with comment #3, you employ the sort() function to order alphabetically the names of the countries bordering Hungary. You then print the final alphabetical list with numbered items. Figure 7.3 shows you the output of Listing07_03.

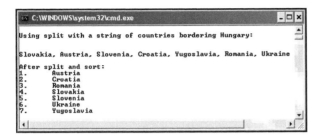

Figure 7.3
The split() function allows you to separate items in strings into array elements.

Joining Elements from an Array

Using the join() function, you can extract elements from an array to form a string. As you know from a previous chapter, the join() function allows you to join elements into a string. You can use it to access elements in an array in the same way that you use it to access elements in a list enclosed between parentheses. Listing07_04 explores some of the ways you can use the join() function to form a scalar that includes line returns.

```
#Listing07_04
#1 Form arrays
@CountryArrayM = qw(Macedonia Madagascar Malawi);
@CountryArrayN = qw(Namibia Nepal Nicaragua Norway);
@CountryArrayP = qw(Pakistan Palau Panama);


#2 Iterate through all the arrays
$Itr = 0;
foreach $Country (@CountryArrayM, @CountryArrayN, @CountryArrayP){
print "\n" . ++($Itr) . ". $Country";
}


#3 Form a scalar with line returns
$AllCountries = join(" ", @CountryArrayM, "\n",
                         @CountryArrayN, "\n",
                         @CountryArrayP);
#Print the scalar
print "\n\nCountries ($Itr):\n ".
                         $AllCountries . "\n\n";
```

Figure 7.4 illustrates the output of Listing07_20.

Figure 7.4
You can retrieve elements
from arrays and join them
into a string.

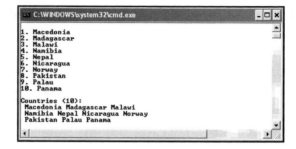

Extracting Elements from the Front of an Array

The `shift()` function removes elements from the beginning of the arrays. To understand how this works, consider Figure 7.5. When you create an array using, for example, the `list()` function, the first element you assign to the array is associated with the index position of 0. The second element you assign to the array is associated with the index position of 1. The array continues to grow in this way as you add elements. When you employ the `shift()` function, you automatically remove the element associated with the lowest index. At the same time, as you remove the element using the `shift()` function, all the elements in the array are shifted toward the front (or zero index) of the array.

Figure 7.5
`shift()` removes the
first element of the array.

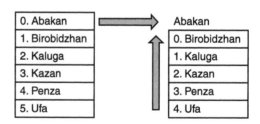

Listing07_05 explores the basic operations of the `shift()` function.

```
#Listing07_05
#1 Set up an array of Russian cities
@CitiesInRussia = qw(Abakan Birobidzhan Kaluga Kazan Penza Ufa);
print "\n Cities in Russia: ";
```

```perl
for ($Itr = 0; $Itr < scalar(@CitiesInRussia); $Itr++){
    print "\n " . $Itr . ". $CitiesInRussia[$Itr]";
}


#2 Remove an element
$City = shift(@CitiesInRussia);
print "\nCity removed from array: $City";
print "\n Cities in Russia: ";
for ($Itr = 0; $Itr < scalar(@CitiesInRussia); $Itr++){
    print "\n " . $Itr . ". $CitiesInRussia[$Itr]";
}


#3 Remove element from
$City = shift(@CitiesInRussia);
print "\nCity removed from array: $City";
print "\n Cities in Russia: ";
for ($Itr = 0; $Itr < scalar(@CitiesInRussia); $Itr++){
    print "\n " . $Itr . ". $CitiesInRussia[$Itr]";
}
print "\nWith shift(), the first element in is the first element out.";
```

At comment #1 in Listing07_05, you set up an array of Russian cities. The first item you store in the index is Abakan. Having set up the array, you then employ a `for` statement to iterate through the scalar form of the array to retrieve its elements according to the index position they have been assigned.

With comment #2, you call the `shift()` function. You provide the function with one argument, the array containing the names of Russian cities (`@CitiesInRussia`). Following the call to `shift()`, you then iterate through the items in the array once again. As Figure 7.6 reveals, the array now lacks its first element, Abakan. The element has been removed from the front or top of the array.

In the lines trailing comment #3, you call the `shift()` function and afterward use the scalar form of the array so that you can use their index values to retrieve them for display. Again, it is evident, as Figure 7.6 shows, that the element at the top or front of the array has been removed (Birobidzhan). The last statement in the program repeats the message that `shift()` applies to the first element you put in the array. Given this scheme, the element entered first is the first element out.

Figure 7.6
As the shift() function is called, elements are removed from the head of the array.

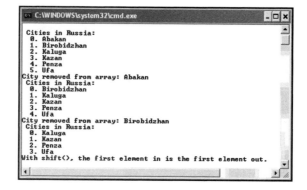

Inserting Elements into the Front of an Array

The unshift() function performs an action that is the reverse of the shift() function. Rather than removing the first element in an array, the unshift() function inserts an element into the first or zero position of an array. Consider Figure 7.7. When the unshift() function inserts a new element into an array, the indexes of the existing elements increase in value by one. They are "unshifted" from the front or head of the array toward its tale or end.

Figure 7.7
The unshift() function moves all the elements further from the head of the array when it adds a new element.

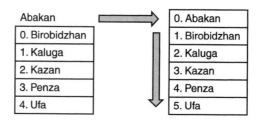

unshift( ) inserts an element
into the array at its top or head.

Listing07_06 explores the fundamental use of the unshift() function.

```
#Listing07_06
#1 Set up an array of Russian cities
@CitiesInRussia = qw(Kaluga Kazan Penza Ufa);

print "\n Cities in Russia: ";
for ($Itr = 0; $Itr < scalar(@CitiesInRussia); $Itr++){
    print "\n " . $Itr . ". $CitiesInRussia[$Itr]";
}
```

```
$City = "Abakan";
#2 Add an element to the front of the array
unshift(@CitiesInRussia, $City);
print "\nCity added to array: $City";

print "\n Cities in Russia: ";
for ($Itr = 0; $Itr < scalar(@CitiesInRussia); $Itr++){
    print "\n " . $Itr . ". $CitiesInRussia[$Itr]";
}

#3 Add an element to the front of the array
$City = Birobidzhan;
unshift(@CitiesInRussia, $City);
print "\nCity added to array: $City";
print "\n Cities in Russia: ";
for ($Itr = 0; $Itr < scalar(@CitiesInRussia); $Itr++){
    print "\n " . $Itr . ". $CitiesInRussia[$Itr]";
}
```

In the lines that comment #1 identifies in Listing07_06, you create an array containing the names of cities in Russia. You start with a short list, one consisting of four items. You then print the array. To print the array, you employ the scalar form of the array (@CitiesInRussia) so you can see the elements in the array displayed with their associated index values, which tells you their positions in the array.

With comment #2, you call the unshift() function and insert a new city into the array (Abakan). To accomplish this, you provide the unshift() function with two arguments. The first argument consists of the name of the array to which you want to add a new element (@CitiesInRussia). The second, in this instance, consists of a scalar identifier ($City) to which you have assigned the name of the city you want to add (Abakan). Having completed the call to the shift() function, you then iterate through the array to confirm the values. As Figure 7.8 shows, the shift() function has added the new city to the top or head of the array, and all previously existing elements have been shifted so they possess index values greater by one.

In the lines trailing comment #3, you repeat the actions performed in association with comment #2. This time, you add Birobidazhan to the array. As before, you use this value assigned to the $City scalar as the second argument of the unshift() function. Following insertion of the name of the city into the array, you again iterate through the array to confirm that the new element has been assigned a zero index. Figure 7.8 reveals that this is so.

Figure 7.8

The unshift() function inserts a new element at the front of an array.

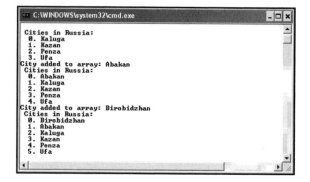

Removing Elements from the End of an Array

The pop() function takes an element away from the end of an array. The pop() function takes only one argument, the name of the array from which you want to remove an element. As Figure 7.9 illustrates, when you pop an element from an array, the other elements in the array retain their index value.

Figure 7.9

You take an element from the end or tail of a list when you pop it.

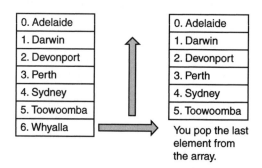

Listing07_07 explores the use of the pop() function to remove the elements from an array that stores the names of cities in Australia.

```
#Listing07_07
#1 Set up an array of Australian cities
@CitiesInAustralia = qw(Adelaide Darwin Devonport
                        Perth Sydney Toowoomba Whyalla);

print "\n Cities in Australia: ";
```

```
for ($Itr = 0; $Itr < scalar(@CitiesInAustralia); $Itr++){
    print "\n " . $Itr . ". $CitiesInAustralia[$Itr]";
}


#2 Remove an element
$City = pop(@CitiesInAustralia);
print "\nCity removed from array: $City";

print "\n Cities in Australia: ";
for ($Itr = 0; $Itr < scalar(@CitiesInAustralia); $Itr++){
    print "\n " . $Itr . ". $CitiesInAustralia[$Itr]";
}


#3 Remove element from
$City = pop(@CitiesInAustralia);
print "\nCity removed from array: $City";

print "\n Cities in Australia: ";
for ($Itr = 0; $Itr < scalar(@CitiesInAustralia); $Itr++){
    print "\n " . $Itr . ". $CitiesInAustralia[$Itr]";
}
```

The lines comment #1 designates define an array that consists of seven cities in Australia. You employ a for statement immediately after defining the statement to iterate through the elements in the array and display them. To iterate through the elements, you use the scalar ($) form of the array so that you can view the elements in the array according to their index values.

At comment #2, you call the pop() function to remove an element from the end or tail of the array. The pop() function requires only one argument, the name of the array (@CitiesInAustralia). You then report the name of the city you have removed from the array and again iterate through the array using the scalar form of the array. This is to verify the contents of the array according to index positions. As Figure 7.10 shows, as a result of the call to the pop() function, Whyalla has been removed from the list.

With the lines trailing comment #3, you perform largely the same actions you performed in the lines associated with comment #2. This time, the call to the pop() function results in the removal of Toowoomba from the array. This city occupies the highest index value and so is the target of the pop() function. As result of the call to the pop() function, as Figure 7.10

illustrates, the size of the array decreases by one, and all elements except the popped element remain unaffected.

Figure 7.10
As each element is popped from the list, the highest index value in the list decreases by one.

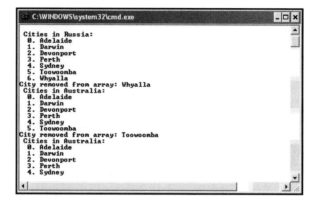

Adding Elements to the End of an Array

You employ the push() function to add an element to the end of an array. The push() function does not affect any of the existing elements in an array. It serves only to increase the number of elements in the array by one each time you call it. As Figure 7.11 illustrates, as the push() function appends the new element onto the array, it assigns the element an index value one greater than the existing size of the array.

Figure 7.11
You push elements onto the end of an array.

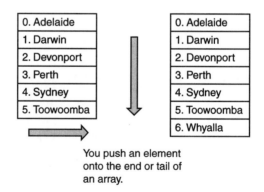

You push an element onto the end or tail of an array.

Listing07_08 explores the use of the push() function by adding elements to an array that consists of the names of Australian cities.

```
#Listing07_08
#push elements onto an array
```

```
#1 Set up an array of Australian cities
@CitiesInAustralia = qw(Adelaide Darwin Devonport
                        Perth Sydney);

print "\n Cities in Australia: ";
for ($Itr = 0; $Itr < scalar(@CitiesInAustralia); $Itr++){
    print "\n " . $Itr . ". $CitiesInAustralia[$Itr]";
}


$City = "Toowoomba";
#2 Add an element to the front of the array
push(@CitiesInAustralia, $City);
print "\nCity added to array: $City";

print "\n Cities in Australia: ";
for ($Itr = 0; $Itr < scalar(@CitiesInAustralia); $Itr++){
    print "\n " . $Itr . ". $CitiesInAustralia[$Itr]";
}


#3 Add an element to the front of the array
$City = "Whyalla";
push(@CitiesInAustralia, $City);
print "\nCity added to array: $City";
print "\n Cities in Australia: ";
for ($Itr = 0; $Itr < scalar(@CitiesInAustralia); $Itr++){
    print "\n " . $Itr . ". $CitiesInAustralia[$Itr]";
}
```

The lines affiliated with comment #1 in Listing07_08 allow you to set up an array consisting of the names of five Australian cities. You then use the scalar form of the array to iterate through its elements. The scalar form of the array allows you to access the array elements by their index values, and in this way you can see clearly where the pop() function adds new elements.

Having set up the array of Australian cities, you then proceed at comment #2 to call the push() function. The push() function requires two arguments. The first argument consists of the array to which you want to append an element (@CitiesInAustralia). The second is the element you want to append. While the element can be a literal value, in this instance it is a scalar ($City) that contains the name of a city (Toowoomba). After pushing the name into

167
❋ ❋ ❋

the array, you then iterate through the array to verify that it has increased in size by one element. As Figure 7.12 shows, this is the case. The index value of the new element reveals the push() function has augmented the size of the array by one and assigned the new element to the position designated by the largest index value.

In the lines trailing comment #3, you repeat the actions of the code associated with comment #2. This time around, you add Whyalla to the array. Again, you iterate through the list using the scalar form of the array and display the index values of the list elements. In the data display Figure 7.12 provides, you can see that the new element possesses the highest index value.

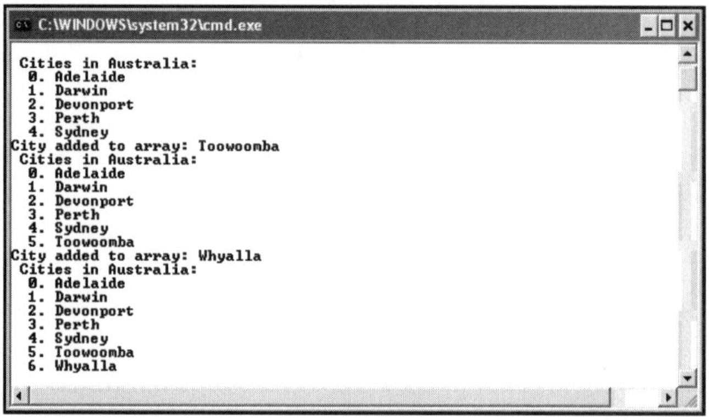

Figure 7.12
As each element is pushed onto an array, it assumes the highest index value.

```
C:\WINDOWS\system32\cmd.exe
Cities in Australia:
  0. Adelaide
  1. Darwin
  2. Devonport
  3. Perth
  4. Sydney
City added to array: Toowoomba
Cities in Australia:
  0. Adelaide
  1. Darwin
  2. Devonport
  3. Perth
  4. Sydney
  5. Toowoomba
City added to array: Whyalla
Cities in Australia:
  0. Adelaide
  1. Darwin
  2. Devonport
  3. Perth
  4. Sydney
  5. Toowoomba
  6. Whyalla
```

Uses of Dynamic Arrays

The array Perl provides is known technically as a *dynamic* array. Dynamic arrays grow automatically. In other words, you can add items to them whenever you want, at any time during the execution of your program. In contrast, in other programming languages, you find *static* arrays, which are arrays that you set up once, with a fixed number of elements, and cannot change afterward. Perl does not provide such arrays. Its arrays are dynamic. You can add to them at any time.

The question then becomes *how* you want to add items to your arrays. How you add items to an array changes the array into a *container*. In simple terms, a container can be viewed as an array that you use in a special way, as when you add items to its beginning only or to its end only. The push(), pop(), shift(), and unshift() functions allow you to use arrays as containers. Among the containers are such entities as stacks, queues, lists, and vectors. Each of these containers is also known as a *data structure*. Data structures (containers) allow you to control the way that you add data to or remove data from an array.

Two frequently used data structures are called *stacks* and *queues*. You can apply the push() and shift() functions to the dynamic array Perl furnishes to transform it into a

168

queue. You can apply the push() and pop() functions to the dynamic array Perl furnishes to transform it into a stack. Using these two containers, you can then write some programs that allow you to fully comprehend the usefulness of data containers. The closing sections of this chapter involve you in such activities.

Controlling Shuttles with Stacks

As Figure 7.13 illustrates, a stack constitutes a container in which you add elements to the end and then, at a given moment, remove elements from the end. Generally, programmers say that they *push* elements into a stack or *pop* elements from a stack. The push() and pop() functions reviewed in previous sections perform actions on arrays that correspond to common stack operations. One other operation common to stack containers is that of obtaining the length of the stack. The scalar() function or the procedure you use to assign the @ array value ($Length = @some array) serves this purpose.

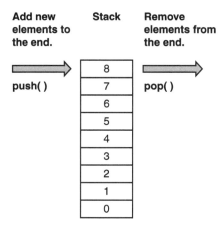

Figure 7.13
Stacks involve pushing, popping, and knowing the length of the stack.

Uses of stacks extend into every area of the computer industry. The reason for this is that a stack serves as a way that you can join the accumulated actions of individuals acting in isolation into a meaningful whole. You can then translate the meaningful whole to other actions relating to time, grouping, or the demand to make a decision.

A key concept in the use of stacks usually involves the notion of a threshold. A threshold is an accumulated quantity. Consider, for example, a situation in a factory in which you want to relate the actions of two production lines. One line supplies plastic dolls. The other supplies crates that contain plastic dolls. A stack allows you to do so. You can create a computer program that records the actions of an electronic detection device that monitors the output of the line that produces the dolls. Each time a doll emerges from the line, you can add an element to a stack. When the elements in the stack grow to a given point, you can "pop" the stack. When you pop the stack, you signal that a crate for the dolls is needed. Yet another stack might be used to track the number of crates that emerge so that the workers in the factory know when pallets for the crates are needed.

Using a Stack as an Accumulator

To create a brief program to illustrate how to use the stack as an *accumulator*, it is possible to use the example of the doll factory as a starting point. The goal involves people at an airport arriving at one of several stops located around the airport. A service representative attends each stop and sends a message to a computer in the central office each time a new passenger arrives needing a shuttle ride. During peak hours, the central office dispatches a shuttle to stops when the computers show that eight people are waiting. Figure 7.14 illustrates the situation.

Figure 7.14
The computer dispatches a shuttle when it finds that eight people are waiting.

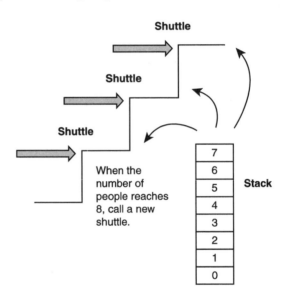

A specification for Listing07_09 might be along the following lines:

 ❄ Record each passenger who comes to one of the shuttle stops and requests transportation.
 ❄ Accumulate the requests (in a stack).
 ❄ When the stack reaches the designated maximum (8), issue an order to dispatch a shuttle.

Granted, in a commercial setting, much more might be involved in developing any such dispatch system, but in this situation, the scenario provides a context in which it is possible to see how the stack works as an accumulator to relate two activities: passengers arriving at a shuttle stop and dispatching shuttles to pick up passengers.

```
#Listing07_09
#Setting up a stack as a shuttle schedule
#1 Define a passenger list
@Passengers =      qw (Ali Mo Stu Ed Ira Abe Todd Ham
                        Si Lil Min Lo Dli Regi Cal Hal
                        Su Len Joy Jay Xi Chi Tan Nu);


#Obtain a general number for the passengers
$Length = scalar(@Passengers);
print "\nNumber of passengers: $Length \n";
$ShuttleCount = 0;
$SHUTTLEMAX = 8; # Capacity of shuttle


#2 Set up "peak hours" with a for loop
for($Itr = 0; $Itr < $Length; $Itr++){

    #Comment out one of the following options
    # a. manual $AnyChar = <STDIN>;
    # b. delay the program's execution by one second
    sleep(1.0);

    #This involves a queue, passengers are taken on a first arrived,
    #first served basis

    #3 Use the push function to push passenger names into the stack
    push(@ShuttlePassengers, shift(@Passengers));

    #Accumulate shuttle passengers
    $WLength = scalar(@ShuttlePassengers);
    print "\n Waiting: $WLength)";
    if($WLength >= $SHUTTLEMAX )
    {
        print "\n Please notify passengers: \n";
        for($Itr = 0; $Itr < $WLength; $Itr++){
        #4 When the stack is full, pop the passengers
            print "\t" . pop(@ShuttlePassengers);
        }
```

```
#4.1 Augment the shuttle count and call for the shuttle
$ShuttleCount++;
print "\n Summon shuttle " . $ShuttleCount . "\n";
print "\n Current group: " . $WLength . "\n";
#4.2 Subtract the number who have left on the shuttle
# from the total count
$CurrentGroup = ($Length - ($ShuttleCount * $WLength));
print "\n Passengers still waiting: $CurrentGroup\n";
#4.3 Clear the stack array so the accumulation can start over
undef(@ShuttlePassengers);
if ($CurrentGroup <= 0){
    print "\n Passengers accommodated.\n";
    print "\n";
    print "\n";
    exit(0);
}
    }
}
```

Figure 7.15 illustrates the output of Listing07_09. In the lines trailing comment #1, you set up a mock set of passengers. Such a list represents passengers who have registered at the shuttle stops. You store the list in the @Passengers array, and to obtain a count of this list of passengers, you employ the scalar() function to extract the length of the array, which you assign to the scalar $Length. At this point, you also declare a scalar, $ShuttleCount, which you use momentarily to store the number of dispatched shuttles. You also set up a scalar ($SHUTTLEMAX) that establishes the maximum number of people a shuttle holds. In this case, the maximum number needs to be adjusted, so the threshold you set is 8.

In the lines trailing comment #2, the number of times the for statement iterates in this instance is controlled by the total number of passengers ($Length). Inside the for loop, you set up two options for controlling how the program works. One option (a) allows you to operate the program manually. You press Return to add a customer to the waiting list. The other option automates the program, so that it executes, adding customers at a rate of one per second.

At comment #3, you employ the push() function in conjunction with the shift() function to extract the name of a passenger from the general passenger list and place it in the stack you have set up to accumulate the names of passengers who seek a shuttle. Each time the for loop iterates, the size of the @ShuttlePassengers array grows by one passenger name. Following this operation, you then use the scalar() function to obtain the size of the waiting list, and this you assign to the scalar $WLength. You use the print() function to display this information.

As you proceed at comment #4, you are in an if statement. The if statement evaluates the number of passenger names in the stack ($WLength) to determine whether it is greater than or equal to the maximum number of passengers a shuttle can hold ($SHUTTLEMAX). If so, then the code inside the if statement executes. The first order of business involves *popping the stack*. When you pop the stack you use the $WLength scalar to control a for statement that calls the pop() function as many times as $SHUTTLEMAX allows. This pops the name of each person currently waiting, which you print for display.

At comment #4.1, you increment the number of shuttles summoned ($ShuttleCount++) and then display the new count. You also note the number of people climbing aboard.

Comment #4.2 marks some bookkeeping details. You determine the number of people who have left by multiplying the current number of people who depart with each shuttle by the number of shuttles that have departed and subtract the product from the total passenger count. This gives you the value of $CurrentGroup, which you display as the number of passengers still waiting.

In the lines trailing comment #4.3, you clear the current stack (@ShuttlePassengers). This is a precautionary measure. People sometimes complain about being stuck in the queue or stack. This way they can complain if they do not receive service or see their names in a reasonable amount of time. The pop() function should have cleared it. You are then ready to either iterate through another group of passengers or exit the program. The exit() function, which you furnish with an argument of 0, exits the program and returns a value of zero as it does so.

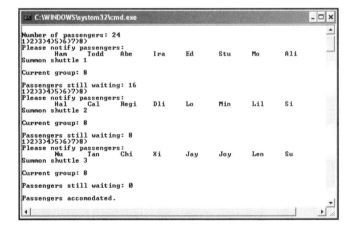

Figure 7.15
Popping the stack allows you to know when to call the shuttles.

Tracking Customers with a Queue

A queue is a container that is analogous to a group of people standing in line at a movie theater. The theater receptionists sell tickets to people on the basis of their positions in the line. The first person in the line receives a ticket first. When you arrive, you line up last in line.

An array can work like a queue if you control it using the push() and shift() functions. As Figure 7.16 illustrates, the push() function inserts a new element into the array in an index position greater than those of existing members. The shift() position extracts the element of the array that occupies the lowest index position.

Figure 7.16
The push() and shift() functions turn an array into a queue.

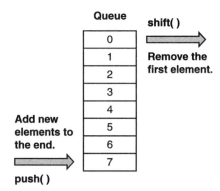

Like stacks, queues receive use throughout the programming world as accumulators. Consider a situation in which a large group of people show up at a bank and want to receive help filling out forms. The banking associates who provide this service must prepare background material so that they can serve those whom they counsel. Further, they wish to have the customers who arrive distributed fairly evenly among the available service representatives. Also, the principle stands that the first person to arrive should be the first person served. Figure 7.17 illustrates the situation.

To provide for the distribution of work among the three service representatives and likewise to ensure that each person received service on a first-come-first-serve basis, Listing07_10 implements a queue. People get in line, and then the program directs them to an available service representative. The program ensures that the service representatives receive customers on an equally distributed basis.

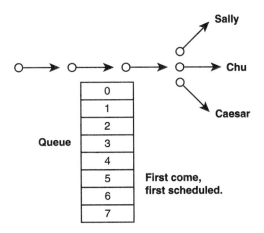

Figure 7.17
A queue accumulates customer names for distribution among service representatives.

```
#Listing07_10
#Distribute customers among representatives using a queue
#1 Define a customer list
@Customers = qw (Ali Mo Stu Ed Ira Abe Todd Ham
                 Si Lil Min Lo Dli Regi Cal Hal
                 Su Len Joy Jay Xi Chi Tan Nu);


#Formatting
$LINE = "\n" . "=" x 60 ;
#Obtain the number of customers
$CustomerCount = scalar(@Customers);


#2 Distribute the customers
for($Itr = 0; $Itr < $CustomerCount; $Itr++){

    #3 use the push function to push customer names into service queues
    push(@SallyCustomers, shift(@Customers));
    push(@ChuCustomers, shift(@Customers));
    push(@CaesarCustomers, shift(@Customers));

    #Obtain a general number for the passengers
    $ScheduledCustomers = scalar(@Customers);
```

```
#4print the customers
print "$LINE \n \n Sally: \n \n " ;
for($Itr = 0; $Itr < scalar(@SallyCustomers); $Itr++){
    print " \n " . $Itr + 1 . " " . $SallyCustomers[$Itr] . " ";
}
print "$LINE \n \n Chu: \n \n " ;
for($Itr = 0; $Itr < scalar(@ChuCustomers); $Itr++){
    print " \n " . $Itr + 1 . " " . $ChuCustomers[$Itr] . " ";
}
print "$LINE \n \n Caesar: \n \n " ;
for($Itr = 0; $Itr < scalar(@CaesarCustomers); $Itr++){
    print " \n " . $Itr + 1 . " " . $CaesarCustomers[$Itr] . " ";
}
print "$LINE";
    print "\n \n \n";


#5 Check for whether to refresh the display
    if($ScheduledCustomers >= 3){
    sleep(1.0);
    print "\n \n";
    system("cls");

    # print "$LINE";
     print "\n \n \n Thank you for your patience.";
    }
#6 Exit when done
if($ScheduledCustomers == 0){
    print "\n \n";
    exit(0);
}
}
```

In the lines that comment #1 in Listing07_10 designates, you create an array of customers called @Customers. (This is the same customer group from Listing07_09.) You use the qw() function in this case for convenience. In addition to setting up the customer array, you also create a formatting line and use the scalar() function to obtain the number of elements in the @Customers array and assign this to a scalar, $CustomerCount.

Next you turn to creating a for statement to attend to the primary activities of the program. In the lines accompanying comment #2, to control the for loop, you employ the value stored in $CustomerCount. This approach to controlling the loop is a crude measure. You could, in fact, do without it.

Through the operations that the code affiliated with comment #3 performs, you use the push() function to push customers into three arrays you create to accommodate the three customer representatives. The shift() function extracts the names of customers from the front of the @Customer array. In this way, the customers who arrived first are given attention first. The push() function inserts their names into the arrays that represent the customer service representatives.

Each customer service array serves as a queue. Each name is pushed into one of the customer service arrays from the back or end of the queue. It then migrates up the queue as other names are push()ed into the queue.

In this instance, rather than using the shift() function to remove the name of the customer from the queue, you go only so far as to display the name of the customer in the order in which it entered the queue. To accomplish this, as you can see at comment #4, you employ the scalar form of each of the queues you have set up for the customer service representatives. You iterate through the scalar using a for loop controlled by the number of customers stored in the queues you have set up for the customer representatives. By using the scalar() function you are able to continuously monitor the number of customer names each queue stores.

The actions associated with comment #5 allow you to use the sleep() function to pause the display every second before refreshing it. You also make a call to the system() function, which allows you to issue commands to the operating system. In this instance, you issue the cls command, which clears the screen so the display of queued customers can be refreshed.

As a final measure, with the code introduced by comment #6, you check the number of customers (@SheduledCustomers) to see whether it has been reduced to zero. If so, you stop the action of the program. Figure 7.18 illustrates the output of Listing07_10.

Figure 7.18
The program assigns customers to the service representatives.

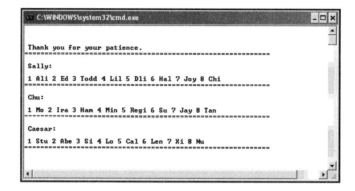

Conclusion

In this chapter you have worked through several functions that allow you to view how the array can be used as a data container. Beginning with the reverse() and sort() functions, you explored the extent to which the elements in an array can be manipulated as a complete set.

Given a start with reversing and sorting arrays, you then moved on to examine how the split() function allows you to easily break the contents of strings into array elements. Along the same lines, you also dealt with the join() function, which you viewed in an earlier chapter in relation to string manipulations. In this chapter, the join() function allowed you to merge the contents of several arrays.

The step beyond merging arrays involved a set of four functions that allow you to make the array into a data container. These four functions consist of the shift(), unshift(), push(), and pop() functions. By using these functions with arrays in different ways, you can transform arrays into such data containers as stacks and queues. The uses of such data containers prove endless. In this chapter, you developed a simple stack program that allowed you to load passengers into shuttles. You developed a simple queue program that allowed you to distribute the customers in a bank among three service representatives.

8 } Hashes

This chapter introduces you to hashes. Hashes consist of containers that hold key-value pairs. When you work with hashes, you associate a unique key with a value. The keys in any given hash must be unique, but the values need not be. When you add a duplicate key to a hash, the hash automatically replaces the old key with the new. Many basic functions allow you to work with hashes. Some of these are familiar if you have worked with Perl arrays. Others are new. Among those familiar from working with arrays are the shift() and pop() functions. Among those new with hashes are the keys(), values(), and each() functions. The programs and activities presented in this chapter include the following:

* Approaches to defining hashes
* Implicit and scalar forms of hashes
* Keys and values in hashes and how to access them as arrays
* How to access both keys and values using the each() function
* Building tables to display the contents of hashes
* Fetching values from hashes in specific orders

Basics of Hashes

A hash resembles an array, but rather than storing items in association with a set of indexes, it stores items in *key-value pairs*. Hashes are sometimes called *associative containers*. As Figure 8.1 reveals, a container provides a way that you can collect data into a single group. Hashes and arrays are containers that work according to different logics of organization. The array that Perl provides is a dynamic array that stores its items one after another, on a logic based on the value of its indexes, from zero to whatever constitutes the largest index in the array. It is referred to as a *sequential container*.

Figure 8.1
A hash is an associative container.

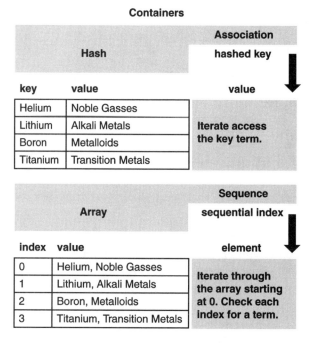

A hash constitutes an associative container because it does not necessarily store the elements it contains using a logic based on the sequence of the indexes. Instead, you access the elements in a hash according to an order that the content of the elements establishes. The order the content establishes creates a situation in which association among the elements, rather than sequence, characterizes the logic that characterizes the container.

The elements in a hash can be said to be organized according to hashed keys. When you place a key in a hash, as Figure 8.1 indicates, you see a recognizable word. However, when you insert this word into the hash, the hash transforms (or hashes) it to make it so that it can serve, in essence, as a kind of encrypted index. This index might be placed in the container in any number of positions. An algorithm embedded in the programming behind the container determines this position. Given an effective design of the algorithm, when you search a hash for a given key, the hash retrieves the item more quickly than it could using a sequential search (which is the approach often employed with arrays).

Each key serves as a hashed index to a value. Perl hashes provide unique keys. When a hash provides unique keys, if it finds that you are inserting a key that the hash already contains, it replaces the old key with the new one. In Figure 8.2, when you insert the second and third elements with the key of Alkali, the third key displaces the first two, and when you examine the contents of the hash afterward, you find only the third entry, which in this case is associated with `Potassium`. The same form of displacement characterized the two `Metalloid` keys. In the end, you find only the key associated with `Silicon`.

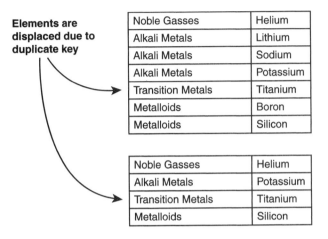

Elements are displaced due to duplicate key

Noble Gasses	Helium
Alkali Metals	Lithium
Alkali Metals	Sodium
Alkali Metals	Potassium
Transition Metals	Titanium
Metalloids	Boron
Metalloids	Silicon

Noble Gasses	Helium
Alkali Metals	Potassium
Transition Metals	Titanium
Metalloids	Silicon

Figure 8.2
Perl hashes allow no duplicate keys.

What pertains to keys, however, does not pertain to values. As Figure 8.3 illustrates, as long as you insert unique keys, a hash stores multiple identical values.

Helium	Noble Gasses
Lithium	Alkali Metals
Sodium	Alkali Metals
Potassium	Alkali Metals
Titanium	Transition Metals
Boron	Metalloids
Silicon	Metalloids

A hash allows multiple indentical values.

Figure 8.3
You can have many duplicate values.

The order in which the hash replaces duplicated keys is predictable. The most recently entered duplicate key displaces the older key. As for the organization of values in a hash, the situation depends on the algorithm behind the hash. When you display the items in a hash, it is difficult to predict the order of display. Consider the elements shown in Figure 8.3. This could be the order in which you see elements as you print them from a hash. The order of elements is not alphabetical. Nor is it the order in which you add values to the hash.

Identifying and Initializing Hashes

Hashes have two contexts of use. One context is the implicit context. The other is the scalar context. When a hash appears in an implicit hash context, you identify it with a percent sign (%).

When you use a hash in a scalar context, you identify it with a dollar sign ($). Listing08_01 shows you hashes initialized in both implicit and scalar contexts. The program produces no output.

```
#Listing08_01


#1 Implicit initialization using the
# correspondence operator (0=>)
#Parentheses
%Elements = (Hydrogen => H,
             Helium => He,
             Manganese => Mn);


#Implicit initialization using a list
%Elements = ("Oxygen" , "O",
              "Nitrogen" , "N",
              "Potassium" , "K");


#2 Scalar initialization using
#Curly braces
    # correspondence operator (0=>)
$Elements{Carbon}=C;
$Elements{Calcium}=C;
$Elements{Aluminum}=Al;
```

At comment #1 you first initialize a hash using the correspondence operator. To effect such an initialization, you prefix the percent sign to the hash identifier (%Elements). This designates an implicit hash. You then use a list operation (parentheses enclosing the keys and values) to designate the key-value pairs you want to assign to the hash. If you do not use the parentheses, the initialization will still work, but only for the first element (Hydrogen). The second form of implicit initialization using a list involves using commas rather than the correspondence operator. This approach works just as well as the first.

The lines associated with comment #2 allow you to continue the work of initializing the %Elements hash using the scalar, or lookup, form of initialization. In this case, you prefix a dollar sign to the hash identifier ($Elements) and employ curly braces ({}) to enclose the key you want to designate. You then follow with an assignment operator and the value you want to associate with the key.

Order of Initialization

When you initialize hashes using implicit and lookup forms of the hashes, you follow implicit form with the lookup form. Consider the following order of initialization:

```
#1 Lookup following implicit form works
%Elements = (Hydrogen =>    H);    #implicit
$Elements{Aluminum} = Al;          #lookup
```

When the lookup follows the implicit form, you see the following output if you print the contents of @Elements with formatting:

```
Aluminum Al
Hydrogen H
```

The Perl interpreter allows you to initialize a hash implicitly and then to add more elements to the hash with the scalar or lookup statement. You add Aluminum after Hydrogen, and when you print the contents, you see both elements.

This situation changes when you reverse the order. If you begin with a lookup form of initialization and then follow with an implicit form of initialization, the Perl interpreter does not add elements to your hash. Instead, it allows the implicit initialization to cancel the contents previously assigned. Consider initializations in the following lines:

```
#2 Implicit following lookup does not work
$Elements{"Calcium"}=       "Ca";         #lookup
$Elements{Aluminum}=        "Al";         #lookup
%Elements = ("Oxygen" , "O");             #implicit - cancels previous
```

When you follow the two scalar expression with the implicit initialization, if you print the contents of @Elements with formatting, you see only one element:

```
Oxygen O
```

With the implicit initialization, you lose the contents of the hash as previously defined.

> ❄ It might seem that the behavior of Perl is arbitrary when you consider the way that you go back and forth between the implicit (%) and (scalar) explicit ($) forms. One way to counter this notion involves remembering that when you use explicit ($) form, you are dealing with an item in the hash as a single scalar. When you use the implicit form (%), you are dealing with the item as a part of the whole hash structure. It is as though you have thrown a switch.

Variations on Initialization

When you employ either the implicit form of initialization or the scalar (lookup) form of initialization for hashes, you can represent the data you are dealing with in a number of ways. Listing08_02 provides examples of several somewhat random approaches to data representation. The program produces no output.

```
#Listing08_02
#1 Implicit initialization -- variations


# Scalar
$TableElement = "Hydrogen";


# A scalar and interpolated and literal strings
%Elements = ($TableElement =>  "H",
              "Helium" =>        'He',
              'Manganese' =>     "Mn");


#2 Initialization using the scalar
$Elements{"Carbon"} = "C";
$Elements{"Calcium"} = "Ca";
$Elements{Aluminum} = "Al";


#3 Keys and values consisting of more than one word
#requires quotes
$CompoundName = "Carbon Monoxide";
%Compounds = ($CompoundName          =>      "CO",
               q(Plumbous Oxide)     =>      'PbO',
               qq(Copper Hydroxide) =>      "CuOH");
$Compounds{"Calcium Oxide"}          =       "CaO";
```

At comment #1 in Listing08_02 you first assign an interpolated string to a scalar ($TableElement). Then, in the implicit form of initialization that follows, you insert the scalar in the position in the list that designates the key for the first element. For the value for the first element, you follow the correspondence operator (=>) with an interpolated string containing a single character, H, which designates the abbreviation for Hydrogen in the Table of Elements.

After inserting an element for Hydrogen, when you initialize the elements immediately following it, you first use an interpolated string ("Helium") for a key and a character string

('He') for a value. Then you use a character string ('Manganese') for a key and an interpolated string for the value ("Mn").

No advantage rests with scalars, character strings, interpolated strings, or the approach shown in Listing08_01, which involves no quotes at all. When you encounter situations in which the keys or elements you are adding to a hash consists of several words, then the situation changes. At comment #2, for example, you assignment a character string consisting of two words to a key ("Carbon Monoxide"). When you assign two or more words to a scalar, you can then insert the scalar into the initialization list, and no problems arise.

When you deal with literal values, you need quotes. For this reason, the compound names in the initialization of the %Compounds hash are enclosed in quotations or processed through the qq() and q() functions, which transform them into strings that can then serve as either keys or values.

Accessing Hash Elements

To access hash keys, you can take a multitude of approaches. To start with, it is useful to know a few of the most basic approaches that often prove helpful in debugging procedures. Listing08_03 provides a few examples of these simple approaches to accessing the data in a hash.

```
#Listing08_03

#Simple approaches to accessing elements

$Elements{"Carbon"}=          "C";
$Elements{"Calcium"}=         "Ca";
$Elements{"Aluminum"}=        "Al";

#1 Print the value using the key
print "\n 1. Just the values: ";
print "\n " . $Elements{"Carbon"};
print "\n " . $Elements{"Carbon"};

#2 Print as a crude list
print " \n 2. Crude list: ";
print(%Elements);
print " \n";
```

```
#3 Use printf
print "\n 3. Use printf and \%s to extract keys and values: \n";
printf(" %s - %s , %s - %s, %s - %s ", %Elements);


#4 Assign the implicit form of the hash to an array
print " \n 4. Assign the hash to an array and print: \n";
#Print the array -- See subsequent sections
@ElementArray = %Elements;
print "\n Listed: @ElementArray";
print "\n ... or on separate lines: \n";
foreach $LocVal (@ElementArray){
        print "\n " . $LocVal;
}


print "\n 5. Far-fetched formatting:\n ";
print "\n 5. Far-fetched formatting:\n ";
foreach $LocVal (@ElementArray){ #read to end of array
    if($Flag == 0){
        printf ("\n Element %-15s", $LocVal); #left align 15 char
        $Flag = 1; #reset flag
        next; #skip the rest of the foreach loop
      }
    if($Flag == 1){
        printf ("Symbol %-25s", $LocVal);
        $Flag = 0; #reset flag
    }
}
```

Figure 8.4 illustrates the output of Listing08_03. In the lines that accompany comment #1, you use the lookup form of the hash to access the value of a given key. You place the key of the hash element between the curly braces. In this way, you retrieve the value the hash element contains.

At comment #2, you use a crude approach to printing the contents of an array as a list. This approach provides you with a way to confirm the contents of a hash, but it proves unwieldy if you are dealing with a large collection of elements.

The `print()` function comment #3 identifies allows you a bit more control over the element from the hash. In this instance, as Figure 8.4 shows, you see the first few elements of the array as keys and values. The `printf()` function accesses keys and values sequentially. You employ a `%s` specifier for each item you want to see. You also employ the implicit form (`%`) of the hash.

Comment #4 introduces the most convenient approach to accessing the keys and values stored in a hash. You first assign the implicit form of the hash to an array (`@ElementArray`). As the `printf()` example discussed previously reveals, the hash stores the key-value pairs in a continuous list, so when you use the assignment operator, you transfer an alternating list of keys and values to the array.

You can then print the list. One approach involves printing the contents of the interpolated array. As Figure 8.4 illustrates, the result appears as a somewhat unsightly series of terms, but you still see spaces between the items. Alternatively, you can use a `foreach` statement to iterate through the list and print each of its elements on separate lines. The `foreach` statement continues to read the array until it reaches an undefined element that marks the end of the array.

Comment #5 introduces an innovation that you are not likely to use, but it shows you that you can fold in control statements, flags, and the `printf()` function for formatting. This example allows you to fetch the elements from an array (`@ElementArray`). Using the `foreach` statement, you iterate through the array as before, but this time, you employ selection statements inside the `foreach` loop to retrieve keys and values alternatively and display them in formatted columns.

The example following comment #5, as well as the other examples shown in Listing08_03, are intended purely as introductory demonstrations. The Perl functions and control statements provide much more elegant approaches to accessing keys and values in a hash. Subsequent sections of this chapter, along with examples in Chapters 9 and 10, provide further discussion. Here are a few common approaches:

✳ Use the `keys()` function to transfer the keys to an array.

✳ Use the `values()` function to transfer the values to an array.

✳ Employ the `each()` function to access both the keys and the values.

Figure 8.4
Simple ways of accessing data in hashes make it easy to test your code.

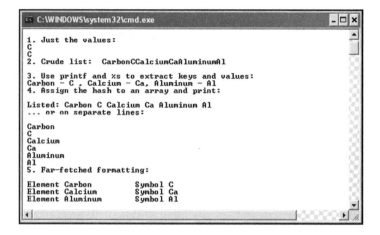

Using the keys() Function

The keys() function allows you to access all the keys in a hash. Its sole argument consists of the implicit form of the hash. Its two principal uses involve converting the keys of a hash into an array. You can then iterate through the array and fetch the values of the array using the lookup form of the hash. You can also make use of the keys() function for hash slicing (see the section titled "Slicing Hashes," in Chapter 9). Listing08_04 illustrates the basic use of the keys() function to retrieve an array of hash keys.

```
#Listing08_04


# 1 Formatting elements for the table
$NL = "\n ";
$DC = "=";              #character for top and bottom lines of table
$TW = 55;               #Table width
$DL = sprintf( "%55s", $NL . $DC x $TW); #top and bottom lines
$COLAHEAD = "Element";
$COLBHEAD = "Atomic Weight";
#2 Set up the data using an implicit hash
%ElementsAtomicWeights = (Oxygen, 15.9994, Fluorine, 18.9984032,
                          Neon, 20.1797, Sodium, 22.989770,
                          Magnesium, 24.3050, Aluminum, 26.981538,
                          Silicon, 28.0855, Phosphorus, 30.973761,
```

```
                    Sulfur, 32.065, Chlorine, 35.453,
                    Potassium, 39.0983, Calcium, 40.078,
                    Vanadium, 50.9415 , Manganese, 54.938049);
#3 Print the table
   printf("$DL");
   printf("\n %-15s %-15s", $COLAHEAD , $COLBHEAD);
   printf("$DL");


#4 Assign the elements to an array
@ElementNames = keys(%ElementsAtomicWeights);


#5 Use an inner foreach loop and a selection statement
#to retrieve the names of elements
   foreach $EName (@ElementNames){
        printf("\n %-15s %-15s",
        $EName,
        $ElementsAtomicWeights{$EName});
}
```

At comment #1 in Listing08_04 you set up some formatting scalars for use later in the program. At comment #2, you use the implicit form of initialization of a hash to create a hash containing the names of elements as keys and the associated atomic weights of the elements as values. The name of the hash is %ElementsAtomicWeights.

Following the creation of the hash, you then print it. Printing the heading of the table is taken care of in the few lines accompanying comment #3. At comment #4 you call the keys() function and use the name of the hash to create an array (@ElementNames) that contains all the keys in the hash.

The lines trailing comment #2 then make use of the array of keys. You use a foreach statement to iterate through the array. The foreach statement sequentially extracts each key from the array and stores it temporarily in a scalar ($EName). The scalar $EName then allows you to employ the lookup form of the hash to access the value associated with each key ($ElementsAtomicWeights{$EName}). When you employ the print() function, you can readily display the key-value pairs, as Figure 8.5 illustrates. You can also make use of the sprintf() function to create separate formatted strings containing both the key and values of each element (see "Converting a Hash into a String," in Chapter 9).

Figure 8.5
The keys() function allows you to retrieve key-value pairs with the lookup operation.

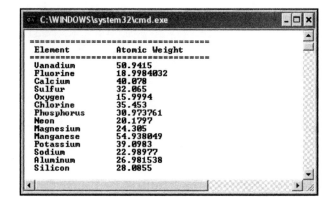

Using the values() Function

The values() function returns all the values in a hash, which you can conveniently assign to an array. Like the keys() function, the sole argument of the values() function consists of the implicit form of the hash. If you use the values() function to retrieve key-value pairs, you must perform more work than you do if you employ the keys() function. As Listing08_05 illustrates, however, you can still make use of the values() function in this role. Used alone, the values you obtain are like answers for which you do not know the questions. Recall *The Hitchhiker's Guide to the Galaxy* and the infamous answer of "42" to the "ultimate question." The characters asked the most powerful computer in the universe what the answer to the ultimate question might be. After a long while, the computer answered, "42," leaving the characters hanging with respect to the question.

```
#Listing08_05
# 1 Formatting elements for the table
$NL = "\n ";
$DC = "=";                    #character for top and bottom lines of table
$TW = 55;                     #Table width
$DL = sprintf( "%55s", $NL . $DC x $TW); #top and bottom lines
$COLAHEAD = "Element";
$COLBHEAD = "Atomic Weight";

#2 Set up the data using an implicit hash
%ElementsAtomicWeights = (Oxygen, 15.9994, Fluorine, 18.9984032,
                          Neon, 20.1797, Sodium, 22.989770,
                          Magnesium, 24.3050, Aluminum, 26.981538,
                          Silicon, 28.0855, Phosphorus, 30.973761,
```

```
                    Sulfur, 32.065, Chlorine, 35.453,
                    Potassium, 39.0983, Calcium, 40.078,
                    Vanadium, 50.9415 , Manganese, 54.938049);
#3 Print the table
   printf("$DL");
   printf("\n %-15s %-15s", $COLAHEAD , $COLBHEAD);
   printf("$DL");


#4 Assign the elements to an array
@ElementsAW = values(%ElementsAtomicWeights);
@ElementNames = keys(%ElementsAtomicWeights);


#5 Use an inner foreach loop and a selection statement
#to retrieve the names of elements
foreach $EName (@ElementNames){
    foreach $AtomicWeight (@ElementsAW){
        #Look up the atomic weight and see if there is a match
        #If so, you know you have the name corresponding
        #to the atomic number - note the use of ==
        if($AtomicWeight == $ElementsAtomicWeights{$EName}){
           printf("\n %-15s %-15s",
           $EName,
           $AtomicWeight);
        }#end if
    }#end inner
 }#end outer
```

In Listing08_05, you face the same problem the characters in *Hitchhiker's Guide to the Galaxy* face when they learn the ultimate answer. You still need to find the question. In this case, one approach to finding the answer involves employing a selection statement.

To start things off, at comment #1 you create a few scalars containing formatting strings for a table. Then, at comment #2, you use the implicit form of assignment to define an array that consists of the elements of the Table of Elements and their weights. With the lines accompanying comment #3, you print the column heads of a table to display the elements and their weights. (See Figure 8.6.)

The assignment operations shown at comment #4 involve both the keys() and values() functions. You access and assign the keys and values in the hash to two arrays (@ElementsAW and @ElementNames).

At comment #5 you employ two foreach control statements. The outer foreach statement allows you to iterate through the @ ElementNames array on the basis of the keys (names of elements) it contains. When you iterate through this array, you assign each element name temporarily to a scalar, $EName.

The inner foreach statement allows you to iterate through all the values (atomic weights) in the @ElementsAW array. When you iterate through the @ElementsAW array, you assign each atomic weight temporarily to a second scalar, $AtomicWeight.

Given that you now have the name of the element (assigned to $EName) you can set up an if selection statement that involves supplying the name to the lookup hash operation. For each atomic weight you retrieve from the @ElementsAW array in the inner loop, you use the if statement to evaluate whether it equals the atomic weight the lookup returns. If the two are equal, then you have identified a key-value pair ($EName and $AtomicWeight). As Figure 8.6 illustrates, these you print in formatted columns.

Figure 8.6
If you employ a selection statement, you can use the values() function to retrieve key-value pairs.

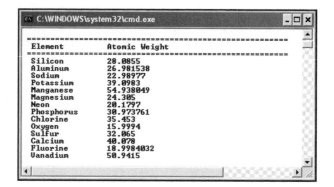

Using the pop() Function

The pop() function applies to arrays, but when you pop items from an array, you diminish the size of the data container you are dealing with. If you are dealing with large collections of data, for this reason the pop() function offers a way to increase the performance of your program.

You can employ the pop() function in conjunction with an array of keys you create using the keys() hash function. As Listing08_06 shows, you can employ the sort() and reverse() functions so that you can alphabetize key-value pairs as you access them. The reverse()

function reverses the order of keys in an array so that as you pop them, you see them in ascending order.

To accent the example, Listing08_06 makes use of the melting temperatures of chemical elements. As many chemists can relate, in 1742 Anders Celsius figured out how to convert degrees Celsius into degrees Fahrenheit. The formula that he presented reads as follows:

```
Fahrenheit = 9/5(Celsius) + 32
```

You can fold this formula into a program to add a column to an output table that shows the Fahrenheit values for the melting points of selective elements (see Figure 8.7). In the process, you can check your program for sanity by using the Celsius temperature at which water boils (100). On the Fahrenheit scale, water boils at 212 degrees.

```
#Listing08_06
# 1 Formatting elements for the table
$NL = "\n ";
$DC = "=";                  #character for top and bottom lines of table
$TW = 55;                   #Table width
$DL = sprintf( "%55s", $NL . $DC x $TW); #top and bottom lines
$COLAHEAD = "Element";
$COLBHEAD = "Celsius";
$COLCHEAD = "Fahrenheit";


#2 Set up the data using an implicit hash
%ElementsCelMeltingPts = ( (Water), 100,
                        Aluminum, 659, Carbon , 3600,
                        Chromium, 1615, Copper, 1083,
                        Gold, 1946, Hydrogen, -259,
                        Iron, 1530, Lead, 327,
                        Magnesium ,670, Manganese, 1260,
                        Nickel, 1452, Phosphorous, 44,
                        Silicon, 1420, Silver, 961,
                        Tin, 232, Titanium, 1795,
                        Tungsten, 3000, Zinc, 419);

#3 Print the table
   printf("$DL");
   printf("\n %-25s %-15s %-15s", $COLAHEAD , $COLBHEAD, $COLCHEAD);
   printf("$DL");
```

```
#4 Assign the elements to an array
@Elements = keys(%ElementsCelMeltingPts);
#Arrange the elements alphabetically
@Elements = sort(@Elements);          #Sort the elements
@Elements = reverse(@Elements);       #Reverse for the pop() function


#5 Use a while control statement to iterate through
#the array, calling the pop() function to remove elements
#from the end of the array
while($ElementName = pop(@Elements)){
   $CelsiusValue = $ElementsCelMeltingPts{$ElementName};
   printf("\n %-17s %15.2f %15.2f", $ElementName ,
                #Display Celsius
                $CelsiusValue,
                #Display Fahrenheit
                (9/5) * $CelsiusValue + 32
                );
}#end while
```

At comment #1 in Listing08_06 you set up scalars containing table formatting information. In the lines comment #2 identifies, you use the implicit form of hash initialization to create a hash containing key-value pairs representing a few elements and their melting points. At comment #3, you display the column heading of the table (see Figure 8.7).

The lines associated with comment #4 perform three actions relating to arrays. First, you assign the elements of the hash (%ElementsCelMeltingPts) to an array (@Elements) and then proceed to first sort and reverse the elements using the sort() and reverse() functions. These functions apply to arrays, so in this case, you deal only with the keys (element names) you have acquired from the hash. Since the sort() function arranges the names alphabetically, you use the reverse() function to transform the array so that the items in the array are organized in descending order: Aluminum is at the end rather than the beginning of the array.

In the lines comment #5 identifies, you use a while loop to iterate through the @Elements array. You accomplish this using the array pop() function, which pops the name of the element at the end of the array. You temporarily assign the popped element name to a scalar, $ElementName.

Inside the while block, you submit the name of the element as the argument of the lookup hash operation ($ElementsCelMeltingPts {$ElementName}), which retrieves the Celsius

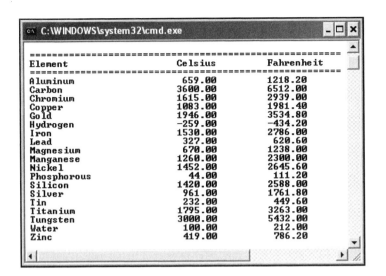

Figure 8.7
The pop() function applies to arrays, but you can use it to access elements in a hash.

value of the melting point of the named element. You assign the Celsius value to a scalar $CelsiusValue.

Given this work, you are then in a position to employ the printf() function to display three values in table columns. In the first column, you display the name of the element ($ElementName). In the second column, you display the melting point in degrees Celsius. To create the value for the final column, you insert the formula for converting degrees Celsius to degrees Fahrenheit as the last argument of the printf() function. As Figure 8.7 illustrates, you see the elements arranged alphabetically, with their melting points displayed in degrees Celsius and Fahrenheit.

Reversing Keys and Values

The reverse() function works with both arrays and hashes. With a hash, it reverses keys and values. The reverse() function takes only one argument, the name of the hash in its implicit form (%). When you use it with hashes, you assign the return value of the hash back to the hash. Listing08_07 reverses a hash to create a table that displays chemical elements according to the descending order of their melting points.

```
#Listing08_07
# 1 Formatting elements for the table
$NL = "\n ";
$DC = "=";                #character for top and bottom lines of table
$TW = 55;                 #Table width
$DL = sprintf( "%55s", $NL . $DC x $TW); #top and bottom lines
```

```
$COLAHEAD = "Element";
$COLBHEAD = "Celsius";
$COLCHEAD = "Fahrenheit";

#2 Set up the data using an implicit hash
%ElementsCelMeltingPts = ( Water, 100,
                           Aluminum, 659, Carbon , 3600,
                           Chromium, 1615, Copper, 1083,
                           Gold, 1946, Hydrogen, -259,
                           Iron, 1530, Lead, 327,
                           Magnesium, 670, Manganese, 1260,
                           Nickel, 1452, Phosphorous, 44,
                           Silicon, 1420, Silver, 961,
                           Tin, 232, Titanium, 1795,
                           Tungsten, 3000, Zinc, 419);

#3 Print the table
    printf("$DL");
    printf("\n %-25s %-15s %-15s", $COLAHEAD , $COLBHEAD, $COLCHEAD);
    printf("$DL");

#4 HASH: Reverse the Keys and Values in the hash
%ElementsCelMeltingPts = reverse(%ElementsCelMeltingPts);


#Set up a key array using the melting points and sort them
@MeltingPoints = keys(%ElementsCelMeltingPts);
@MeltingPoints = sort{$a <=> $b}(@MeltingPoints); #Sort the elements
# @MeltingPoints = reverse (@MeltingPoints); #ARRAY Reversal for ascending

#5 Use a while loop and the hash lookup operation
#to retrieve the names of elements
while ($CelsiusMP =pop(@MeltingPoints)){
        #Look up name of the element
        $EName = $ElementsCelMeltingPts{$CelsiusMP};
        printf("\n %-17s %15.2f %15.2f", $EName ,
```

```
        #Display Celsius
        $CelsiusMP,
        #Display Fahrenheit
        (9/5) * $CelsiusMP + 32);
}#end while
```

At comment #1 in Listing08_07, you create scalar identifiers to provide formatting for the table. The lines comment #2 identify create a hash containing the names of elements and their melting points. (Water is included as a test value.) The lines accompanying comment #3 print the column headings for the table.

At comment #4 you use the `reverse()` function to reverse the key-value pairs in the `%ElementsCelMeltingPts` hash. To accomplish this, as mentioned previously, you assign the return value of the `reverse()` function back to the name of the hash.

Given the reversal of the keys and values, the keys of the hash now consist of the temperatures at which the elements melt. You use the `keys()` function to assign these values to an array, `@MeltingPoints`.

The lines at comment #4 apply the `sort()` function to the array of melting temperature. Notice the form of the `sort()` function:

```
    sort {$a < = > $b}( @MeltingPoints)
```

This form of the `sort()` function applies to numbers, and you must use it in this context or the temperatures are not sorted correctly. The `sort{$a< = > $b)` function sorts the temperatures so that they are in ascending order. The `pop()` function, used in the `while` loop, reverses this order. If you want to see ascending order, uncomment the following line:

```
# @MeltingPoints = reverse(@MeltingPoints); #ARRAY Reversal for ascending
```

In this instance, the `reverse()` function is used on an array, not a hash.

The `while` loop that comment #5 identifies iterates through the `@MeltingPoints` array and pops elements from it. This is why you see the default sorted array as descending rather than ascending. You use the lookup hash operation and the popped melting temperature as its argument to retrieve the name of the element. With the `printf()` function, you display the name of the element, the Celsius melting point, and then, embedding the conversion formula as the third argument of the `printf()` function, the Fahrenheit melting point. Figure 8.8 illustrates the output of Listing08_07.

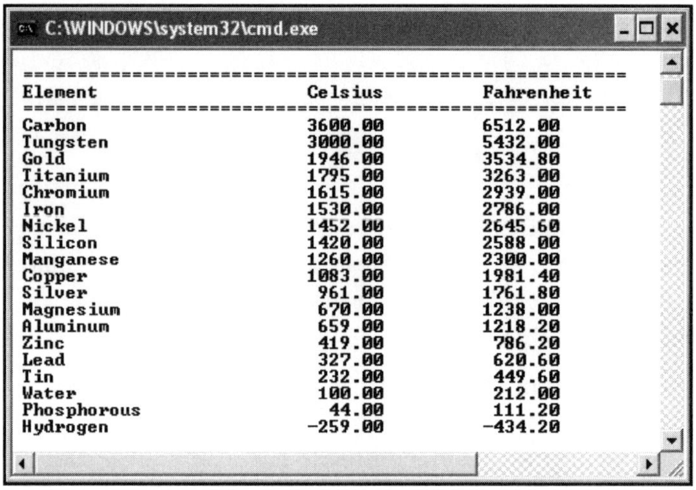

Figure 8.8
The reverse() function when applied to hashes reverse the key-value designations of the items in the hash.

```
C:\WINDOWS\system32\cmd.exe

============================================
Element              Celsius      Fahrenheit
============================================
Carbon               3600.00       6512.00
Tungsten             3000.00       5432.00
Gold                 1946.00       3534.80
Titanium             1795.00       3263.00
Chromium             1615.00       2939.00
Iron                 1530.00       2786.00
Nickel               1452.00       2645.60
Silicon              1420.00       2588.00
Manganese            1260.00       2300.00
Copper               1083.00       1981.40
Silver                961.00       1761.80
Magnesium             670.00       1238.00
Aluminum              659.00       1218.20
Zinc                  419.00        786.20
Lead                  327.00        620.60
Tin                   232.00        449.60
Water                 100.00        212.00
Phosphorous            44.00        111.20
Hydrogen             -259.00       -434.20
```

Using the shift() Function

The shift() function applies to arrays. You can use it in the same way you use the pop() function to access array keys that you use in common with the lookup function to retrieve values for display. The only difference between the pop() and shift() functions is that the pop() function extracts items from the end of an array while the shift() function extracts elements from the beginning of an array. As mentioned previously in relation to the pop() function, given that the shift() function actually removes items from an array, you can enhance the performance of a program by using it. Listing08_08 illustrates the use of the shift() function.

```
#Listing08_08
# 1 Formatting elements for the table
$NL = "\n ";
$DC = "=";                 #character for top and bottom lines of table
$TW = 45;                  #Table width
$DL = sprintf( "%45s", $NL . $DC x $TW); #top and bottom lines
$TableTitleText = ' Melting Points of Elements';
$COLAHEAD = "Element";
$COLBHEAD = "Celsius";


#2 Set up the data using an implicit hash
%ElementsMeltingPts = (Aluminum, 659, Carbon, 3600,
                       Chromium, 1615, Copper, 1083,
                       Gold, 1946, Hydrogen, -259,
```

```
                        Iron, 1530, Lead, 327,
                        Magnesium, 670, Manganese, 1260,
                        Nickel, 1452, Phosphorous,44,
                        Silicon, 1420, Silver, 961,
                        Tin, 232, Titanium, 1795,
                        Tungsten, 3000, Zinc, 419);


#3 Print the table
    printf("$DL");
    printf("\n %-25s %-15s", $COLAHEAD , $COLBHEAD);
    printf("$DL");
#4 Assign the elements to an array
@Elements = keys(%ElementsMeltingPts);
#Arrange the elements alphabetically
@Elements = sort(@Elements);


#Use a while control statement to iterate through
#the array, calling the shift() function to remove elements
#from the top
while($ElementName = shift(@Elements))
{
    printf("\n %-25s %-15s", $ElementName ,
                            $ElementsMeltingPts{$ElementName});

}
```

At comment #1 in Listing08_08, you declare some scalar identifiers and define them for use as table formatting elements. At comment #2 you define a hash using the implicit form of definition. The lines associated with comment #3 make use of the formatting elements previously defined and print the column headers of the table.

The keys() function as used after comment #4 assigns the names of the elements to an array, @Elements. Immediately after defining the @Elements array, you make it the argument of the sort() function, which organizes the element names it stores in ascending alphabetical order.

At comment #5, you set up a while loop and employ the shift() function to retrieve the elements from the @Elements array. With each iteration of the while loop, the shift() function extracts one element name from the front of the array. You assign this value temporarily to a scalar, $ElementName. Given the default order of element names the sort() function creates, the first element out is Aluminum.

To print the element name and the corresponding melting point, you submit two values to the print() function. The first is $ElementName; the second is the returned temperature you retrieve when you use the hash lookup operation using, again, $ElementName. Figure 8.9 illustrates the output of Listing08_08.

Figure 8.9
The shift() function can be used with the lookup operation to access elements in a hash.

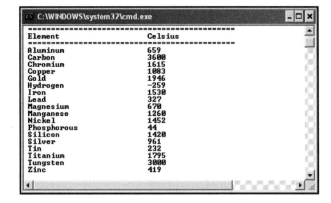

Working each() to Retrieve Keys and Values

Of all the functions used specifically for hashes, the each() function proves to be the most useful when you seek to retrieve both the keys and values from an array. The each() function takes the array in its implicit form (%) as its argument. It returns a key-value pair each time it is called. Listing08_09 illustrates the use of the each() function to create a table that displays the names of legendary chemists and their achievements.

```
#Listing08_09
# 1 Formatting elements for the table
$NL = "\n ";
$DC = "=";              #character for top and bottom lines of table
$TW = 55;               #Table width
$DL = sprintf( "%45s", $NL . $DC x $TW); #top and bottom lines
$TableTitleText = 'Leading Chemists of History';
$COLAHEAD = "Chemist";
$COLBHEAD = "Achievement";
$TableTitle = sprintf("%45s", $DC x int(($TW - length($TableTitleText))/2) .
                  $TableTitleText .
                  $DC x int(($TW - length($TableTitleText))/2));
```

```
# 2 Define the keys and values for a table
%Chemists = ("Trevisan", "Ancient alchemist",
             "Paracelsus", "Physician who cured diseases",
             "Priestly", "Discovered oxygen",
             "Lavoisier", "Father of modern chemistry",
             "Dalton", "Invented the atomic theory",
             "Woehler", "Father of organic chemistry",
             "Mendeleev", "Created the first table of elements",
             "Curies", "Isolated radium",
             "Thomson", "Discovered the electron"
             );
#3 Print the table
   printf("$DL");
   printf("%s", $NL . $TableTitle);
   printf("$DL");
   printf("\n %-15s %-20s", $COLAHEAD , $COLBHEAD);
   printf("$DL");


# 4 Use each to retrieve key - value pairs
   while(($Name, $Achievement) = each(%Chemists)){
       printf("\n %-15s %-20s", $Name , $Achievement);
   }
```

The lines that comment #1 identify create elements that you can use to format a table. To create the string that the $TableTitle identifier contains, you form a string consisting of three parts. The first and third parts are padding. The second part is the string you want to use for a title. To create the padding parts, you subtract the length of the string used for the title of the table from the width of the table. You divide the remainder by two so that you can pad the title on either side. You then concatenate the parts using sprintf() and assign it to $TableTitle.

The lines trailing comment #2 define a hash, %Chemists, that contains keys identifying famous chemists and values that name their greatest accomplishments. At comment #3 you print the table header. To accomplish this, you print the title line you have assigned to $TableTitle and follow with the column headers.

At comment #4, you use a while control statement to iterate through the hash. To access the key-value pairs in the hash, you employ the each() function. You assign the return value of the each() function to a list of two scalars, $Name and $Achievement. Notice that you separate the scalars using commas. You assign the return value from the each() function to this list. For the each() function itself, it is optional to enclose the array name in parentheses, but using them can render the order of operations clearer. When the each() function iterates through all the key-value pairs, it reaches an undefined element, and this terminates the action of the while control statement.

As you access the key-value pairs, you then feed them to the printf() function. The formatting capabilities of the printf() function allow you to set up columns 15 and 20 characters wide. Figure 8.10 illustrates the output of Listing08_09.

Figure 8.10
The each() function allows you to access both keys and values simultaneously.

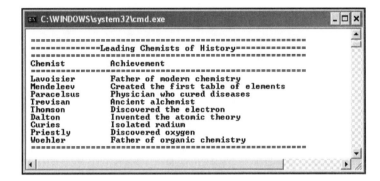

Conclusion

This chapter explored the basics of hashes as associative containers. An associative container employs an algorithm that does not involve storing data on a strictly sequential basis, as you see, for example, when you inspect the indexes of an array. One item does not necessarily follow another according to how you have placed them in the container. Instead, the algorithm is constructed to organize data according to its own characteristics. The characteristics remain hidden in the algorithm, but it remains that it makes it possible for you to quickly access the information the hash stores.

When you initialize a hash, you can use both scalar and implicit forms of the hash as you do so. The result depends to a great extent on the context you are working in. Still, the basics remain the same. You can recognize the implicit form of a hash by the business "at" sign (@). The scalar, or lookup, form of a hash is associated with the dollar sign.

When accessing items in a hash, you have a variety of options. Two easy ones involve employing the keys() or values() function to access the keys or values in a given hash and assigning them to an array. You can then use repetition control statements such as while or foreach to traverse the array. Used with the lookup form of the hash, traversing an array of keys or values allows you to easily access all the elements in the hash.

This chapter also explored how functions familiar from work with arrays prove useful when dealing with hashes. Among these functions are the `shift()`, `pop()`, and `reverse()` functions. When you use the `reverse()` function with a hash as its argument, you reverse the key-value relationship of the items in the hash. In essence, you are reading a list backward, but in relation to a hash, this means that you are also reading the key-value pairs backward. Reversing key-value pairs allows you to easily organize data in varying ways, as when you display chemical elements in an order established by their melting points.

9 } Extending Hash Applications

In this chapter you further explore the use of hashes. Among the functions you explore are the `defined()`, `exists()`, `scalar()`, `delete()`, and `reverse()` functions. Some of these functions are also used with arrays. When used with hashes, they might perform the same basic activity they perform with arrays, but they have different visible results. This is the case with the `reverse()` function, which reverses the key-value associations you see when you access items in a hash. One of the more complex activities you perform with hashes involves slicing hashes. When you slice hashes, you insert one hash into another. You can use a number of approaches to slicing. The same applies to converting hashes into strings or strings into hashes. To accomplish this work, you use the `split()` and `join()` functions. Among the activities this chapter addresses are the following:

❈ Exploring different ways to determine whether hash elements have been defined

❈ How to delete a key-value pair from a hash

❈ Sorting and reversing items as you retrieve them from a hash

❈ Converting the key-value pairs in a hash to a string

❈ Converting a sting into key-value pairs

❈ Merging hashes through slicing

Checking for Existence

The `exists()` function checks for the existence of a hash key. If the key exists, it returns true (1). If the key does not exist, it returns false (0). It does not test for the existence of values. The `exists()` function requires one argument. This argument consists of the hash lookup operation with the name of the key that you target for your query.

Listing09_01 makes use of the tables of elements created by the chemists John Newlands and Dmitri Mendeleev. In 1866, Mendeleev created what is generally recognized as the modern

Periodic Table of Elements. To arrive at his scheme, he took an approach that improved on the approach that John Newlands employed. Listing09_01 uses the `exists()` function to test for differences in the data the two chemists used.

```
#Listing09_01
#Note : The DzSoft editor reports an error if you use the exists()
#function. To use the DzSoft editor, press Shift F9.
#Or run the file in DOS to see it execute.


# 1 Formatting elements for the table
$NL = "\n ";
$DC = "=";               #character for top and bottom lines of table
$TW = 55;                #Table width
$DL = sprintf( "%55s", $NL . $DC x $TW); #top and bottom lines
$COLAHEAD = "Element";
$COLBHEAD = "Status";
$COLCHEAD = "Chemists";


#2 Set up the data using an implicit hash
%MendeleevElements = (H, D, Li, D, Be, D, B, D, C, D, NB, D, O, D,
                      F, D, Na, D, Mg, D, Al, D, Si, D, P, D, S, D,
                      Cl, D, K, D, Ca, D, Ti, D, V, D, Cr, D, Mn, D,
                      Fe, D, Co, D, Ni, D, Cu, D, Sn, D, As, D,
                      Se, D, Dr, D, Ru, D, Rh, D, Pd, D, Ag, D, Cd, D,
                      In, D, Sb, D, Te, D, I, D, Cs, D, Ba, D);

%NewlandsElements = (H, D, Li, D, B, D, C, D, N, D, O, D, F, D, Na, D,
                     Mg, D, Al, D, Si, D, P, D, S, D, Cl, D, K, D,
                     Ca, D, Cr, D, Ti, D, Mn, D, Fe, D, Co, D, Ni, D,
                     Cu, D, Zn, D, Y, D, In, D, As, D, Se, D, Dr, D,
                     Rb, D, Sr, D, La, D, Ce, D, Zr, D, Nb, D, Mo, D, Ru, D,
                     Rh, D, Pd, D, Ag, D, Cd, D, U, D, Sn, D, Sb, D,
                     Te, D, I, D, Cs, D, Ba, D, V, D);

#3 Print the table
   printf("$DL");
   printf("\n %-15s %-15s %-15s" , $COLAHEAD , $COLBHEAD, $COLCHEAD);
   printf("$DL");
```

```
#4 Assign the elements to an array
@MElementNames = keys(%MendeleevElements);

#5 Use an inner foreach loop and a selection statement
#to retrieve the names of elements
     $Itr = 1;
     foreach $MEName(@MElementNames){
         if(exists($NewlandsElements{$MEName})){
             printf("\n %-15s %-15s %15s",
                 $MEName,
                 $NewlandsElements{$MEName},
                 "Mendeleev and Newlands");
         }
     }

print "\n";
print "\n";
#Allows the file to execute in DOS without closing
system("pause");
```

At comment #1 you set up some formatting elements for the table the program creates. The lines associated with comment #2 create two hashes. The first, %MendeleevElements, consists of the names of the elements Mendeleev considered valid. You employ the "Ds" to signify "defined." The second hash, %NewlandsElements, offers a list of elements John Newlands considered valid. The "Ds," as before, signify elements he "defined."

At comment #3 you print the column headers of the table. At comment #4, you create an array using the keys() function, @MElementNames. The array consists of the names of elements Mendeleev used.

At comment #5, you use a foreach control statement to iterate through the @MElement-Names array, which names the elements Mendeleev considered valid. You temporarily assign the name of each element to a scalar, $MEName.

At this point, you make use of the exists() function inside an if control statement. The procedure involves first making use of the %NewlandsElements hash. This hash, you recall, contains the data Newlands considered valid. You want at this point to see if the element names Mendeleev used can also be found in the collection of data Newlands used. To accomplish this, you employ the exists() function and provide as its argument a lookup operation that uses the $NewlandsElements hash. For the key in the lookup operation, you use the element name you have obtained from the Mendeleev list ($MEName).

As the foreach statement traverses the elements in the array, the exists() function checks the element name from the Mendeleev list against the element name in the Newlands list. If exists() returns true, then you print the name of the element along with its status. As Figure 9.1 illustrates, you also see a column confirming that the element appears in both the Mendeleev and Newlands sets of data.

As a final note, the program includes a call to the system() function, which allows you to issue a DOS command. In this case, since you might want to run the program straight from Windows to test it, the pause command prevents the command prompt window from immediately closing when the program completes its execution.

Figure 9.1
Uses the exists()
function to establish that
elements appear in two
hashes.

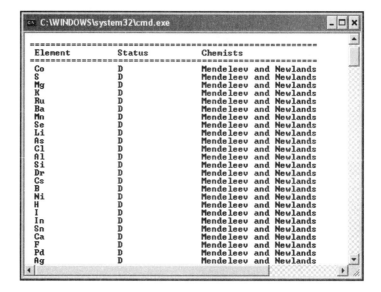

Determining if Elements Are Defined

You use the defined() function in precisely the same way that you use the exists() function. As an argument, you employ the hash lookup operation. You include as the argument of the lookup function the key you want to test. The defined() function discovers whether a key has been defined. Listing09_02 pursues the same scenario described in the previous section. Dmitri Mendeleev and John Newlands used different data sets in their investigations of the Periodic Table of Elements. The program seeks to establish the differences between the two sets of data. (For a background discussion of the program, see the section titled "Checking for Existence.")

In this case, the goal is to find the elements that appear in John Newlands' set of data that do not appear in Dmitri Mendeleev's set of data. Toward this end, you employ the NOT form of the `defined()` function (`!defined()`). If Newlands names data that Mendeleev does not, then you print this in a table.

```
#Listing09_02
# 1 Formatting elements for the table
$NL = "\n ";
$DC = "=";                    #character for top and bottom lines of table
$TW = 55;                     #Table width
$DL = sprintf( "%55s", $NL . $DC x $TW); #top and bottom lines
$COLAHEAD = "Element";
$COLBHEAD = "Status";
$COLCHEAD = "Chemist";


#2 Set up the data using an implicit hash
%MendeleevElements = (H, D, Li, D, Be, D, B, D, C, D, NB, D, O, D,
                      F, D, Na, D, Mg, D, Al, D, Si, D, P, D, S, D,
                      Cl, D, K, D, Ca, D, Ti, D, V, D, Cr, D, Mn, D,
                      Fe, D, Co, D, Ni, D, Cu, D, Sn, D, As, D,
                      Se, D, Dr, D, Ru, D, Rh, D, Pd, D, Ag, D, Cd, D,
                      In, D, Sb, D, Te, D, I, D, Cs, D, Ba, D);


%NewlandsElements = (H, D, Li, D, B, D, C, D, N, D, O, D, F, D, Na, D,
                     Mg, D, Al, D, Si, D, P, D, S, D, Cl, D, K, D,
                     Ca, D, Cr, D, Ti, D, Mn, D, Fe, D, Co, D, Ni, D,
                     Cu, D, Zn, D, Y, D, In, D, As, D, Se, D, Dr, D,
                     Rb, D, Sr, D, La, D, Ce, D, Zr, D, Nb, D, Mo, D, Ru, D,
                     Rh, D, Pd, D, Ag, D, Cd, D, U, D, Sn, D, Sb, D,
                     Te, D, I, D, Cs, D, Ba, D, V, D);

#3 Print the table
   printf("$DL");
   printf("\n %-15s %-15s %-15s" , $COLAHEAD , $COLBHEAD, $COLCHEAD);
   printf("$DL");
```

```
#4 Assign the elements to an array
@NElementNames = keys(%NewlandsElements);
#5 Use an inner foreach loop and a selection statement
#to retrieve the names of elements
      $Itr = 1;
      foreach $NEName(@NElementNames){
          if(!defined($MendeleevElements{$NEName})){
              printf("\n %-15s %-15s %-15s",
                  $NEName,
                  $NewlandsElements{$NEName},
                  "Newlands");
          }
      }
system("pause");
```

To format the output table, at comment #1 you define several identifiers with information relative to formatting. At comment #2, you set up two hashes. The first hash contains data Mendeleev used. The second hash contains data Newlands used. At comment #3, you print the heading of the output table.

In the lines associated with comment #4, you assign the keys of the hash that contain the data Newlands used to an array, @NElementNames. With this array in place, you then proceed in the lines trailing comment #5 to employ a foreach control statement to traverse the items in the @NElementNames array. As you access the names of the elements, you temporarily assign them to the $NEName identifier.

After assigning the name of an element to the $NEName identifier, you can then use the identifier in the hash lookup operation, which you evaluate using the NOT form of the defined() function (!defined()). The purpose of this operation is to test for keys that are not defined in the hash that contains the data Mendeleev used (%MendeleevElements).

You test each of the elements Newlands used. Each time you find one that is not present in the Mendeleev data, you print it. In addition to the element name, you print the status associated with it. In each case, the status is "D." You also print "Newlands" to confirm that the data was used only by Newlands. Figure 9.2 displays the output of Listing09_02.

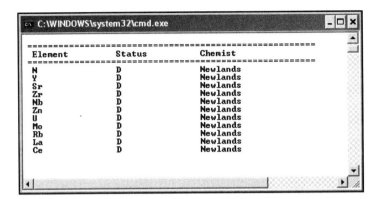

Figure 9.2
Use the defined()
function to determine if
elements in two hashes
are the same.

Ascertaining the Number of Key-Value Pairs

To ascertain the number of key-value pairs in a hash, you can use an approach that involves
the keys() function and the scalar() function. The procedure involves first assigning the
keys in a hash to an array. Then you use the scalar() function to extract the number of
elements in the array. Listing09_03 provides an example of this procedure that involves the data
used by Newlands and Mendeleev. For a background discussion of the program, see the section
titled "Checking for Existence."

```
#Listing09_03
# 1 Formatting elements for the table
$NL = "\n ";
$DC = "=";                #character for top and bottom lines of table
$TW = 55;                 #Table width
$DL = sprintf( "%55s", $NL . $DC x $TW); #top and bottom lines
$COLAHEAD = "Mendeleev";
$COLBHEAD = "Newlands";


#2 Set up the data using an implicit hash
%MendeleevElements = (H, D, Li, D, Be, D, B, D, C, D, NB, D, O, D,
                      F, D, Na, D, Mg, D, Al, D, Si, D, P, D, S, D,
                      Cl, D, K, D, Ca, D, Ti, D, V, D, Cr, D, Mn, D,
                      Fe, D, Co, D, Ni, D, Cu, D, As, D,
                      Se, D, Dr, D, Ru, D, Rh, D, Pd, D, Ag, D, Cd, D,
                      In, D, Sn, D, Sb, D, Te, D, I, D, Cs, D, Ba, D);
```

```
%NewlandsElements = (H, D, Li, D, B, D, C, D, N, D, O, D, F, D, Na, D,
                     Mg, D, Al, D, Si, D, P, D, S, D, Cl, D, K, D,
                     Ca, D, Cr, D, Ti, D, Mn, D, Fe, D, Co, D, Ni, D,
                     Cu, D, Zn, D, Y, D, In, D, As, D, Se, D, Dr, D,
                     Rb, D, Sr, D, La, D, Ce, D, Zr, D, Nb, D, Mo, D, Ru, D,
                     Rh, D, Pd, D, Ag, D, Cd, D, U, D, Sn, D, Sb, D,
                     Te, D, I, D, Cs, D, Ba, D, V, D);

#3 use keys to extract the unique keys
$MLenK = scalar(keys(%MendeleevElements));
$MLenV = scalar(values(%MendeleevElements));


$NLenK = scalar(keys(%NewlandsElements));
$NLenV = scalar(values(%NewlandsElements));


#Display the result
    printf("$DL");
    printf("\n %-30s %-30s" , $COLAHEAD , $COLBHEAD);
    printf("$DL");
    printf("\n %-15s %-15s%-15s %-15s", "Keys" , "Values",
                                        "Keys", "Values");
    printf("$DL");
    printf("\n %-15s %-15s%-15s %-15s", $MLenK, $MLenV ,
                                        $NLenK, $NLenV);


system("pause");
```

This program uses the same approach to the data and the presentation of the data that the two previous programs used. In the lines that comment #1 identifies, you set up formatting elements for the presentation table. At comment #2, you create two hashes. One, %MendeleevElements, holds keys and values for the data Mendeleev used. The second hash, %NewlandsElements, holds keys and values for the data Newlands used. The "D's" designate "defined."

At comment #3, you employ the scalar() function to determine the number of keys and values in each hash. The sole argument of the keys() function consists of the hash from which you want to access the keys. The return value of the keys() function consists of all the keys in an array. When you cascade the keys() function into the scalar() function, the result is a value representing the number of keys.

A similar procedure characterizes your use of the `values()` function. The `values()` function accesses all the values in a hash, and if you cascade the `values()` function into the `scalar()` function, you get a count of all the values in a hash.

For the two hashes representing the data used by Mendeleev and Newlands, you use the `scalar()` function and the cascaded `keys()` and `values()` functions to define four scalar identifiers (`$MLenV`, `$MLenK`, `$NLenK`, `$NLenV`). Having obtained these values, you can then proceed to print them. Figure 9.3 shows you the table that results from Listing09_03.

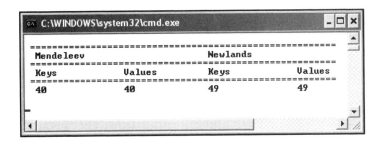

Figure 9.3
Use the `scalar()` function to retrieve the number of elements.

Slicing Hashes

When you use a slice operation, you can insert the contents of one or more other hashes into a hash. You can improvise an endless number of approaches to hash slicing. The procedure usually involves the use of the lookup form of the target hash. You follow this with an assignment operation involving a list of items to be sliced into the target hash. In other cases, you can avoid using the lookup operation and employ instead assignment of a list alone. Listing09_04 presents three possibilities:

❋ Use the hash lookup operation with a series of keys separated by commas. Assign a list of values to the keys. See comment #4.

❋ Use the hash lookup operation. As the argument for the lookup, use `keys()` with the hash from which you want to derive keys for splicing. Follow with the assignment operator and a list containing the `values()` function. For the argument of the `values()` function, you use the same hash you used in the `keys()` function. See comment #5.

❋ Use the assignment operator to assign a list of hashes to the target hash. As the first item in the list, name the target list. See comment #6.

```
#Listing09_04
# 1 Formatting elements for the table
$NL = "\n ";
$DC = "=";                  #character for top and bottom lines of table
```

```
$TW = 55;                #Table width
$DL = sprintf( "%55s", $NL . $DC x $TW); #top and bottom lines
$COLAHEAD = "Element";
$COLBHEAD = "Atomic Number";


#2 Set up the data using an implicit hash
%RareEarthElements = (Lanthanum, 57, Cerium, 58,
                      Praseodymium, 59, Neodymium, 60,
                      Promethium, 61, Samarium, 62);




#3 Create a second hash
    %AlkaliMetals = (Lithium, 3, Sodium, 11,
                     Potassium, 19, Rubidium, 37,
                     Cesium, 55, Francium, 87);


#4 SLICE some elements into a hash in an array context
    # Curly braces precede list parentheses. As keys are
    # added, you iterate through the list to add the values.
@InertGases{"Helium" , "Neon", "Argon"}
                = (2, 10, 18);


#4.1 Create a hash
    %Gasses = (Helium , 2, Neon, 10,
                Argon , 18, Xenon, 54);


# 5 SLICE with keys() and Values()
# Use the keys and values functions to add elements
# keys() iterates through the hash and pulls all the
# keys from it; values() does this in tandem to
# assign the values.
    @Elements{ keys(%Gasses)} =
                values(%Gasses);


# 6 SLICE hashes together
  # Basic iteration through the items in the list
```

```
    %Elements = (%Elements,
                 %InertGases,
                 %AlkaliMetals,
                 %RareEarthElements);

# 7 Print the table
    printf("$DL");
    printf("\n %-17s %3s", $COLAHEAD , $COLBHEAD);
    printf("$DL");
    foreach $ElementName (keys(%Elements))
    {
        printf("\n %-17s %3.0f", $ElementName,
                            $Elements{$ElementName});
    }
```

In the lines associated with comment #1, you set up a few formatting elements for the table that displays the sliced data. At comment #2, you create a basic hash, %RareEarthElements. This hash contains the names of six rare earth elements and their corresponding atomic numbers. At comment #3, you create a second hash, %AlkaliMetals, which provides six alkali metals and their atomic numbers. These two hashes remain in the background for a moment.

In the lines accompanying comment #4, you defined a third hash using a slicing technique. The slicing technique ostensibly employs the lookup form of the hash. You prefix the name of the hash with the implicit hash identifier (@). (Normally, you use a dollar sign for lookup operations.) Inside the curly braces, you provide a list of keys you want to slice into the hash. You then assign a list of items that you want to slice into the hash as values. The list of keys corresponds to the list of values.

In the lines trailing comment #4.1 you add another hash definition to the program (%Gasses). This definition includes four elements and their corresponding Celsius melting points.

Comment #5 identifies a second form of slicing. In this instance, you employ the keys() and values() functions to slice the keys and values of the %Gasses hash into the %Elements hash. The keys() function accesses all the elements in the %Elements hash. You call the keys() function inside the curly braces of the lookup operation.

For the corresponding values, you use an assignment operator to assign the items the values() function returns inside the list parentheses. As the argument for the values() function, you again use the %Gasses hash. The operation is basically the same as if you had a set of comma-delimited items.

The final slice operation occurs in association with comment #6. There, you use the list function alone. To effect the slice, you assign a list of hashes to the target hash. The only stipulation is that the first hash in the assigned list must be the target hash. In this case, the target hash is %Elements. Figure 9.4 illustrates that when you print the contents of %Elements, you obtain all the elements from all of the hashes in Listing09_04.

Figure 9.4
Slicing operations allow
you to merge hashes.

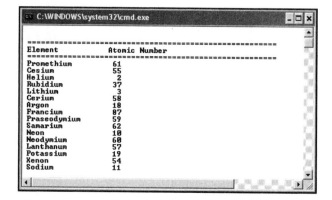

Converting a String into a Hash

You can employ the split() function to convert a string into a hash. This procedure proves useful when you process the results of Internet transmissions, which arrive as strings. The split() function takes two arguments. The first argument names the expression to use to separate the items in the string. The second argument consists of the string you want to operate on. Listing09_05 provides an example of how to translate a string into a hash. In this instance, the string consists of key-value pairs joined by colons. Commas separate the pairs.

```
#Listing09_05
#1 Set up the data using an implicit hash
#It is important not to introduce extra line returns and the like ...
 $ElementsString ="Aluminum:659, Carbon:3600, Chromium:1615, Copper:1083,".
          "Gold:1946, Hydrogen:-259, Iron:1530, Lead:327, " .
          "Magnesium:670, Manganese:1260, Nickel:1452, " .
          "Phosphorous:44, Silicon:1420, Silver:961, " .
          "Tin:232, Titanium:1795, Tungsten:3000, Zinc:419";

#2 Use the split() function and a regular expression to split
#the string. The expression calls for a comma followed by a space
@ElementList = split(", ", $ElementsString);
```

```perl
$ListLength = scalar(@ElementList); #read length of array
print "\nNumber of items : $ListLength\n";

#3 At the colons, separate the elements and melting points
# The expression calls for a colon with no spaces
foreach $Item (@ElementList){
    ($Element, $MeltingPt) = split(":",$Item );
    # Two steps that could be one: create a hash with the two parts
    $NewElementList{$Element} = $MeltingPt;
}#end foreach
# 4 Print the hash as a string; use each to retrieve keys and values
print "\nThe element list follows:\n";

$Itr = 1;
while(($Element, $MeltingPt) = each(%NewElementList)){
    printf "\n %-4s %-25s %-10.0f", $Itr++, $Element, $MeltingPt;
}#end while
```

The lines accompanying comment #1 in Listing09_05 create a string that consists of a number of chemical elements and their melting points. Commas separate the element-temperature pairs that constitute the string. To display this program in this book, it is necessary to break the string into a set of concatenated elements. You can derive a lesson from this. It remains essential not to introduce newline characters into a string you want to split. The split() function usually processes your string, but unless you tell it otherwise, it assumes you want to leave escape sequences alone. This can create problems.

In the lines comment #2 designates, you use the split() function to divide the string into items that consist of the element-value sets. To divide the string, you supply as a first argument to the split() function a comma followed by a blank space. You enclose these in double quotation marks. (You can also use forward slashes (//), the q() function, the qq() function, or single quotation marks.) The split() function returns the items that result when the string is divided as stipulated, and you assign these items to an array, @ElementList. You use the scalar() function to ascertain the number of items in the array, and as Figure 8.14 shows, you print this so that you can check the displayed elements against it.

At comment #3, you employ a foreach control statement to traverse the items in the @ElementList array. The foreach statement allows you to access each item in the array and assign it to a scalar, $Item. Within the foreach block, you then again use the split()

function to separate the element and temperature components the $Item identifier temporarily stores. To accomplish this, the first argument you supply to the split() function consists of a colon enclosed in double quotes.

You assign the return value of the split() function to the list that consists of two scalar identifiers ($Element, $MeltingPt). These two elements you then supply to a lookup hash operation featuring the %NewElementList hash. Between the curly braces, the $Element identifier supplies the key for each hash item. The $MeltingPt identifier supplies the assigned value.

At comment #4, you employ the returned values of the each() function as arguments in a while control statement to iterate through the %NewElementList hash. You assign the accessed values to the same scalar identifiers used before ($Element, $MeltingPt). You can then employ the printf() function to display the contents of the hash in a formatted, numbered form. To number the items you display, you include an incremented identifier ($Itr) inside the while block. Figure 9.5 illustrates the resulting table.

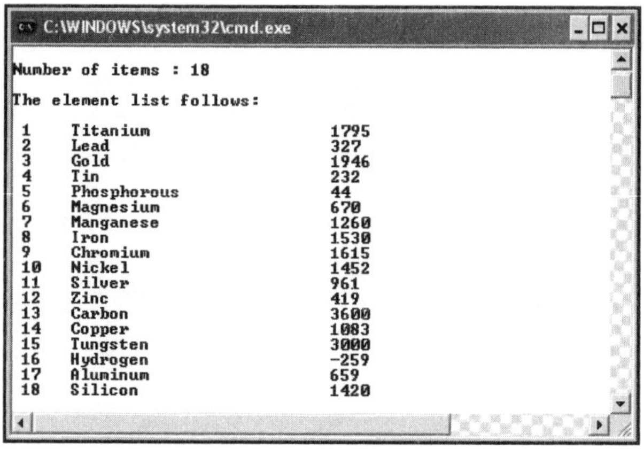

Figure 9.5
Use the split() function to place items from a string into a hash.

```
C:\WINDOWS\system32\cmd.exe

Number of items : 18

The element list follows:
1       Titanium            1795
2       Lead                327
3       Gold                1946
4       Tin                 232
5       Phosphorous         44
6       Magnesium           670
7       Manganese           1260
8       Iron                1530
9       Chromium            1615
10      Nickel              1452
11      Silver              961
12      Zinc                419
13      Carbon              3600
14      Copper              1083
15      Tungsten            3000
16      Hydrogen            -259
17      Aluminum            659
18      Silicon             1420
```

Deleting Elements

To delete items from a hash, Perl provides you with the delete() function. The delete() function requires one argument, the lookup form of the hash you are working with supplied with the key for the key-value pair you want to delete. Listing09_06 provides an interactive program you must execute from the DOS command line. You can either open a command prompt window or just click on the program in Windows Explorer. The program prompts you to supply the name of a chemical element (Aluminum) to be deleted from a list of chemical elements. Figure 9.6 shows you a complete round of interaction with the program.

```
#Listing09_06
 #1 Create a hash
%ElementsCelMeltingPts = (Aluminum, 659, Carbon , 3600,
                          Chromium, 1615, Copper, 1083,
                          Gold, 1946, Hydrogen, -259);
#2 Print it
print "\n\nBefore:";
$Itr = 1;
while(($Element, $MeltingPt) = each(%ElementsCelMeltingPts)){
    printf "\n %-4s %-25s %-10.0f", $Itr++, $Element, $MeltingPt;
}


#3 To delete an element get some input from the program user
#Delete "Aluminum"
print "\n From the list above, type the KEY (try \"Aluminum\") " .
                  "\n you want to delete: ";
$KeyToDelete = <STDIN>;
chomp($KeyToDelete);

if(!defined( $ElementsCelMeltingPts{$KeyToDelete} ) ){
   print "\nThe element you've typed isn't in the list. Try again.";
}



#4 Use the delete() function to delete the element
delete($ElementsCelMeltingPts{$KeyToDelete});

print "\n\nAfter:";
$Itr = 1;
while(($Element, $MeltingPt) = each(%ElementsCelMeltingPts)){
    printf "\n %-4s %-25s %-10.0f", $Itr++, $Element, $MeltingPt;
}
```

The lines associated with comment #1 in Listing09_06 create a hash that consists of six chemical elements and their associated melting points. At comment #2, you use a while control statement in conjunction with the each() function to access the element-temperature pairs in the hash. These you display in a tabular, numbered form, as Figure 9.6 shows.

Figure 9.6
Use the delete() function to remove key-value pairs from a hash.

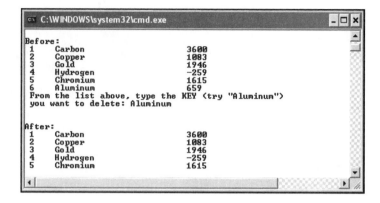

```
C:\WINDOWS\system32\cmd.exe                                    _ □ ×
Before:
1       Carbon                  3600
2       Copper                  1083
3       Gold                    1946
4       Hydrogen                -259
5       Chromium                1615
6       Aluminum                659
From the list above, type the KEY (try "Aluminum")
you want to delete: Aluminum

After:
1       Carbon                  3600
2       Copper                  1083
3       Gold                    1946
4       Hydrogen                -259
5       Chromium                1615
```

At comment #3, you prompt the program user to type the name of a chemical element to be deleted from the list. You use the <STDIN> handle to obtain the input from the user. You assign the input to a scalar identifier, $KeyToDelete. You then follow with a call to the chomp() function. You provide $KeyToDelete as the argument. The chomp() function removes the newline character that is appended to input when you press Enter.

You then use an if control statement to check whether the data typed at the prompt exists in the hash. To accomplish this, you call the defined() function. In this case, you prefix a NOT operator to the defined() function (!) so that the selection statement proves true only if the element has not been correctly typed or in some other way is not in the hash. The argument you supply to the defined() function consists of a lookup hash operation. You submit the $KeyToDelete identifier to this operation.

The lines associated with comment #4 employ the delete() function. The procedure involves using the lookup hash operation as an argument. The argument for the lookup operation itself is the key that designates the hash item to be deleted ($KeyToDelete).

Given the completion of the deletion, you then use a while control statement along with the each() function to iterate through the hash and confirm the deletion. Figure 9.6 shows the items in the hash following the deletion.

Converting a Hash into a String

Converting a hash to a string often proves useful when you want to display the contents of database or Internet interactions in a webpage. Converting a hash to a string involves using the join() function in association with the sprintf() function. In many cases, you might forego the use of the sprintf() function, but it remains a handy auxiliary function if you want to format the items you extract from a hash. Listing09_07 illustrates a procedure you might use to convert the key-value items in a hash into a single formatted string that you can display as a table.

```
#Listing09_07
#1 Create a hash
%ElementsAtomicWeights = (Oxygen, 15.9994, Fluorine, 18.9984032,
                          Neon, 20.1797, Sodium, 22.989770,
                          Magnesium, 24.3050, Aluminum, 26.981538,
                          Silicon, 28.0855, Phosphorus, 30.973761,
                          Sulfur, 32.065, Chlorine, 35.453,
                          Potassium, 39.0983, Calcium, 40.078,
                          Vanadium, 50.9415 , Manganese, 54.938049);
# Formatting elements for the table
$NL = "\n ";
$DC = "=";       #character for top and bottom lines of table
$TW = 55;        #Table width
$DL = sprintf( "%55s", $NL . $DC x $TW); #top and bottom lines
$COLAHEAD = "Element";
$COLBHEAD = "Weight";


#2 Use the join() function to repeatedly join the string with
#itself. Use the printf() function to form the keys and values
#into manageable components
#manageable

while(($Element, $Weight) = each(%ElementsAtomicWeights)){
    $EString = join("\n ", $EString, sprintf("%-15s %-15s",
                                        $Element , $Weight));
}


#3 Print the table heading . . .
printf("$DL");
printf("\n %-15s %-15s " , $COLAHEAD , $COLBHEAD );
printf("$DL");

# Print the string . . .
print "\n" . $EString;
```

The lines comment #1 identifies create a hash (%ElementsAtomicWeights) that consists of the names of chemical elements and their atomic weights. You follow the definition of the table with the definition of a set of identifiers you can use to format a table to display the data in the hash.

At comment #2, you create a while control statement. To generate arguments for the while statement, you use the hash each() function. As the argument for the each() function, you submit the %ElementsAtomicWeights hash. The while statement iterates until it reaches an undefined value that marks the end of the hash. As it iterates, the each() function repeatedly accesses the key-value pairs in the hash and assigns them to a pair of listed identifiers ($Element, $Weight). These identifiers provide the element name and atomic weight of each chemical element the hash contains.

You use the $Element and $Weight identifiers as arguments to the sprintf() function. The sprintf() function in this instance formats a string 30 characters long that provides 15-character fields for two data items it includes.

The return value of the sprintf() function supplies the second of two arguments to the join() function. As the first argument of the join() function, you provide a line return and a space enclosed in double quotation marks. The first argument provides the expression you want to use as you join the items into a string. In this case, as you form the string, you join the formatted columns the sprintf() function creates using line returns and blank spaces. In effect, you are creating rows of a table.

In the lines comment #3 identifies, you print a table. As Figure 9.7 shows, first you print a line of equals signs. Then you print the column heads and another line of equals signs. As a final gesture, you employ a brief print statement to print the string assigned to the $EString identifier.

Figure 9.7
Use the join() function with the sprintf() function to convert hash items into a single string that displays in a tabular form.

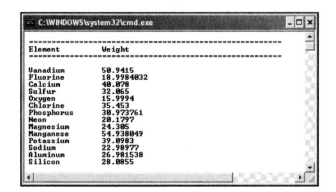

Reversing Keys and Values

The reverse() function works with both arrays and hashes. With a hash, it reverses keys and values. The reverse() function takes only one argument, the name of the hash in its implicit form (%). When you use it with hashes, you assign the return value of the hash back to the hash. Listing09_08 reverses a hash to create a table that displays chemical elements according to the descending order of their melting points.

```
#Listing09_08
# 1 Formatting elements for the table
$NL = "\n ";
$DC = "=";        #character for top and bottom lines of table
$TW = 55;         #Table width
$DL = sprintf( "%55s", $NL . $DC x $TW); #top and bottom lines
$COLAHEAD = "Element";
$COLBHEAD = "Celsius";
$COLCHEAD = "Fahrenheit";


#2 Set up the data using an implicit hash
%ElementsCelMeltingPts = ( Water, 100,
                           Aluminum, 659, Carbon, 3600,
                           Chromium, 1615, Copper, 1083,
                           Gold, 1946, Hydrogen, -259,
                           Iron, 1530, Lead, 327,
                           Magnesium, 670, Manganese, 1260,
                           Nickel, 1452, Phosphorous, 44,
                           Silicon, 1420, Silver, 961,
                           Tin, 232, Titanium, 1795,
                           Tungsten, 3000, Zinc, 419);


#3 Print the table
    printf("$DL");
    printf("\n %-25s %-15s %-15s", $COLAHEAD , $COLBHEAD, $COLCHEAD);
    printf("$DL");


#4 HASH: Reverse the Keys and Values in the hash
%ElementsCelMeltingPts = reverse(%ElementsCelMeltingPts);
```

223

```
#Set up a key array using the melting points and sort them
@MeltingPoints = keys(%ElementsCelMeltingPts);
@MeltingPoints = sort{$a <=> $b}(@MeltingPoints); #Sort the elements
# @MeltingPoints = reverse (@MeltingPoints); #ARRAY Reversal for ascending

#5 Use a while loop and the hash lookup operation
#to retrieve the names of elements
while ($CelsiusMP =pop(@MeltingPoints)){
    #Look up name of the element
    $EName = $ElementsCelMeltingPts{$CelsiusMP};
    printf("\n %-17s %15.2f %15.2f", $EName ,
      #Display Celsius
      $CelsiusMP,
      #Display Fahrenheit
      (9/5) * $CelsiusMP + 32);
}#end while
```

At comment #1, you create scalar identifiers to provide formatting for the table. The lines comment #2 identifies create a hash containing the names of elements and their melting points. (Water is included as a test value.) The lines accompanying comment #3 print the column headings for the table.

At comment #4 you use the `reverse()` function to reverse the key value pairs in the `%ElementsCelMeltingPts` hash. To accomplish this, as mentioned previously, you assign the return value of the `reverse()` function back to the name of the hash.

Given the reversal of the keys and values, the keys of the hash now consist of the temperatures at which the elements melt. You use the `keys()` function to assign these values to an array, `@MeltingPoints`.

The lines at comment #4.5 apply the `sort()` function to the array of melting temperature. Notice the form of the `sort()` function:

```
sort {$a < = > $b}( @MeltingPoints)
```

This form of the `sort()` function applies to numbers, and you must use it in this context or the temperatures are not sorted correctly. The `sort{$a< = > $b)` function sorts the temperatures so that they are in ascending order. The `pop()` function, used in the `while` loop, reverses this order. If you want to see ascending order, uncomment the following line:

```
# @MeltingPoints = reverse(@MeltingPoints); #ARRAY Reversal for ascending
```

In this instance, the `reverse()` function is used on an array, not a hash. The `while` loop that comment #5 identifies iterates through the `@MeltingPoints` array and pops elements from it. This is why you see the default sorted array as descending rather than ascending. You use the lookup hash operation and the popped melting temperature as its argument to retrieve the name of the element. With the `printf()` function, you display the name of the element, the Celsius melting point, and then, embedding the conversion formula as the third argument of the `printf()` function, the Fahrenheit melting point. Figure 9.8 illustrates the output of Listing09_08.

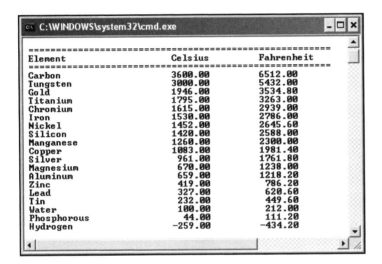

Figure 9.8
The `reverse()` function when applied to hashes reverses the key-value designations of the items in the hash.

Conclusion

In this chapter, you have explored a number of ways to extend your use of hashes. You first examined the uses that you can make of the `defined()` and `exists()` functions to establish whether a named key exists in a hash. You moved from this to approaches you can use to obtain the number of elements in a hash. From obtaining the number of elements, you then explored how to slice hashes. A number of approaches to hash slicing are available. One involves using the lookup hash operation. Another involves using the list operation to merge the contents of different hashes.

Two important activities you perform when using hashes involve uses of the `join()` and `split()` functions to translate hashes into strings or strings into hashes. When combined with the `sprintf()` function, you can transform key-value pairs into fully formatted strings ready for display. In addition to operations relating to strings, you also investigated the use of the `delete()` function, which used in combination with the `defined()` and `exists()` functions allows you to remove items from hashes.

225

❄ ❄ ❄

10 } Control Structures

This chapter provides an introduction to conditional statements. In this chapter, you concentrate on sequence and selection statements. Sequence, repetition, and selection characterize the actions that all programs perform. When a program performs actions sequentially, it executes one statement after another. Sequential execution of programs can become somewhat involved if you introduce such items as `goto` operators, arrays, and incremental operators. When a program performs actions governed by selection, it uses control expressions to determine whether one or more alternate courses of action might be introduced into the flow of the program. Among the sequential control statements are `if`, `unless`, `if...else`, and `if...elsif...else` statements. To make effective use of selection (and repetition) control statements, you employ relational and Boolean operators. You frequently use these two types of operators to create involved control expressions. This chapter provides discussion of the following topics:

* The basics of statements and compound statements
* Blocks and control blocks
* Sequence, selection, and repetition as programming fundamentals
* Relational and Boolean operators as they apply to control expressions
* Sequential use (or abuse) of `goto`, arrays, parentheses, and incremental operators
* Selection using `if`, `unless`, `if...else`, and `if...elsif...else` statements

Expressions and Statements

To review a few items, a declaration involves typing an identifier and associating it with a type of data. In Perl, you work primarily with scalars (`$`), array (`@`), and hash (`%`) data types. When you declare an identifier in Perl, you usually assign data to it. You define or initialize the identifier upon first use.

An expression involves a single item of data, such as a word or a number. It can consist of an identifier and operators. It does not go so far as to actually process the combination of identifiers and operators. Listing10_01 provides a few expressions (note that this program does not provide output, but you can use it to explore statements):

```
#Listing10_01
$Tax + $Sales
$Mass * $Acceleration
$FirstString . $SecondString
$Item++
```

Such expressions stop short of doing anything other than presenting the potential for an action. For this reason, you seldom code an expression in isolation. Even in the instance of the unary operator (Item++), nothing happens until you add a semicolon to the line on which it appears. At that point, the expression can become a statement. A statement provides a line of code that causes your computer to perform an action.

As mentioned in Chapter 3, you terminate a statement in Perl with a semicolon. A statement allows you to effect some action that in some way transforms the data in your program. The following statements make use of the expressions shown previously:

```
$Item = 1;
$Item++; #increments the value of $Item by one.
$Force = $Mass * Acceleration; #Calculates $Force
$ThirdString = $FirstString . $SecondString;
    #Creates a third string from two others
```

When you combine two or more statements, you create a compound statement. Curly braces often enclose compound statements. Such an enclosed set of statements is also known as a *block*. Consider the following excerpt of code:

```
if($Item == 1)
{
    print "\nHello";
    print "\nAgain.";
    $Sum++;
}
```

The three statements within the braces serve as a compound statement. In this case, the compound statement is executed only when a condition is fulfilled. The first line of the excerpt sets this condition. Since it does not lie inside the curly braces, the first line is known as a control statement. The control statement is not a part of the compound statement. Instead, the control statement transforms the compound statement into what is known as a *conditional* block. Conditional blocks usually create compound statements; at the same time, you often introduce compound statements using control statements.

Control Statements

Control statements provide the entryways to conditional statements or blocks of statements. As Figure 10.1 illustrates, a control statement consists of a word that designates the type of control you want to apply to a given block of statements. Figure 10.1 illustrates an if control statement. Logical expressions characterize control statements. The logical expression usually appears between parentheses that follow a keyword that identifies the control statement. A logical operator characterizes the logical expression that appears between the parentheses.

Following the control designation and its accompanying logical expression, you usually encounter the opening brace of the two braces that establish the scope of a controlled block of statements. Whether the block of statements enters the flow of your program depends on the behavior of the control statement.

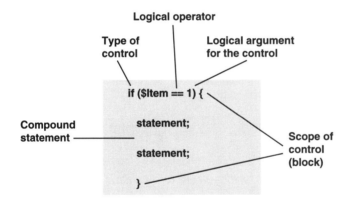

Figure 10.1
Conditional statements serve as gateways to other statements.

Program Flow

Program flow consists of the path of logic your program follows when you execute it. The path of logic can vary from program execution to program execution due to the logical decisions you embed in your program. Control statements embody logical decisions, but both using and not using control statements serve to guide the flow of your program. Given this situation, three patterns of activity characterize the flow of most programs:

❋ **Sequence.** The statements a program contains execute one after another. It might be said that statements execute as the program presents them, but if you use goto operators to call functions, you can create a program in which the order of the statements in the text no longer corresponds to the sequence of their execution.

✻ **Selection.** You can embed decisions in a program that determines whether given blocks of the program are to be entered. The flow of the program depends on the outcomes of the decisions. Selection can involve single decisions or multiple decisions.

✻ **Repetition.** A program can execute such that certain blocks of its statements execute over and over again, according to a set number of repetitions that a counter controls or according to given conditions. If a condition is true, a block of your program repeatedly executes. If the condition becomes no longer true, then the repeated executions cease.

Flow and Sequence

Programs flow sequentially when one statement after another executes until you reach the end of the program. Usually, the statements in a program that employ only sequential logic execute in the order in which you see them in the text of the program. You can alter this situation if you use labels and "go to" instructions, but even then it remains that your program executes according to a sequential logic. No decisions occur. Rather, you set a path, and the program follows it. Figure 10.2 illustrates the actions of a program that executes according to sequential logic.

Figure 10.2
When a program executes sequentially, it moves invariably from one statement to another from beginning to end.

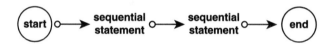

Table 10.1 provides discussion of a few of the terms related to sequential statements. The sequential flow of a program can include subroutines (also known as functions or methods). Chapter 12 covers the use of functions. The use of functions also relates to modules (see Chapter 13).

Table 10.1   Discussion of Sequential Terms

Term	Discussion
The semicolon (;)	You employ the semicolon to create a statement. A sequence consists of a set of statements.
Operator precedence	Operators possess precedence. In Chapter 5, Table 5.1 provides a summary of the operators Perl provides. The table also indicates their precedence.

Term	Discussion
Parentheses	Use of parentheses can group operations. Parentheses deserve special notice because they provide a way to override the precedence of operators. You exert control over their associations.
goto	Perl provides a goto operator. When you use this operator, you guide the flow of the program using target labels.
Blocks	A block is a labeled sequence of statements defined by some type of name and usually enclosed in parentheses.
Subroutines	Subroutines are also known as functions or methods. A function can be viewed as a labeled block. The label of the block identifies the block, and when you "call" the block in the flow of a program, you in essence continue to sequentially execute the program.

You can find programming examples and extended explanations of items in subsequent sections of this chapter and in Chapter 11.

goto Problems

Programs that involve solely sequential operations tend to be rare, but it remains that sequence lies at the basis of all programs. Statements execute one after another. As is the case with those that employ selection and repetition control structures, a program that uses only sequential statements can still present programmers with problems relating to duration and order. The order of execution brings to light the widely accepted notion that use of the goto operator tends to create problems.

The goto operator redirects the flow of a program to a point in a program that a label designates. When you use the goto operator to redirect the flow of the program, the flow goes from the statement containing goto to the point designated by the label. Convention dictates that you should capitalize labels. To define a label, you type the name of the label followed by a colon. You can access labels in any order.

At one time, programmers posed no particularly strong objections to the use of goto operations. The reason for this was that programs tended to lack subroutines (functions or methods), were short and simple, and were characterized by fairly extended commentary. Over time, this situation has changed. Now programmers usually consider use of the goto operator unacceptable. Listing10_02 illustrates the use of the goto operator.

```
#Listing10_02
goto AUTHOR;
TITLE:
($Lines =<<TITLE);
            The Goal
```

```
TITLE
print"\n".$Lines;


STANZA1:
($Lines=<<STANZA1);
I sprang on life's free course, I tasked myself,
    And questioned what and how I meant to be;
And leaving far behind me power and pelf,
    I fixed a goal-nor farther could I see.
STANZA1
print"\n".$Lines;
goto NOTE1;


STANZA2:
($Lines=<<STANZA2);
For this I toiled, for this I ran and bled,
    And proudly thought up my laurels there.
                        .  .  .
STANZA2
print"\n".$Lines;
goto SOURCE;


AUTHOR:
($Lines=<<AUTHOR);
Ellen Sturgis Hooper (1812-1848)
AUTHOR
print"\n".$Lines;
goto TITLE;


SOURCE:
($Lines=<<SOURCE);
Perry Miller, ed. The American Transcendentalists
(Baltimore: Johns Hopkins U. Press, 1957), p. 274.
SOURCE
print"\n".$Lines;
goto END;
```

```
NOTE1:
($Lines=<<NOTE1);
[Vocabulary "Pelf": Wealth or riches dishonestly acquired.
NOTE1
print"\n".$Lines;
goto STANZA2;

END:
```

Listing10_02 uses seven labels. The flow the program maintains remains sequential, but the labels dictate the order of the flow. To understand the program, you must trace it from beginning to end following the labels and the statements that incorporate `goto` operators. Figure 10.3 illustrates the output of Listing10_02. The order of the information the program presents appears simple when displayed: author, title, stanza, note, stanza, source. Each time you use the `goto` operator, the program jumps to the designated label.

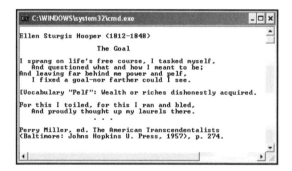

Figure 10.3
Sequential execution can be altered using `goto` operators.

Functional Ordering

Sequential organization of a program extends to the use of functions. A function creates a means of reordering statements in a program because it creates blocks of flow associated with the name of the function. A function provides both a block of flow and a set of parentheses that allow you to introduce specified values (arguments) into the functional block. Listing10_03 demonstrates the use of the `join()` function in this context. Variables defined earlier in the program are organized into output through the `join()` function. The sequence of their definition has little to do with the order in which you access them when you join and display them.

```
#Listing10_03

$SetA =
"\nHath this world, without me wrought,".
```

```
"\nOther substances than my thought?";

$SetB =
"\nLives it by my sense alone,".
"\nOr by essence of its own?";

$SetC =
"\nWill its life, with mine begun,".
"\nCease to be when that is done,".
"\nOr another consciousness".
"\nWith the self-same forms impress?";

$Title ="\nQuestionings";
$Author = "\nFrederic Henry Hedge 1805-1890";
$Source=
"\nPerry Miller, ed. The American Transcendentalists".
"\n(Baltimore: Johns Hopkins U. Press, 1957), p. 271.";

print "\n" . join(" ", ($Author, $Title, "\n",
                        $SetA, $SetC, "\n", $Source));
```

The poem by Frederic Hedge and the information relating to it can be set up in a series of scalars that the `join()` function organizes for display. See Figure 10.4. In Chapter 12, approaches to using functions to reorganize the sequential flow of a program receive extensive discussion.

Figure 10.4
A function uses its block and parentheses to organize flow of a program.

As the discussion in Chapter 5 emphasizes, the precedence of the parentheses in organizing numeric operations remains paramount. Consider the difference the position of the parentheses creates in Listing10_04.

❈ ❈ ❈

```
#Listing10_04

$Result = 6 + (5 + 8) * (9 + 4) * 2;
print "\n A: " . $Result ;


$Result = (6 + 5 + 8) * 9 + (4 * 2);
print "\n B: " . $Result ;


$Result = (6 + 5) + (8 * 9) + (4 * 2);
print "\n C: " . $Result ;
```

The output of Listing10_04 reveals that the parentheses create a wide discrepancy between the different results:

```
A: 344
B: 179
C: 91
```

Sequence and Incremental Operations

Incremental operations involve unary operators. The sequential actions of a program can drive incremental operations. If you employ incremental operations in relation to array indexes, the sequential flow of a program can affect how you retrieve elements from an array. Listing10_05 sets up a block of text representing a poem by Amos Alcott. It then makes use of the split() function and a regular expression to divide the poem into elements of an array. (Chapter 15 provides an extended discussion of regular expressions.) It then allows the sequential flow of the program to drive an iterator that retrieves the lines of the poem and displays them.

```
#Listing10_05
#1 Set up the data for the poem
($ABAlcottMan=<<ABALLCOTT);
He omnipresent is,
All round himself he lies,
Osiris spread abroad,
Upstarting in all eyes:
Nature has globed thought,
Without him she were not,
Cosmos from Chaos were not spoken,
And God bereft of visible token.
ABALLCOTT
```

```
$Title ="\nMan";
$Author = "\nAmos Bronson Alcott 1799-1888";
$Source=
"\nPerry Miller, ed. The American Transcendentalists".
"\n(Baltimore: Johns Hopkins U. Press, 1957), p. 257.";


#2 Split the array using the punctuation marks
@ABAlcott = split(/:|,|:/, $ABAlcottMan);


#3 Print the introductory lines
#Increment through the lines of the poem
#Print the source
$Itr = 0;
print "\n" . join("", $Author, $Title, "\n\n",
            $ABAlcott[$Itr], $ABAlcott[++($Itr)],
            $ABAlcott[++($Itr)], $ABAlcott[++($Itr)],
            $ABAlcott[++($Itr)], $ABAlcott[++($Itr)],
            $ABAlcott[++($Itr)], $ABAlcott[++($Itr)],
            "\n", $Source);
```

At comment #1 you use a text block to create a scalar that stores the text of a poem by Amos Alcott. You also create scalars that identify the author, title, and source text of the poem. In the lines that comment #2 identifies, you use the split() function to separate the lines of the poem into elements of an array (@ABAlcott). The split() function contains a regular expression that consists of three punctuation marks, a semicolon, a comma, and a colon (/ : | , | : /). The two slashes serve to bound the regular expression. The pipes (|) separate the items and indicate that any one of them can be used as a separator for the text the split() function processes.

In the lines associated with comment #3, you allow the sequential flow of the program to determine the order in which the print() function accesses its arguments. You begin by accessing the author and title information. Then, with each subsequent appearance of the @ABAlcott array in its scalar form, you retrieve an element from the array. After the poem, you identify the source. Figure 10.5 illustrates the output of Listing10_05.

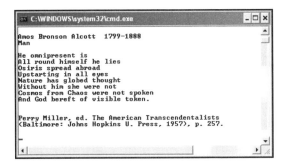

Figure 10.5
Arrays in combination with incremental operators add dimensions to sequential programs.

Relational and Logical Operators

In Chapters 3 and 5, you reviewed operators that relate to manipulating strings and numbers. Selection and repetition statements require continuous use of relational and Boolean operators. They also make use of the return values of such functions as the `exists()` and `defined()` functions.

Relational operators test for some form of equality, inequality, or identity. Figure 10.6 provides a summary view of the relational operators included in the discussions Chapters 3 and 5 presented. The return value designated by the open quotes signifies false. For practical purposes, the open quotes can be understood as zero, but their significance is to designate what can be viewed as a condition of being undefined. If a value is undefined and you submit it to a selection or sequence expression, it returns false.

Description	Numbers	Text	True/False Return	
Equal to	==	eq	1	" "
Not equal to	!=	ne	1	" "
Less than	<	lt	1	" "
Less than or equal to	<=	le	1	" "
Greater than	>	gt	1	" "
Greater than or equal to	>=	ge	1	" "
Comparatively equal to	<=>	cmp	−1 if left is less than right 0 if equal 1 if left is greater than right	

Figure 10.6
Relational operators underlie control expressions.

You evaluate sets of relational operations using Boolean AND and OR operators. Figure 10.7 illustrates the common Boolean approach to evaluating expressions.

The use of Boolean operations usually involves test conditions in which you have multiple criteria for verifying a given identity. For example, if you operate a website that retrieves

Figure 10.7
Boolean operators supplement relational operators.

AND &&

T	T	Two true statements are **true**.	T
T	F	A true statement and a false statement are **false**.	F
F	F	A false statement and a false statement are **false**.	F

OR ||

T	T	Two true statements are **true**.	T
T	F	A true statement and a false statement are **true**.	T
F	F	Two false statements are **false**.	F

Exclusive OR ^^

T	T	Two true statements are **false**.	F
T	F	A true statement and a false statement are **true**.	T
F	F	Two false statements are **false**.	F

information on American Transcendentalist poets, you might make use of the names of authors and poems to retrieve and print data. In such situations, a combination of relational and Boolean operators might arise. Listing10_06 provides a program that explores a version of this scenario.

```
#Listing10_06
#1 Data the user provides
$QueryAuthorName = "Christopher Cranch";
$QueryTitle = "Gnosis";

#2 Data retrieved
$Title = "Gnosis";
$Author = "Christopher Cranch";

($StanzaA=<<STANZA);
Thought is deeper than all speech,
    Feeling deeper than all thought
```

```
Souls to souls can never teach
    What unto themselves was taught.

        . . .

STANZA

($Source=<<SOURCE);
Perry Miller, ed. The American Transcendentalists
(Baltimore: Johns Hopkins U. Press, 1957), p. 262.
SOURCE

#3 Boolean evaluation combining relational operators
if( $QueryAuthorName eq $Author && $QueryTitle eq $Title
                    && defined($Author)){
    $Lines = join("\n",$Author, $Title, $StanzaA, $Source);
    print "\n\n$Lines ";
}
```

❄ **Note**
If you are not comfortable using the Boolean && and || operators, you can also use the words and
(for &&) and or (for ||).

Figure 10.8 illustrates the output of Listing10_06. At the start of the program, you simulate the
data that the user provides that you acquire from the database. At comment #3, prior to printing
the data, you check the information in three ways. The first two verifications involve checking
the name of the author and the name of the poem. The third involves verifying that any data at
all has been accessed. For two of the verifications, you employ string relational operators. For
the third you employ the defined() function, which causes the if selection statement not to
print if no data at all has been entered or retrieved. Figure 10.8 illustrates the result of the query
for Christopher Cranch.

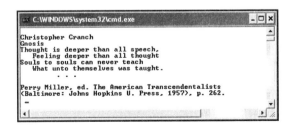

Figure 10.8
Simple selection can incorporate several forms of control.

Flow and Selection

Programs flow selectively when you place points of decision in them. A point of decision allows the flow of a program to take one or more alternate courses of action. The occasion for the alternate course of action consists of an expression or a statement. The selection control statement evaluates the information you provide to it and then renders a decision concerning whether to take an alternate course of action.

In simple selection control statements, you face a situation in which only one alternative exists: Perform a given action or do not perform it. Consider an analogous situation. As you walk along a street, you approach a storefront. You either go in or you continue to walk. Either you perform an action or you do not perform an action. Figure 10.9 illustrates this form of selection statement.

In more complex forms of selection statements, you select from among a range of alternatives. As an analogy, think of walking along a supermarket aisle. You come to the section of the supermarket dedicated to canned soup. You select from among many candidates. In complex selection statements, several alternatives are at hand. Figure 10.9 illustrates only a simple form of selection statement.

Figure 10.9
A selection control statement diverts the flow of a program if it finds a given condition to be true.

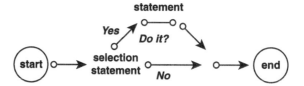

Table 10.2 provides discussion of keywords, concepts, and operators that you are likely to encounter as you work with selection statements in Perl.

Table 10.2 Discussion of Selection Terms

Term	Discussion
if	The if control statement is known as a *single-entry/single-exit control statement*. You follow it with an expression in parentheses to be evaluated. You then follow up the statement with a block you create with curly braces.
if else	The if else statement provides a categorical form of selection. If one course of action is not taken, then another course of action is taken. You are limited to two mutually exclusive actions.
if/elsif/else	In Perl the expression does not read else if. Rather it is elsif (minus the "e"). The only time you type else is for the final tested condition. You can test several cases or alternative courses of action. If one course of action is not taken, then any among several others might be taken. This is known as a *multiple case selection statement*.

Term	Discussion
unless	The unless control statement allows you to base a selection on a false condition, so given the presence or identification of a given value, you can determine not to perform a given action.

*You can find programming examples and extended explanations of items in subsequent sections of this chapter and in Chapter 11.

Selection Using the if Control Statement

The if control statement is known as a single-entry, single-exit control statement. The reason for this is that it sets one condition and allows you to access one block of statements. The if statement tests for the truth of a given condition. If the expression the statement evaluates does not render true, then statements that follow in the control block are not performed. To be true, the result of a condition must possess a value that is not undefined or a zero. The if statement can on this basis handle expressions that test strings and numbers. As shown previously in the example relating to retrieving a poem from a data store, it can easily handle expressions that combine Boolean and relational operators. Listing10_07 provides examples of selection statements used with both relational and Boolean operations.

#Listing10_07

```
#1 block containing text
$Itr = 1;
($OrphicSayings=<<ORPHICSAYINGS);
1. Enthusiasm
Believe, youth, that your heart is your oracle...
2. Hope
Hope deifies man; it is the apotheosis of the soul;
the prophecy and fulfillment of her destinies.
3. Immortality
The grander my conception of being, the nobler any future.
4. Vocation
Engage in nothing that cripples or degrades you.
Your first duty is self-culture, self-evaluation. . .
5. Sensualism
He who marvels at nothing, who feels nothing to be
mysterious, but must needs bare all things to sense,
lacks both wisdom and piety.
6. Aspiration
```

The insatiableness of her desires is an augury of the soul's eternity.
ORPHICSAYINGS

```
#2 Split the text at numbers
@ABAlcott = split(/\d.\s/, $OrphicSayings);


#3 Set up strings for display
# Create random numbers

$Title ="
Orphic Sayings";
$Author = "\nAmos Bronson Alcott 1799-1888";
$Source=
"\nPerry Miller, ed. The American Transcendentalists".
"\n(Baltimore: Johns Hopkins U. Press, 1957), pp. 86-88.";


$Itr = 0;
$Itr = 1 + int(rand(6));
print "\n(---)" . $Itr;


#4 Various forms of selection statement
# Compounded

if($Itr != 2 && $Itr != 4){
    print "\n(***)" . $Author. $Title . "\n"
            . $ABAlcott[$Itr] . "\n". $Source;
}
#5 valuation of equality

if($Itr == 2){
    print "\n(**)" . $Author. $Title . "\n"
            . $ABAlcott[$Itr] . "\n". $Source;
}


#6 Compound: less than greater than
if($Itr > 3 && $Itr < 5)
```

```
{
    print "\n (*)" . $Author. $Title . "\n"
              . $ABAlcott[$Itr] . "\n". $Source;
}
```

In line lines trailing comment #1 in Listing10_07, you set up a labeled block, including a few aphorisms extracted from Amos Alcott's writings. Numbers followed by periods and spaces separate the aphorisms. The name of the block is ORPHICSAYINGS, which is derived from the name of the work from which the aphorisms have been taken ("Orphic Sayings"). You assign the block to a scalar identifier ($OrphicSayings).

At comment #2 you employ the split() function with a regular expression as its first argument to extract elements from the block and store them in an array (@ABAlcott). The split() function and its arguments are as follows:

```
@ABAlcott = split(/\d.\s/, $OrphicSayings);
```

The regular expression (/\d.\s/) designates that the split should occur when the function detects a combination of any number (\d) followed by any character (.), followed by a white space (\s). The action of the split() function creates six elements in the array, one for each aphorism.

In the lines associated with comment #3, you create strings to hold author, title, and source information. You also generate a random number. Six items reside in the array, and the index of the first value is 1. You must generate a range of values that extends from 1 to 6. When you use the int() function to transform the output of the rand() function set at 6 into an integer and then add 1, the numbers that result range from 1 to 6. (Recall from the discussion in Chapter 5 that the highest value you obtain with 6 as the control consists of a number just short of 6. To obtain six, you add 1 and then remove the digits to right of the decimal point.)

The lines trailing comment #4 provide an expression that uses the AND (&&) operator to join the actions of two relational operators. Each relational operator tests for values not equal to (!=) 2 and 4. If the value the rand() function generates and assigns to $Itr equals neither of these numbers, then the expression evaluates to true, and the print statement that follows processes the result.

To attend to the two numbers the first selection statement excludes, at comment #5 you employ a test for equality with the integer 2. If the expression evaluates to true, then the aphorism associated with 2 is printed. At comment #6, you use an elaborate approach to printing the aphorism associated with 4. This approach again employs the AND operator. In this case, the expression isolates a value that is less than 5 and greater than 3. Figure 10.10 illustrates the output of Listing10_07.

Figure 10.10
Different expressions em-
bedded in if selection
statements allow you to
display a range of six
items.

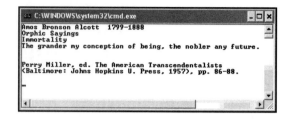

The unless Structure

The unless selection statement tests for a negative condition. Whereas the if statement processes statements in its block when an expression is true, the unless statement processes
statements only when the expression is *not* true. Listing10_08 provides an example of the use
of unless to provide a slightly different appearance for quotes from Henry D. Thoreau's
Walden.

```
#Listing10_08
#1 block containing text
$Itr = 1;
($WaldenLines=<<WALDENLINES);
1. The mass of men live lives of quiet desperation.
2. Most of the luxuries, and many of the so-called
comforts of life, are not only not indispensable,
but positive hindrances to the elevation of mankind.
3. Every child begins the world again, to some extent,
and loves to stay outdoors, even in wet and cold.
4. If I knew for a certainty that a man was coming to
my house with the conscious design of doing me good,
I should run for my life . . . .
5. The heroic books, even if printed in the character
of our mother tongue, will always be in a dead
language to degenerate times . . . .
6. No man ever followed his genius until it misled him.
WALDENLINES

#2 Split the text at numbers
@HDThoreau = split(/\d.\s/, $WaldenLines);

#3 Set up strings for display
```

```
|# Create random numbers
$Author = "\nHenry D. Thoreau 1817-1862";
$Source=
"\nHenry D. Thoreau, Walden ".
"\n(Philadelphia: Courage Press, 1990).";


$Itr = 0;
$Itr = 1 + int(rand(6));
print "\n(---)" . $Itr;

#4 Various forms of selection statement

#Can be 1 2 3
unless($Itr == 6 || $Itr == 5 || $Itr == 4){
    print "\n(***)" . $Author . "\n".
            $HDThoreau[$Itr] . "\n" . $Source;
}
#5 valuation of equality
#It can be 4 5 6
unless($Itr == 1 || $Itr == 2 || $Itr == 3 ){
    print "\n(**)" . $Author. "\n"
            . $HDThoreau[$Itr] . "\n". $Source;
}
```

At comment #1 in Listing10_08, you set up a block of text and assign it to a scalar, $Walden-Lines. Six quotes from Thoreau's *Walden* appear in the block. A number, a period, and a space separate them from each other. At comment #2, you use the split() function to separate the quotes in the text into elements of an array (@HDThoreau). The first argument of the split() function designates the criteria you want to use to separate a body of text into segments. In this case, you provide a regular expression (/\d.\s/), which designates that whenever the function finds a number (\d), any character (.), and a blank space (\s) together, it should break the text.

The lines associated with comment #3 define scalars to identify the author and his work and then generate a random number using the rand() function. The rand() function generates a range of numbers that is greater than or equal to zero and less than the number you supply as an argument to the rand() function. For this reason, you "shift" the value by one, so the range becomes 1 to 6. You do not need 0 because the 0 index of the @HDThoreau array holds no data.

In the lines trailing comment #4, you set up two `print()` functions. The print functions possess slightly different adornments. The user of the program sees different adornments, depending on where the quote lies in the @HDThoreau array. The first `unless` selection statement determines that unless the number of the quote lies in the range of 4, 5, and 6, you see vertical lines, as Figure 10.11 shows. The second `unless` selection statement excludes the range of 1, 2, and 3. If you execute the program several times, you can see the adornments change.

Figure 10.11
Use of `unless` statements
allows you to implement
controls that resemble the
`if` statements.

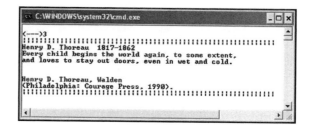

The if...else Selection Structure

The `if...else` selection structure accommodates exclusive choices. You can use it to make one choice or another. To make a choice, you set up one condition. If the condition proves true, then the selection statement directs the flow of the program to the primary `if` block. If the condition does not prove true, then the statement directs the flow to a catch-all `else` block. No conditional expression governs the `else` portion of the structure. Listing10_09 explores the use of the `if...else` selection structure, but it adds to the basic use by embedding a second `if...else` selection structure in the first `if...else` selection structure.

```
#Listing10_09
#1 Generate a random number
#convert it to a character
$Itr = 0;
$Itr = 1 + int(rand(3));
$Itr += 96; #Make it 97, 98, 99;

$Char = sprintf("%c", $Itr);

#2 Set up two strings with the names of poems
#Ralph Waldo Emerson
$RWE = join("\n ", " Ralph Waldo Emerson",
                "The Apology", "Uriel", "Destiny",
                "Each and All", "The Eternal Pan",
```

```
                              "Hamatreya", "Earth-Song", "Brahma");
#Henry D. Thoreau
$HDT = join("\n " , " Henry D. Thoreau ",
                      "Sympathy ", "Sic Vita",
                      "Friendship", "Prayer",
                      "Independence", "The Inward Morning",
                      "My Love Must Be as Free");


#Sarah Margaret Fuller
$SMF = join ("\n " , " Sarah Margaret Fuller ",
                      "Encouragement" , "Dryad Song",
                      "The Highlands", "Winged Sphinx",
                      "The Passion-Flower");
#3 Make an exclusive choice with an embedded
# selection statement and print
if($Char eq 'a'){
        $ToPrint = $RWE;
}
else{
    if($Char eq 'b'){
        $ToPrint = $SMF;
    }
    else{ #only with c
        $ToPrint = $HDT;
    }
}
print "\n(" . $Char . ")". $ToPrint;
```

The lines in Listing10_09 that comment #1 identifies generate a random number each time the program executes. The number falls in a range that extends from 1 to 3, and you add 96 to it so that the three resulting integer possibilities are 97, 98, and 99. As is discussed in Chapter 5, these three values represent the ASCII values for lowercase "a," "b," and "c." To convert the numbers to characters, you use the sprintf() function and the %c type specifier. You assign the resulting letter to a scalar, $Char.

In the lines associated with comment #2, you create three strings using the join() function. The strings identify one of three Transcendentalist poets, Emerson, Fuller, or Thoreau, and then name a few of their poetical works. For the first argument of the join() function, you designate the character you want to use to separate items as the function concatenates them into a string. You assign a new line character to this argument.

At comment #3 you set up an if...else selection statement. The control expression for the if statement tests $Char for the letter a. If the expression evaluates to true, then inside the if block, you assign the string that stores information related to Emerson ($RWE) to another scalar, $ToPrint. The flow of the statement then exits the conditional blocks, and the next statement it encounters is the print() function. The print() function prints the string you have assigned to $ToPrint.

If the evaluation of $Char for the letter a renders a false outcome, then the flow of the program passes to the else block. When the flow enters this block, another if...else selection statement awaits it. This time $Char is evaluated in relation to b. If the evaluation results in true, then information on Margaret Fuller is assigned to $ToPrint, and as you see in Figure 10.12, her name and the list of her works appear as the program's output.

The else block of the embedded loop accepts the program flow whenever the control expression of the embedded if selection renders false. Only the third value (c) causes this to occur. With this occurrence, as Figure 10.12 illustrates, you see the information on Thoreau appear as output.

Figure 10.12
The if...else statement provides an exclusive form of selection.

The if...elsif...else Statement

When you use the if...elsif...else selection statement, it is important to notice that the spelling of the middle term is "elsif" rather than "else if." Likewise, the terminating statement is spelled "else." This is known as a *cascading* or *multiple-case* selection structure. The structure works on a fairly efficient basis. The flow of the program enters the if statement that heads the structure. If the control expression evaluates to true, then the first block executes. Following this, the flow of the program exits the structure completely.

If the first evaluation renders a false outcome, then the flow of the program passes to the first elsif control statement. If this proves true, the statements in this first block are executed. When this activity concludes, the flow of the program exits the structure completely.

You set up only one if statement in the structure. You likewise set up only one else statement. The else statement is a *default* condition. Since it does not support an evaluation expression, when the flow of the program enters the `else` block, it does so because all the explicit evaluations the structure supports have been exhausted.

> **Note**
> You do not have to have an `else` statement at the end of the `elsif` chain. If you do not include a default, it is a good idea to provide an `elsif` selection that covers exceptions. See the Geology Review example in Chapter 11.

Listing10_10 explores the use of the cascading case structure and allows the `else` statement to process the statements related to the last of four random letters the program generates. This is an acceptable approach to processing the flow of the program, but it might not be the safest. The safest approach is to use the `else` statement to process exceptional conditions (conditions outside those expected).

> **Note**
> Experienced programmers usually try to anticipate all conditions. When you set up a structure that tests a narrow range of possibilities, it is a good practice to make it so that your program also knows what to do with the values that do not fall within this range. You can accomplish this using the `else` statement at the end of an `elsif` chain.

You can place as many `elsif` statements in a cascading structure as you want. If the number of cases becomes extremely large, it is best to turn to the use of a hash lookup. Chapter 11 provides discussion of this topic.

```
#Listing10_10
#1 Generate a random number
#convert it to a character
$Itr = 0;
$Itr = 1 + int(rand(4));
$Itr += 96; #Make it 97, 98, 99, 100;
$Char = sprintf("%c", $Itr);

#2 Set up strings with the names of authors and poems
#Ralph Waldo Emerson
$RWE = join("\n ", " Ralph Waldo Emerson",
                "The Apology", "Uriel", "Destiny",
```

```
                        "Each and All", "The Eternal Pan",
                        "Hamatreya", "Earth-Song", "Brahma");
#Henry D. Thoreau
$HDT = join("\n " , " Henry D. Thoreau ",
                        "Sympathy ", "Sic Vita",
                        "Friendship", "Prayer",
                        "Independence", "The Inward Morning",
                        "My Love Must Be as Free");


#Sarah Margaret Fuller
$SMF = join ("\n " , " Sarah Margaret Fuller ",
                        "Encouragement" , "Dryad Song",
                        "The Highlands", "Winged Sphinx",
                        "The Passion-Flower");


#Caroline Sturgis Tappan
$CST = join ("\n " , " Caroline Sturgis Tappan",
                        "Lyric" , "Life" ,
                        "Art and Artist" ,
                        "Lines" , "The Hero");


#3 Make a choice
    if($Char eq 'a'){
        $ToPrint = $RWE;
    }
    elsif($Char eq 'b'){
        $ToPrint = $SMF;
    }
    elsif($Char eq 'c'){
        $ToPrint = $HDT;
    }
    else{
        $ToPrint = $CST;
    }
print "\n(" . $Char . ")". $ToPrint;
```

At comment #1 in Listing10_10, you employ the `rand()` function to generate random numbers in a range extending from 1 to 4. To accomplish this, you set the argument of the `rand()` function to 4. You employ the `int()` function to convert the rational number the `rand()` function returns to an integer. You then add 1 to the integer value to shift it so that its minimum is 1 and its maximum is 4. You assign the result to `$Itr`.

Given the conversion of the random value to an integer, you add 96 to the value of `$Itr` so that the resulting number corresponds to the ASCII values of the lowercase letters "a," "b," "c," and "d." These letters become random values that allow you later in the program to use the cascading selection structure to choose from among a set of four poets.

In the lines comment #2 identifies, you set up four scalar identifiers with strings containing information on nineteenth century writers associated with American Transcendentalism. To create the strings, you employ the `join()` function. For the first argument of the `join()` function, you insert a newline character. The string the function joins consists of the names of the poets and the titles of a number of their poems. The strings that result from the four calls to `join()` are assigned to four scalars, each representing one of the writers (`$CST`, `$SMF`, `$HDT`, `$RWE`).

At comment #2 you create a selection structure. The structure evaluates the random characters generated by the lines associated with comment #1. The `if` selection statement contains an expression that tests for the validity of "a." If this proves true, the flow of the program passes into the first block, and the value of `$RWE` is assigned to `$ToPrint`. The flow of the program then exits the structure, and the next statement encountered is the `print()` function. The `print()` function prints the string that has been assigned to `$ToPrint`.

If the first selection statement results in a false evaluation, the control passes to the first `elsif` statement. The control expression of this structure evaluates `$Char` in relation to "b." If the evaluation renders a true outcome, then control passes into the first `elsif` block, and the string associated with Margaret Fuller is assigned to `$ToPrint`. Following the assignment, the flow of the program exits the selection structure, and the `print()` function is called.

If the first `elsif` renders a false result, the second `elsif` is evaluated. The actions that characterize the `if` statement and the first `elsif` statement characterize all subsequent `elsif` statements. The procedure always involves exiting the selection structure following the performance of actions in a given structure if the control expression allows the flow of the program to enter a given block.

Unless all control expressions in the selection structure render false, the flow of the program never reaches the `else` statement at its tail. In the case of Listing10_10, the `else` statement is reached only if the random character generated for the program is "d." Since none of the other explicit control expressions evaluate `$Char` for this value, the control passes implicitly to the else statement if the value is "d." As mentioned previously, this does not constitute the safest course of action, but in this instance it poses no risk. Figure 10.13 illustrates the output of Listing10_10 when the selection structure defaults to true for the information relating to Caroline Sturgis Tappan. The "d" indicates control passed to the else selection statement to process information relating to her.

Figure 10.13
Multiple case selections accommodate extensive bodies of information.

Conclusion

This chapter has provided the first two parts of a three-part treatment of control structures. In Chapter 11, the discussion continues with repetition statements. In this chapter, you have concentrated on statements that involve sequence and selection in the flow of programs. At the start of the chapter, you reviewed the notion that a program consists of a set of statements. Unless you introduce controls that force it to do otherwise, when a program executes, it processes one statement after another. Such basic program activity is known as the sequential flow of a program.

You can introduce involved procedures into the sequential flow of a program if you make use of such features as functional subroutines, parentheses, array storage, and goto operations. The extent to which you can alter a sequential flow becomes evident when you make heavy use of the goto operator. Given the use of labels and frequent jumps from one place in a program to another, a program can become nearly impossible to understand. This situation has been responsible for a widespread trend among programmers to avoid using goto operators.

When you introduce selection statements, you again have the option of performing a wide variety of activities not possible with sequential statements alone. Among the selection statements available to you are the single and exclusive selection statements (if and if...else). You can also use a negative form of selection, the unless statement. For more involved operations, you have the cascading or multiple case structure. This is the if...elsif...else statement.

Control expressions involve using relational and Boolean operators. You can combine such operators into compound statements. Such statements can be used in all forms of selection, and as Chapter 11 shows, extend to repetition structures as well.

This text incorporates quotations from writers usually associated with a literary movement known as Transcendentalism that flourished during the 1800s. Here are the texts used as sources:

Miller, Perry, editor. *The American Transcendentalists: Their Prose and Poetry*. Baltimore: Johns Hopkins University Press, 1957 (1981).

Thoreau, Henry David. *Walden*. Philadelphia: Running Press, 1990.

11 } Control Structures and Applications

Chapter 10 introduced compound statements and selection control statements. In this chapter, you continue to explore control statements as they apply to repetition in programming. Repetition is the third primary form in which the flow of a program can be controlled. Perl provides some forms of repetition that can be applied to almost any situation. Among these are `for`, `while`, `until`, `do...while`, and `do...until`. Other control statements work especially well with arrays. The chief among these is the `foreach` control statement. The `each` control statement provides a ready way to access keys and elements in a hash. A number of Perl operators supplement repetition and other control activities. Among these operators are `next`, `last`, `redo`, and `continue`. In addition to standard programming controls statements, Perl also provides block tags and the controls you can apply to them. In relation to these and other concerns, the topics this chapter explores are as follows:

- ❈ Basic uses of the `for` control statement
- ❈ Basic uses of the `while` control statement
- ❈ Using infinite loops with routines that break out of the loop
- ❈ Using control expressions and the ends of control blocks
- ❈ Creating blocks and relating them to sequential selection
- ❈ Creating applications that allow you to explore control

Flow as Repetition

Repetition characterizes the flow of a program that at some point repeatedly executes a given statement or compound statement. Figure 11.1 illustrates the simplest type of repetition control statement. The statement involves a single block or loop of statements (bounded by curly braces). The control statement precedes the loop and includes an expression that is evaluated as the flow of the program enters the loop and as it iterates through the statements in the loop. As long as

❈ ❈ ❈

the expression evaluates true, the flow of the program continues to iterate through the loop. An analogy might be feeding coins into a parking meter to make it register the longest parking interval possible. You have in hand a number of coins. You feed in a coin. The meter clicks, and you the see the time indicator rise. You feed in another coin, and the indicator rises again. When the indicator reaches a maximum, you exit your loop of activity and go on to the next item on your agenda.

Figure 11.1
Repetition in a program involves repeated execution of a statement or block of statements according to an expression that continually evaluates to true.

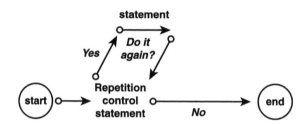

Repetition statements become more complex when they involve embedded loops. An embedded loop consists of a loop within a loop. An analogy might be that you approach a parking meter with a friend. You want to max out the meter, but your supply of change is limited. You turn to your friend. She searches her purse for coins, and each time she finds one, she hands it to you. Your loop of activity contains her loop of activity. Table 11.1 provides general discussion of operators and keywords that relate to repetition statements in Perl.

Table 11.1   Discussion of Repetition Terms

Term	Discussion
while	This statement comes at the beginning of a loop. The expression you use for a while statement checks for a result of true. As long as the expression results in true, the while block continues to execute. When the statement renders a false result, then the flow of the program exits the while block.
until	This statement comes at the beginning of a loop. This statement repeats until the test expression is true. When the expression becomes true, it discontinues the loop.
do...while	This statement places the test expression at the end of the loop. The flow of the program enters its block without being tested. When the flow of the program reaches the end of the block, however, it's then tested. If the test evaluates to true, then the block statements are performed again. The process repeats while the test expression evaluates to true. If it evaluates to false, the flow of the program exits the block.
do...until	This statement resembles the do...while statement. In this case, however, it repeats the statement or statements in the block only if the tested expression is false. When the test expression is true, it exits the loop.

Term	Discussion
for	A `for` loop can be set up in a number of ways. It can use expressions, separated by semicolons, for initialization, setting the loop condition, and establishing the step expression. You have the option of leaving one or all of these out of the `for` statement. You must always use two semicolons as part of the test expression, even if you leave everything else out. The `for` statement precedes the block and allows the statement or statements in the block to continue to execute as long as its control conditions are true. If you set no conditions, then you create an infinite loop.
loop controls	If you set no conditions to control a loop, then you create an infinite loop. If your program enters an infinite loop, you have no option but to terminate its execution by using the operating system.
next	If you place a `next` operator anywhere inside a loop, it causes the flow of your program to skip the remaining statements in the loop. It does not skip out of the loop entirely, however. Instead, it causes the flow of activity to go back to the point of control. You can use a label with the `next` operator. To employ `next` with a label, you follow it with the name of a label (usually in capital letters). The label itself can be placed at a point of control. You follow a label with a colon (`LABEL:`).
last	This operator allows you to entirely exit a loop. It can also allow you to access a label in the same fashion employed with the `next` operator.
redo	The `redo` operator causes the flow of the program to jump back to the beginning of a loop without evaluating the control expression of the loop. The result is that the statements in the loop execute even if the control expression if normally evaluated would cause the loop to terminate.
continue	The `continue` operator is another version of a break. It causes the flow of the program to immediately exit a loop. The flow of the program continues from after the closing brace of the loop. Subsequent statements in the loop are ignored.

You can find programming examples and extended explanations of items in subsequent sections of this chapter.

Repetition and the for Statement

The `for` statement provides the quintessential vehicle for elementary repetition in a program. It proves convenient to use because it provides you with the chance to introduce three arguments into your repetition activities. Refer to Figure 11.2 as you review the items in the following list:

❋ **The control value.** The control value is a scalar identifier that establishes a starting value. The starting value is often set at zero (0).

❋ **The limit.** A second expression uses a relational operator to compare the value of the control identifier with a another value, one that you often provide as a constant value.

❋ **The incremental expression.** The incremental expression usually consists of the control value suffixed or prefixed by an incremental operator.

Figure 11.2
The basic for control
allows three arguments.

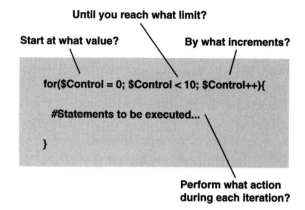

Listing11_01 demonstrates a few variations on the for statement. The basic for statement uses three arguments separated by semicolons. Depending on the problem you seek to solve, you can place these argument inside or outside the parentheses. You can increment the control within the control block, for example, or you can initialize the counter prior to the for statement.

```
#Listing11_01

#1 Basic for repetition statement
#Control, Limit, and Counter

$Example = 1;
@Minerals = qw(Covelite Galena Stibinite
               Molybdenite Graphite Pyrolusite Basalt);

$LIMIT = scalar(@Minerals);

# 1 Set the counter at 0 to accommodate the array
print "\n\n Example " . $Example++ .
': for($Itr = 0; $Itr < $LIMIT ; $Itr++)' ." \n ";

for($Itr = 0; $Itr < $LIMIT ; $Itr++)
{
    print "\n " . $Itr . " $Minerals[$Itr].";
}
# 2 Increment inside the loop by increments of 2
print "\n\n Example " . $Example++ .
```

```
': for($Itr = 0; $Itr < $LIMIT ;)' ." \n ";

for($Itr = 0; $Itr < $LIMIT ;)
{
    print "\n " . $Itr . " $Minerals[$Itr].";
    $Itr = $Itr + 2;
}


# 3 Pre-decrement operator inside the loop ; set limit outside
print "\n\n Example " . $Example++ .
': for(; $Itr >=0;)' ." \n ";
$Itr = $LIMIT;
for(;$Itr > 0 ;)
{
    --($Itr);
    print "\n " . $Itr . " $Minerals[$Itr].";
}
```

At comment #1, you set up an array consisting of the names of a few elements. You also employ the scalar() function to access the number of elements in the array, which you assign to the $LIMITS identifier. Given that you have assigned the number of elements to $LIMIT, you then proceed to implement a for repetition statement that assumes what might be called the standard form of a for test expression. And identifier, $Itr, is set at 0. You control the maximum value $Itr can achieve by setting a condition that restricts it to values less than $LIMIT. To move the counter, you employ the increment operator ($Itr++). The results follow Example 1 in Figure 11.3.

At comment #2, you set up a for statement that places the incremental operation inside the for block. The statement that advances the counter does so in increments of 2. You see the results following Example 2 in Figure 11.3.

A still different approach appears in the lines trailing comment #3. With this implementation of the for statement, you decrement the loop. After setting the maximum value for the repetition statement, you use the middle condition of the control expression to limit the values of the counter to those that are greater than 0. Inside the for block, you decrement the counter in decrements of 2. The results appear after Example 3 in Figure 11.3.

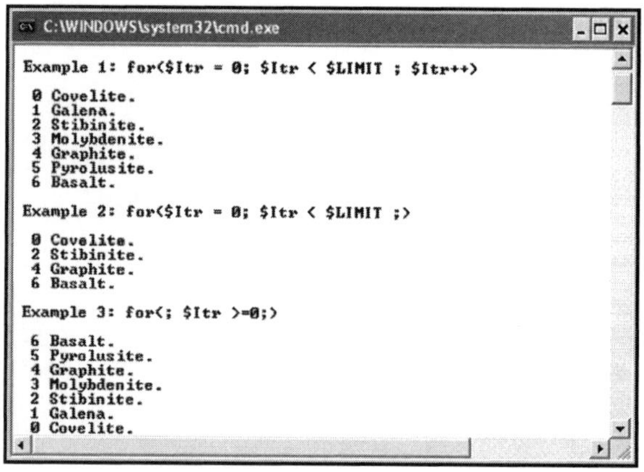

Figure 11.3
You can position the
control elements of a for
statement inside and out-
side the for block.

Exiting for Loops Using last

In addition to using the for statement control, you can implement loops that employ the
last operator. The last operator causes the flow of the program to exit a repetition block.
Listing11_02 provides examples using the if and unless selection statements.

```
#Listing11_02
#1 Set up some data
$Example = 1;
@Minerals = qw(Covelite Galena Stibinite
               Molybdenite Graphite Pyrolusite);
$LIMIT = scalar(@Minerals);

print "\n\n Example " . $Example++ .
': for(;;){unless(){last;:}}' ." \n ";
#2 Set the counter at 0 to accommodate the array
$Itr = 0;
for(;;)
{
    print "\n " . $Itr . " $Minerals[$Itr++].";
    unless($Itr < $LIMIT)
    {
        last;
    }
}
```

```
print "\n\n Example " . $Example++ .
': for(;;){if(){last;}}' . " \n ";
#3 Use an if selection statement to exit using last
$Itr = 0;
for(;;)
{
    print "\n " . $Itr . " $Minerals[$Itr++].";
    if($Itr >= $LIMIT)
    {
        last;
    }
}
```

At comment #1 in Listing11_02, you set up an array (@Minerals) to use for the for loops in the program. You also use the scalar() function to derive the number of elements in the array.

The lines trailing comment #2 implement a for control statement that features no control statement between the parentheses. The counter ($Itr) is set up prior to the for statement. Inside the statement block, you use an unless selection statement to assess when the counter becomes greater than the limit. When this happens, you invoke the last operator. The last operator exits the for loop.

In the lines that comment #2 identify, you again set up a for repetition statement that contains no controls between the parentheses. You define the iterator prior to the control statement. Inside the for block, you employ an if selection statement to assess when the counter exceeds the limit. When it exceeds the limit, you exit the for block. Figure 11.4 illustrates the output of Listing11_02.

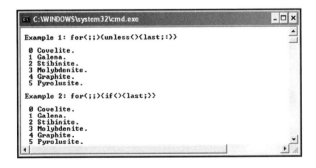

Figure 11.4
You can employ if and unless selection in conjunction with last to exit repetition blocks.

Infinite for Loops with Controls

Infinite loops allow programs to continue operating until you issue an instruction that breaks the looping activity. To break out of a loop, as discussed previously, you can use the `last` operator. Listing11_03 provides an example of an application that performs its work inside an infinite `for` loop. As the loop executes, it repeatedly encounters a temporary halting point. This is a handle. The handle pauses the program until you enter a number or letter to tell a multiple selection structure embedded in the loop what you want to do next. Figure 11.5 illustrates the opening view of the program. The program provides information about igneous, metamorphic, and sedimentary rocks. When you enter a number, you select a body of information.

Figure 11.5
When the program displays the menu, type a number to view data of a given type of rock.

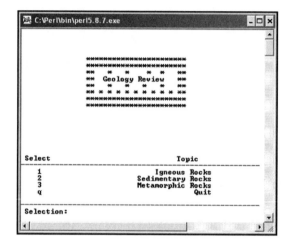

Figure 11.6 (following Listing11_03) shows you the information you can retrieve for sedimentary rocks. Obviously, in a world in which you can set up webpages or use windows and any number of other tools to create applications that retrieve and display data, the geological data program Listing11_03 presents leaves much to be desired. Still, it serves to show you one use of an infinite loop, the `last` operator, and a cascading selection structure. Even the most sophisticated Windows applications in the end use this same type of control.

```
#Listing11_03
#1 Block for the opening
system('cls');
$NL = "\n" ;

($RockType[0] = <<ROCKS);
```

```
* * * * * * * * * * * * * * * * * * * * * *
* * * * * * * * * * * * * * * * * * * * * *
* *     *     *     *     *     * *
* *    Geology Review     * *
* *     *     *     *     *     * *
* * * * * * * * * * * *
* * * * * * * * * * * * * * * * * * * * * *
* * * * * * * * * * * * * * * * * * * * *
```

```
ROCKS
#----------------------------------------------------------
#2 Create blocks to serve as data
($RockType[1] = <<ROCKS);


        1. Igneous Rocks


    Rocks and minerals that originate
    as magma are igneous. Magma is rock
    that has been heated to the melting
    point by tectonic pressures.
        Magma is a common feature of volcanic
    eruptions, but it exists only in the
    upper crust of the Earth. Deeper in the
    earth, pressures prevent rock from melting.
        Examples: porphyry, granite, pegmatite,
    gabbro. These rocks form the cores
    of mountains and are exposed by weathering.



ROCKS
#----------------------------------------------------------
```

```
($RockType[2] = <<ROCKS);
```

2. Sedimentary Rocks

Igneous rocks are exposed to erosion
in the form of wind and water. This is
known as weathering. Weathering causes
rocks to deteriorate (they crumble or
decompose).
    Decomposed rocks can be dissolved in
water or they can remain in small particles
and chunks that wind, earth movements,
glaciers or other events can move.
    Dissolved or decomposed rocks can be deposited
in layers at the bottoms of lakes or in
other places. They harden into layers to
    form new rocks. Sedimentary rocks almost
always have fossils in them.
    Examples: coal, shale, limestone, sandstone.

```
ROCKS
#----------------------------------------------------------
($RockType[3] = <<ROCKS);
```

3. Metamorphic Rocks

Metamorphic rocks are often formed
when the forces of the earth pulverize
igneous and sedimentary rocks and transform
them in to new rocks. The new rocks have new
textures and often consist of new minerals.
    Pressure significantly influences the
creation of metamorphic rocks, as do
chemical reactions.
    Examples: gneiss, schist, slate, marble,
quartzite.

```
ROCKS
#-----------------------------------------------------------
#A block for errors
($RockType[4] = <<ROCKS);



            ***********************
            ***********************
            **    *    *    *    *    **
            **    Geology Review   **
            **    *    *    *    *    **
            ** * * * * * * * * **
            ***********************
            ***********************


        Not a valid choice. Valid
        options are 1 to 3
        ...or q to quit.



ROCKS
#-----------------------------------------------------------
#3 Display the opening screen

print "$RockType[0]";      #First view of the program
for(;;) {                    #Infinite loop using for()
    print( "$NL");
    printf("%-15s %25s"," Select", "    Topic");
    printf("$NL" . "-" × 55 . $NL);
    printf( "%-20s %25s","    1" ,  "Igneous Rocks $NL");
    printf( "%-20s %25s","    2" ,  "Sedimentary Rocks $NL");
    printf( "%-20s %25s","    3" ,  "Metamorphic Rocks $NL");
    printf( "%-20s %25s","    q" ,  "Quit $NL");
    printf( "$NL" . "-" × 55);
    print( "$NL Selection: ");
```

265

❊ ❊ ❊

```
    $ControlChar = <STDIN>;
    chomp($ControlChar);
    system(cls);            #Call to the DOS system


#4 multiple case structure for the options displayed
    if(lc($ControlChar) eq 'q'){            #last exits the for loop
        last;                               #Exits the loop
    }elsif($ControlChar eq '1'){
        print "$RockType[1]";           #Retrieve from array
    }elsif($ControlChar eq '2'){            #Zero index is not used
        print "$RockType[2]";
    }elsif($ControlChar eq '3'){
        print "$RockType[3]";
#Replaces the else: you need to exclude everything except
#Valid options
    }elsif($ControlChar > 3 || $ControlChar < 1){
        print "$RockType[4]";
    }#end elsif
}#end menu for
```

At comment #1 of Listing11_03, you begin setting up blocks of text such as those you see displayed in the upper part of Figure 11.6. Clearly, storing text in a separate file or database and then introducing it to a program provides a better approach, but in this case, no damage results from creating a program wholly contained in one file. (See Chapter 12 for file IO procedures that help you reduce the size of a program that performs actions similar to those of Listing11_03.)

You set up a total of five blocks. Two of these blocks you dedicate to cosmetic effects. The first block you see at comment #1 provides the opening screen of the program (see Figure 11.5). At comment #2, you see the first of the next three blocks defined. These blocks provide narratives concerning three fundamental rock types. In each case, you create blocks of precisely the same number of lines. This allows the program user to refresh data to the screen without seeing fluctuations or changes in the position of the title, text, menu, or input line. Each display area includes 18 lines.

To define a display area, you count from the line following the line on which the block is defined. The block definition for metamorphic rocks is as follows:

```
    ($RockArray[3] = <<ROCKS);
```

As previous chapters have discussed, you assign the label (ROCK) using the assignment operator and the shift operator. When you define a block, you assign it to the index of an array, @RockType. You assign the blocks sequentially, beginning with the zero (0) index, which holds the opening screen message (as shown in Figure 11.6). Storage of the narratives on igneous, sedimentary, and metamorphic rocks corresponds to array indexes (1 through 3), and these are also the menu items used to retrieve the narratives. You store the error message screen in the array element corresponding to index 4.

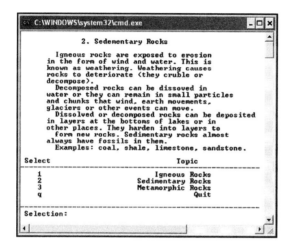

Figure 11.6
The block allows you to view the formatted text.

At comment #3 you begin the process of setting up the program for display. The first action the program visibly displays consists of printing the opening block to the monitor. This is the block shown in Figure 11.6.

The next action after displaying the starting block of the program involves creating an infinite loop:

```
for(;;) {
    #Lines left out
}
```

Such a loop proves hazardous unless you implement ways to halt it or break out of it. In this case, you are more than amply covered. As Figure 11.7 shows, you first pause the loop using the <STDIN> handle. This serves to prompt the user to enter a menu selection. The program user is afforded this opportunity once during each cycle of the for loop.

The user types a number (1, 2, 3) or a letter (q). A cascading selection structure processes this information a few lines later.

Figure 11.7
You halt the loop to solicit
input from the user.

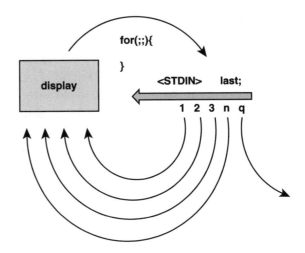

The specific lines that accomplish the work of halting the loop and prompting you for input are as follows:

```
$ControlChar = <STDIN>;
chomp($ControlChar);
system(cls);          #Call to the DOS system
```

When the program encounters the handle (<STDIN>), it immediately halts its execution while it waits for input. To process the input, you assign it to a scalar ($ControlChar). At the same time, when you press the Enter key to transmit the input to the program, you append a newline character to the data you enter. To eliminate this extra character, you call the chomp() function.

After removing the extra character from the input, you call the Perl system() function. The system() function allows you to interact with the operating system. The cls argument of the system() function is a DOS command that clears the screen.

> ❋ Using such a call in a command line application presents no problem; however, if you develop a Perl program for use in a browser, then calls of system() can create major problems. Among other things, because it calls directly to the operating system, it creates a "security violation." Browsers are not supposed to interact directly with your operating system.

Prior to halting the loop to provide input to the program, you make several calls to the print() and printf() functions to display the options available to the program user. These options appear in the bottom of the screenshot Figure 11.6 displays. To print the options to the screen, you might easily use another block. You could also use the join() function to create a single string that would require a single call to `print()`. As it is, the calls to `print()` and `printf()` represent a needed refinement.

The menu provides you with four input options. The three numerical options display information on metamorphic, sedimentary, and igneous rocks. The letter option allows you to exit. Comment #4 identifies the lines that attend to processing the input. A cascading selection structure provides five selection statements. As Chapter 11 discussed, each block of the selection structure allows you to process a different control expression.

The `if` selection statement processes the "q" character. When you type this character, you indicate you want to quit the program. As mentioned previously, quitting the program involves exiting the infinite `for` loop. The `last` operator provides a vehicle to accomplish this. When the program flow reaches the `last` operator, it immediately reroutes the flow of the program outside the most immediate repetition loop. Since the program contains only one repetition loop, this means that the execution of the `last` operator effectively ends the program.

Taking care of exceptional data input events also forms part of the work the selection structure performs. The final `elsif` statement provides a control expression that disallows any input that does not lie in the narrow range extending from 1 to 3. The letter "q" falls outside this range, but you avoid preempting its processing by processing exceptions at the end of the selection structure rather than the beginning.

> ❄ Providing "handlers" (such as the final `elsif` statement) for unexpected input is a basic precaution all experienced programmers take as they develop programs. A handler is a statement that accounts for data that falls outside the data you expect the user to submit to your program. It keeps the program under the programmer's control and prevents it from wandering off in unanticipated directions.

The use of a character operator (`eq`) to process the numerical values as character values makes no difference in the performance of the program. On the other hand, the final `elsif` statement handles the input as numbers rather than characters. One justification for processing exceptional input as numbers is that the numerical operators can at least ostensibly deal with a much larger range of values than the character operators. Figure 11.8 shows the error message you receive if you type any characters other than those specified in the menu.

Figure 11.8
Error messages guide the
user.

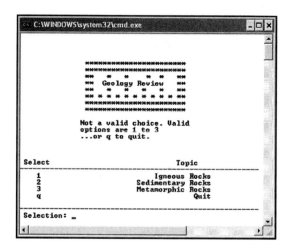

The while Statement

The control condition you assign to the while repetition statement determines whether the flow
of your program can enter the statement controls. It then tests the condition with each repetition,
and until the condition chances to false, the repetition continues. As Figure 11.9 illustrates, one
common approach to working with a while control statement involves using a counter. You
must place the counter inside the while block. You evaluate it in relation to a limiting value
with each cycle of the block.

Figure 11.9
The control for the
while loop can be a
single expression.

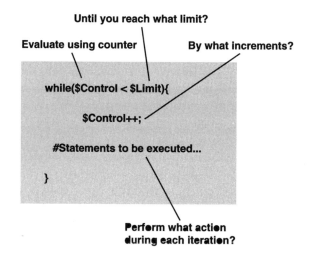

Listing11_04 shows the use of a while control statement to traverse the items stored in an array. With such programs, you combine the work of the counter with that of the test expression for the while statement.

```
#Listing11_04
#Using a while statement with a counter

#1 Formatting elements for the table
$NL = "\n ";
$DC = sprintf("%c",212);      #cast using sprintf to make a special character
$TW = 40;                     #Table width
$DL = sprintf( "%55s", $NL . $DC x $TW); #top and bottom lines
$COLAHEAD = "Name of Quartz";
$COLBHEAD = "Value";

#2 Set up data for quartz types using an implicit hash and a list
%QuartzValues          = (Amethyst,       "Modest",
                          Citrine,        "High",
                          Rose,           "High",
                          Colorless,      "Low",
                          "Cat's-eye",    "Low",
                          Chalcedony,     "High",
                          Adventurine,    "Modest",
                          );
#3 The hash keys function creates an array (@QuartzNames)
@QuartzNames = keys(%QuartzValues);

#Set up the header to the table
print "$NL A Table Describing Quartz values. $NL";
printf("$DL $NL");
printf("$NL %-20s %-20s $NL ", $COLAHEAD , $COLBHEAD);
printf("$DL $NL" );

#4 Use a while loop with a control
#Obtain the number of items in the array
$Length = scalar(@QuartzNames);
$Counter = 0;
while($Length > $Counter){
```

```
    printf("$NL %-20s %-15s",
           $QuartzNames[$Counter],
           #Increment the counter and call the next Quartz
           $QuartzValues{$QuartzNames[$Counter++]}
           );
}#end while.
```

In the lines that comment #1 identifies in Listing11_04, you define identifiers with which to format your table. Notice that the sprintf() function allows you to cast a character using the ASCII value of 212. This provides a border character for the table that you do not see displayed on your keyboard.

At comment #2, you create a hash of a few different types of quartz and their relative values. Quartz names serve as keys, and the rankings of High, Low, and Modest provide the values.

The lines trailing comment #3 access the keys in the hash and assign them to an array (@QuartzNames). Following the creation of the array, you print the heading of a table. The heading provides the two column heads defined earlier, Name of Quartz and Value. By using the $DL identifier, you can print bounding lines 55 characters wide that display the character the ASCII value of 212 represents.

As for the while loop that comment #4 introduces, you first obtain the length of the @QuartzNames, which you assign to the scalar $Length. You define another scalar, $Counter. You employ these two values together with a greater than (>) relational operator to create the control expression for the while statement.

The flow of your program enters the scope the while statement defines because the value of $Counter is less than that of $Length. Inside the while block, you use the value of $Counter to access the indexes of the @QuartzNames array. From the array you access the name of the types of quartz. You both display the name you retrieve and, with a second use of the array, use the lookup hash operator to access the value associated with the key the array holds. As you look up the key in the hash operation, you increment $Counter, and this eventually increases the value it represents to the point that it exceeds the value stored in $Length. At that point, the flow of the program does not again enter the block. Figure 11.10 illustrates the output of Listing11_04.

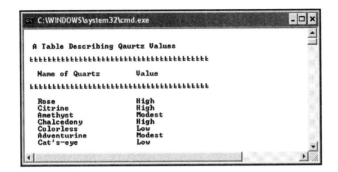

Figure 11.10
You control the while loop at its access point.

The do...while Statement

The do...while statement allows you enter its block without first encountering a control statement. This guarantees that the statements in the block of the control statement execute at least once. You then provide a control statement to determine whether the statements are to execute again. Listing11_05 shows the use of the do...while statement used in conjunction with the keys() function and a hash. The control condition that comes at the end of the bock tests a counter that increases in value with each iteration of the block.

```
#Listing11_05
#Using do...while

#1 Formatting elements for the table
$NL = "\n ";
$DC = sprintf("%c",178);         #cast using sprintf to make a special character
$TW = 60;                        #Table width
$DL = sprintf( "%55s", $NL . $DC × $TW); #top and bottom lines
$COLAHEAD = "Mineral Name";
$COLBHEAD = "Description";

#2 Set up the data for types of quartz implicit hash and a list
%QuartzValues         = (Amethyst,      "Modest",
                         Citrine,       "High",
                         Rose,          "High",
                         Colorless,     "Low",
                         "Cat's-eye",   "Low",
                         Chalcedony,    "High",
                         Adventurine,   "Modest",
                         );
```

```
#3 The hash keys function creates an array (@QuartzNames
# using the hash (%QuartzValues)
@QuartzNames = keys(%QuartzValues);
#Obtain the number of items in the array
$Length = scalar(@QuartzNames);

#4 Print the start of the table
print "$NL A Table Describing $Length Minerals. $NL";
printf("$DL $NL");
printf("$NL %-15s %-15s $NL ", $COLAHEAD , $COLBHEAD);
printf("$DL $NL" );

#5 Use the length to control the number of iterators
$Control = 0;
do{                                        #Enter without question
    $Names = shift(@QuartzNames);      #access items from the top of the array
    printf("$NL %-15s %-15s",
    $Names,                            #The item from the array
    $QuartzValues{$Names});        #lookup for the hash
    $Control++;
}while($Control < $Length);
```

At comment #1 of Listing11_05, you define several identifiers to use in the construction of a table. The sprintf() function allows you to cast the ASCII value of 178 as a character you can use to create bounding lines for your table. You employ the multiplier character (×) to create these lines, which you assign to the $DL identifier.

At comment #2, you create a hash that contains the names of quartz as keys and estimations of worth as values. In the lines associated with comment #3, you make use of this hash to create an array (@QuartzNames). To accomplish this, you employ the keys() functions, providing @QuartzValues (the hash) as it argument. Given the creation of an array that contains all of the keys the hash provides, you can then call the scalar() function to obtain the number of keys from the array.

After setting up the table heading in the lines trailing comment #4, you then generate the rows of the table using a do...while repetition statement (see comment #5). Prior to the start of the do...while block, you define an identifier to use as a counter ($Counter). Inside the block, your first action is to call the shift() function to retrieve the first quartz name stored in the @QuartzNames array. You assign the name to an identifier ($Names). $Names then serves as an argument for the `printf()` function. First it furnishes the data for the first column the `printf()` function defines. Next, it serves as an argument to the lookup hash operation, which accesses the value associated with the quartz name in the `%QuartzValues` array (represented in its scalar form).

Following the `printf()` function, you increment the `$Control` identifier. You then submit the incremented identifier to the control expression in the parentheses following the closing braces of the repetition block. As long as the value of `$Control` remains less than the value `$Length` represents, the flow of the program loops through the do...while block. Figure 11.11 shows you the table that results from Listing11_05.

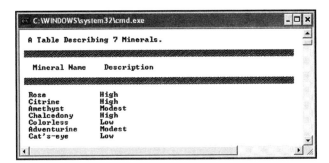

Figure 11.11
The do...while statement allows you to test a control condition after you enter a block.

The until Statement

Like the `while` repetition statement, the `until` repetition statement allows you to test a condition prior to allowing the flow of your program to enter the block associated with the condition. Unlike the `while` statement, the `until` statement tests for the falsehood of a condition. Listing11_06 illustrates how you can use the `until` statement to print a table of data that identifies gems according to general classifications.

```
#Listing11_06
#Using an until repetition structure
#1 Formatting elements for a table
$NL = "\n ";
$DC = sprintf("%c",221);        #cast using sprintf to make a special character
$TW = 60;                       #Table width
$DL = sprintf( "%55s", $NL . $DC × $TW); #top and bottom lines
$COLAHEAD = "Gem Name";
$COLBHEAD = "Gem Type";
```

```
#2 Set up data for gems and their general categories
%GemCategories = (Alexandrite,  "Chrysoberyl",
                        Cymophane,      "Chrysoberyl",
                        "Red Spinel",   "Spinel",
                        "Blue Spinel",  "Spinel",
                        "Pink Topaz",   "Topaz",
                        "Blue Topaz",   "Topaz",
                        Emerald,        "Beryl",
                        Aquamarine,     "Beryl",
                        );
#3 The hash keys() function creates an array (@GemNames
# using the hash (%GemCategories)
@GemNames = keys(%GemCategories);
$Length = scalar(@GemNames);


#4 Print the start of the table
printf("$DL $NL");
printf("$NL %-15s %-15s $NL ", $COLAHEAD , $COLBHEAD);
printf("$DL $NL" );


#5 until tests before it allows you to enter
$Count = 0;
until($Count > $Length){
    printf("$NL %-15s %-15s",
        $GemNames[$Count],              #The item from the array
        $GemCategories{$GemNames[$Count++]});  #lookup for the hash
}#end until block
```

In the lines associated with comment #1 of Listing11_06, you define formatting identifiers for the table. The `sprintf()` function allows you to cast the ASCII value of 221 to a character, which you then use with the multiplier character (×) to create a bounding line for a table heading ($DL).

In the lines trailing comments #2 and #3, you use the implicit form of hash initialization to create a hash that consists of the names of gems (as keys) and categories to which experts often assign gems (as values). The `keys()` function allows you to access the names of the gems and assign them to an array (@GemNames). On the next line, you employ the `scalar()` function to obtain the number of gem names the array contains. This value you assign to the $Length identifier.

After printing the table heading (see the lines associated with comment #4), you then proceed at comment #5 to create a repetition loop using the until statement. To accomplish this, you first create a control identifier ($Count), which you initialize to zero. Then you enter the until control condition. The conditional expression you create relates $Count to $Length, using the greater than relational operator. As long as $Count remains less than or equal to $Length, the loop continues to iterate.

Having entered the until block, you call the printf() function to create the table rows. To retrieve the names of the gems for the first column, you use $Count to access the indexes of the @GemNames array. As a second argument to printf(), to create the second table column, you employ the lookup hash operation. To access the data for this column, you again use the scalar form of the @GemNames array, this time with $Count incremented using the unary (incremental) operator. The gem name you retrieve from the array becomes the key you use to loop up the corresponding gem category. Figure 11.12 shows you the resulting table of gems and their categories.

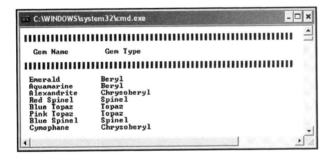

Figure 11.12
The until statement iterates while a given condition proves false.

The do…until Statement

The do…until control statement allows you to place your control expression at the end of the control block. In this way, the flow of your program can enter the block area without being tested, performing the statements within the block at least once. Statements in the block continue to execute as long as the control statement remains false. Listing11_07 explores the use of the do…until statement to create a table of minerals and brief descriptions of them.

```
#Listing11_07
#Using do…until
#1 Formatting elements for the table
$NL = "\n ";
```

```
$DC = sprintf("%c",247);   #cast using sprintf to make a special character
$TW = 60;                  #Table width
$DL = sprintf( "%55s", $NL . $DC x $TW); #top and bottom lines
$COLAHEAD = "Mineral Name";
$COLBHEAD = "Description";


#2 Set up the data on minerals using a hash
%MineralDescriptions = (Natrolite, "Colorless, white; nonmetallic luster",
                        Colemanite, "Colorless, white; nonmetallic luster",
                        Corundum,   "Bluish gray; nonmetallic luster",
                        Topaz, "Colorless, yellow, blue; nonmetallic luster",
                        Vanadinite, "Orange; nonmetallic luster",
                        Serpentine, "Green; nonmetallic luster",
                        Turquoise,  "Blue, green; nonmetallic, luster",
                        );


# The hash keys function creates an array (@MineralNames)
# using the hash (%MineralDescriptions)
@MineralNames = keys(%MineralDescriptions);
# Obtain the number of items in the array
$Length = scalar(@MineralNames);
@MineralNames = sort(@MineralNames);      #order the elements alphabetically


#3 Print the start of the table
print "$NL A Table Describing $Length Minerals. $NL";
printf("$DL $NL");
printf("$NL %-15s %-15s $NL ", $COLAHEAD , $COLBHEAD);
printf("$DL $NL" );



#4 Use do...while to print the table
$Control = 0;
do{                                   #Enter without question
    $Names = shift(@MineralNames);    #access items from the top of the array
    printf("$NL %-15s %-15s",
    $Names,                           #The item from the array
```

```
    $MineralDescriptions{$Names}); #lookup for the hash
    $Control++;
}until($Control > $Length);        #Check the control here
```

With the lines that comment #1 identifies, you create formatting elements for the table. Notice that you use `sprintf()` to cast the ASCII number 247 to create a character to use for the header lines. You employ the multiplier character (×) to define a character line 60 characters long that you assign to the $DL identifier.

At comment #2, you create a hash (@MineralDescriptions) that consists of keys that contain the names of a variety of minerals and values that contain information on the minerals. You then employ the keys() function to assign the names of the minerals to an array (@MineralNames). After assigning the mineral names, you then use the scalar() function to obtain the number of items the array contains, and this value you assign to a scalar ($Length). To alphabetically organize the elements in the array, your next call involves the sort() function. You must assign the array back to itself when you employ the sort() function.

After setting up the table heading in the lines associated with comment #3, you move on at comment #4 to employ the do...until control structure to print the columns of the table. The control condition you set up for the do...until structure uses the length of the array ($Length) and a control ($Control) that you declare immediately before the flow of the program enters the control block. You set the control to zero.

Through each iteration of the do...until block, the control expression confirms that the value of $Control does not exceed the value of $Length. As long as this expression remains false, the block continues to execute. Inside the loop, you increment $Control. When the incremental action at last increases its value so that it is greater than $Length, making the expression true, the flow of the program exits the loop.

To retrieve the name of minerals from the array, you employ the shift() function. The shift() function removes elements from the beginning of an array. The first element you retrieve is Corundum, as Figure 11.13 illustrates. (Were you to employ the pop() function, you would see Topaz first.) You assign each shifted mineral name to the $Name identifier. You then use the $Name identifier as an argument in the hash lookup operation to obtain the description that corresponds to the mineral name. The printf() function prints the name of the mineral in the first column and the corresponding description in the second.

Figure 11.13
The do...until control
allows you to enter the loop
and tests for false.

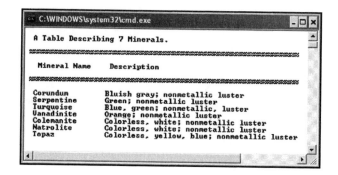

The foreach Control Statement

The foreach repetition statement allows you to sequentially access items in a list or an array. As you access the items, you can assign them to an identifier that you place immediately after foreach and before the list or array you are using foreach to access. While you place the list or array identifier inside parentheses, the identifier you use to extract items remains outside parentheses. In this respect, foreach differs from other control statements. Listing11_08 illustrates the use of foreach to create a table of mineral names and corresponding descriptions of the minerals.

```
#Listing11_08
#Using foreach with arrays and hashes
#1 Formatting elements for the table
$NL = "\n ";
$DC = sprintf("%c", 197);      #cast using sprintf to make a special character
$TW = 60;                      #Table width
$DL = sprintf( "%55s", $NL . $DC x $TW); #top and bottom lines
$COLAHEAD = "Mineral Name";
$COLBHEAD = "Description";


#2 Set up the data on minerals using an implicit hash list
 %MineralDescriptions = (Natrolite, "Colorless, white; nonmetallic luster",
                         Colemanite, "Colorless, white; nonmetallic luster",
                         Corundum, "Bluish gray; nonmetallic luster",
                         Topaz, "Colorless, yellow, blue; nonmetallic luster",
                         Vanadinite, "Orange; nonmetallic luster",
                         Serpentine, "Green; nonmetallic luster",
                         Turquoise, "Blue, green; nonmetallic, luster",
                         );
```

```
#The hash keys() function creates an array (@MineralNames)
# using the hash (%MineralDescriptions)
@MineralNames = keys(%MineralDescriptions);

#3 Print the start of the table
printf("$DL $NL");
printf("$NL %-15s %-15s $NL ", $COLAHEAD , $COLBHEAD);
printf("$DL $NL" );

#4 The foreach statement accesses each item in the
# array until it reaches an undefined item at the end
foreach $Descriptions (@MineralNames){
        printf("$NL %-15s %-15s",
                $Descriptions,                  #The item from the array
                $MineralDescriptions{$Descriptions});   #lookup for the hash
}#end of foreach
```

At comment #1 in Listing11_08, you set up formatting elements for a table to display minerals and their descriptions. You make use of the sprintf() function to cast the ASCII number 197 to use as character for the table heading. The multiplier character (×) allows you to replicate this character for a line 60 characters wide. In addition to heading lines, you also set up identifiers for the column headings ($COLAHEAD, $COLBHEAD).

In the lines associated with comment #2, you set up a hash (%MineralDescriptions) that contains the names of minerals and their descriptions. You employ an implicit form of hash initialization. The items appear between parentheses and are separated by commas. For items of more than one word, you use double quotes. You then use the keys() function to retrieve the names of the minerals from the hash and assign them to a list (@MineralNames).

At comment #3, you print the heading of the table. By employing the $DL identifier as an argument for printf(), you can conveniently print the lines that define the heading. You employ the identifiers you set up earlier to assign Mineral Name and Description to the column headings (see Figure 11.14).

In the lines trailing comment #4, you attend to printing the table using a foreach control statement. The form of the statement varies from others, such as for, while, and until, which require you to enclose the control statement entirely in parentheses. In essence, you perform the same operation here, but you employ an identifier ($Description) to momentarily store the mineral name you retrieve from the array (@MineralNames). The foreach control statement accesses each successive mineral name in the array. It then assigns the mineral name to $Description. You can then employ descriptions inside the control block to print the table.

Control of the foreach statement resides in the array. Undefined elements terminate arrays, so the foreach statement traverses the array, retrieving successive elements, until it reaches the undefined element. When it reaches the undefined element, it terminates its iterative actions, and the flow of the program exits the foreach block.

Printing the mineral names and their accompanying descriptions involves using the $Description identifier combined with the lookup hash operator. You assign $Description as an argument to printf() to print the name of the element in the first column of the table. You assign $Description to the lookup form of the hash to retrieve the description that corresponds to the mineral name. You then pass the resulting string to the printf() function as a second argument, and this appears in the second column of the table. Figure 11.14 illustrates the output of Listing11_08.

Figure 11.14
The foreach control provides a simple way to access arrays.

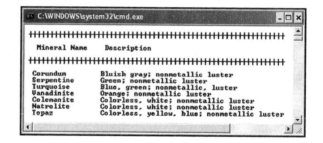

Using a Block with last and redo

You have experimented before with blocks in relation to capturing strings that you can print directly or assign to scalar identifiers. You can use blocks as controls, also. A control block consists of a control block target name and then one of the Perl operators that redirects the flow of the program relative to the blocks' target names. Listing11_09 provides an example of how to use target blocks combined with the redo and last identifiers to create a program in which you randomly explore gems and their ratings.

```
#Listing11_09
#Using block targets and blocks
#1 Set up data for gems and their ratings
%QuartzValues        = (Amethyst,      "Modest",
                        Citrine,       "High",
                        Rose,          "High",
                        Colorless,     "Low",
```

```
                              "Cat's-eye",        "Low",
                              "Chalcedony",       "High",
                              "Adventurine",      "Modest",
                              "Heliodore",        "High"
                              );

# Use the keys function to create an array (@QuartzNames)
@QuartzNames = keys(%QuartzValues);
#3 set up a block tag
QUARRYTAG:{
        print "\nChoose a quartz quarry (1 2 3 4 5 6 7 8): ";
        $Quarry = <STDIN>;
        chomp($Quarry);
    if($Quarry eq '3'){
        print "\nYou picked $Quarry!";
        print "\n $QuartzNames[$Quarry] :" .
                        " $QuartzValues{$QuartzNames[$Quarry]}";
#2go to the tag - several instances in the selection structure
        redo QUARRYTAG;
    }elsif($Quarry eq '4'){
        print "\nYou picked $Quarry!";
        print "\n $QuartzNames[$Quarry] :" .
                        " $QuartzValues{$QuartzNames[$Quarry]}";
        redo QUARRYTAG; #go to the tag
    }elsif($Quarry eq '5'){
        print "\nYou picked $Quarry!";
        print "\n $QuartzNames[$Quarry] :" .
                " $QuartzValues{$QuartzNames[$Quarry]}";
        redo QUARRYTAG;    #go to the tag
    }elsif($Quarry eq '7'){
        print "\nYou picked $Quarry!";
        print "\n $QuartzNames[$Quarry] :" .
            " $QuartzValues{$QuartzNames[$Quarry]}";
        redo QUARRYTAG; #go to the tag
    }else{
        print "\nYou picked $Quarry!";
        print "\nOops! Bottomless pit...!\n";
```

```
#3exit the block
        last;
    }#end else
  }#end of block QUARRYTAG
```

At comment #1 in Listing11_09, you set up a hash that contains the names of quartzes (except Heliodore, which is not usually identified as a quartz) and their values as assessed by experts. You call the hash %QuartzValues. You then assign the names of the quartzes to an array (@QuartzNames) so that in the selection structure that follows you can easily access items from the array using numbers the program user enters.

At comment #2, you set up a block tag, QUARRYTAG. You can use any name you please to create a tag. By convention, programmers capitalize tags. You follow the tag with a colon. You then create a block that corresponds to the tag. The block in Listing11_09 begins with the curly brace immediately following the colon after QUARRYTAG and extends to the last line of the program (note the comment: #end of block QUARRYTAG). All the statements lying between the opening curly brace and the closing curly brace fall into the block the tag establishes.

Within the QUARRYTAG block, you construct a cascading selection structure that tests for numerical input. At the opening of the block, you call the print() function to prompt the program user to input a number. You assign this input to a scalar, $Quarry. You then call the chomp() function to remove the newline character that the system usually appends to data entered from the keyboard.

Through a series of selection statements, you then test the value the user has entered to discover which item in %QuartzValues corresponds to it. If the user enters 3, 4, 5, or 7, the program reports the discovery of a quartz (or Heliodore). If the user enters any other number, as Figure 11.15 reveals, the program responds by reporting that the quarry consists of a bottomless pit and exits.

To make the program iterate as it selects among the safe entries, you use the redo operator. As the lines trailing comment #2 show, you follow the redo operator with the name of the tag that names the block. When the flow of the program encounters the tag name, it returns to it and commences to redo the statements following it. Each of the winner options in Listing11_09 provides a redo directive to cycle the program back to the block's name tag.

If the user types a number other than 3, 4, 5, or 7, an inclusive else statement catches the number and redirects the flow of the program using the last operator. The last operator works with repetition and selection statements to allow you to cause the flow of the program to exit the block that contains the last statement. In this case, the curly braces associated with QUARRYTAG constitute the block for last. When the flow of the program encounters this operator, it jumps beyond the block, and the program terminates.

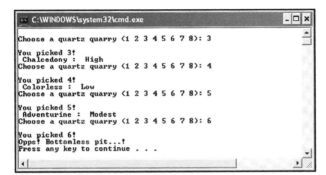

Figure 11.15
Block tags can emulate a
control structure.

Using continue with while, last, and next

The `continue` operator creates a block that extends a repetition block. The `continue`
operator allows you to extend the block to which you append it and add additional statements.
If you append it to a `while` statement, for example, and use the `next` operator, the flow
of the program returns to the top of the `while` statement. If you use the `last` operator inside a `continue` block that extends a `while` block, you can exit from the `while` block.
Listing11_10 experiments with selection and repetition statements and includes the use of
`continue` blocks. It prompts the user to enter a number. Based on the number (ostensibly
identifying a quarry), it retrieves a quartz sample.

```
#Listing11_10
#1 Set up the data quartz values
%QuartzValues       = (Amethyst,       "Modest",
                        Citrine,        "High",
                        Rose,           "High",
                        Colorless,      "Low",
                        "Cat's-eye",    "Low",
                        Chalcedony,     "High",
                        Adventurine,    "Modest",
                        );


# The hash keys function creates an array (@QuartzNames)
@QuartzNames = keys(%QuartzValues);
#2 set up an infinite for structure
for(;;){
```

```
    print "\nChoose a quartz quarry (0 1 2 3 4 5 6 7 8): ";
    $Quarry = <STDIN>;
    chomp($Quarry);
#3 Check for exit or valid numbers
    if($Quarry == '0'){last;}
    if($Quarry <= '8' && $Quarry > '0'){
    print "\n You picked " .
      "$QuartzNames[$Quarry] :" .
                " $QuartzValues{$QuartzNames[$Quarry]}";
      }
    while($Quarry){
#4 Continue the while
      }continue{
        print "\n Okay so far...\n";
#5 Exit the while loop to the for loop
        last;
      }#end continue
#6 Numbers over 8
$Count = 0;
    if($Quarry > 8){
        print "\n Woops, nothing but an...";
        while($Count < $Quarry ){
#7 Continue the while only if $Count has been reset above
      }continue{
        print "\n echo...";
        $Count++;
        if($Count == $Quarry){
            last;
        }
#8 go back to while
        next;
            }#end continue
      }#end continue


}#end for
```

At comment #1 in Listing11_10, you set up a hash that contains a number of quartzes and the rating experts assign them. You then use the keys () function to assign the names of the quartzes to an array, @QuartzNames. At comment #2, you set up an infinite for loop. The opening and closing braces of the for loop enclose all actions the program performs other than those involved in defining the hash and the array.

Immediately following the opening curly brace of the for loop, you use the print () function to prompt input from the user. You assign the input to the $Quarry identifier. You call the chomp () function to remove newline characters from the input. The input includes numbers from 0 to 8.

If the user types 0, the program terminates. A selection statement that handles 0 immediately follows comment #3. This is an if selection statement, and its sole activity involves executing the last operator. The last operator causes the flow of the program to break out of the for loop, and the program terminates.

After the if selection statement that handles 0, you find two other selection statements. The first handles numbers from 1 to 8. The other handles numbers over 8. As Figure 11.16 illustrates, if the program user types a number in the range from 1 to 8, the program responds with the name and rating of a quartz and continues to cycle.

A while loop follows the selection statement that evaluates numbers from 1 to 8, and the controlling expression for this statement is the $Quarry identifier, which holds the input from the program user. As long as the program user types a number, the flow of the program enters this while loop. If the user simply presses Return, $Quarry remains undefined, so the flow of the program does not enter this while loop.

The sole action this while loop performs amounts to serving as a gateway to the continue block attached to it. In the attached continue block, you call the print () function, which prints Okay so far... to the monitor. You then execute the last operator. This operator breaks the flow of the program from the while loop and returns it to the main for loop (see comment #5).

At comment #6, you proceed with another selection statement. This one tests for numbers greater than 8. If the test condition proves true, you call the print () function to print a message: Woops, nothing but an... You then move into a while loop. The expression that controls entrance to the while loop involves two identifiers. One is $Count, and the other is $Quarry. $Count receives its definition in the for block just prior to the if statement at comment #6.

The first time the flow of the program enters the while loop, it does so because $Count is less than $Quarry (the value of 0 is less than 8, for example). The while block serves as an entry to the `continue` block. After the flow of the program enters the `continue` block, you then increment $Count using the increment operator ($Count++).

$Count continues to increment until it reaches a value equal to $Quarry. When it equals $Quarry, you execute an `if` selection statement that allows the last operator to execute. The last operator causes the flow of the program to return to the `for` block.

Before the $Count identifier reaches a value equal to $Quarry, the flow of the program bypasses the selection statement that contains the `last` operator. Instead, the flow moves on and encounters the `next` operator. The `next` operator directs the flow of the program to the top of the `while` loop, and as long as the conditional expression of `while` finds that the value of $Count does not exceed the value of $Quarry, it allows the block to repeat. Each time the block repeats, $Count is incremented, and as Figure 11.16 illustrates, you see the `echo...` message.

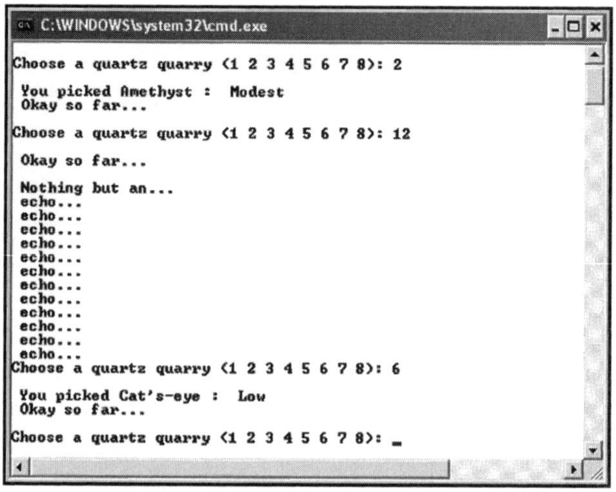

Figure 11.16
continue blocks allow
you to extend repetition
blocks.

Mineral Luck Using while and Selection Statements

You can use the `while` control statement, like the `for` control statement, to create infinite loops. As in the example shown for the Geology Review program, you can exit such a loop using the `last` operator. Listing11_11 provides an example of an infinite `while` loop that allows you to explore the names of minerals and their descriptions while battling with the chance generation of numbers.

```
#Listing11_11
#1 set up for random numbers and formatting
# data on minerals using an implicit hash list
```

```perl
%MineralDescriptions = (Natrolite,  "Colorless, white; nonmetallic luster",
                        Colemanite, "Colorless, white; nonmetallic luster",
                        Corundum,   "Bluish gray; nonmetallic luster",
                        Topaz, "Colorless, yellow, blue; nonmetallic luster",
                        Vanadinite, "Orange; nonmetallic luster",
                        Serpentine, "Green; nonmetallic luster",
                        Turquoise,  "Blue, green; nonmetallic, luster",
                        );

srand;
# The hash keys function creates an array (@MineralNames)
# using the hash (%MineralDescriptions)
@MineralNames = keys(%MineralDescriptions);
$NL = "\n ";
$TW = 55;
$DC = sprintf("%c",240);
$DL = sprintf( "%55s", $NL . $DC x $TW);


#2 Start the program
 system(cls);
 $TRUE = 1;
 $Score = 1;
 print "$DL $NL The Mineral Name game. How's your luck? $DL $NL";


 while($TRUE){      #Set perpetually true.
    #Number from 1 to 7
    $Number = 1 + int(rand(7)); #generate number
    print "$NL The number is: $Number ";
#3 A selection structure for different numbers
        if($Number == 1){
            print "$NL $MineralNames[$Number]?";
            print "$NL $MineralDescriptions{$MineralNames[$Number]}.";
            print "$NL Go again! $NL";
            enterData();
        }
        elsif($Number == 2){
            print "$NL $MineralNames[$Number]?";
```

```
            print "$NL $MineralDescriptions{$MineralNames[$Number]}.";
            print "$NL Go again! $NL";
            enterData();
        }
        elsif($Number == 3){
            print "$NL $MineralNames[$Number]?";
            print "$NL $MineralDescriptions{$MineralNames[$Number]}.";
            print "$NL Go again! $NL";
            enterData();
        }
        elsif($Number == 4){
            print "$NL $MineralNames[$Number]?";
            print "$NL $MineralDescriptions{$MineralNames[$Number]}.";
            print "$NL Go again! $NL";
            enterData();
        }
        elsif($Number == 5){
            print "$NL $MineralNames[$Number]?";
            print "$NL $MineralDescriptions{$MineralNames[$Number]}.";
            print "$NL Go again! $NL";
            enterData();
        }
        elsif($Number == 6){
            print "$NL $MineralNames[$Number]?";
            print "$NL $MineralDescriptions{$MineralNames[$Number]}.";
            print "$NL Double score! Go again! $NL";
            $Score++;
            enterData();
        }
#4 Isolate processing in the loop for the terminating event
    if($Number == 7){
            print "$NL Pyrite? Too Bad!\n";
            print "$NL Your final score is: $Score";
            print "$NL Type \'g\'to go on or <Enter> to quit. ";
        $ControlChar = <STDIN>;
        chomp($ControlChar);
```

```
        unless(lc($ControlChar) eq 'g'){ #last exits the program
            last;
        }
        $Score = 1; #rest the score
        system(cls);
        next; #back to the top of the loop
    }
#5 Isolate processing in the loop for the winning event
    if($Score == 12){
        print "$NL You Win!!!!!.\n";
        print "$NL Press <Enter> for a new game or \'q\' to quit. ";
        $ControlChar = <STDIN>;
        chomp($ControlChar);
        if(lc($ControlChar) eq 'q'){ #last exits the program
            last;
        }
        $Score = 1; #reset the score
        system(cls);
        print "$DL $NL The Mineral Name game. How's your luck? $DL $NL";
        next;                       #back to the top of the loop
    }
  }#end while


#6 An example of how to write a function.
sub enterData{
        print "$NL Score now $Score. ";
        $Score++;
        print "$DL";
        print "$NL Press <Enter>.\n";
        $ControlChar = <STDIN>;
}
```

In the lines trailing comment #1 in Listing11_11, you set up a hash that contains the names of minerals and their corresponding descriptions. You also create a number of identifiers to help with text formatting details. Using the sprintf() function, you cast the ASCII value of 240 to create the triple-dashed character you see in Figure 11.17. You also call srand. In this context, this is largely unnecessary, but srand supplements the rand() function and allows it to generate unique values.

After setting up data and formatting details, you then turn to defining two identifiers that prove important to the execution of the program. Comment #2 identifies the lines that attend to these tasks. You set up an identifier, $TRUE, to allow the while control statement that creates the overall block for the program to run indefinitely. You also define an identifier ($Score) to track the progress of the player. Prior to defining these two identifiers, you call the system() function to clear the screen.

In the lines just prior to comment #3, you use the rand() function to generate numbers in the range from 1 to 7. You assign the random number to an identifier ($Number). You print the number so the player can see it with each iteration of the while block. Following the generation of the random number, you set up a sequence control structure that tests the generated value against constant values. In each case, if the number corresponds to any number in the range from 1 to 6, you print a message that names one of the minerals and includes information about how to identify the mineral. It also congratulates the player on a successful find.

To retrieve information, you use the array @MineralNames in its scalar form and submit the value the $Number identifier contains to locate the mineral name to display. To access information for the mineral, you employ the lookup hash operation for %MineralDescriptions. For the argument of the operation, you use the mineral name you retrieve from the @MineralNames array.

Two if selection statements follow the cascading selection structure. One (at comment #4) tests for when the value assigned by the random number generator equals 7. The other (at comment #5) tests for when the number assigned to $Score equals 12.

Losing with 7

In the lines trailing comment #5 in Listing11_11, you test for whether $Number is equal to 7. When you test for 7, you are testing for the number that ends the game. If the player can avoid this number for long enough to accumulate a score of 12, then the player wins. Even if the player's luck has proven bad, you allow the player to continue to play. The player can type "q" to quit or press Enter to go on. You assign the input to $ControlChar.

If the player presses Enter, the value assigned to $ControlChar consists only of a line return. When you apply the chomp() function to $ControlChar immediately after you assign the line return to it, you end up with an undefined value.

The unless selection statement allows you to evaluate $ControlChar to exclude everything except a defined value. This defined value is "q." (The lc() function transforms the uppercase version into lowercase if the player has typed "Q.") Given a defined value of "q," the unless condition directs the flow of the program into its block, and the last operator causes the flow to return to break out of the while loop. The game terminates.

If the player presses Enter, the flow of the program passes over the unless statement. You then assign a new starting score of 1 to the $Score identifier, call the system() function to clear the screen, and execute the next operator. The next operator causes the flow of the program to return to the top of the while loop.

Winning with 12

At comment #5 in Listing11_11, you deal with winners. Winning brings a humble accolade, nothing more. You allow the player the option of continuing to play or to exit. The player presses Enter to continue or types "q" to quit. You assign the result of the action to $ControlChar and then use the lc() and chomp() functions to eliminate the return from the input and to reduce the input to lowercase characters if necessary.

If the player has entered "q," you provide an if selection statement that calls the last operator. The last operator causes the flow of the program to skip out of the while loop, so the game ends.

If the player presses Enter (or any character other than the "q" key), then you reset the value of $Score, call the system() function to clear the screen, and execute the next operator to cause the flow of the program to return to the top of the while loop.

As a final point, at comment #6 you see a Perl function (subroutine). Its name is enterData, and since it is a function, in this book it is identified as enterData(). Since subsequent chapters explain functions in detail, it is appropriate for now to point out only the selections that cover the numbers 1 through 6. It is called wherever you see its name. It momentarily halts the game and prompts the players to press Enter. As Figure 11.17 illustrates, you can tell when this function executes whenever you see the expression Score now followed by the score.

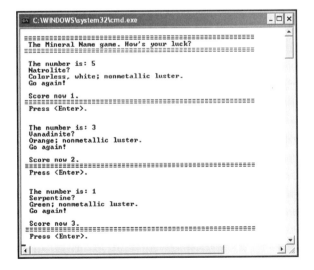

Figure 11.17
Combining controls allows you to create a mineral ID game.

Using each to Count Word Occurrences

Listing11_12 counts the number of times specific terms occur in a list. A scenario for such an array might involve a geology lab. A lab instructor might divide a class into teams and then solicit from the teams lists of mineral samples studied during a term. Rather than counting the items one-by-one, the instructor might create a list and then use a Perl program to discover the number of times the teams as a whole accessed specific lab samples. Using the same model, it becomes possible to create a much more involved program that goes through a text, finds the pages on which words occur, and records them in a file. Listing11_12 provides a minimal program that shows a few starting routines.

```perl
#Listing11_12
#Using foreach, while, and each.
#compendium, concordance, count


#1 Create an array of items
@MineralSamples = qw( Flourite Rhodonite Roodochrosite
                      Siderite Strontianite Smithsonite
                      Colemanite Natrolite Feldspare
                      Siderite Natrolite Strontianite
                      Topaz Borax Magnesite Turquoise
                      Colemanite Siderite Natrolite
                      Flourite Rhodonite Natrolite Feldspare
                      );


#2 foreach counts all the items in the array
foreach $Sample(@MineralSamples){
    #access value and increment it for each occurrence found
    $SampleCount{$Sample} = $SampleCount{$Sample} += 1;
}


#3 Formatting elements for the table
$NL = "\n ";
$DC = sprintf("%c",236);    #cast using sprintf to make a special character
$TW = 60;                   #Table width
$DL = sprintf( "%55s", $NL . $DC x $TW); #top and bottom lines
$COLAHEAD = "Mineral Name";
```

```
$COLBHEAD = "Number of Samples";


#Print the header
print "$NL Number of Lab Mineral Samples $NL";
printf("$DL $NL");
printf("$NL %-15s %-15s $NL ", $COLAHEAD , $COLBHEAD);
printf("$DL $NL" );
$Control = 0;




#4 Print the resulting count by accessing hash keys and values
while (($Sample, $Number) = each(%SampleCount)){
    printf("$NL %-15s %-15s",        #
    $Sample,                         #The item from the array
    $Number);
}
```

At comment #1 in Listing11_12, you create an array of mineral samples (@MineralSamples).
Some samples occur several times, others only once. At comment #2, you use a foreach
statement to traverse the array and translate it into a hash. The translation involves accessing
each sample the array stores and assigning it to the scalar $Sample. You then use $Sample
to create both keys and values in a hash called %SampleCount. Here's the code:

```
$SampleCount{$Sample} = $SampleCount{$Sample} += 1;
```

As you traverse the array, you continuously assign the name of the sample to the
%SampleCount hash. As you assign the mineral name to the hash, you use the default behavior
of the hash lookup operation to do one of two things:

❋   If the sample already resides in the hash, then the name you submit accesses the value from
    this sample. By adding 1 to the value and then assigning it back to itself, you augment the
    count of the number of occurrences.

❋   If the sample does not exist, the lookup operation creates a key-value pair and assigns it to
    the hash. A 1 is assigned to the value.

Given the creation of the %SampleCount hash, you then proceed in the lines accompanying
comment #3 to print the results of the count. To accomplish this task, you set up some formatting
elements. To create lines for the table header, you employ the sprintf() function to cast the

ASCII number 236. You use the character multiplication operator to create lines of these characters for the table.

At comment #4, you use a while control structure along with the hash each function to extract and print the sample names and their counts from the hash. The each function extracts the keys and values from the hash and assigns them to a list consisting of two scalars, $Sample and $Number. Given these temporary assignments, you can then employ the printf() function to create the table that Figure 11.18 illustrates.

Figure 11.18
Translating an array into a hash allows you to count occurrences of items in the array.

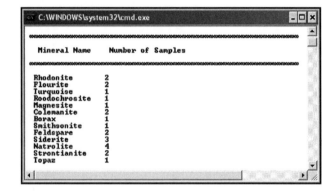

Conclusion

This chapter began with an exploration of the basic concept of repetition. It then moved on to explore the most fundamental of repetition control statements, the for control statement. From there, it moved into such control statements as while, until, do...while, and do...until. Such repetition control statements tend to be generic, lending themselves to any types of applications you want to make of them.

Other controls investigated in this chapter tend to be more specific. Among these are the foreach and each controls. The foreach statement extracts items from an array until it reaches an undefined element that marks the end of the array. The each control statement performs a similar action with relation to hashes, with the difference that it reads key-value pairs rather than single array items.

In addition to control statements, this chapter explored the next, redo, last, and continue operators. The next operator returns you to the head of a repetition control block. The last operator exits you from a block. You can use the redo operator with block target tags to control the flow of a program in a fairly arbitrary way. The continue operator allows you to extend a repetition block. Used with selection statements and next and last, continue statements become effective ways of implementing involved program flows.

12 } Functions

This chapter provides discussion of how to create and use functions. You first investigate the fundamental properties of functions, such as returned values, arguments to functions, the `sub` keyword, and function blocks. These elements in place, you then turn to creating functions with no return values and no arguments. From this starting point, you explore functions that accept scalar values as arguments and likewise return scalar values. Next, you turn to functions that involve arrays and hashes. You explore how you can use function arguments to convert hashes into arrays and then retrieve the hashes through operations you establish in the block scope of the function. Contextualization allows you to make use of the returned values of functions. As for returning values, you can do so both explicitly and implicitly. Explicit return of values involves using the `return` keyword. Among the central topics of this chapter:

* Functions as vehicles for simplifying programs
* The elements involved in defining functions
* Creating functions with scalar arguments and return values
* Creating functions with array arguments and return values
* Creating functions that use hashes
* Different approaches to process return values

Abstraction and Functional Decomposition

Perl identifies functions with the keyword `sub`, which stands for *subroutine*. Programmers also refer to subroutines as *methods*, but a method is usually also associated with object-oriented programming and *classes*. A class is a way to organize a group of functions into operational wholes. You can develop classes with Perl, but they are beyond the scope of the discussion this chapter presents.

A function is a subroutine. A subroutine provides a way that you can conveniently break a program into parts to make its development and maintenance much more convenient than would be possible otherwise. In fact, without subroutines, it would not be possible to write programs of any but a fairly elementary level of sophistication. The reason for this is that programs constitute information systems. An information system consists of a collection of processes that accomplish a given task or provide a given service. As a system becomes more complex, the number of processes it includes can after a time become too complex for any given individual to understand as a whole.

> ※ In much of the documentation pertaining to Perl, you often read about functions as built-in functions. It remains, however, that the functions you create are also functions. Another term for the functions you developed are "user-defined" functions.

Complexity provides a measurement of how many things you must be conscious of at any given moment to accomplish a given task or provide a given service. Consider a situation in which you have ten tasks to perform. If you try to think about all ten tasks at once, you are not likely to meet with success. Even if you can think of ten things at once, sustaining ten simultaneous thoughts is probably not a good use of your time.

To deal with complexity, you use what is known as abstraction. Abstraction allows you to group the 10 tasks into subtasks. A subtask is a group of tasks that possess a common theme. Consider in general terms the work involved in composing a computer program. Suppose, for example, that you have at hand the work of creating a program to display information about ecological science. Figure 12.1 provides a possible scenario.

Figure 12.1 represents a longer list of tasks broken down into a shorter list of tasks. The shorter list represents *abstractions*. Each abstraction helps you view the task in a given context of activity. Researching ecological biomes now constitutes an initial project activity. Testing the main features of the program the project becomes a task you associate with the end of the project. In the middle lie tasks involving assimilating and categorizing information and attending to the specifics of writing a computer program.

When you create abstractions, you develop ways to more easily understand a project. Remembering four headings requires less effort than remembering ten. Assessing priorities becomes easier when the work of assessment involves four tasks rather than ten. Likewise, when you analyze how tasks relate to each other, if you can view sets of tasks as a given type of activity (planning, research, design and development, testing), then you are in a better position to know how to organize tasks that emerge as you pursue your project.

In Figure 12.1, each abstraction can be considered a subroutine of the larger group of tasks. Each subroutine results from what is sometimes called *functional decomposition*. Functional

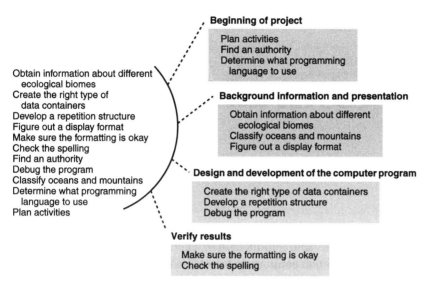

Obtain information about different
  ecological biomes
Create the right type of
  data containers
Develop a repetition structure
Figure out a display format
Make sure the formatting is okay
Check the spelling
Find an authority
Debug the program
Classify oceans and mountains
Determine what programming
  language to use
Plan activities

Beginning of project

  Plan activities
  Find an authority
  Determine what programming
    language to use

Background information and presentation

  Obtain information about different
    ecological biomes
  Classify oceans and mountains
  Figure out a display format

Design and development of the computer program

  Create the right type of data containers
  Develop a repetition structure
  Debug the program

Verify results

  Make sure the formatting is okay
  Check the spelling

Figure 12.1
Abstraction generally allows you to view large sets of tasks in smaller sets.

decomposition involves, among other things, asking a fairly rudimentary question: What is the order of the tasks to be performed? With the designation of an order of tasks comes the designation of *dependencies*. You know what you need for each task to be fulfilled. In Figure 12.1, for example, it makes little sense to check the spelling if no textual content exists.

Abstraction serves to eliminate dependencies. It accomplishes this feat by *encapsulating* code. Encapsulation ends up being an enormous asset in most industrial situations. Consider this: If you set up your programs so that the different functions you create are not tangled up with other functions, then you can more easily change one thing in isolation. This is one of the major benefits of encapsulation. Programmers can make isolated changes. The technical terms for this are loosely coupled and highly cohesive. In other words, the code in a function coheres: It makes sense when examined in isolation. A function is also loosely coupled with other functions, meaning that if you make changes to one function, you do not have to make changes in other functions.

Functional Abstraction in Programs

Figure 12.2 illustrates how you can use decomposition of the functionality to address the project depicted in Figure 12.1. The analysis involves four abstractions. Each abstraction relates to a task or set of tasks the program might perform as it provides the envisioned service. To access information involves in some way obtaining the information from some source. The source might be the program itself, a file containing text, or a database. Organizing information might involve sorting it or being able to select specific items from it. Processing user selections might involve taking input from the terminal. Displaying information might involve working with a DOS character display, creating a window component, or using a browser. In each instance, you can create functions that isolate a specific task so that it can be seen in isolation from others.

Figure 12.2
Functions in computer programs provide ways that you can break down complexity.

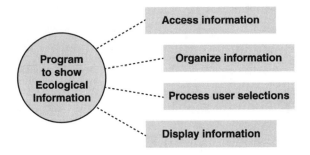

When you develop a computer program, you can try to create the program as a single flow of activity that proceeds from a beginning to an end. As Figure 12.3 illustrates, in this light, you can decompose the program in terms of the sequence of tasks it performs and the abstractions that identify different segments of the sequence of tasks. In this respect, you have analyzed the program so that it now consists of functional subroutines.

Figure 12.3
Analysis allows you to view a sequence as a set of functional subroutines.

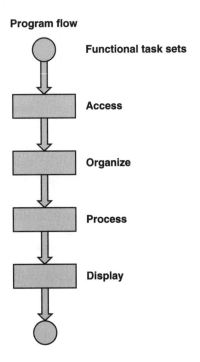

Identifying Functional Subroutines

To create a functional subroutine (from here on referred to as a function) in Perl, you employ a combination of program syntax and convention. The syntax and conventions apply to both the specific development of functions and the broader layout of programs in which you include functions. Table 12.1 provides a summary.

Table 12.1   Syntax and Conventions for Functions

Item	Discussion
sub	This is a keyword that allows you to designate the word that follows it as the name of a function.
Name	Functions have names. The name of a function can be almost any expression you choose. You cannot use words reserved for other purposes in Perl (continue, for, while, and so on). The function name should not be a number or consist of operators or controls. It should begin with an alphabetical character. Function names can include underscores and dashes, among other characters (A_Za_z0), but they must always begin with a character and cannot include hyphens.
Block	In this context, block refers to a set of curly braces ({}). You must enclose the statements that compose the body of the function in curly braces. The curly braces follow the name of the function.
return	You can use the return keyword with functions. The return keyword closes out the function so that you can predict the precise value the function makes available in the flow of the program. The return value allows you to specify the value that the function passes back to the calling code.
Arguments	When you create a function, you can define a list of arguments you can pass to the function. You can pass these arguments to the function inside a set of parentheses that follow the name of the function. When you define a function, you can make it clear what arguments the function receives by following a coding standard that identifies the arguments.
Program organization	You can organize a program on a structural, package, or modular basis. On a modular basis, you place functions in separate files or groups of files known as modules. If you use a package approach, you divide a single file into separate parts using package labels. If you use a structural approach, you try to place all the code that constitutes a program into functions and then, to set up the program, call the functions.

Basic Program Organization for Functions

When you develop functions, you can use any of a number of programming techniques. One that many programmers favor requires that you organize your programs structurally. Structural organization of a program entails placing a program in a file so that you see calls to functions first and then the definitions of the called functions. Figure 12.4 illustrates the practical consequences of this type of organization.

Figure 12.4
Structural organization of a program submerges complexity.

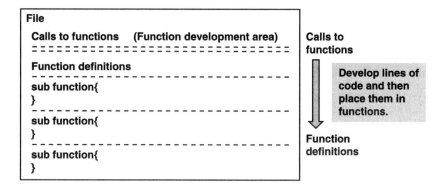

Organized structurally, a program hides the details involved in the definition of functions. When you hide details, you make it simpler to understand your code. You likewise make it possible to make repairs to your program without having to become involved in functions other than those you need to fix.

When you define a function, you compose the lines of code that constitute the function. The definition of a function, then, consists of a body of code enclosed in curly braces and preceded by the name of the function and the appropriate keyword (usually sub). In a structurally organized program, as Figure 12.5 illustrates, you employ the top of the program for calling functions. You reserve the remainder of the program for the functions you have developed.

During the development cycle of a program's life, you can employ the top of the program as a development area. Using this approach, you can have a fairly clear view of the overall program, but as the need arises, you can "open" a functional space and either add to it or create new functionality.

For more involved programs, the structural approach to development still pertains, but rather than placing functions in a submerged area of a single file, you move them to separate files. The separate files become modules or packages. Figure 12.6 illustrates this situation.

When you create a function, you attempt to hide complexity, making the operations the function contains visible to the user of the function only through the calls made to the function. The structural organization of the program accommodates both abstraction and development. It

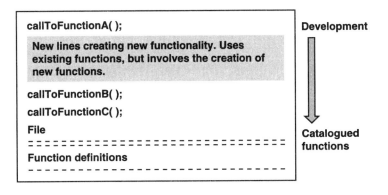

Figure 12.5
The development of the program takes place at the top of the program.

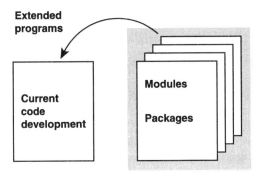

Figure 12.6
Programs consisting of multiple files place defined functions in modules or packages.

accommodates abstraction because it allows the person who maintains the program to understand it according to the functions it uses. It accommodates development because it allows you to create programs in a staging area at the top of the program, thus avoiding the necessity of digging into what might amount to hundreds or thousands of lines of code that constitute the program.

Functions with No Arguments

The most fundamental type of function in Perl can be characterized as taking no arguments and providing no return values. Such a function resembles the blocks developed in Chapter 11, with the difference that they can be used more flexibly. Listing12_01 employs functions to replace the opening, menu, and display options. All the functions used employ no arguments and do not explicitly return values.

```
#Listing12_01
#Functions without arguments
system('cls');
$NL = "\n" ;
$ML = $NL x 5; #Multiple line returns for displays
```

```
#1 See the definitions of the functions; call to opening view
viewOpening();


for(;;) {                       #Infinite loop using for()
#3 Call to function to view menu options
        viewMenu();
        $ControlChar = <STDIN>;    #User input
        chomp($ControlChar);
        system(cls);              #Call to the DOS system
#5 Function calls for each display option   1 - 4 and errors
        if(lc($ControlChar) eq 'q'){
            last;                              #Terminate the program
        }elsif($ControlChar eq '1'){
            viewMarine() ;                #Function call
        }elsif($ControlChar eq '2'){
            viewFreshwater();             #Function call
        }elsif($ControlChar eq '3'){
            viewTerrestrial();            #Function call
        }elsif($ControlChar eq '4'){
            viewDomesticated();             #Function call
        }elsif($ControlChar > 4 || $ControlChar < 1){
            viewError();                    #Function call
        }#end elsif
    }#end menu for


#2 Definitions
#--------------- Definition of viewOpening() ---------------
sub viewOpening{
print(<<ECOSYS);
$ML
                ** * *   * *  **
                **     Ecosystems    **
                ** * *   * *   **
$NL
ECOSYS
}
```

```
# 4
#-------------- Definition of viewOpening() ---------------
sub viewMenu{
        print( "$NL");
        printf("%-15s %25s"," Select", "    Topic");
        printf("$NL" . "-" x 55 . $NL);
        printf( "%-20s %25s"," 1" ,    "Marine $NL");
        printf( "%-20s %25s"," 2" ,    "Freshwater $NL");
        printf( "%-20s %25s"," 3" ,    "Terrestrial $NL");
        printf( "%-20s %25s"," 4" ,    "Domesticated $NL");
        printf( "%-20s %25s"," q" ,    "Quit $NL");
        printf( "$NL" . "-"x 55 . "$NL >> " );


}
# 6
#-------------- Definition of viewMarine() -------------
sub viewMarine{
print(<<ECOSYS);
$ML
                1. Marine
                Open oceans, continental shelf,
                fisheries, deep sea, estuaries
$NL
ECOSYS
}
#-------------- Definition of viewFreshwater() -------------
sub viewFreshwater{
print(<<ECOSYS);
$ML
                2. Freshwater
                Lakes and ponds, rivers and streams,
                marshes and swamps
$NL
ECOSYS
}
#-------------- Definition of viewTerrestrial () -------------
sub viewTerrestrial{
```

```
print(<<ECOSYS);
$ML
                3. Terrestrial
                Tundra, coniferous forests,
                deciduous forests, grasslands, savanna,
                desert, semi-evergreen, tropical rainforests

ECOSYS
}
#-------------- Definition of viewDomesticated () -------------
sub viewDomesticated{
print(<<ECOSYS);
$ML
                4. Domesticated
                Corporate farms, plantation forests,
                transportation corridors, towns, industrial
                parks, urban industrial areas

ECOSYS
}
#-----------------------------------------------------------
sub viewError{
print(<<ECOSYS);
$ML
Not a valid choice. Valid
                options are 1 to 3
                ...or q to quit.
$NL
ECOSYS
}
```

In the lines immediately preceding comment #1, you define a few formatting characters. Using the multiplication operator for characters, you create an identifier ($ML) that contains five new lines. This identifier allows for spacing in the displays the program creates but saves space in the program itself. You also call to the system() function and use the DOS cls command to clear the screen to display the first view of the program.

The Basics of Calling and Defining a Function

At comment #1, you call the `viewOpening()` function. The form of the function call resembles that of the built-in functions (such as `print()`). It is not necessary, but when you call a function, a good practice involves following the function name with a set of parentheses. Likewise, when you place the function on a separate line and treat it as a separate statement, you close the line with a semicolon.

Comment #2 appears in the definitions section of the program. At comment #2, you see first a typical program comment line used to identify a function. In this case, the comment line consists of dashes and the name of the function. Programmers often insert a few sentences at this point describing the use of function. To save space, such comments do not appear in this section.

The definition of `viewOpening()` characterizes the definition of many basic functions. The first element of the definition consists of the keyword `sub`. This keyword designates that the word immediately following it names a function. The function name, `viewOpening`, represents a convention. The convention involves combining at least two words. You allow the first word to remain in lowercase letters while you capitalize the second word and, in the event that you use still more words, every subsequent word. Here are a few more examples:

```
viewOfOpening
determineQuantity
showPreliminaryResults
calculateNetGainFromLoss
```

In each case, the words appear in their entirety, not abbreviated. The use of such *verbose* function names constitutes a coding convention that characterizes the work of many programmers. Generally, this approach results in programs that are easier to understand and maintain.

Following the name of the function, you create what is known as the *function block*. Two curly braces, an *opening brace* and a *closing brace*, define the *scope* of the function block. Within the function block you place any statements you choose. The essential features of the function are as follows:

```
sub viewOpening{
}
```

The lines that fall within the scope of the `viewOpening` function consist first of a call to the `print()` function and a text bock. The lines here differ slightly from those in the Geology Review program of Chapter 11 (Listing11_03). In addition to the use of the `print()` function, the name of the block in this instance is `ECOSYS`, and to create blank lines, you use the $ML and $NL identifiers, which hold newline characters.

More Functions and Scope Specifics

At comment #3 in Listing12_01, you call the viewMenu() function. You call this function at the top of the infinite for loop that defines the primary framework of the application. As a result, the program user has the menu options continuously in view, as Figure 12.7 illustrates.

Figure 12.7
Placing a call to the viewMenu() function keeps the menu continuously in view.

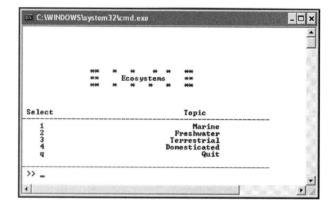

Along with the call to the viewMenu() function, you also prompt the user for input to determine the ecological information to display. To prompt for information, you use a handle (<STDIN>). You can use the handle operator alone (<>), but the convention of using STDIN to identify the handle follows a convention that ensures others can readily understand your program. You assign the input from the prompt to the $ControlChar identifier and then call the chomp() function to remove the line return that pressing Enter adds to the input. Failure to use chomp() often results in a value that your selection statements cannot understand correctly because they usually test for numerical or alphabetical equivalency with a single character. Likewise, you also call the system() function with cls as the argument to ensure that the data you display appears in the same location each time you refresh the window by making a menu selection.

The definition of the viewMenu() function at comment #4 shows you largely the same lines you saw in Chapter 11 in Listing11_03. Now, instead of three options, you have four (see Figure 12.7).

At comment #5, the selection structure provides six options. One option allows the user to exit the program. The other options process the numerical input. In each case, the selection statement calls a function, and the function in turn displays the information the user has requested. Each function definition, as you can see in the lines following comment #6 (in the definition portion of the program), provides largely the same appearance. The function block contains a tagged block. You call the `print()` function to print the contents of the tag. You use the $ML and $NL identifiers to position the text for display.

Functions That Accept Arguments

You can create functions that handle one or more arguments. To accomplish this, you make use of the *argument array* that is associated with every Perl function. You identify the argument array using a special array notation, which consists of the array sign followed by a single underscore:

    @_

You can use the argument array in a variety of ways, but at least initially passing it the values it contains to an array you name in the context of your function makes the flow logic in your function clearer. For this reason, in Figure 12.8, the contents of @_ are passed to @functionArray. This array then contains all the values passed to the function through the argument array (@_).

When you define a function that accepts parameters, you do not have to process the argument array in such an explicit manner. Instead, you can use the argument array directly, with no intermediate array (as with @functionArray).

In Figure 12.8, the programmer passes `argument1` and `argument2` to the `showTwo()` function. In the definition of the function, you see that the contents of the argument array (@_) are assigned to a local array (@functionArray). Then, to use the values in the local array, the two print functions take as their argument the first (0) and second (1) elements of @functionArray (used in its scalar form).

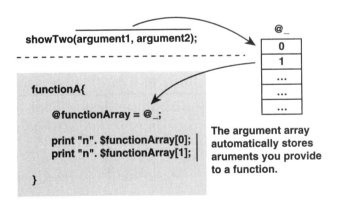

Figure 12.8
A function that uses parameters automatically passes them to the argument array.

Passing an argument to a function involves passing a value from the general scope of a program to the local scope of the function. Listing12_02 explores the use of arguments with two functions, viewMarine() and viewFreshwater(). The first function, viewMarine(), accepts one argument, the text that you want to display as a menu item. The second function, viewFreshwater(), accepts three arguments, the text of the menu item and the spacing before and after the text. Both functions make use of the argument array by assigning its contents to an array defined in the scope of the function.

```
#Listing12_02
#Functions without scalar arguments
#1. define two formatting identifiers
# and two blocks of text

$NL = "\n" ;
$ML = $NL × 5; #Multiple line returns for displays


#Assign text for the first menu item to a scalar
($MarineMenu = <<ECOSYS);
                1. Marine
                Open oceans, continental shelf,
                fisheries, deep sea, estuaries
ECOSYS


#Assign text for the first menu item to a scalar
($FreshWaterMenu = <<ECOSYS);
                2. Freshwater
                Lakes and ponds, rivers and streams,
                marshes and swamps
ECOSYS



#2 Pass one argument to the function as you call it

viewMarine($MarineMenu);                    #Function call

#4 Pass three arguments to the function as you call it
viewFreshwater($ML, $FreshWaterMenu, $NL );


#===============================================================
# Function Definitions
```

❄ ❄ ❄

```
#3
#-------------- Definition of viewMarine() ----------------
#Use:
#viewMarine(string menu_text)
sub viewMarine{

   @LocalArray = @_;            #retrieve argument array locally
   print("$ML $LocalArray[0] $NL"); #retrieve argument array locally
}


#5
#-------------- Definition of viewFreshwater() -------------
#Use:
#view Freshwater(string space_before, string text, string space_after)
sub viewFreshwater{

   @LocalArray = @_;                  #retrieve argument array locally
                                      #retrieve three arguments
   print("$LocalArray[0] $LocalArray[1] $LocalArray[2]");
}
```

At comment #1 in Listing12_02, you define two formatting identifiers. One ($NL) contains one newline character. The other ($ML) contains five. Following the definition of these two formatting identifiers, you then create two identifiers to store the text for the menu items ($MarineMenu and $FreshWaterMenu). Given the definition of the formatting and textual element, you then proceed into the main body of the program.

Comments #2 and #4 identify the content of the main body of the program. Accompanying both of these comments you see calls to functions. The call at comment #2 involves the following syntax:

```
viewMarine($MarineMenu);
```

With this line, you call the viewMarine() function and submit one argument to it. The argument consists of the scalar that stores the text for the information relating to the marine ecosystem.

Later in the program, at comment #3, you find the definition of the function. Here are the lines:

```
#Use:
# viewMarine (string menu_text)
```

```
sub viewMarine{
    @LocalArray = @_;# retrieve argument array locally
    print("$ML $LocalArray[0] $NL"); # retrieve argument array locally
}
```

The first two lines of the definition provide comments that show its use. The comments represent programming conventions rather than any strict syntax that might be said to apply to Perl. You simply show in parentheses following the function name the arguments that the function accepts. Following the comments, you proceed with the definition of the function. The first line inside the function block assigns the general argument array (@_) to a local array (@LocalArray). The second line calls the print() function to print the one item you retrieve from @LocalArray. You accomplish this by using the scalar form of the array and retrieving the item stored at index 0. This is the text that you submitted to the function as an argument when you called it. To format the display, you insert the $ML identifier before the text and follow with the $NL identifier. Figure 12.9 illustrates the resulting display.

For the second function, viewFreshwater(), at comment #4, you see that the call to the function involves three arguments:

```
viewFreshwater($ML, $FreshWaterMenu, $NL );
```

The first argument consists of the identifier to which you assigned five newline characters previously. The second provides the text to be displayed. The third furnishes the identifier to which you have assigned a single newline character.

In the definition of the viewFreshwater() function (see comment #5), you again provide a line of comments to show how the function is used:

```
#Use:
#view Freshwater(string space_before, string text, string space_after)
sub viewFreshwater{
    @LocalArray = @_;                    #retrieve argument array locally
                                         #retrieve three arguments
    print("$LocalArray[0] $LocalArray[1] $LocalArray[2]");
}
```

The comment line that you use to explain a function is, again, a matter of convention rather than required Perl syntax. It shows that the function accepts three strings as arguments. The suggested use stipulates space before the text, the text itself, and space after the text. Inside the function block, as before, you assign the general argument array to a local array. You then call the print() function. This time for the arguments to the print() function, you retrieve three items from the local array. Each item represents one of the arguments you submitted to the array. The first, at index 0, represents the first ($ML) argument to the function call in the main body of the program. The second index (1) presents the text block you assigned to $Fresh-WaterMenu. This leaves the third index (2) to retrieve the new line assigned to $NL. Figure 12.9 shows the resulting display. For both the viewMarine() and viewFreshwater() functions, the text appears with five new lines preceding it and one new line following. The only difference is that one of the functions takes three arguments, whereas the other takes one.

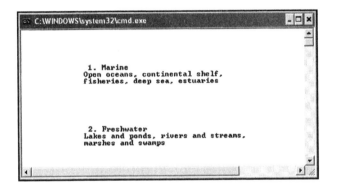

Figure 12.9
Functions that take arguments allow you to create displays.

Passing an Array and Efficiency Measures

Whether you pass a lone scalar or an entire array, the arguments you pass to a function all pass through the argument array. Creating a local array as you define a function provides a way that people reading your programs can more readily recognize its features. Creating a local array involves declaring an array within the function block and then assigning the argument array to it. Such an operation might take the following form:

```
sub objectFunction{
    @LocalArray = @_    #Argument array passed to local array
}
```

At the same time, assigning the argument array in this manner often tends to create needless redundancy. To avoid this, you can adopt the practice of using the argument array directly. When you employ the argument array directly, you enjoy two options. As you might expect, the two options involve using either the implicit form or scalar form of the array. Listing12_03 provides examples of both types of use in a context involving data relating to the greenhouse effect, which scientists regard as the result of rapid accumulation of certain types of gasses in the atmosphere.

```
#Listing12_03
#Using the argument array without renaming it locally

#1 Set up the data on greenhouse gasses
```

313

```
@GreenhouseGasses =
                (@GreenhouseGasses,
                "Carbon Dioxide", "Fossil fuel combustion; ".
                        "deforestation",
                "Methane",
                "Animal wastes, wetlands oil and gas production",
                "CFCs-halogenated compounds", "Refrigerants, foam ".
                        "production",
                "Nitrous oxides", "Fossil fuel, fertilizers, ".
                        "forest destruction",
                 Ozone, "Sunlight reacting with pollutants "
                 );


#2 Create the table heading -- three argument function
makeTableHeading("Type of Gas",
                "Description",
                "Greenhouse Gasses");



#4 Print the table; submit the array to the function
printTable(@GreenhouseGasses);


#=====================================================================
#3 --------------- Definition of makeTableHeading() -------------
#Use:
#makeTableHeading(col head 1, col head 2, table title)
sub makeTableHeading{
  #1 Formatting elements for the table
  $NL = "\n ";
  $DC = sprintf("%c", 177); #cast using sprintf to make a special character
  $TW = 64;                 #Table width
  $DL = sprintf( "%55s", $NL . $DC x $TW); #top and bottom lines
  $COLAHEAD = $_[0];
  $COLBHEAD = $_[1];
  print "$NL $_[2] $NL";
  printf("$DL $NL");
  printf("$NL %-15s %-40s $NL ", $COLAHEAD , $COLBHEAD);
```

```
  printf("$DL $NL" );
}
#5 --------------- Definition of printTable() -------------
#Use:
# printTable(array to print)
sub printTable{
  $NL = "\n ";
  $Control = 0;
  foreach $Gas (@_){    #access the argument array here
    if($Control % 2 == 0){printf("$NL %-30s", $Gas);
    }
    else{printf("$NL %-15s %-40s $NL", "", $Gas);
    }
    $Control++;
  }
}
```

In Listing12_03, at comment #1 you declare an array that consists of the names of the major greenhouse gasses and brief summaries of their ecological sources. Quotation marks enclose each item. Commas separate the items in the list, and when the descriptions require more than one line, the second line is concatenated and appears indented. At comment #2, you call the makeTableHeading() function. Arguments to the function include, in the first two positions, the two titles for column headings and, as the third argument, the title of the table, Greenhouse Gasses.

In the definition of makeTableHeading() in the lines trailing comment #3 (see the lower part of the program), you directly use the argument array in its scalar form to define the identifiers for formatting the table. Here are the lines:

```
    $COLAHEAD = $_[0];
    $COLBHEAD = $_[1];
    print "$NL $_[2] $NL";
```

In each instance, the scalar form of the argument array consists of a dollar sign followed by an underscore and index brackets containing the index number of the element you want to retrieve from the argument list of the function. Given that you state in the comments preceding the function definition the order and purpose of the function arguments, you can easily map the indexes you use to the information they represent.

Back in the top of the program, at comment #4, you call the printTable() function. You supply the @GreenhouseGasses array to the function as its sole argument. In the definition of the function shown trailing comment #5, in the definition section of the program, you make use of the implicit form of the argument array to access the items in the @GreenhouseGasses array. This use appears in the argument following the foreach repetition statement. It allows you to print the items in the array in table rows. Here are the lines:

```
foreach $Gas (@_){ #lines left out
```

You do not require the scalar form of the array in this instance because you have no need to access items specifically, as is the case when you process the column heads and the table title in the makeTableHeading() function. Here, by traversing the array and printing each item successively, you fulfill the requirements set for the function.

You can use the scalar and implicit forms of the argument together or exclusively in any given function definition. Figure 12.10 shows the table that results from the use of the two approaches to passing the argument array.

Figure 12.10
You can use the argument array directly without copying it locally.

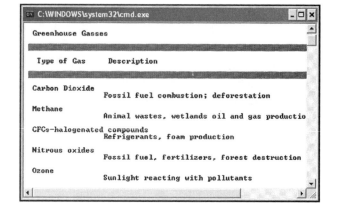

Passing a Hash as an Argument

When you pass a hash to a function, the argument array converts the hash into an array. To process the hash in the function definition, you must convert the items that the argument array provides back into a hash. You can accomplish this by assigning the argument array to a hash. Listing12_04 processes data that shows atmospheric increases in parts per million (PPM) of CO_2 over the past few centuries. The program involves passing a hash containing atmospheric data to a function. The function retrieves data from the argument array, converts it back into a hash, and then prints the data by year in tabular form using the lookup hash operation.

```
#Listing12_04
#Passing a hash to a function
```

```
#1 Set up data on CO2 in the atmosphere
%CO2Changes = ("1750", "180",
               "1970", "320",
               "1980", "330",
               "2000", "360",
               "2025", "450");


#2 Pass arguments for the table heading
makeTableHeading("Year",
                 "CO2 Parts Per Million",
                 "Rise In Atmospheric Carbon Dioxide");


#4 Pass the hash to a function
makeTable(%CO2Changes);


#==================================================================
#3
#--------------- Definition of makeTableHeading() -------------
#makeTableHeading(col head 1, col head 2, table title)
sub makeTableHeading{
  #4 Formatting elements for the table
  $NL = "\n ";
  $DC = sprintf("%c", 247); #cast using sprintf to make a special character
  $TW = 50;                 #Table width
  $DL = sprintf( "%55s", $NL . $DC × $TW); #top and bottom lines
  $COLAHEAD = $_[0];
  $COLBHEAD = $_[1];
  print "$NL $_[2] $NL";
  printf("$DL $NL");
  printf("$NL %-15s %-40s $NL ", $COLAHEAD , $COLBHEAD);
  printf("$DL $NL" );
}


#5--------------- Definition of makeTable() -------------
#makeTable(hash for table)
sub makeTable{
  $NL = "\n ";
```

```
%LocalCO2 = @_;                    #Assign argument array to hash
@CO2Years = keys(%LocalCO2);                #extract keys for sorting
@CO2Years = sort{$a<=>$b}(@CO2Years);       #perform the sort
#Use the sorted years (array) to extract the values (hash)
foreach $Year (@CO2Years){                     #access the argument array here
    printf("$NL %-15s %-40s $NL", $Year, $LocalCO2{$Year});
}
}
```

In the lines that comment #1 in Listing12_04 identifies, you set up a hash (%CO2Changes) that lists dates and CO_2 levels for the past few centuries. Immediately after defining the hash, at comment #2, you call the makeTableHeading() function and supply it with three arguments. As Figure 12.11 reveals, these name the table and supply Year and CO2 Parts Per Million as the column headings.

In the lines associated with comment #4, you pass the %CO2Changes to the makeTable() function. You supply the hash to the function in its implicit form. In the lower part of the program, at comment #5, you retrieve the hash from the argument array by assigning it to a local hash identifier, %LocalCO2. Assignment automatically translates the items in the hash into key-value pairs.

Following the definition of the local hash, you use the keys() function to assign the years (keys) in the local hash to a local array (@CO2Years). In the line following the definition of this array, you sort the years using the numerical form of the Perl sort() function. You then proceed into a foreach repetition statement in which you employ the sorted years in @CO2Years to access the items in the %LocalCO2 hash. To accomplish this, you use the hash lookup operation. When you employ the sorted array to retrieve the values (CO_2 levels) from the hash, the years unfold in the table in ascending order. As Figure 12.11 reveals, it is also the case that the level of CO_2 grows with the passing years. Note that the data for 2025 is projected.

Figure 12.11
Passing a hash to a function requires that you re-create the hash in the context of the function.

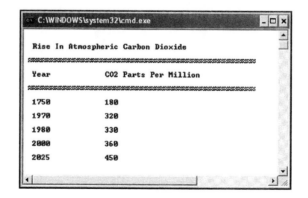

Functions That Return Values

You can return values from functions in two ways. One way involves using the keyword `return` followed by the argument you want to return. The other approach is to allow the function to return the result of its last active statement. Listing12_05 works with the conversion of acres to hectares. Ecologists measure the ecological footprint of the human population in terms of the number of hectares needed to support consumption levels. Listing12_05 generates a table that shows figures for acres in one column and hectares in another. The definition and call to a function that converts acres to hectares demonstrate the use of the `return` keyword. On the other hand, the definition and call to a function that returns a string that serves to identify the source of the information the function contains demonstrate how you can implicitly return the results of the final statement in a function.

```
#Listing12_05
#Passing and returning a value
#1 Footprints for US in acres
    %Footprints = ("Fossil/Nuclear Power",   14.5,
                   "Built-up Areas",  0.9,
                   "Growing Crops",  3.7,
                   "Grazing Animals",  0.8,
                   "Harvesting Fish and Sea Food",  0.8);
#Source of information
@FPInfoSource = ("Source: M. Wackernagel, C. Monfreda, D. Deumling,",
                 "\"Ecological Footprint of Nations.\" November, 2002.",
                 "Redefining Progress www.redefiningprogress.org.");


#2 Pass arguments for the table heading
makeTableHeading("Footprint Type",
                 "Acres",
                 "Hectares",
                 "Ecological Footprints for the US");


#4 Pass the hash to a function
makeTable(%Footprints);


#8 Cascading functions: print calls to printTableNote
#  See #9 - printTableNote returns implicitly
print(formatTableNote(@FPInfoSource));
```

```
#======================================================================
#3 --------------- Definition of makeTableHeading() --------------
#makeTableHeading(col head 1, col head 2, table title)
sub makeTableHeading{
  #4 Formatting elements for the table
  $NL = "\n ";
  $DC = sprintf("%c", 254);  #cast using sprintf to make a special character
  $TW = 52;                  #Table width
  $DL = sprintf( "%60s", $NL . $DC x $TW); #top and bottom lines
  $COLAHEAD = $_[0];
  $COLBHEAD = $_[1];
  $COLCHEAD = $_[2];
  print "$NL $_[3] $NL";
  printf("$DL $NL");
  printf("$NL %-30s %-10s %-10s $NL ", $COLAHEAD , $COLBHEAD, $COLCHEAD );
  printf("$DL $NL" );
}


#5 --------------- Definition of makeTable() -------------
#makeTable(hash for table)
sub makeTable{
  $NL = "\n ";
  %LocalFP = @_;                  #Assign argument array to hash
  @FPAcres = keys(%LocalFP);    #extract keys for sorting
 #Use the sorted years (array) to extract the values (hash)
  foreach $Acres (@FPAcres){    #access the argument array here
      printf("$NL %-30s %-10.2f %-10.4f $NL ",
                                    $Acres,
                                    $LocalFP{$Acres},
#6 Call conversion function
                                    convertAcreToHectare($LocalFP{$Acres})
                                    );
  }#end foreach
}#end makeTable


#7 --------------- Definition of convertAcreToHectare() -------------
#convertAcreToHectare(hash for table)
```

```
sub convertAcreToHectare{
  #Use the return keyword to explicitly return the value
  return($_[0]/2.42);
  #or without return, the last active statement returns a value
  #($_[0]/2.42);
}


#9 --------------- Definition of formatTableNote() -------------
#formatTableNote(string for table note)
sub formatTableNote{
    $NL = "\n";
    $CH = "-" × 52;
    #Join elements into a string
    #$TableNote =
    join("$NL ", $NL, $CH, @_);
    #or
    #return($TableNote);
}
```

At comment #1 in Listing12_05, you create a hash (%Footprints) that contains the names of ecological "footprints," which are areas of the earth's surface required to support given human consumption patterns. Following the definition of the data hash, you then create an array that provides information relating to the source of information in the %Footprints array.

At comment #2, you call the makeTableHeading() and provide four arguments to the function. The first furnishes the heading for the column that names the footprints. The second names the Acres column. The third names the Hectares column. For the last argument, you supply the name of the table, Ecological Footprints for the US.

The code associated with comment #3 (in the definition section of the program) reveals that you provide no return statement for the makeTableHeading() function. You require no return value from this function since it serves only to print the table heading, not to process information passed to other functions.

In the lines trailing comment #4, you call the makeTable() function and supply it with the %Footprint array as its lone argument. The argument array picks up the items in the hash, and at comment #5, in the definition section of the program, you assign the items from the argument array to the %LocalFP hash to restore them to their original key-value pairs. This then allows you to make use of the each repetition statement to print the items in the hash.

The Explicit Use of return

At comment #6, which identifies lines inside the makeTable() definition block, you call a function that converts acreage to hectares (convertAcreToHectare()). To employ this function, you supply it with the lookup hash operation for %LocalFP. When you provide the key ($Acres) to the lookup operation, it provides the number of acres for the footprint the key identifies. The convertAcreToHectare() function performs its work and then returns a value to the printf() function through the makeTable() function, and as Figure 12.13 illustrates, you see the result displayed under the Hectares column heading.

You return this value explicitly (with the use of the return keyword). To return the value explicitly, in the definition of the convertAcreToHectare() function (see the lines following comment #7), you provide only one statement for the entire body of the function:

```
return($_[0]/2.42);
```

The return keyword accesses the result of the calculation and makes it available when the flow of the program reaches the end of the function and returns the value to the main flow of the program. If it is your task to maintain this code, the keyword enables you to recognize precisely how and where the function returns its value. When the return statement executes, it terminates the action of the function. Lines following it are not processed.

As a contrast, in the comment following the return statement, the program provides an example of how you can implicitly return the converted number.

```
#($_[0]/2.42);
```

Commenting out this line make no difference in the performance of the function because the function terminates with the execution of the return statement. However, it is good form to comment the line to show that it is not intended as a duplication of the return statement. Were you to comment out the return statement, this statement would take its place and implicitly return the result of the calculation.

On the other hand, as Figure 12.12 illustrates, if you reverse the order of the statements so that the explicit return statement follows the calculation, the return statement remains the last statement in the program. The flow of the program reaches the calculation, performs it, and without returning passes on to the following line, which contains the return statement. It then performs the calculation again and this time returns the result.

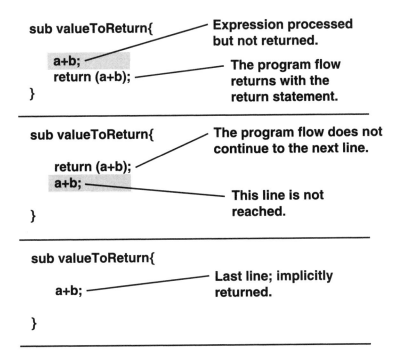

Figure 12.12
If the `return` operation is implicit (no use of the `return` keyword), it must be the last statement in the function.

The Implicit Use of return

The function call associated with comment #8 involves a cascading set of functions. The built-in Perl `print()` function takes as its argument the value that the `formatTableNote()` function returns. As an argument to the `formatTableNote()` function, you supply the `@FPInfoSource` array. The purpose of the `formatTableNote()` function involves processing the array you furnish to it so that it can be printed as a single string.

At comment #9, in the section of the program dedicated to the definition of the `format-TableNote()` function, you employ the `join()` function to create a string using the elements of the array you have passed to the function. The function returns the string implicitly. Here is the code:

```
$TableNote = join("$NL ", $NL, $CH, @_);
```

No `return` statement follows this statement. The performance of the `join()` operation stands as the last (uncommented) line of the function, and for this reason, as Figure 12.13 illustrates, the result of the `join` operation becomes the value the function returns. You can reduce the complexity of the code even further if you eliminate the assignment operation:

```
join("$NL ", $NL, $CH, @_);
```

The function continues to perform its work because the join() function returns a string, and this action provides the value the formatTableNote() function supplies. Figure 12.13 illustrates the formatted string.

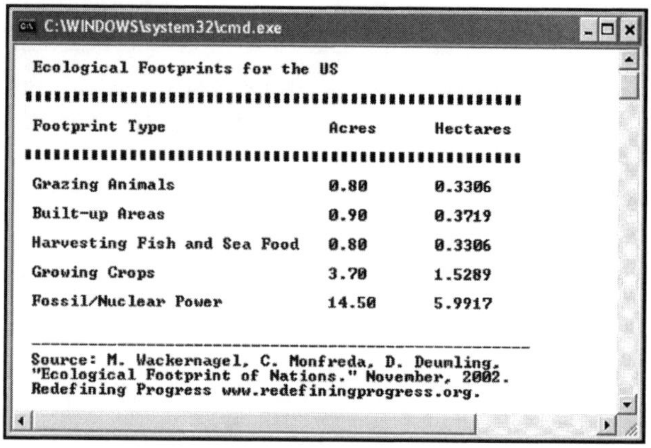

Figure 12.13
You can return values implicitly or using the return keyword.

Contexts and Returning Arrays and Hashes

As previous examples of using the argument array demonstrate, the context into which you introduce the returned value of a function determines how it is "cast." In other words, if you use the returned value as a string, then it becomes a string. If you use it as a number, then it becomes a number. (If you cast a word as a number, the value of the word is 0.) This same relationship applies to hashes and arrays. Listing12_06 demonstrates how this works using an array that contains information relating to the way the biosphere dissipates solar radiation. The sortRows() function receives a hash as its argument. It processes the values in the hash and returns them as an array. The displayTable() function then displays the sorted data.

```
#Listing12_06
#Using contexts to process data in hashes and arrays
#1 set up table of media and percentages
%MediaOfDissipation = ("Reflected", 30,
                       "Direct Conversion to Heat", 46,
                       "Evaporation and Precipitation", 23,
                       "Wind, Wave, Currents", 0.2,
                       "Photosynthesis", 0.8
                       );
```

```
@InfoSource = ("Source: Eugene P. Odum, Ecology: A Bridge Between",
                "Science and Society. Sunderland, MA: Sinauer Associates,",
                "Inc., Publishers, p. 86");

#2 Pass arguments for the table heading - print heading
makeTableHeading("Medium ",
                "\% Solar Radiation",
                "Biospheric Dissipation of Heat");

#3 Pass the hash to a function that orders its elements
#   and returns an array (see #4). Assign the array...
@SortedMedia = sortRows(%MediaOfDissipation);

#5 Pass the array to a function that prints the table rows
#   (see #6)
printTable(@SortedMedia);

#7 Print the note for the table
print(printTableNote(@InfoSource));


#===================================================================
#-------------- Definition of makeTableHeading() -------------
#makeTableHeading(col head 1, col head 2, table title)
sub makeTableHeading{
  #4 Formatting elements for the table
  $NL = "\n ";
  $DC = sprintf("%c", 254);   #cast using sprintf to make a special character
  $TW = 52;                   #Table width
  $DL = sprintf( "%60s", $NL . $DC x $TW); #top and bottom lines
  $COLAHEAD = $_[0];
  $COLBHEAD = $_[1];
  print "$NL $_[2] $NL";
  printf("$DL $NL");
  printf("$NL %-30s %-10s $NL ", $COLAHEAD , $COLBHEAD);
  printf("$DL $NL" );
}
```

❄ ❄ ❄

```
#4 -------------- Definition of sortRows() -------------
#sortRows(string for table note)
sub sortRows() {
%LocalHash = @_; #array passed to a hash

#Access keys (names of media) and values (percents)
@DissipationKeys = keys(%LocalHash);
@DissipationValues = values(%LocalHash);

#Sort the numbers
@DissipationValues = sort{$a <=> $b}(@DissipationValues);

#Use the sorted numbers to reorganize the keys
  foreach $Value (@DissipationValues){
      foreach $Key (@DissipationKeys){
            if($Value == $LocalHash{$Key}){
            #      printf("\n %-30s %-10s", $Key, $Value);
            @OrderedArray = (@OrderedArray , $Key, $Value);
            }#end if
      }#end inner
  }#end outer
  #Return an array in which items are ordered numerically
  return @OrderedArray;
}


#6 -------------- Definition of printTable() -------------
#printTable(@array to print)
sub printTable{
  @SortedMedia = @_;
  for($Itr = 0; $Itr < scalar(@SortedMedia); $Itr += 2){
      printf("$NL %-30s %-10.2f $NL ", $SortedMedia[$Itr],
                                        $SortedMedia[$Itr+1]);
  }
}


# -------------- Definition of printTableNote() -------------
# printTableNote(string for table note)
```

```
sub printTableNote{
    $NL = "\n";
    $CH = "-" × 52;
    #Join elements into a string
    $TableNote = join("$NL ", $NL, $CH, @_);
    #or
    #return($TableNote);
}
```

With the lines that comments #1 and #2 identify, you set up first a hash that stores information about the different ecological media that filter solar radiation (%MediaOfDissipation). You also define an array that contains information identifying the source of this information. In addition, you set up the headings you see in Figure 12.14, Medium and % Solar Radiation. You must use an escape sequence to display the percent sign.

At comment #3, you call the sortRows() function and furnish it with the %MediaOfDissipation hash as its only argument. The purpose of the sortRows() function is to translate the hash into an array and order the items in the array so that the data representing percentages of solar radiation appear in ascending order.

To contextualize the results of the operation that sortRow() performs, you assign the return value of sortRows() to an array (@SortedMedia). The specifics of the conversion between contexts unfold at comment #4, which identifies the definition of sortRows(). To re-create the hash that you have passed to the function, you assign the contents of the argument array to the hash identifier, %LocalHash. You then call the keys() and values() functions to access the media (keys) and percentages of radiation (values) in the local hash.

To order the resulting display of the table, you first order the percentage values. To accomplish this, you call the numeric form of the sort() function and sort the items in the @DissipationValues array. This array then becomes the controlling array in the outer of two foreach statements. The inner foreach statement accesses the names of the media. Within the inner loop, you employ the lookup hash operation and use the percentages to retrieve the names of the media from the local hash. With each retrieval, you employ an if selection statement to determine if the retrieved percentage conforms to the ascending order that the percentage array establishes. If it does, then you assign the percentage, preceded by the name of its associated medium, to a new array (@OrderedArray). You then explicitly return @OrderedArray.

Given the returned array that contains the media is now ordered according the ascending values of their percentages, at comment #3 you assign the returned array to @SortedMedia and then employ @SortedMedia as the argument for printTable() (see comment #5).

In the lines associated with comment #6, you define printTable(). In this case, you assign the argument array to a local array only to make things a little clearer to anyone who might be reading the code. You traverse the items in the array through a repetition statement that you advance in increments of 2 using the counter. When you advance the counter in increments of 2, you can access items two at a time. The first item corresponds to the value of the counter. The second item is the item that corresponds to the value of the counter plus 1. Retrieving items from the array in this way, you can assign them simultaneously as two arguments to the printf() function. In this fashion, you display media and percentages in ascending order, as Figure 12.14 illustrates.

Figure 12.14
Contextual uses of arrays and hashes allow you to organize items for display.

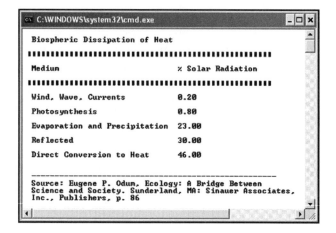

Conclusion

In this chapter, you have explored the use of functions. Functions provide a way to organize the statements that constitute a program into manageable units. When you set up a Perl program, it is beneficial to make use of some of the lessons of structural programming. Accordingly, you designate a space in your program in which you place function definitions. You make calls to these defined functions in another area of your program. The area you set aside for calling functions provides the working area of your program. Set up in this way, you can pursue development activities in the working area while reserving the defined area for code you consider stable.

Definitions of functions range from those that employ no return values and accept no arguments to those that employ many arguments and return values and even incorporate arrays and hashes. When you pass values to a function, you pass the values through the Perl argument array. The argument array translates all the arguments you pass to a function into a single array. To access the values you have provided as arguments to a function, you must retrieve them through array operations you implement within the function definition block.

To retrieve values from the argument array, you can assign the array to a local array or hash. After completing this assignment, you can then use standard array and hash functions to perform operations. The operations you implemented in this chapter included sorting, printing, formatting, and performing simple calculations. Regardless of the operation performed, you can return the results. When you return the results of your operations, you can do so explicitly, using the `return` keyword, or you can allow the last operation performed to return its result implicitly.

13 } References

This chapter explores references, which among other activities allow you to pass complex arguments to functions and to create data structures that involve storing arrays in arrays or arrays in hashes. References work in direct and indirect ways. From a direct approach, you create a reference and assign a value directly to it. From an indirect approach, you assign a value to an identifier and then assign the identifier to the reference. In addition to constructing references for scalar, array, and hash values, you can also create references to functions. In addition to function references, you can make use of typeglobs, which are a more basic form of reference. One good use of typeglobs involves creating constant values. Here are a few of the topics this chapter covers:

* How to create references
* Dereferencing references
* Storing arrays in hashes
* Storing hashes in arrays
* Creating and using function references
* Typeglobs and the `ref()` function

References in General

In previous chapters, you saw that when you create a function with multiple parameters, the parameters are merged into the argument array. When you define a function, you must unpack the argument array if you want to retrieve individual elements from it. If you pass a series of scalar values to an array, you can easily retrieve the values by employing the indexes of the argument array. When you pass several different data types to a function, unpacking the argument array becomes more problematic. Consider Listing13_01.

```
#Listing13_01

#1 Define different identifiers of different types
$ExtraVegetable = "Cabbage";
@Vegetables = ("Green beans", "Broccoli", "Brussels sprouts");
@Fruits = ("Apple", "Apricot", "Banana", "Cantaloupe", "Grapefruit");
%Cereals = ("Bran Buds" , 110, "Raisin Bran" , 150, "Grapenuts" , 100);

#2 Call a function to submit the identifiers
printItems(@Vegetables, @Fruits, %Cereals, $ExtraVegetable);



#======================================================================
#3 --------------- Definition of printItems() -------------
#printItems(array to print)
sub printItems{
  $NL = "\n ";
  foreach $Item (@_){ #access the argument array here
          printf("$NL %-30s", $Item);
  }
}
```

At comment #1 in Listing13_01, you define a series of identifiers of different types. The identifiers consist of a scalar, two arrays, and a hash. At comment #2, you call the printItem() function and pass all of these identifiers to it as arguments. With the definition of printItem() that follows comment #3, you employ a foreach statement to access the argument array and print the items it contains. As you can see in Figure 13.1, the result consists of a single, merged array from which it would prove difficult to extract individual items.

Figure 13.1
Arrays, hashes, and scalars merge as you submit them as arguments.

When you use a hash, an array, and a scalar as arguments to the printItems() function in Listing13_01, they are all merged into one large array. The items in the hash (%Cereals) lose their key-value identity. The items in the arrays (@Vegetables, @Fruits) merge into one massive array. The lone scalar ($ExtraVegetable) is likewise tossed in, and when you see the list Figure 13.1 shows, you have lost track of the initial groupings the hash, arrays, and scalar provided. How do you retrieve these items in the same form that you submitted them? You use references to make this possible.

What you do when you pass arguments to functions extends to building complex bodies of data that involve putting hashes inside arrays or arrays inside hashes. In each instance, you need a convenient way to maintain the identity of your data. At the same time, you can use references to make it so that you can store and retrieve data without having to use explicit names for it. The same power that allows you to maintain the identity of data as you pass it to functions allows you to maintain the identity of data when you store it in complex forms in arrays or hashes. How references allow you to accomplish this work becomes the topic of later topics in this chapter (see, for example, "Anonymous Hash References as Data Containers").

The term "reference" applies to the process of referring one thing to another. When applied to data, a reference identifies a place in the memory of your computer. When you work with Perl, the reference identifies a place in memory that stores the values you create for your programs. This place in memory is characterized by a table. The table can relate your values to all the data types that Perl supports and allows you to perform operations such as accessing an array element as a scalar or working back and forth between numbers and strings. Figure 13.2 provides a crude representation of a reference table.

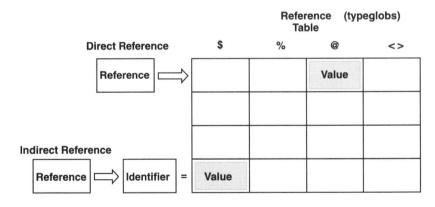

Figure 13.2
A reference allows you to access values more immediately than is otherwise possible.

Creating References

To create a reference, you use a special operator called the reference operator. The reference operator consists of a backslash (\). When you prefix it to an identifier, it issues a directive for the Perl interpreter that the identifier should be recognized as a reference. When you use the reference operator, you can do so in two ways. One way involves assigning a reference to another identifier. This involves what is known as *indirect* or *symbolic* reference and provides an excellent way to work with references if you are encountering them for the first time. The other approach involves direct or hard references, and this approach is preferable after you understand how to use references.

To create references in an indirect way, you can use the approach Listing13_02 provides. Accordingly, you define an identifier as you do normally. You then employ the reference operator to create a reference. The reference is the address or place in memory of the value you have defined for your identifier. You then assign this value to yet another identifier. See Figure 13.2.

```
#Listing13_02


#1 Define different identifiers of different types
$ExtraVegetable = "Cabbage";
@Fruits = ("Apple", "Apricot", "Banana");
%Cereals = ("Bran Buds" , 110, "Raisin Bran" , 150);


$NL = "\n\n";
$DL = "-" x 50;
#2 Define references
#  In each case, the scalar stores the reference
# You assign the reference to the scalar


#2.1 Define a reference for a scalar
$RefToExtraVegetable = \$ExtraVegetable;


print "$NL 2.1.1. Value in \$ExtraVegetable -- " . $ExtraVegetable;
print "$NL 2.1.2. Reference in \\\$ExtraVegetable -- " . $ExtraVegetable;
print "$NL 2.2.3. Reference in \$RefExtraVegetable -- " . $ExtraVegetable;


print $NL . $DL;
```

```
#2.2 Define a reference for an array
$RefFruits = \@Fruits;

print "$NL 2.2.1. Value in \@Fruits -- @Fruits";
print "$NL 2.2.2. Reference in \\\@Fruits -- " . \@Fruits;
print "$NL 2.2.3. Reference in \$RefToFruits -- " . $RefFruits;

print $NL . $DL;

#2.3 Define a reference for a hash
$RefToCereals = \%Cereals;

print "$NL 2.3.1. Value in %Cereals -- ";
print %Cereals;
print "$NL 2.3.2. Reference in \\\%Cereals -- " . \$Cereals;
print "$NL 2.3.3. Reference in \$RefToCereals -- " . $RefToCereals;
```

As Figure 13.3 shows, Listing13_02 provides output that traces the assignment process. At comment #1, you define three standard identifiers ($ExtraVegetable, @Fruits, and %Cereals). You then proceed at comment #2 to use the reference operator to access the reference for each of these identifiers. In each instance, you assign the reference to a scalar identifier that you prefix with Ref. As Figure 13.3 illustrates, printing the value that you have assigned to each identifier echoes the value back to you.

When you apply the reference operator or the identifier (items 2.1.2, 2.2.2, and 2.3.2), you see the reference identifier. You can refer to this form of the identifier as its typeglob readout. The typeglob readout is an analytical tool that usually has few places in basic Perl programs, but it proves useful if you are curious to see how the identifier reference table identifies any given identifier in your program.

In every instance, the typeglob characterization consists of the address of the identifier and its type. For the @Fruits array, then, you see ARRAY(0×35f00) in Figure 13.3. For the %Cereals hash, you see HASH(0×1833e7c) in Figure 13.3. When you execute Listing13_03 on your computer, you see different numbers (the 0× indicates that they are hexadecimal numbers) because your computer assigns the memory locations to the identifiers when the program executes, and each computer on which a program runs is likely to designate different memory locations.

Figure 13.3
Definition of references allows you to see the location in memory of different identifiers.

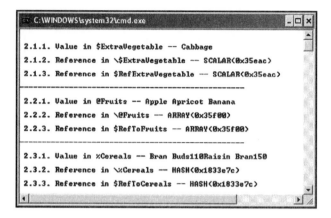

```
C:\WINDOWS\system32\cmd.exe                                    _ □ ×

2.1.1. Value in $ExtraVegetable -- Cabbage
2.1.2. Reference in \$ExtraVegetable -- SCALAR(0x35eac)
2.1.3. Reference in $RefExtraVegetable -- SCALAR(0x35eac)
_____

2.2.1. Value in @Fruits -- Apple Apricot Banana
2.2.2. Reference in \@Fruits -- ARRAY(0x35f00)
2.2.3. Reference in $RefToFruits -- ARRAY(0x35f00)
_____

2.3.1. Value in %Cereals -- Bran Buds110Raisin Bran150
2.3.2. Reference in \%Cereals -- HASH(0x1833e7c)
2.3.3. Reference in $RefToCereals -- HASH(0x1833e7c)
```

The typeglob readouts for items 2.1.2, 2.2.2, and 2.3.2 in Figure 13.3 provide direct references. In other words, you are directly accessing the reference itself. The direct reference results when you use the reference operator on the identifier that holds the value. On the other hand, the typeglob readouts for items 2.1.3, 2.2.3, and 2.3.3 represent indirect or symbolic references. The indirect reference results when you print the value that you have assigned to a scalar.

When you use the symbolic form of an identifier (its name), you see the form of the identifier that gets merged into the argument array of your function. When data is identified in this indirect way, the interpreter sees no need to distinguish it on the address level—the level of the reference. But, if you move to a direct approach to identifying the data, then the interpreter can always know precisely where the data you are dealing with begins and ends based on its location in memory. It can use this address to preserve the identity of the data. You then submit the address rather than the data the address points to (or references).

Using the ref() Function

Perl provides a function that allows you to check the typeglob status of any given reference. In this way, you can see the reference the interpreter stores for each data item. Also, you can see how you might make use of this form of the data as you approach the problem of preserving groups of data as you pass them to functions. This is the ref() function. Listing13_03 illustrates the basic use of the ref() function. To use it, you submit the identifier you want to explore, prefixed with the reference operator.

```
#Listing13_03
#1 Define different identifiers of different types
$ExtraVegetable = "Cabbage";
@Fruits = ("Apple", "Apricot", "Banana");
%Cereals = ("Bran Buds" , 110, "Raisin Bran" , 150);
```

```
$NL = "\n\n";
$DL = "-" × 50;
#2 Define references
#Use ref to return a string that tells you the reference type

#2.1 Define a reference for a scalar
$RefToExtraVegetable = \$ExtraVegetable;
print "$NL 2.1.4. ref(\\\$ExtraVegetable) -- " . ref(\$ExtraVegetable);
if( ref(\$ExtraVegetable) eq "SCALAR"){ print "$NL Okay."};

print $NL . $DL;
#2.2 Define a reference for an array
$RefFruits = \@Fruits;
print "$NL 2.2.4. ref(\\\@Fruits) -- " . ref(\@Fruits);
if( ref(\@Fruits) eq "ARRAY"){print "$NL Okay."};

print $NL . $DL;
#2.3 Define a reference for a hash
$RefToCereals = \%Cereals;
print "$NL 2.2.4. ref(\\\%Fruits) -- " . ref(\%Cereals);
if( ref(\%Cereal) eq "HASH"){print "$NL Okay."};
```

At comment #2.1 in Listing13_03, as Figure 13.4 shows, you print the typeglob standing of $ExtraVegetable. Since you have prefixed the identifier with the reference operator, the ref() function reports that the reference is to a SCALAR. When you use an if selection statement to test the string the ref() function returns, the selection evaluates true, and you see "Okay" printed to the screen. The same applies to the use of the ref() function with the array and the hash identifiers.

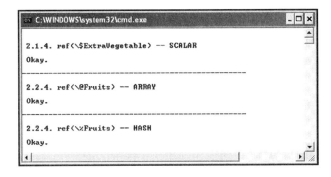

Figure 13.4
The ref() function returns the typeglob standing of your reference.

Dereferencing References

When you print the scalar to which you have assigned a reference, you see only the memory locations of the information the reference guides you to. What you usually require is not the location of the information but the information itself. To access the information a reference designates, you must dereference the reference. To dereference a reference, you employ the dereference operator.

As Figure 13.5 illustrates, the dereference operator for each type of reference consists of its type identifier. You prefix the type identifier to the reference:

* Dereference a scalar: `$$RefToExtraVegetable`
* Dereference an array: `@$RefToFruits`
* Dereference a hash: `%$RefToCereals`

In each case, extracting the value a reference represents involves applying a type identifier to the reference identifier. In Listing13_04, you apply the dereference operators to the scalar identifiers to which you have assigned references.

```
#Listing13_04


#1 Define array and hash
$ExtraVegetable = "Cabbage";
@Fruits = ("Apple", "Apricot", "Banana");
%Cereals = ("Bran Buds" , 110, "Raisin Bran" , 150);


#2 Define references
#For a scalar
$RefToExtraVegetable = \$ExtraVegetable;
#For an array
$RefToFruits = \@Fruits;
#For a hash
$RefToCereals = \%Cereals;



$NL = "\n\n";
$DL = "-" x 50;
#3Show dereferences
#Scalar
print "$NL Scalar: $NL Value in \$ExtraVegetable -- " . $ExtraVegetable;
```

```
print "$NL Reference: \$RefToExtraVegetable -- " . $RefToExtraVegetable;
print "$NL Dereference: \$\$RefExtraVegetable -- " . $$RefToExtraVegetable;
print $NL . $DL;

#Array
print "$NL Array: $NL Value in \@Fruits -- @Fruits";
print "$NL Reference: \$RefToFruits -- " . $RefToFruits;
print "$NL Dereference: \@\$RefToFruits-- ";
print "@$RefToFruits";

print $NL . $DL;

#Hash
print "$NL Hash: $NL Value in %Cereals -- ";
print %Cereals;
print "$NL Reference: \\\%Cereals -- " . \%Cereals;
print "$NL Dereference: \%\$RefToCereals -- ";
print %$RefToCereals;
```

At comment #1 in Listing13_04, you set up three identifiers: a scalar, an array, and a hash. At comment #2, you define references for each of the identifiers. In the lines following comment #3, you print the values the non-reference identifiers store, the memory location of the reference, and then the dereferenced values. You use the $ type identifier to dereference a scalar, a @ type identifier to dereference an array, and a % identifier to dereference a hash. Figure 13.5 shows you that the dereferenced values match the values stored in the standard identifiers.

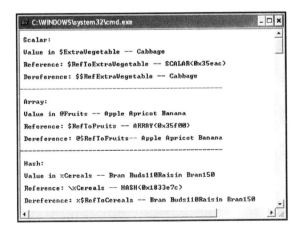

Figure 13.5
Dereferencing a reference involves using the type identifier.

Accessing Items in References to Arrays

To access values in referenced arrays, you can use two approaches. One approach involves dereferencing the array. In this instance, you apply the dereference operator (@) and then access items in the array just as though you were dealing with a standard array. The other approach involves using the pointer operator (->). When you use the pointer operator, you do not dereference the array. Instead, you access the item from the reference itself. If the item you are seeking is not a reference, then it appears in a non-referenced form. Listing13_05 explores using both dereferencing an array to retrieve items in it and accessing values directly from an array reference.

```
#Listing13_05
#Accessing items in arrays
#1 Define an array
@Vegetables = ("Green beans", "Broccoli", "Brussels sprouts");



#2 Define reference
$RefToVegetables = \@Vegetables;
$Size = scalar(@$RefToVegetables);

makeTableHeading("Vegetables", "1. Dereferenced Array \@\$", "");
#3. using Dereference
foreach $Item (@$RefToVegetables){
    printf(" %10s ", $Item);
}


makeTableHeading("Vegetables", "2. Dereferenced Index []", "");
#4. Dereference
$Count = 0;
while($Count < $Size){
    printf(" %10s ", @$RefToVegetables[$Count++]);
}
makeTableHeading("Vegetables", "3. Pointer Operator ->", "");
#5 Pointer Operator
$Count = 0;
while($Count < $Size){
    printf(" %10s ", $RefToVegetables->[$Count++]);
}
```

```
#===================================================================
#-------------- Definition of makeTableHeading() -------------
#makeTableHeading(col head 1, col head 2)
sub makeTableHeading{
    $NL = "\n ";
    $DC = sprintf("%s", "-");
    $TW = 50;
    $DL = sprintf( "%55s", $NL . $DC x $TW); #top and bottom lines
    $COLAHEAD = $_[0];
    $COLBHEAD = $_[1];
    printf("$NL $DL $NL %-25s %-25s $DL $NL", $COLAHEAD , $COLBHEAD);
}
```

In the lines associated with comments #1 and #2 in Listing13_05, you define an array
(@Vegetables) and then define a reference for the array that you assign to a scalar
($RefToVegetables). You use the scalar() function to access the number of items in
the array. To access the array, you dereference the scalar that stores the reference to the array
(@$RefToVegetables).

At comment #3, you again employ a dereferencing strategy to access the items in the array
(@$RefToVegetables). As is evident following Heading 1 in Figure 13.6, you can then use
the dereferenced array in a foreach structure and retrieve items from it as though it were a
regular array.

At comment #4, you dereference the array still again, and this time the result is that you can
retrieve items from the array using their indexes. To accomplish this task, you create a scalar
that you can use to traverse the array ($Count). You likewise employ the scalar, defined earlier,
that stores the size of the array ($Size). Using a while repetition statement, you then traverse
the indexes of the array and print them. The listing following Heading 2 in Figure 13.6 shows
the results.

In the lines trailing comment #5, you make use of the pointer operator in conjunction with the
index brackets ($RefToVegetables->[$Count++]). The pointer operator allows you to
retrieve items directly from the array reference. Using the incremented values of the
$Counter identifier to access the array items, you can print them without further ado because
they do not themselves represent referenced values. Only the array container is referenced. You
access the name of the vegetables through the referenced array. The list following Heading 3 in
Figure 13.6 shows the output of this operation.

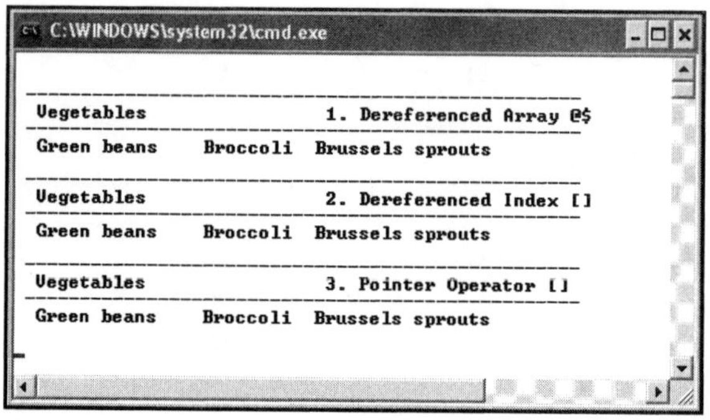

Figure 13.6
You can use dereferencing
or the pointer operator to
access items in an array.

Accessing Hash Keys and Values

To access keys and values in reference to a hash, you can dereference the hash and then use the `each` repetition statement to retrieve key-value pairs. A second approach entails employing the `keys()` function to retrieve keys from a dereferenced version of the hash. You assign the keys to a standard array and then use items from the array in a `foreach` repetition statement that traverses the hash by feeding the array items to the hash lookup operation. To implement the lookup operation, you dereference the hash. A third approach involves using the pointer operator in combination with the `keys()` function. Listing13_06 explores this approach to accessing key-value pairs in a hash.

```
#Listing13_06
#Accessing items in a hash
#1 Define a hash
%Cereals = ("Bran Buds" , 110, "Raisin Bran" , 150);
#2 Define references
$RefToCereals= \%Cereals;


makeTableHeading("Cereals and Calories", "1. Dereferenced Hash \%\$", "");
#3. Using Dereference
while(($Key, $Value)= each(%$RefToCereals)){
    printf(" %-10s %-10s ", $Key, $Value);
}


makeTableHeading("Cereal and Calories", "2. Dereferenced lookup \%\$ {}", "");
#4. Dereference
@CerealNames = keys(%$RefToCereals);


foreach $Name (@CerealNames){
```

342

```
        printf(" %-10s %-10s ", $Name, @$RefToCereals{$Name})
}


makeTableHeading("Cereal and Calories", "3. Pointer Operator ->{}", "");
#5 Pointer Operator
foreach $Name (@CerealNames){
        printf(" %-10s %-10s ", $Name, $RefToCereals->{$Name})
}


#===================================================================
#--------------- Definition of makeTableHeading() -------------
#makeTableHeading(col head 1, col head 2)
sub makeTableHeading{
        $NL = "\n ";
        $DC = sprintf("%s", "-");
        $TW = 50;
        $DL = sprintf( "%55s", $NL . $DC x $TW); #top and bottom lines
        $COLAHEAD = $_[0];
        $COLBHEAD = $_[1];
        printf("$NL $DL $NL %-25s %-25s $DL $NL", $COLAHEAD , $COLBHEAD);
}
```

In the line comment #1 identifies, you define a hash (%Cereals) consisting of two items. At comment #2, you assign a reference for the hash to a scalar ($RefToCereals). Using the hash reference, at comment #3 you employ a while repetition statement in conjunction with the each selection statement to retrieve key-value pairs from the dereferenced hash (%RefToCereals).

In the lines affiliated with comment #4, you again use the dereferenced hash, this time as the argument of the keys() function. You assign the keys of the hash to a standard array, @CerealNames. You then use the array in a foreach selection statement, retrieving the names of the cereals to use in a hash lookup operation. For the hash lookup operation, you employ a dereferenced form of the hash reference (%$RefToCereals).

In the lines trailing comment #5, you again make use of the array of cereal names, but this time, rather than employing them in a dereferenced form of the hash, you use the pointer operator. Accordingly, after retrieving the cereal names from the @CerealNames array using a foreach control statement, you submit each cereal name to the hash lookup operation. In its pointer form, the lookup operation allows you to access values directly from the reference. Figure 13.7 illustrates the output of Listing13_06.

Figure 13.7
You can use different approaches to dereferencing hashes and accessing the information they contain.

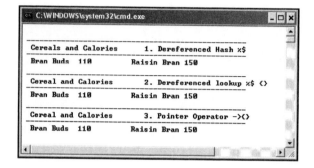

Passing Hash References to a Function

When you submit hash references as arguments to a function, each reference becomes an item in the function's argument array. To retrieve a hash from the array, you retrieve the reference to the hash from the argument array and then access the key-value pairs in the hash either by dereferencing the hash or by using the pointer operator to retrieve the items it contains. Listing13_07 makes use of both dereferencing and the pointer operator to process the key-value pairs of three hashes passed to a function. The hashes contain information on food groups.

```
#Listing13_07
#Pass Hashes to a Function
#1 Define hashes

%Cereals = ("Bran Buds" , 110, "Raisin Bran" , 150);
%Fruits = ("Apple" , 80, "Apricot", 50);
%CookedLegumes = ("Kidney beans" , 110, "Lima beans" , 95);

#Create references for the hashes
$RefToCereals = \%Cereals;
$RefToFruits = \%Fruits;
$RefToCookedLegumes = \%CookedLegumes;

makeTableHeading("Food Name", "Calories per Serving");

#2 Use the references to the hashes as arguments to a function
showData($RefToCereals, $RefToFruits, $RefToCookedLegumes );
```

```
#==============================================================
#3 --------------- Definition of showData()---------------------
#showData (Hash, Hash ...)
sub showData{
    @ArrayInSub = (@_);
    $NumOfHashes = scalar(@ArrayInSub);
    $NL = "\n ";
    #Traverse all the hash references
    for($Itr = 0; $Itr < $NumOfHashes; $Itr++){
        print "$NL $NL Category $Itr $NL";
    #Retrieve each reference sequentially
        $Ref = $ArrayInSub[$Itr];
    #Retrieve the names of the foods and categories
        foreach $Name (keys(%$Ref)){
            printf("$NL %-25s %-25s ", $Name,
                                    $ArrayInSub[$Itr]->{$Name})
        }#end foreach
    }#end for
}#end of showData()


#--------------- Definition of makeTableHeading() -------------
#makeTableHeading(column head 1, column head 2)
sub makeTableHeading{
    $NL = "\n ";
    $DC = sprintf("%s", "-");
    $TW = 50;
    $DL = sprintf("%55s", $NL . $DC x $TW); #top and bottom lines
    $COLAHEAD = $_[0];
    $COLBHEAD = $_[1];
    printf("$NL $DL $NL %-25s %-25s $DL ", $COLAHEAD , $COLBHEAD);
}
```

The lines trailing comment #1 in Listing13_07 first define three hashes and then create scalars that hold references to them. The three hashes contain information relating to three food groups. To create the references, you employ the reference operator (\) in conjunction with the names of the hashes.

At comment #2, after calling the makeTableHeading() function and setting up two column headings (Food Names and Calories per Serving), you call the showData() function, a function that allows you to processes references to hashes to print the items the hashes contain. How this is accomplished becomes apparent at comment #3, which introduces the definition of the function.

To process the hash references, you assign the elements from the argument array to a local array (@ArrayInSub). You then employ the scalar function to determine the number of items the array contains, and this you assign to a scalar ($NumOfHashes). Given that you know the number of hashes in the local array, you can create an embedded repetition structure. The embedded structure consists of a for repetition statement that traverses @ArrayInSub and a foreach repetition structure that retrieves the key terms in the hashes that the array contains.

Prior to accessing the information the hashes contain, you employ the print() function to print the Category of the data. This amounts to the current value of $Itr, which serves to set the index values of $ArrayInSub as you traverse its elements. As Figure 13.8 shows, the category number allows you to identify the contents of each hash passed to showData(). To retrieve individual hash references from @ArrayInSub, you assign each reference to a scalar, $Ref. You then make a dereferenced version of this identifier (%$Ref) the argument of the hash keys() function. The keys() function retrieves the names of foods from the hash, and you submit these to the hash lookup operation in its pointer form to retrieve calorie information from the hash currently represented by @ArrayInSub.

Each iteration of the for loop provides @ArrayInSub in sub with a different reference, so the inner foreach repetition statement traverses each array in the order in which the argument array for showData() transfers the arrays to @ArrayInSub. There is nothing spectacular in this representation of data, but it does suffice to maintain and display the hashes as separate entities.

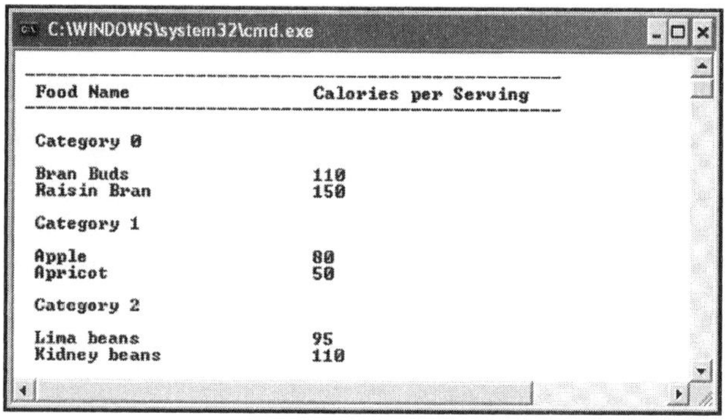

Figure 13.8
Retrieve hash references from the argument array and print them separately.

```
C:\WINDOWS\system32\cmd.exe                              _ □ ×

Food Name                    Calories per Serving
-------------------------------------------------

Category 0

Bran Buds                    110
Raisin Bran                  150

Category 1

Apple                        80
Apricot                      50

Category 2

Lima beans                   95
Kidney beans                 110
```

Passing Arrays to a Function

When you pass references to arrays to a function, each reference is assigned a separate index in the function's argument array. If you try to print the contents of the array argument, you find only the address values representing the arrays. To access the contents of the arrays, you must dereference the arrays. Listing13_08 explores passing and dereferencing references to three arrays that contains the names of foods in different food groups. When the showData() function accesses the references, it dereferences them in reverse order.

```
#Listing13_08
#Pass Arrays to a function
#1 Define arrays
@Vegetables = ("Green beans", "Broccoli", "Brussels sprouts");
@Fruits = ("Apple", "Apricot", "Banana", "Cantaloupe", "Grapefruit");
@Legumes =("Kidney beans", "Lima beans", "Navy beans");

$RefToVegetables = \@Vegetables;
$RefToFruits = \@Fruits;
$RefToCookedLegumes = \@Legumes;

#Print the heading
makeTableHeading("Food Name", "");
#2 Pass the references to a function
showData($RefToVegetables, $RefToFruits, $RefToCookedLegumes);

#===============================================================
#3 --------------- Definition of showData()---------------------
#showData(array ref, array ref...)
sub showData{
    @ArrayInSub = (@_);
    $NumOfArrays = scalar(@ArrayInSub);
    $NL = "\n";
    #Traverse all the hash references -- in reverse order
    for($Itr = $NumOfArrays - 1; $Itr >= 0; $Itr--){
        print "$NL $NL Group $Itr $NL";
    #Retrieve each reference sequentially
        $Ref = $ArrayInSub[$Itr];
    #Retrieve the names of the foods and categories
```

```
        foreach $Name (@$Ref){
            printf("$NL %-25s", $Name,)
        }#end foreach
    }#end for
}#end of showData()


#--------------- Definition of makeTableHeading() -------------
#makeTableHeading(col head 1, col head 2)
sub makeTableHeading{
    $NL = "\n ";
    $DC = sprintf("%s", "-");
    $TW = 50;
    $DL = sprintf("%55s", $NL . $DC x $TW); #top and bottom lines
    $COLAHEAD = $_[0];
    $COLBHEAD = $_[1];
    printf("$NL $DL $NL %-25s %-25s $DL ", $COLAHEAD , $COLBHEAD);
}
```

In the lines trailing comment #1 in Listing13_08, you first define three arrays that name foods from the vegetable, fruit, and legume groups. You then create references to these arrays using the reference operator (\) and assign the references to scalars ($RefToVegetables, $RefToFruits, and $RefToCookedLegumes). You then proceed to set up the printing of a table to display the contents of the arrays. To accomplish this, in the line preceding comment #2, you call the makeTableHeading() function. This takes only one argument, Food Name.

Trailing comment #2, you call the showData() function. The function accepts three arguments, the references to the three arrays you defined previously. In the lines associated with comment #3, you define the function.

Your first task as you define the function involves assigning the contents of the argument array to a local array (@ArrayInSub). You then call the scalar() function to establish the number of elements the array contains and assign this number to a scalar identifier, $NumOfArrays. This identifier then becomes the initializing value for the counter of a for repetition statement ($Itr). When you initialize the counter using $NumOfArrays, you set the total number of references @ArrayInSub contains, so the operation of the repetition statement becomes one of decrementing from this number.

With the for block, you first print a line using the value in $Itr to identify the number of the group. The numbers in this case, as Figure 13.9 shows, begin with 2. With each iteration of the loop, you print the food group number and then proceed to print the names of the food items included in the group. To print the names of the items, you first retrieve the reference from @ArrayInSub. To accomplish this, you use the scalar version of the array and the current value of $Itr to access the index of the reference and then assign the reference temporarily to a scalar identifier ($Ref).

You then dereference $Ref and make it the target of the foreach repetition statement. You assign the food names that the dereferenced array (@$Ref) contains to the $Name identifier and then call the printf() function to print it. With each iteration of the for loop, you access a new reference, and given the work of the foreach traversal of the names, you print the contents of the three arrays. That you print them in an order that is the reverse of their position in the argument array serves only to show that you can access references to arrays and readily manipulate them.

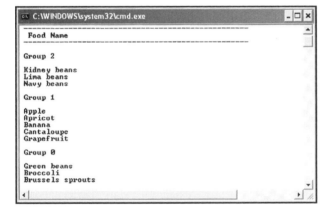

Figure 13.9
You can access array references passed to a function and work with them in any number of ways.

References to Functions

You can make use of the fact that every set of function blocks is in essence a reference. To create a reference to a function, you need only assign the nameless address of the function to a scalar. Here is an example of how this works:

```
$addFoods = sub{
    return join(" ", @_);
};
```

In this example, you assign the nameless function sub to the $addSub identifier. Given this bit of preparation, you can then call the function. To call a function using a reference, you have two options:

❅   Dereference it using the & sign:

```
&$addFoods();
```

❅   Use the pointer operator before the parentheses (->):

```
$addFoods->();
```

Listing13_09 explores the creation of three function references. One prints a list of vegetables when you call it. The other two modify this basic version of the function so that when it appends the names of foods, it adds characters between them. To explore one use of function references, you assign the two forms of the functions into an array and then call the functions using the name of the array and index numbers corresponding to the positions of the function references in the array.

```perl
#Listing13_09
#Function references
#1 Define an array
@Vegetables = ("Green beans", "Broccoli", "Brussels sprouts");
$NL = "\n";


#2 Definition of anonymous functions before their use
$addFoods = sub{
    return join(" ", @_);
};


#3 Definition and assignment to an array
$addMoreFoods[0] = sub{
    return join(" | ", @_);
};


$addMoreFoods[1] = sub{
    return join(" * ", @_);
};


#-----------------------------------------------------------
printf(" %25s", "$NL $NL $NL Use of addFoods()");

#4 Using a dereferenced anonymous function
printf("$NL %15s $NL" . &$addFoods(@Vegetables));
```

```
#5 Using pointer notation
printf("$NL %15s $NL" . $addFoods->(@Vegetables));
printf(" %25s", "$NL $NL $NL Use of addMoreFoods()");


#6 Accessing function references in an array
printf("$NL %15s $NL" . $addMoreFoods[0]->(@Vegetables));
printf("$NL %15s $NL" . $addMoreFoods[1]->(@Vegetables));
```

In the lines that comment #1 in Listing13_09 indicates, you define an array (@Vegetables). At comment #2, you define the first of three anonymously defined functions. The definition of the function involves the sub keyword followed by opening and closing curly braces to form the scope of the function. A semicolon follows the closing curly brace. In the scope of the function, you place only one statement. The statement returns a string that joins arguments submitted to the function into a string and then returns them. To join the arguments, you employ the join() function. The first argument to the function consists of quotation marks that designate blank spaces to separate the items in the string the function returns. For the second argument, you provide the argument array character (@_).

The two function definitions following comment #3 involve statements similar to the first. In the first, you assign a pipe (|) as a separator for the items the join() function forms into a string. In the second, you assign an asterisk (*) as a separator.

At comment #4, you call the addFoods() function using the dereference operator (&). You submit the @Vegetables array as the argument to the function. As Figure 13.10 shows, the output consists of the items the array contains displayed in a single line and separated by white spaces.

In the lines associated with comment #5, you employ the pointer operator (->) to access the function. When you employ the pointer operator, the type is a dollar sign alone. Once again, you submit the @Vegetables array as the sole argument. The result, shown in Figure 13.10, is the same as the first call.

With the calls to the @addMoreFoods array, the results differ according to the value of the index. In the lines trailing comment #6, you first access the function reference at index 0. Then you access the function reference at index 1. As Figure 13.10 reveals, you see the items from the @Vegetables array that you saw before, but this time pipes separate those in the first line while asterisks separate those in the second.

Figure 13.10
You can store references to
functions in an array.

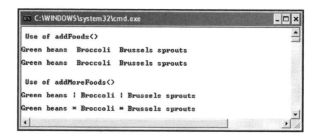

```
C:\WINDOWS\system32\cmd.exe

Use of addFoods()
Green beans   Broccoli   Brussels sprouts
Green beans   Broccoli   Brussels sprouts

 Use of addMoreFoods()
Green beans : Broccoli : Brussels sprouts
Green beans * Broccoli * Brussels sprouts
```

Anonymous Array References as Data Containers

You can create data structures that consist of arrays within arrays if you use anonymous array references. One reason that programmers use anonymous references is that such references enable them to avoid the need to name arrays within arrays. If you use an anonymous reference, you can concentrate on perfecting the work of a few sets of braces instead of a large number of different identifier names. As the next few programs reveal, without anonymous references, you might end up with dozens of identifier names that would make it almost impossible to manage the code in your programs.

An anonymous array reference consists of square braces inside of square braces. The outer set of braces constitutes a "container" for as many arrays as you want to add inside them. You can view the arrays inside the outer braces as "records." You can view the elements within these record arrays as "fields." Figure 13.11 illustrates the arrangement of the arrays that results and how two sets of index braces are involved when you access any given field in a record.

Figure 13.11
An outer container array
involves two sets of
indexes.

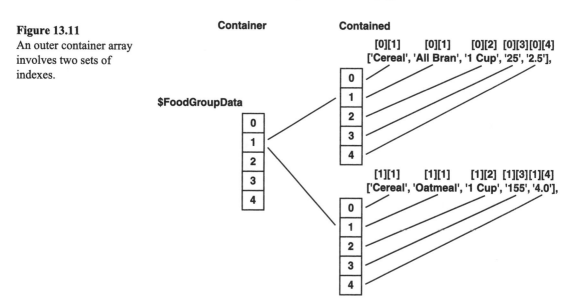

As Figure 13.11 shows, the indexes that identify the first element (Cereal) in the first array are 0 for the array and 0 for the element ([0][0]). For the third element in the second array (1 cup), you use 1 for the array and 2 for the element ([1][2]). This type of container-contained array structure becomes possible when you create a reference within a reference. Listing13_10 experiments with such a structure. You store arrays containing information on different foods inside an array called @FoodGroupData. Each data item is a field within a record, and you dereference the arrays to access the information the fields contain.

```
#Listing13_10
#1 Create an array using anonymous references (square brackets).
        # Food Group Food Serving KCalories
Grams of Fiber
    $FoodGroupData =
        [ #Container array
            [Cereal, 'All Bran', '1 Cup', '25', '2.5'], #Arrays contained
            [Cereal, 'Oatmeal', '1 Cup', '155', '4.0'],
            [Vegetables, 'Green Beans', '0.5 Cup', '15', '1.0'],
            [Vegetables, 'Broccoli', '0.5 Cup', '20', '3.0']
        ];


#2 Insert a record
    $FoodGroupData->[4] = [Fruits, 'Apple', '1 Medium', '80', '3.0'];


#3 Insert items into a record and insert record in larger array
  $FoodGroup = 'Fruits';
  $FoodName= "Apricot";
  $Serving = "3 medium";
  $kCalories = "50";
  $DietaryFiber = "1.8";
    $insertRecord = [$FoodGroup, $FoodName,
                        $Serving, $kCalories, $DietaryFiber];
    $FoodGroupData->[5] = $insertRecord;


#4 Obtain the number of records; dereference the
    #container array
    @Ref = @$FoodGroupData;
```

```
    #Obtain the number of items in the container array
    $Length = scalar(@Ref);
 print "\n Number of Records: " . $Length . "\n";;
    #Traverse both 'dimensions' of the array
    for($Itr = 0; $Itr < $Length ; $Itr++){
        print("\n");
        $Record = $FoodGroupData->[$Itr];
        $NumOfFields = scalar(@$Record);
        for(my $Itr = 0; $Itr < $NumOfFields ; $Itr++){
            printf(" %-12s", $Record->[$Itr]);
        }
    }


    #5 Retrieve a reference for a given array
    $Ref = @$FoodGroupData->[0];
    #Obtain the number of items (fields or columns) in the array
    $Length = scalar(@$Ref);
    print "\n\n Number of Columns: " . scalar(@$Ref) . "\n";
    print("\n");
    for($Itr = 0; $Itr < $Length ; $Itr++){
        printf(" %-12s", $FoodGroupData->[0][$Itr]);
    }
```

The lines accompanying comment #1 involve two levels of square braces. The first set of braces creates the container array (refer to Figure 13.11). The set of four braces the first set contains creates contained arrays. Each contained array provides five fields. Descriptions of the fields precede the array definitions. The lines following comment #2 provide an example of explicitly inserting a fifth anonymous array. You insert the fifth array using index 4 because array indexes start at zero.

In the lines comment #3 introduces, you work with fields indirectly, first creating a series of scalar identifiers to which you assign string constants. You then position the identifiers in an anonymous array structure and assign them to yet another scalar identifier. This scalar identifier you then assign to the container array at index 5.

The assignment operation trailing comment #4 involves dereferencing the container array and assigning the dereferenced array to an array identifier (@Ref). You then employ the scalar() function to obtain the number of records the container array contains. You assign this value to the $Length identifier, and as Figure 13.12 shows, when you call the print() function to print this value, you see that the container now contains six records.

Given that you know the number of records in the container array, you can create a for repetition structure and traverse the records, printing each field in each record. To accomplish this task, you first access the @FoodGroupData array using the pointer operator and obtain a reference to the first contained array (or record). You assign this reference to a scalar identifier, $Record.

You then employ the scalar() function to obtain the number of fields in the record. For its argument, you use @$Record, which dereferences the array. You assign the return value of the scalar() function to $NumOfFields.

At this point, you are ready to create a second for repetition statement and embed it in the first. To control the inner for repetition, you use $NumOfFields. You traverse the record array and use the pointer operator to access each field in the record. As Figure 13.12 reveals, you see all the fields in all the records.

The lines following comment #5 provide examples of how to access records in isolation. To start with, you employ the pointer operator to access the reference stored in index 0 of the @FoodGroupData array. In this instance, you dereference in a more efficient manner than you employed before; you apply the array dereference operator directly to the name of the containing array (@$FoodGroupData[0]). You assign the reference you obtain in this way to the identifier $Ref.

Using the $Ref identifier as its argument, you call the scalar() function and obtain the number of elements or fields the record corresponding to index 0 contains. Given this information, you can then traverse the record corresponding to index 0 and print the fields in it. To access each field, you employ two indexes ($FoodGroupData->[0][$Itr]) along with the pointer operator. While the first index is set at 0 for the record, you allow the second index to traverse the fields. The result is the Cereal line at the bottom of Figure 13.12.

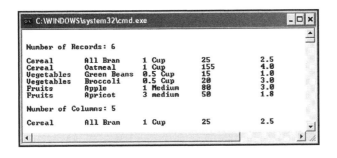

Figure 13.12
Anonymous arrays allow you to create data containers.

❊ ❊ ❊

Anonymous Hash References as Data Containers

You can employ anonymous references with hashes in much the same way that you employ them with arrays. One approach involves using the hash key as a lookup for an embedded array reference. When you employ this approach to accessing records, you can obtain a given record through what might be a unique serial or account number consisting of a combination of letters and numbers. As Figure 13.13 illustrates, to create a container that involves a combination of a hash and an array reference, you combine the capacity to access a hash key with a given word and the indexes the arrays provide.

Figure 13.13
A hash reference can contain array references.

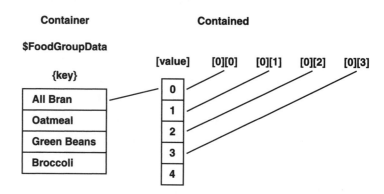

To create anonymous hashes, you employ curly braces. On the other hand, to create anonymous arrays, you use square brackets. Listing13_11 provides an example of using a hash to create records identified by a given food name. For each food name (a hash key), you create an anonymous array. The array provides information such as calories and fiber content. You insert the reference to the array into the value position of the hash and then use the each hash function to retrieve the key and its associated array reference.

```
#Listing13_11
#1 Create an array using anonymous references -- square brackets [ ]
# Embed the array in an anonymous reference -- hash curly braces {}


        #{ Food } [Group Food Serving KCalories Grams of Fiber]
    $FoodGroupData =
        { # key                value
          'All Bran',    [Cereal, '1 Cup', '25', '2.5'],
          'Oatmeal',     [Cereal, '1 Cup', '155', '4.0'],
          'Green Beans', [Vegetables, '0.5 Cup', '15', '1.0'],
          'Broccoli',    [Vegetables, '0.5 Cup', '20', '3.0']
        };
```

```
#2 Array for table headings
    $NL = "\n";
    @Headings = ("Food" , "Group", "Serving", "kCalories", "Grams fiber",);

    foreach $Heading (@Headings){
        printf(" %-12s ", uc($Heading));
    }


#3 Retrieve key and
    while(($Food, $FoodData) = each(%$FoodGroupData)){
            print($NL . "-" x 62 . $NL);
            printf("$NL %-12s " ,uc($Food));
            #Find out how many fields there are
            $Fields_Count = scalar(@$FoodData);
            $Count = 0;
            while($Count < $Fields_Count){
                #Retrieve the fields from the array reference
                printf(" %-12s ", $FoodData->[$Count++]);
            }#end inner while
    }#end outer while
      print($NL . "-" x 62 . $NL);
```

At comment #1 in Listing13_11, you create an anonymous hash reference using curly braces. For the hash keys, you provide a series of four food names (All Bran, Oatmeal, Green beans, Broccoli). For the hash values, you create anonymous arrays. To create the arrays, you employ square brackets. Each array forms one value. Each value in this case provides access to four fields of data for each food. Commas separate the items with the arrays. You assign the structure formed by the hash and its associated arrays to a scalar, $FoodGroupData.

In the lines associated with comment #2, you set up a series of column headings and immediately afterward employ a for repetition statement to print the table heading (see Figure 13.14). You employ the uc() function to capitalize the column headings.

In the lines trailing comment #3, you employ two while repetition statements, one embedded in the other, to traverse the keys and the fields in the arrays associated with the keys. To accomplish this, in the outer while block, you employ the each statement to access the container hash. To dereference the container hash, you apply the hash dereference operator to the scalar representing the reference to the container (%$FoodGroupData). You retrieve the key-value pairs and assign them to $Food and $FoodData. Given that you have dereferenced the key

($Food), you can then proceed to print it in the outer while block. When you do so, you print a divider line on the preceding line and use the uc() function to capitalize the name of the food. At the same time, you print the food name so that no line return follows it. It forms the first column of the table.

To print the information the remaining four columns provide, you begin by dereferencing the value ($FoodData), which is the reference to the array associated with the food name. You employ the scalar() function to ascertain the number of items in the array and assign this value to $Fields_Count identifier. You then proceed to set up a counter, $Count, which services as an iterator for the index of items in the @FoodData array. You employ the pointer operator along with the index brackets to accomplish this work. With the iteration of the inner while block, the four columns associated with each food unroll, as you see in Figure 13.14. The only remaining task involves printing the closing line of the table.

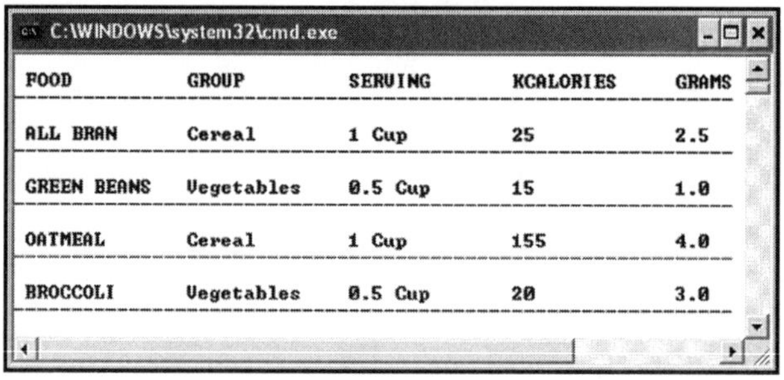

Figure 13.14
You can associate anonymous arrays with the values of hash key-value pairs.

FOOD	GROUP	SERVING	KCALORIES	GRAMS
ALL BRAN	Cereal	1 Cup	25	2.5
GREEN BEANS	Vegetables	0.5 Cup	15	1.0
OATMEAL	Cereal	1 Cup	155	4.0
BROCCOLI	Vegetables	0.5 Cup	20	3.0

Returning References

Listing13_12 presents a function, compareGroups(), that compares two arrays you pass to it. The function processes the arrays and then returns a scalar value and a reference to an array. Both of these values are stored in an array, and you return a reference to the array. By dereferencing the returned reference, you have access to the two items of information.

```
#Listing13_12
#1. Create arrays
@GroupA = ("Apple", "Apricot", "Banana", "Cantaloupe", "Grapefruit");
@GroupB =("Kidney beans", "Lima beans", "Navy beans",
          "Apple", "Apricot", "Banana");
$NL = "\n";
print($NL. $NL . "=" × 60 . $NL);
```

```
$Row = 4;
$Count = 0;
foreach $Food (@GroupA, @GroupB){
    printf(" %-15s", $Food);
    $Count++;
    if($Count == $Row){
        print($NL);
        $Count=0;
    }
}
print($NL. $NL . "=" x 60 . $NL);
#Create the references
$GroupARef = \@GroupA;
$GroupBRef = \@GroupB;


#2.          Pass the references to the function that compares the groups
$ResultArray = compareGroups($GroupARef, $GroupBRef);


#4 Print the first item in the dereferenced array
print "$NL Number of matches: @$ResultArray[0]:" ;


#5 Dereference individual items.
for($Itr = 0; $Itr < @$ResultArray[0]; $Itr++)
{
        print "$NL $$ResultArray[1]->[$Itr]";
}
print($NL. $NL . "=" x 60 . $NL);


#=================================================================


#3 --------------- Definition of compareGroups() --------------
#compareGroups(@Array , @Array)
sub compareGroups{
        ($xArray, $yArray) = @_;
          $Count = 0;
          foreach $ItemA (@$xArray)
          {
```

```
        foreach $ItemB (@$yArray)
        {
          if($ItemA eq $ItemB){
            @ MatchingItems = (@MatchingItems, $ItemB);
            $Count++;
          }#end if
        }#end inner
    }#end outer
    #Build the array to return
    @ReturnList = (@ReturnList, $Count);
    #Add a reference as index 1
    @ReturnList = (@ReturnList, \@ MatchingItems);
  return \@ReturnList;
}
```

At comment #1 in Listing13_12, you set up two arrays that contain the names of foods. If you inspect the lists, you see that a few redundancies characterize the arrays. To verify the foods named in the arrays, as Figure 13.15 illustrates, you print them as a complete set using the list operation combined with the foreach repetition statement. You then create references to both arrays.

In the lines trailing comment #2, you pass the references to the two arrays to the compare-Groups() function. At this point, notice that the function has a return value and that you assign the returned value to a scalar ($ResultArray). This assignment accommodates a reference.

How you create the reference is a mystery exposed in the lines following comment #3, where you define the compareGroups() function. The definition of the function involves first retrieving the references to the two arrays from the argument array. When you retrieve the two references, you use the list operation, which enables you to avoid having to use array indexes later in the function definition. You simultaneously assign the references to two identifiers ($xArray and yArray).

You then define a counter ($Count) with a starting value of 0 and proceed into a repetition structure that includes one foreach repetition statement embedded in another. The outer foreach statement sequentially accesses each element in the dereferenced @xArray and assigns it to the $ItemA identifier. The inner foreach statement sequentially accesses each element in the dereferenced @yArray and assigns it to the $ItemB identifier. Given the embedded statements, the inner loop traverses every item in the @yArray for every item in the @xArray. As the inner loop traverses the $xArray, you set up an if selection statement to compare each item retrieved in the inner loop ($ItemB) with the current outer loop item

($ItemA). When the `if` selection statement finds a match, you assign the matched item to a new array (@MatchingItems). You also increment $Count to tally the number of matching words.

Following the execution of the inner and outer `foreach` blocks, you have collected the matching words in @MatchingItems and the number of words in $Count. You are ready to assign the values of these two identifiers to another array, @ReturnList. You accomplish this using the list function. You assign to the first index of @ReturnList the number of matching words (as an unreferenced scalar). You assign to the second index a reference to the array that stores the matched words. You then use the reference operator to create a reference for the returned array.

Back in the main section of the program, the lines associated with comment #5 make use of the returned value of the compareGroups() function. As noted previously, you assign the returned value to $ResultArray. You know from the definition that this value consists of two elements in a referenced array: a number and a reference to an array. To print the number, you dereference $ResultArray and make it an argument for the print() function. Zero for the index retrieves the number of words.

To retrieve the list of words, you set up a `for` repetition statement. As the limit you dereference the 0 index of $ResultArray array. As before, this gives you the number of words. You then use double dollar signs with the $ResultArray identifier and the pointer operator to access the array of repeated words associated with the second index (1). The counter ($Iter) when used in the second set of square brackets retrieves the individual words.

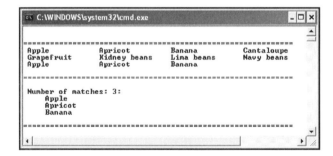

Figure 13.15
A returned reference to an array allows you to track duplicated words.

Conclusion

In this chapter, you have explored references as used with scalars, arrays, hashes, and functions. When you create references, you can pass multiple arrays or hashes to functions. When you pass multiple hashes or arrays, you can then retrieve the items in them without losing track of sources. Ultimately, this proves an extremely useful tool. Among other things, you can then perform actions such as comparing the items in two arrays. You can also create data containers. In this chapter, one such container involved embedding anonymous references in a container array. In this way, you created a data structure that provided a series of fields and records characteristic of databases.

You also created a container that stored anonymous arrays in the value slots provided by a hash. In this way, you could use a key to look up a value, as usual, but you could also dereference the value to gain access to a record containing several fields of information about the key. The exploration of arrays included in this chapter included creation of references for functions. You created among other things function references that you assigned to an array. Given this ability, you could access functions by doing nothing more than inserting an integer into the index brackets of an array.

References allow you to glimpse how the reference table works. The reference table associates each identifier you create with a set of data types. When you understand how the reference table works, you are then in a position to understand how it is that you can change from implicit to explicit forms of identifiers and convert one type of data to another.

14 } File IO

This chapter provides an exploration of the use of functions and operators that allow you to write to and read from files. Input/output (IO) processes involve reading from files. To accomplish this in Perl, you use a file handle. A file handle is a data type you identify using the diamond operator. You associate filenames with file handles and then write to them or read from them using operations that employ the handle as an argument. Among the IO functions you use often are the open(), close(), seek(), and read() functions. Using these functions, you can readily manipulate the data in the files you access. Among the topics this chapter covers are the following:

* Gaining familiarity with IO
* The basics of handles
* The open(), print(), and close() functions
* Seeing and reading data from a file
* Writing records to files
* Reading records from files

Input/Output Streams

Anything beyond the CPU and its associated memory is usually regarded as a "device." The operating system of your computer can identify devices through special memory locations that allow the CPU to communicate with them. When you enter characters at the keyboard, your operating system regards the characters as *input* to your CPU. On the other hand, your operating system regards the signal from the CPU to the monitor as *output*. Together, input and output constitute data input/output (IO) *streams*. The operating system commands the CPU to stream characters from the keyboard to RAM, and when you save the file, the operating system commands the CPU to stream data to your disk drive. The means by which your program file participates in this activity is a special relationship it has with the operating system through an array known as the @ARGV array.

Handles

Perl manages input and output using handles. A handle consists of paired less than and greater than signs (<>). You can refer to this combination of symbols as the *diamond operator* or *file handle operator*. If you supply a file handle identifier to the file handle operator, the operator establishes communication with the file the identifier represents. To define a file handle identifier in association with a file, you use the open() function.

When you associate a file handle identifier with a file, you establish a *data stream*. A data stream allows you to write information to or receive information from another file.

The file handle works within the context of your file to allow you to perform such actions as streaming data from your keyboard to your monitor. In previous chapters, you have used statements in the following form:

```
print("Type something. \n >>");
$Input = <STDIN>;
```

The first line prompts the program user to type something. The second line, containing a handle, captures the input as entered at the keyboard and streams it to the $Input identifier. As a matter of convention, you identify a handle using an expression in capital letters.

Basic IO Interactions

Three primary Perl functions allow you to negotiate activities related to IO operations. These are the open(), print(), and close() functions. The open() function opens a file for reading. One of its primary responsibilities is to associate a file handle you name with the name of a file. In performing this work, it opens a file stream. The close() function closes a file, so one of its primary responsibilities is to close out a stream.

As for the middle part, you deal with a familiar function. This is the print() function. The only difference between how you use the print() function with files and how you use it with the standard activity of printing to the monitor involves redirecting the output of your streaming operations so that it goes not to the monitor but to the disk drive. To accomplish this, you use a file handle in place of the standard quotation marks. Figure 14.1 illustrates the different uses.

Basic Open, Print, and Close Activities

To experiment a little with interactions between a program you write, the monitor, the keyboard, and a file, you can use a handle to collect data from the keyboard and stream it to an external file. Listing14_01 employs the open() function to open a file handle (create a stream) and associate

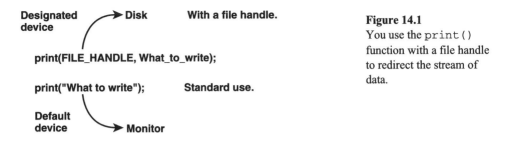

Figure 14.1
You use the print() function with a file handle to redirect the stream of data.

it with an external file. You then employ the print() function to write text to the file, and you call the close() function to close the file. A while loop provides a user session in which you get some practice typing the names of dinosaurs and the period of their existence as prompted.

```
#Listing14_01
#Writing to a file
$NL = "\n";


#1. Display some data
#Repetition for input
do{
system('cls');
#2. Run the main cycle of the program
runMenu();
#-----------------------------------------------------
#5. Open the file -- Creates new or opens old
  open(FILE, "+>>dinoData.txt") || die "Cannot open file. $!";
#5. Write to the file
  print(FILE "$Record $NL");
#7. Close the file
  close(FILE);
#-----------------------------------------------------
#8. Interact with user
}while(checkCycle() eq 'y');


#Automatically open the result file for viewing
system('notepad DinoData.txt');


#================================================================
#--------------- Definition of runMenu() ---------------
```

```
#runMenu() -- no arguments
sub runMenu{
  print (<<MENU);
  Dinosaur Name Period of Existence
  -----------------------------------------
    1. Parasaurolophus        Cretaceous
    2. Tsintaosaurus          Cretaceous
    3. Edmontosaurus          Cretaceous
    4. Allosaurus             Jurrasic
    5. Centosaurus            Jurrasic
    6. Tyrannosaurus          Cretaceous
  -----------------------------------------
MENU
#4 Obtain Data
  print(" Type one of the dinosaur names from the list. $NL >>");
  $Input = <STDIN>;
  chomp($Input);
  $Record = join(" ", $Input);
  print(" Type the period of existence. $NL >>");
  $Input = <STDIN>;
  chomp($Input);
  $Record = join(" ", ($Record, $Input));
  print " $Record $NL";
}
# 9 --------------- Definition of checkCycle() ---------------
#checkCycle() -- returns y or n
sub checkCycle{
  print("$NL File written...");
  print("Write another> ( y n ) ");
  $ControlChar = <STDIN>;
  chomp($ControlChar);
  return $ControlChar;
}
```

In the lines that comment #1 introduces, you set up a while block that contains most of the action the program performs. The checkCycle() function tests the while loop condition each time it repeats, asking you if you want to continue working with the program.

At comment #2, you call the `runMenu()` function. This function first displays the list of six dinosaurs and their periods of existence, as Figure 14.2 shows. To display the list, as the definition of the `runMenu()` function following comment #3 reveals, you create a text block.

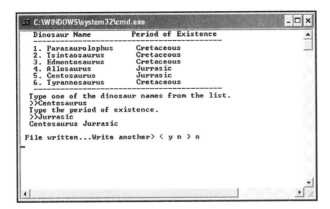

Figure 14.2
With each cycle of interaction, the program writes to a file.

To collect input from the user, at comment #4 (still in the definition), you use a handle (`<STDIN>`) and assign the input to the `$Record` identifier. By employing the `join()` function, you can prompt the user for the period of existence in addition to the name of the dinosaur and concatenate both entries into a single string. You return this string (`$Record`). The explicit `return` statement is not necessary, but it helps show the flow of the program.

Back in the `while` loop, again at comment #2, you assign the return value of the `runMenu()` function to the `$LineToWrite` identifier. You are then in a position to open a file handle to write the contents of `$LineToWrite` to a file.

To open the file for writing, you call the `open()` function. As its first argument, you provide a file handle (`FILE`). The file handle can be any name you choose, and by convention you capitalize it. The second argument to the `open()` function consists of the file to which you want to write (`DinoData.rxt`). In this case, a file specification (`+>>`) precedes the file. This specifier instructs the `open()` function to create a file if one does not already exist. If the file already exists, then it is opened, and anything written to it is appended.

 The information Table 14.1 provides proves essential as you experiment with reading from and writing to files. The `+>>` specifier appends data to your file, but other specifiers cause the data in your file to be overwritten.

In the line associated with comment #5, you employ the print() function to write the contents of the $LineToWrite identifier to the file. To use the print() function, you employ two arguments. The first provides the file handle to which you are writing. The second furnishes the text to be written. In this case, you write $LineToWrite and a newline character ($NL). Each entry appears on a new line, as Figure 14.3 reveals.

Having written a line of text to the file, you call the close() function to close the stream to the file. You call the close() function in the lines associated with comment #6. The close() function requires only one argument, the handle to the file (FILE).

Given the close of the stream, you reach the end of the while block and call the checkCycle() function to determine if the program user wants to enter another record. If not, then the while loop terminates, and you call the system() function to open Notepad to view the contents of the file. Figure 14.3 provides a view of DinoData.txt after a few writing sessions.

Figure 14.3
You write text to a file using the print() function with the file handle as its first parameter.

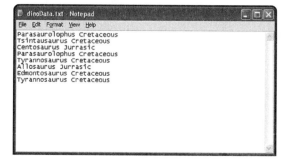

Reading Data from a File

To read data from a file, the most basic approach involves using the open() and close() functions. You need to specify the read function because the file handle provides you with direct access to the contents of the file you have opened. To access the contents of the file, you can, among other actions, place the file handle in a while loop and print each successive line. The while loop repeats, printing successive lines of the file until it reaches the end-of-file (EOF). Here is a rudimentary program to read the contents of a file:

```
#Listing14_02
$NL = "\n";

#1 Open the file handle
open(FILE, "DinoData.txt");
```

```
#2 Iterate through the lines of the file to the EOF
# and print
while($Line = <FILE>){
   print("$Line");
}
#3 Close the file
close(FILE) || "Cannot close file: $!";
```

At comment #1 of Listing14_02, you open the file for reading. You provide a capitalized name for the file handle and a constant string for the name of the file (DinoData.txt). At comment #2, you create a while loop that allows you to repeatedly access the stream that the handle references. In this way, you retrieve lines from the stream and assign them to a scalar identifier ($Line). A line consists of a string of text terminated by a newline character. The number of such lines determines how many times the while loop repeats. When the while loop reaches the EOF character, it terminates. You then call the close() function to close the file. The sole argument of the close() function is the file handle. Figure 14.4 provides a view of such "raw" data.

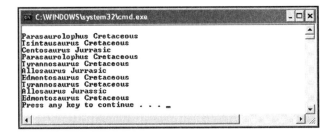

Figure 14.4
Calls to the open() function and use of a while loop and the handle suffice to retrieve data.

Basic Reading and Formatting

When you read data from a file, you usually seek to format it for display. To accomplish this, you can use a variety of approaches. You can, among other things, read the data to a hash or an array. Listing14_03 explores the use of the split() function to divide lines into manageable units. Given that each line in DinosaurData.txt consists of words separated by white spaces and colons, you can employ the split() function to assign the name of each dinosaur, its period of existence, and its family to separate identifiers. You can then use the printf() function to format the display of your dinosaur information.

```
#Listing14_03
#1
$NL = "\n";
```

```
$FileName = "DinosaurSourceData.txt";
#make the table heading
makeHeading();


#2 Open the file and designate a file handle
open(FILE, "$FileName") || die "\n Cannot access file. $!";


#3 Iterate through the lines of the file to the EOF
$Count = 1;
while($Line = <FILE>){
   ($Dino, $Period, $Family) = split(":", $Line);

   printf("%2.0f.%-14s %-14s %-14s $NL", $Count++,
                                    $Dino,
                                    $Period,
                                    $Family);
}


#4 Close the file
close(FILE) || "Cannot close file: $!";


print($NL . "-"×$TW . $NL);
#===========================================================


#--------------------------makeHeading()---------------------
#3 Formatting elements for the table
sub makeHeading{
   $NL = "\n ";
   $DC = sprintf("%c",236); #special character
   $TW = 64;                #Table width
   $DL = sprintf( "%55s", $NL . $DC × $TW); #top and bottom lines
   $COLAHEAD = "Dinosaur";
   $COLBHEAD = "Period";
   $COLCHEAD = "Family";
   #Print the header
   print "$NL Dinosaur Information $NL";
   printf("$DL $NL" );
```

```
printf(" %-20s %-16s %16s", $COLAHEAD ,
                                    $COLBHEAD,
                                    $COLCHEAD);

printf("$DL $NL $NL" );
}
```

The lines trailing comment #1 in Listing14_03 print a table heading and a divider line. Prior to printing the heading, you define an identifier ($FileName) that contains the name of the file you want to access. You then call the makeHeading() function to set up the table heading. It sets up three column headings. (See Figure 14.6.)

At comment #2, you call the open() function. The arguments consist of a file handle (FILE) and the identifier you have defined with the filename ($Filehandle). To ensure that you can generate an informative error message in the event that the program cannot find the file, you employ the die() function. (The next section discusses the use of the die() function.)

Having opened the file, you can then read from it. To accomplish this task, as the lines that trail comment #3 show, you create a counter ($Count) so that you can number items as you print them. You initialize $Count to 1. You then initiate a while block. The control expression for the while statement assigns the successive lines you retrieve from the file to a scalar identifier ($Line). When the control reaches the EOF character, it terminates. With each repetition of the block, you call the split() function.

The first argument for the split() function consists of the expression you want to use to evaluate each line for division. In this case, you use quotation marks enclosing a colon. In this instance, the colon has been used to separate the items in the source file, DionsaurData.txt. Such an approach to separating data allows you read strings that contain spaces. Figure 14.5 shows the data as it appears in the source file.

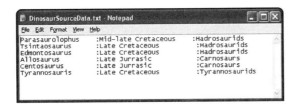

Figure 14.5
Data can be stored with special characters to help with formatting.

To assign the terms to identifiers, you use the list() function. You use three identifiers: $Dino, $Period, and $Family. As the loop repeats, these three identifiers become arguments to the printf() function, which prints them in left-aligned columns. You also create a fourth column, to the left of the others, to contain the values of $Count. As Figure 14.6 shows, in this way you can easily see the number of dinosaur names you have typed, along with their periods of existence and their families.

Figure 14.6
Using the split() function enables you to format data for tabular display.

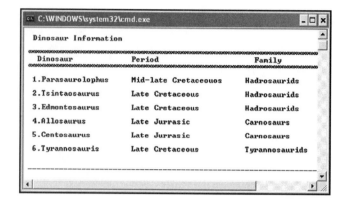

The Use of die and warn

In the listings you have worked with so far in this chapter, you have made use of the die() function. This function allows you to announce that a process has failed. To use the die() function, you precede it with an OR operator, which you can also express with two pipes (| |). With the open() function, for example, when the function fails, it issues an error message. To capture the error message and print it to the terminal as the program terminates, you can use the die() function and a special operator that consists of a dollar sign and an exclamation mark ($!). As an argument for the function, you can include this operator along with any specific text you want to relate to the program user. The die() function channels the failing message to the command line (or the output areas).

Consider Listing14_04. This program accesses the DinoData.txt file and prints dinosaur names and periods of existence to your monitor. Although syntactically correct, the program fails because the name of the data file possesses an extra "n."

```
#Listing14_04
$NL = "\n";
#1
$FileName = "DinnoData.txt"; #Misspelling makes it impossible to
                             #$access the file; Change to DinoData.txt
#2 Open the file and designate a file handle
# Issue an error message using $!
open(FILE, "$FileName") || die("\n See comment #2. Cannot access file. $!");
#The program cannot go and must terminate at this point


#3 Iterate through the lines of the file to the EOF
while($Line = <FILE>){
```

```
   print("$NL $Line");
}
#4 Close the file
close(FILE) || "Cannot close file: $!";
```

At comment #2 in Listing14_04, you name a file from which to obtain information on dinosaurs. The name of the file is misspelled, and for this reason, at comment #3, when you call the open() function, the function fails. Here is the code:

```
open(FILE, "$FileName") || die("\n See comment #1. Cannot access file. $!");
```

To handle the failure, you issue an error message by using the die() function. Its use involves preceding it with an OR operator (!!). As an argument to the function, you include a couple of statements specific to your program. First, you direct the program user to comment #1 (where you name the data file), and you explain that the file cannot be accessed. You also include in the output string the message operator for terminal error messages ($!). The message the operator adds to the output string is the standard failure message that the open() function issues. Figure 14.7 shows you the complete message the die() function issues as viewed in the DzSoft Perl Editor.

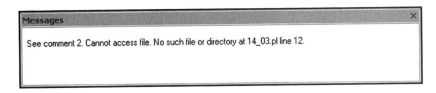

Figure 14.7
The failure message directs you to the comment at #2 in your file, where you find the misspelling of the filename.

The warn() function can be inserted in place of the die() function. The warn() function performs actions similar to the die() function, but it supplements the primary message with details concerning action the program cannot perform due to its premature termination. Figure 14.8 illustrates the output of Listing14_04 after you correct the name of the file to DinoData.txt.

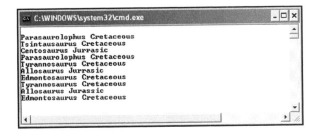

Figure 14.8
Having corrected the file-name, you see the output.

❈ ❈ ❈

Functions Relating to IO

You can make use of a number of functions and operators that relate to file IO. Table 14.1 reviews operators and functions already discussed and adds to these others that enable you to refine basic operations.

Table 14.1   IO Functions

IO Function	Discussion
open()	Opens a file handle. The argument consist of the file handle and the file you want to open. You can also set the specification for read-write permissions. See Table 14.2.
close()	Closes file handles. Terminates the stream. The sole argument is the file handle you want to close.
print()	Use this to write data to a file. The first argument you use is the file handle. The second is the data to be written.
die()	Use this function to close out a program if you encounter a fatal read-write error. Similar to the warn() function.
eof	A special sequence that signals the end of a file. In Windows, this is equivalent to Ctrl + Z.
seek()	Uses three arguments: the file handle, a scalar that stores a value for an offset, and a value that tells the function how to proceed. If you use 0, you indicate that the function should proceed from the start of the file; 2 indicates the end of the file; 1 indicates that the seek() should move from the current position of the pointer.
read()	Uses three arguments: the file handle, a scalar to which you assign data, and the number of characters you want to retrieve from the start of the file.
tell()	Tells you the position of the file pointer. The pointer indicates how far you have read into a file.
pack()	Creates length specifications for fixed-length records. You use field specifiers to set up your data. The most useful is the A specifier, which you can use in a generic way to set up text fields.
getc()	Reads a file one character at a time.
truncate()	Takes the file handle and an integer as arguments. The integer indicates a position in the text of the file after which you want to erase the text.
flock()	You can pronounce the name of this function as f-lock, for "file lock." The function takes two arguments: a file handle and an operator that allows you to control access to

IO Function	Discussion
	the file. The two main locks are LOCK_EX (other programs can access the file while your program is using it) and LOCK_UN (removes exclusive control of the file).
warn()	Similar to the die() function. Use it to close out a file if you encounter a fatal error.

Variations on the open() Function

The open() function takes a file handle and the name of a file as its primary arguments, but you can also specify to the open() function whether you want to define how a file can be used. For example, you can restrict writing to a file, making it so the file you access cannot be written to. You can also overwrite the data in a file. To define such options, you prefix a read-write specifier to the name of the file when you use it as the first argument to the open() function. Table 14.2 provides examples of how to set the permissions relating to files. In each case, *FH* designates a file handle, and *filename* stands for the name of a file.

Table 14.2 Arguments for the open() Function

Use of open	Discussion
open(*FH*, ">*filename*")	Creates a file and writes to it. This overwrites an existing file.
open(*FH*, "<*filename*")	Opens an existing file for reading only.
open(*FH*, "*filename*")	Just the name of the file alone. Opens an existing file for reading only.
open(FH, ">>*filename*")	Adds data to the end of an existing file. If the file does not exist, it creates a file.
open(*FH*, "+<*filename*")	Updates a file. Opens the file for reading and writing. Appends data to the end of the file.
open(*FH*, "+>*filename*")	Creates a file for reading or writing. If the file already exists, it overwrites it.
open(*FH*, "+>>*filename*")	Appends data to the end of the file. If the file does not exist, it creates it.

The tell() Function

When you read a file, you move a pointer through the text of the file. A pointer is an index that tracks the position of characters in a file. It advances from character to character. If you advance through a file line by line, the progress of the pointer is still tracked on a character basis. The tell() function allows you to know the position of the pointer at any time. Its only argument is the file handle. Listing14_05 reads from a file that consists of a number of dinosaur names. To advance the file, you read its contents using a while statement and use the file handle as the argument of the statement. You call the `tell()` function inside the `while` block to report the position of the pointer during each repetition of the block. The program advances the file a line at a time, and the `tell()` function reports the pointer position that marks the end of each line as the file advances. At the same time, a short calculation makes it possible to determine the length of each line as the file advances.

```
#Listing14_05
#1 Formatting definitions and open the file read only
$NL = "\n ";
$DC = sprintf("%c", 236);    #special character
$TW = 44;                    #Table width
$DL = sprintf( "%44s", $NL . $DC x $TW); #top and bottom lines
open(FILE, "<SourceData.txt") or die ("File could not be opened: $!");
print($DL);


#2 Advance through the file a dinosaur name at a time (one line each)
while($Line = <FILE>){
  chomp($Line);
  #Tell how far the pointer has advanced as of the end of the
  #$Line just read
  $FileSoFar = tell(FILE);
  $WordLength = $FileSoFar - $Previous;
  $TotalWordLength += $WordLength;
  printf("\n %-20s %-5s %-5s", $Line, $FileSoFar, $WordLength );
  $Previous = $FileSoFar;
}


#3 Where is the pointer after all the data has been read?
$LengthOfFile = tell(FILE);

# Done reading
close(FILE) || "Cannot close file: $!";

#4 Print total results
print($DL);
```

```
printf("\n %-20s %-5s %-5s", "Length of file:",
                             $LengthOfFile,
                             $TotalWordLength);
print($DL);
```

In the lines associated with comment #1, you attend to a few formatting issues by defining some identifiers to use in the creation of a table. You then call the open() function. You provide the name of the file handle (FILE) as the first argument. For the filename, you supply SourceData.txt and stipulate that it is to be used on a read-only (<) basis.

At comment #2 you proceed into a while block. The control statement for the block consists of an assignment operation in which you repeatedly assign lines from the handle (FILE) to an identifier, $Line. This arrangement retrieves a line at a time from the file, and each line is a portion of the text that proceeds from the start of a line to a return or newline character at the end of the line. For each line, you find the name of one dinosaur.

You employ the chomp() function to remove a newline character attached to each line as it is retrieved from the file. This is the work of the handle, the same type of action that occurs when you enter data from the keyboard. Having removed the extra line return, you can then proceed to call the tell() function. Its argument is the file handle. You assign its return value to the $FileSoFar identifier. The tell() function provides you with the position of the pointer at the end of the line just retrieved. As you can discern from examining the numbers associated with the dinosaur names in Figure 14.9, the first item in the table ends at pointer position 18. This is the position tell() returns during the first iteration of the while block and indicates to you the length of Parasaurolophus.

In each case, to discover the length of a word, you subtract the position tell() reports during the previous iteration from the position tell() currently reports. You assign the difference to the $WordLength identifier. To obtain the total length of the file, you sum the number of characters the pointer advances with each repetition of the block and assign the sum to $TotalWordLength. Since the $FileSoFar identifier reports the actual position of the pointer and $TotalWordLength tells you the cumulative length of all the words, you can check the figures against each other by employing them as the final two arguments of the printf() function. For the first argument to the print() function, you use $Line, which consists of the names of the dinosaurs.

Your last action in the while block involves assigning the current character pointer position to the $Previous identifier so that the current position can be used in the next iteration of the block. The block updates the $Previous identifier with each iteration, and in the end it stores the final pointer position.

At comment #3, you have exited the `while` loop and for good measure call the `tell()` function once again. The pointer has now advanced to the end of the file, so the position the `tell()` function reports marks the character position of the character that corresponds to the end of `Struthiomimus`. To close the file stream, you call the `close()` function. The single argument you provide to the function consists of the file handle.

In the lines trailing comment #4, you call the `print()` function and print the summary data. The `$LengthOfFile` identifier provides information taken directly from the `tell()` function, while the `$TotalWordLength` identifier represents the results of your calculations. Given the equality of the two values, as Figure 14.9 shows, you can conclude that the combined lengths of the lines (or dinosaur names) account for the total length of the file. Such is the work of the `tell()` function.

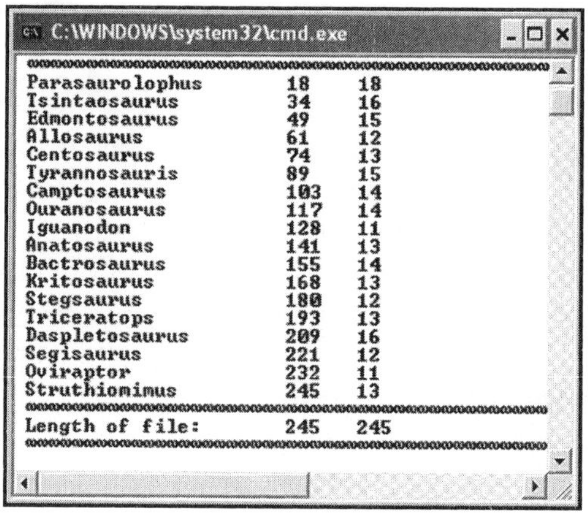

Figure 14.9
As the pointer advances, the `tell()` function allows you to know word lengths.

```
C:\WINDOWS\system32\cmd.exe

Parasaurolophus       18    18
Isintaosaurus         34    16
Edmontosaurus         49    15
Allosaurus            61    12
Centosaurus           74    13
Tyrannosauris         89    15
Camptosaurus         103    14
Ouranosaurus         117    14
Iguanodon            128    11
Anatosaurus          141    13
Bactrosaurus         155    14
Kritosaurus          168    13
Stegsaurus           180    12
Triceratops          193    13
Daspletosaurus       209    16
Segisaurus           221    12
Oviraptor            232    11
Struthiomimus        245    13

Length of file:      245   245
```

The seek() and getc() Functions

You use the `seek()` function to position a pointer in a file. The function takes the following form:

```
Seek(file_handle, offset, [beginning | point_within | end])
```

This function requires three arguments. The first argument is the file handle. The second argument provides the position in the file at which you want to locate the pointer (the offset). The third parameter proves a little more complicated that the first two. It allows three values. It designates what you want to assign as the initial position of your seek activities. The settings for the third parameter are as follows:

※   0 indicates that you want to start at the beginning of the file.

※   1 indicates that you want to start at the current position (a point within the file).

✵ 2 indicates that you want to start at the end of the file and count toward the beginning of the file. If you use this parameter for the current position, you can use a negative number as the second argument to the seek() function to "advance" the pointer.

You must open a file handle prior to calling the seek() function. You then employ the function as many times as you want to reposition the file pointer. Listing14_06 combines the work of the seek() function with that of the getc() function. The getc() function requires one parameter, the integer value representing a given pointer position. It retrieves the character that resides at the pointer position.

Listing14_06 makes use of a do...while repetition structure to retrieve the starting and ending positions of all the dinosaur names in the SourceData.txt file (refer to Figure 14.7). It stores these positions to a hash. For each key-value pair the hash contains, you assign the name of the dinosaur to the key, and then for the value, you create an anonymous array consisting of two items: the beginning pointer position and the end pointer position of the dinosaur name the key stores. Since you have at hand a hash containing the dinosaur names, you extract the names to an array and use the array to sort the names alphabetically for display.

Given the name of the dinosaur, the pointer position at which it begins, and the pointer position at which it ends, you can proceed to set up an embedded repetition structure to retrieve and print your results. In the outer loop of this structure, you use a foreach statement to traverse the keys stored in the hash. Using the keys, you can extract the beginning and end pointer values for each of the dinosaur names. You call the seek() function to set the file pointer at the starting position of the word. You then employ a for repetition statement to move the pointer forward until it reaches the end position of the word. Through each repetition, you call the getc() function to print a character.

```
#Listing14_06
#1 Open source file
$NL = "\n ";
open(FILE, "<SourceData.txt")
                    or die ("File could not be opened: $!");

#2 Set the first value and advance through the file
$WordBeginning = 0;
$Line = <FILE>;
do{

#3 Obtain word beginnings and ends
  $FileSoFar = tell(FILE);
```

```
    #Assign values using an anonymous array reference
    #use a hash to capture beginning and end positions
    $WordPositions{$Line} = [$WordBeginning, $FileSoFar];

    $WordBeginning = $FileSoFar;
}while($Line = <FILE>);


#4 Assign keys to an array and sort
@Dinosaurs = keys(%WordPositions);
@Dinosaurs = sort(@Dinosaurs);


foreach $Name (@Dinosaurs){
print(" ");
#5 Use seek() to put the pointer at the start of each word
# Start the iterator at the pointer position
# And advance to the end of the word


# Use reference lookups to retrieve the values
  seek(FILE, $WordPositions{$Name}->[0], 0);


  #6 Use the getc() function to retrieve a character at a time
    for ($Itr = int($WordPositions{$Name}->[0]);
        $Itr < int($WordPositions{$Name}->[1] - 1);
        $Itr++)
    {
        print (getc(FILE));
    }
}


#7 Close out the session
close(FILE) || "Cannot close file: $!";
```

The lines associated with comment #1 enable you to open SourceData.txt to a read-only (<)
file handle. You then proceed (see comment #2) to define the identifier $WordBeginning,
which serves as a counter in the do...while loop that follows. To retrieve the first line of the
file, you use the diamond operator (<>) to access the file handle and retrieve the first line of
the file to the identifier $Line.

Inside the do...while block, at comment #3 you call the tell() function to obtain the position at which the counter rests after it has read the first line. You assign this value to the identifier $FileSoFar. You then store the information you possess in a hash ($WordPositions). To store the information, you use the hash lookup operation and embed in it an anonymous array reference. Here is the line that accomplishes this work:

```
$WordPositions{$Line} = [$WordBeginning, $FileSoFar];
```

The square brackets create a reference to an anonymous array. You assign the reference for the anonymous array to the value position in the hash key-value pair. The character positions represented by $WordBeginning and $FileSoFar become elements within the anonymous array. $WordBeginning is at index 0 of the array and $FileSoFar is at index 1.

To be able to access the array reference, you associate it with a dinosaur name that you designate as the key of the key-value pair. You create a new pair with each repetition of the loop. When you feed $Line into the curly braces of the hash lookup operation, a dinosaur name becomes the key of the key-value pair.

The last action you perform during each iteration of the do...while loop involves assigning the latest position the seek() function has assigned to the $WordBeginning identifier. This identifier allows you to designate the end position of the current line as the beginning position of the next line.

In the lines associated with comment #4, you perform two operations that enable you to sort the items in the hash alphabetically. First, you employ the hash keys() function to retrieve all the hash keys (the names of the dinosaurs) and assign them to an array (@Dinosaurs). You then call the sort() function to alphabetize the names of the dinosaurs. The sole argument of the sort() function consists of the array you want to sort (@Dinosaurs), and to complete the sort, you assign the array back to itself.

At comment #5, you proceed into a an embedded repetition structure that consists of two loops, one defined by a foreach statement, the other by a for statement. The foreach statement traverses the @Dinosaur array and retrieves the names of the dinosaurs so that you can retrieve the anonymous arrays associated with each dinosaur.

The for loop allows you to retrieve and print the characters that constitute each dinosaur name. To operate the for loop, you must know the position of the first character of each dinosaur name, and you must know the number of characters in the name.

When you know the position of the first character, you can feed it to the seek() function, which repositions the file pointer on the first character. You call the seek() function just prior to the start of the for loop. Here is the line containing the call to the seek() function:

```
seek(FILE, $WordPositions{$Name}->[0], 0);
```

The first argument consists of FILE, the file handle. The last argument is a zero, which indicates that when you reposition the pointer, you do so from the start of the file and move it toward the end. The second argument consists of a hash lookup operation. The $Name identifier designates a dinosaur name for the lookup operation. The lookup operation dereferences the first element (index 0) of the anonymous hash. This element provides the position of the first character. You use the pointer operator (->) to dereference the first element.

At comment #6 you advance into the for loop. For the control expressions of the for loop, you use the hash lookup operation to again retrieve the starting position of the first character of the dinosaur name (index 0). For the limit (the second argument in the control), you use a hash lookup operation that retrieves the value that represents the end of the dinosaur name you want to retrieve (index 1).

The value at index 1 represents the length of a dinosaur name, but you must subtract 1 from the length to accommodate the structure of the loop, which with each repetition would leave you on the first character of the next word if you did not adjust it by subtracting 1.

To advance the loop, you use $Iter++, which allows you to retrieve characters in increments of 1. With each advance of the $Itr identifier, you call the getc() function. The getc() function retrieves the character that lies at the current pointer position and advances the position of the pointer by 1. When you call the print() function with the getc() function as its argument, you see the character displayed on your monitor.

Having used the seek() function to selectively position the pointer as you go and the getc() function to print characters, when you at last exit the foreach block, your only remaining task is to close the file stream. To accomplish this, you call the close() function, which takes the file handle as its sole argument. Figure 14.10 shows you the fruits of your labor.

Figure 14.10
Use the seek() function
with the getc() function
to print the dinosaur
names.

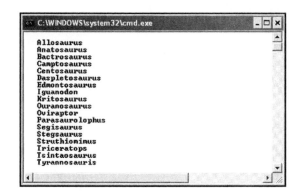

❄ ❄ ❄

The read() Function

The read() function works with either three or four parameters. The first parameter identifies a file handle. The second parameter establishes a string identifier you can use to extract characters from a file during the read operation (the target string). The third parameter designates the number of characters you want to extract. The fourth parameter relates to the identifier you want to store characters in (the target string). It indicates the index position in the target string that you want to use as the beginning point as you transfer characters to it.

To use the read() function, you first call the seek() function to designate the starting point. The read() function reads from the starting point for the number of characters you designate. Listing14_07 experiments with the read() function using the starting positions and lengths of the dinosaurs named in the SourceData.txt file. It moves through the file a word at a time, accessing the words and then placing them in a string in alphabetical order.

```
#Listing14_07

#1 Open source file
$NL = "\n ";
open(FILE, "<SourceData.txt")
                    or die ("File could not be opened: $!");


#2 Set the first value and advance through the file
$WordBeginning = 0;
$Line = <FILE>;
do{
#3 Obtain word beginnings and ends
  $FileSoFar = tell(FILE);
  #Assign values using an anonymous array reference
  #use a hash to capture beginning and end positions
  $WordPositions{$Line} = [$WordBeginning, $FileSoFar];
  $WordBeginning = $FileSoFar;
}while($Line = <FILE>);


#4 Assign keys to an array and sort
@Dinosaurs = keys(%WordPositions);
@Dinosaurs = sort(@Dinosaurs);

$Itr = 0;
foreach $Name(@Dinosaurs){
```

```
#5 Reset the pointer to the start of the word
   seek(FILE, $WordPositions{$Name}->[0], 0);

   read(FILE,
        $DinosaurName,
        ($WordPositions{$Name}->[1]-1) - ($WordPositions{$Name}->[0]),
        0);
   $Itr++;
   $FinalString = join(" ", $FinalString, $DinosaurName);
}


#7 Close out the session
close(FILE) || "Cannot close file: $!";


# Print the alphabetical string
print "$FinalString";
```

For specific discussion of the tasks you perform in Listing14_07 in the lines designated by comments #1 through #5, see the previous section, "The seek() and get() Functions."

At comment #5 of Listing14_07, you have entered into a foreach repetition block that retrieves the name of each dinosaur in the @Dinosaurs array. The @Dinosaurs array contains the alphabetized names of all dinosaurs in the %WordPositions hash. The foreach selection statement retrieves each dinosaur name from the @Dinosaur array and assigns it to the $Name identifier.

When you call the seek() function, you reposition the file pointer so that it designates the first character of the dinosaur name currently assigned to $Name. To obtain the position of the first character for the seek() function, you employ $Name as the key in a hash lookup operation that you use as the second argument to the seek() function. The seek() function moves the pointer to this position, and you are ready to call the read() function, which retrieves all the characters that constitute the name of the dinosaur name.

The seek() function positions the file pointer at the start of a dinosaur name. The read() function, like the getc() function (see the discussion in the previous section), begins to read a file at the pointer position that is valid when you call it.

Given that the read() function knows only its position when you call it, you must provide it information concerning how many characters you want it to read and what you want to do with the characters after it reads them. Accordingly, you provide four arguments to the read() function.

As the lines trailing comment #5 reveal, the first argument consists of the file handle identifier (FILE). The second argument provides a scalar identifier ($DinosaurName) to which you can assign the character string that the read() function retrieves from the file. The last (fourth) argument pertains to this identifier. Set at zero, this argument tells the read() function to use the zero index of the target identifier ($DinosaurName) as the starting position of the character string it copies to the identifier. Generally, then, this argument designates the position in the target string to which you want to transfer the string you copy from the file.

For the third argument of the read() function, you furnish the number of characters you want the read() function to retrieve from the file. To accomplish this, you use an expression that involves subtracting one dereferenced value from another. Here is the expression:

```
$WordPositions{$Name}->[1]-1) - ($WordPositions{$Name}->[0])
```

You use the $Name identifier to identify a given key (dinosaur name) in the %WordPositions hash. Using the key, you retrieve the array associated with the key. The array contains two elements. The first element (at index 0), provides the position of the first character of the dinosaur name. The second element (at index 1) tells you a position in the file one character beyond the end character of the dinosaur name. To obtain the length of the dinosaur name, you subtract 1 from the end and then subtract the beginning from the end. The difference informs the read() function how many characters it is to transfer from the file to the $DinosaurName identifier.

Given that you have assigned the name of a dinosaur to the $DinosaurName identifier, you then call the join() function to concatenate the dinosaur name with other dinosaur names into a single string, ($FinalString). As you concatenate the names, you insert a dash between the dinosaur names as a cosmetic feature.

After the foreach statement traverses all the names in the array, its block terminates, and you close the file stream. To close the file stream, you use the close() function (see comment #6). After that, you call the print() function and provide $FinalString as its only argument. Figure 14.11 displays the result.

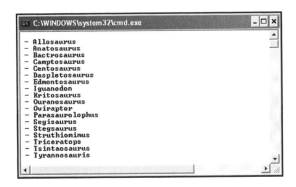

Figure 14.11
Use the read() function to retrieve data and create a string you print to the monitor.

The pack() Function

The pack() function allows you to create a fixed-length record by specifying the data types to be processed and the number of bytes needed to accommodate the data. To create fixed-length records, you first need to establish the length of the record you want to create. Suppose for starters that you want to write records that consist of the following fields:

```
Dinosaur Name     Dinosaur Family     Period of Existence
```

After surveying the basic data, you decide that you are safe if you use the following maximum lengths for the three fields that constitute the record:

```
20 characters     20 characters     20 characters
```

To create a record to accommodate these fields, you use the following approach:

```
$Record = "A20 A20 A20";
my $RecordLength = pack($Record);
```

The pack() function retrieves the information the $Record identifier provides and "packs" it into a single value. The resulting record length for the specifications provided is 60. Now you can use this record definition to write records to a file. Listing14_08 explores this activity in a context that allows you to create a file that contains fixed-length records. The program creates the file every time you execute it and opens the file using Notepad so that you can view it.

```
#Listing14_08
#1 Create anonymous embedded arrays
$DinoRecords =
        [ #Container array
          ['Parasaurolophus', 'Hadrosaurids', 'Late Cretaceous'],
          ['Tsintaosaurus', 'Hadrosaurids', 'Late Cretaceous'],
          ['Allosaurus', 'Carnosaurs', 'Late Jurrasic'],
          ['Centosaurus', 'Carnosaurs ', 'Late Jurrasic',]
        ];
#2 Print the records to preview them
   #Dereference
   @Ref = @$DinoRecords;
   #Obtain the number of items in the container array array
   $Length = scalar(@Ref);
   #Traverse both the array and print its content
   for($Itr = 0; $Itr < $Length ; $Itr++){
       print("\n");
```

```
        $Record = $DinoRecords->[$Itr];
        $NumOfFields = scalar(@$Record);
        for(my $Itr = 0; $Itr < $NumOfFields ; $Itr++){
              printf(" %-20s", $Record->[$Itr]);
        }
   }

#3 Work with formats. Set the fields to alpha length 2 - 20
$Record = "A3 A20 A20 A20";
$RecordLength = length(pack($Record));

print "\n\n Record length:" . $ RecordLength . "\n";

#4 Open a file to write to -- overwrites old data
open(FILE, "+>RecordData.txt") || die "\n\tCannot access file.";

#5 Write a record to the file
#Traverse both dimensions of the array
   for($Itr = 0; $Itr < $Length ; $Itr++){
        print("\n");
        $Record = $DinoRecords->[$Itr];
        #Access each field ...
        $Field = 0;
        $DinoName = $Record->[$Field];
        $FamilyName = $Record->[$Field++];
        $Period= $Record->[$Field++];
        print(FILE pack("A3 A20 A20 A20", "\n",
                                       $DinoName,
                                       $FamilyName,
                                       $Period));

   }

close(FILE);

#6 Close and view the records
print "\n File created....";
system('notepad RecordData.txt');
```

At comment #1 in Listing14_08, you define an anonymous array container. You can discern the container as an array container because it consists of one set of square braces containing another. Two sets of index brackets characterize the container ($DinoRecords[]->[]). As lines later in Listing14_08 reveal, you access a record using the index that precedes the pointer operator while you access fields in the record using the index to which the pointer operator points. The $DinoRecords identifier stores a reference to a container that consists of four records, and each record consists of four fields.

The lines following comment #2 traverse the records and their fields, dereferencing them at is goes, and prints the table that Figure 14.12 displays. Each line constitutes a record. Each item in the lines represents a field. The spacing you see at this point does not represent the designated (fixed) lengths of the fields. Within the inner for loop you call the printf() function and specify 20 characters as the width of all the fields.

The work of creating fixed length records remains to be done. The work begins at comment #3, where you set up a record that consists of four fields (rather than three). The first field provides a three-character field reserved for a newline character. You employ the newline field for aesthetics only, making it so you can see aligned columns when you first view the file (see Figure 14.13).

You specify four columns. The first you set at three alpha characters, and the remaining three you set at 20 alpha characters each. You assign an interpolated string containing these specifications to the $Record identifier. On the next line, you call the pack() function to generate the length of the record for display. You employ the length() function to retrieve the integer length of the record the pack() function defines. As Figure 14.12 shows, after assigning this value to $RecordLength, you call the print() function to print it to the screen immediately following the data table.

At comment #4, you call the open() function to open a file stream. You use a stream specifier (+>) that opens a new file called RecordData.txt if none already exists and overwrites existing data if a file with this name already exists. Having opened a file stream, you then initiate a for loop to write records to the file.

The approach you use here to retrieve the records involves accessing the reference stored in the container array for each record. To accomplish this, you employ the pointer operator to access the reference to the first index ($DinoRecords->[$Itr]). You assign the reference to a scalar identifier ($Record). This identifier now holds a reference that allows you to access data fields.

To access the fields, you set up a counter ($Field). With each repetition of the for block, you set the $Field identifier to zero. After that, with three successive uses of the pointer operator and the $Record identifier, you access the information the fields contain and assign it to three representative identifiers ($DinoName, $FamilyName, and $Period). You then employ these three identifiers as arguments to the print() function. As the first argument to the print() function, you provide a newline character. As explained previously, this is used as a cosmetic element.

The form the print() function assumes involves the file handle identifier (FILE) as its first argument. You follow this with the record field specification as given by the pack() function. (In this case, you do not use the length() function because you are not seeking to output an integer but only to create the record specification.) You use the same field values you used before to create the display value that follows the data table. After the for loop traverses the four records, it terminates. You then call the close() function to close the file stream. Then, to view the results of your work, you employ the system() function to invoke Notepad and display the contents of the file you have created. Figure 14.13 shows you the results.

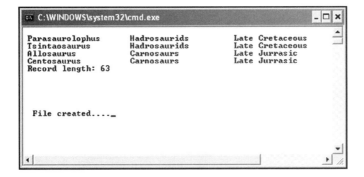

Figure 14.12
You display the data before you write it and indicate the length of the record you intend to create.

Listing14_08 automatically uses a call to the system() function to open Notepad so you can view the file you have created, as Figure 14.13 shows. To exit Notepad, select File > Exit. This leaves the command window for Listing14_08 still open. Press Return to exit.

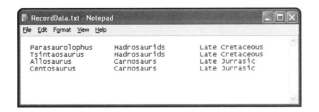

Figure 14.13
The program writes records to the data file in fixed field lengths.

Accessing Fixed-Length Records

To access data in fixed-length records, you again use the pack() function to determine the length of the records you want to read. You then use the seek() function to navigate the file in increments equal to the length of a record. To know where to find a given record, you determine the number of the record in the file and then multiply the record length by this number. You assign the product to the seek() function, and using the length of the record as an argument to the read() function, you retrieve the record for viewing. Listing14_09 explores how to retrieve specific fixed-length records. It introduces no new functions but instead affords you the opportunity to experiment with common uses of functions already introduced.

```
#Listing14_09
#Read fixed length records from a file
#1 Verify the record length
$NL = "\n";
$DC = sprintf("%c", 236);      #Special character
$TW = 63;                      #Line with
$DL = sprintf( "%63s", $NL . $DC x $TW); #top and bottom lines
open(FILE, "<SourceData.txt") or die ("File could not be opened: $!");
print($DL);


$Record = "A3 A20 A20 A20";
$RecordLength = length(pack($Record));
print "$NL Record length: $RecordLength";


#2 Open the data file--read only
open(FILE, "RecordData.txt") || die "\n Cannot access file.";


#3 Set the file at the end (option 2)
   seek(FILE, 0 , 2);
# Obtain the length
   $FileLength = tell(FILE);
   print "$NL The length of the file is $FileLength";
   $NumOfRecords = int($FileLength/$RecordLength);
   print("$NL $NumOfRecords records are in the file.");
  print($DL);
   print "$NL>>Press <Enter>";


#4 Use seek and read to obtain records by multiplying by length
```

```
    for($Itr = 0; $Itr < $NumOfRecords; $Itr++){
        $Count = $Itr + 1;
        $AnyChar = <STDIN>;
        seek(FILE, $Itr * $RecordLength, 0);
        read(FILE, $LineRead, $RecordLength, 0);
        print(" >> $Count $LineRead");
    }
print($DL);


#5 Use seek and record length to find a record for display
    seek(FILE, 0, 0);
    print("$NL $NL Enter a record number. $NL >>");
    $LineNumber = <STDIN>;
    # print "$NL The record length: $RecordLength $NL";
    $SeekPoint = ($LineNumber - 1)* $RecordLength;
    seek(FILE, $SeekPoint, 0);
    read(FILE, $LineRead, $RecordLength);
    # print "$NL The line read is: $NL";
    print "$LineRead\n";

    close(FILE) || "Cannot close file: $!";
```

After setting up some formatting elements in the lines associated with comment #1, you use the pack() function to define a record. You call the length() function to retrieve the integer length of the record and assign it to a scalar identifier, $RecordLength. You call the print() function to display the value assigned to $RecordLength (see the top of Figure 14.14). You then proceed to open the RecordData.txt file. (A copy of the file resides in the code directory for this chapter, ready for use, or you can regenerate it using Listing14_08.)

After you open a stream for RecordData.txt, you call the seek() function and assign 2 to the third argument. This argument instructs the seek() function to move from the end of the file backward. You set the second parameter at 0, indicating that you want to move the pointer to the last position in the file. You then call the tell() function so that you can contain the integer value of the end of the file. You assign this value to the scalar identifier $FileLength.

You now determine the number of records in the file by dividing the length of the file by the length of the records it contains ($FileLength/$RecordLength) and assigning the result to the scalar identifier $NumOfRecords. You can use the int() function to ensure that the value assigned is an integer.

❋ ❋ ❋

At comment #4, you create a `for` repetition statement to iterate through the records in the file and display them for view. As you display the records for view, you print numbers that show their positions. You show the first record as record 1 rather than record 0.

After you display the records, to allow the program user to select a specific record for viewing, you prompt the user to type the number of the record to be viewed. You assign this number to `$LineNumber`. To retrieve the record, you multiply the line number at which a record resides by the length of the fixed record [(`$LineNumber - 1) * $RecordLength`]. You must subtract 1 from `$LineNumber` to compensate for the fact that you listed the records beginning with 1.

The result of the multiplied line and record lengths you assign to `$SeekPoint`, which becomes the second argument in the `seek()` function. The `seek()` function moves the file pointer to the position in the stream that corresponds to the beginning of the record you want to view.

After you reposition the pointer, you can then call the `read()` function. As its second argument, you designate a scalar identifier, `$LineRead`, to receive the string containing the record. For its third argument, you designate the number of characters to be copied to `$LineRead`. The `$RecordLength` identifier provides this value.

Figure 14.14
You combine the work of several IO functions to allow program users to view specific records.

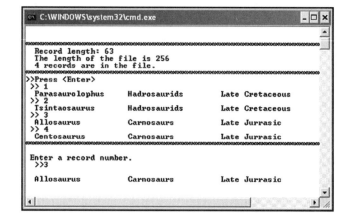

Conclusion

In this chapter, you have reviewed functions and operations relating to file IO. The functions you have reviewed include the `open()`, `close()`, `tell()`, `seek()`, `getc()`, and `read()` functions. These functions allow you to create files, write to files, and retrieve data from files. You have also reviewed the use of the `pack()` function, which allows you to create specifications for fixed-length records. Using fixed-length records, you have created a file containing data on dinosaurs and retrieved data from this file by typing the name of a specific record.

Operations relating to file IO form an important part of any programming language. Perl makes it easy to both read from and write to files, and if you employ data containers you can create using arrays or hashes, working with the IO functions allows you to go as far as you want with the processing of data.

15 } Regular Expressions

In this chapter, you review a number of points relating to regular expressions, which are an effective tool you can use to supplement your Perl programs. When you work with regular expressions, your activities fall into two main categories. One involves matching expressions. A basic matching function and the binding operator allow you to test strings for the existence of words and character patterns. The second activity falls under the heading of substitution. Again, as with matching, a substitution function allows you to search strings for given words or characters. In addition to searching, however, you can also replace characters. Along with matching and substitution, a third area of activity often becomes a part of the work you perform with regular expressions. This involves translation. Translation proves much more limited in scope than matching or substitution, but you can still find handy uses for it. Among the topics this chapter addresses are the following:

* How regular expressions work
* Using the binding operator
* Expressions for matching
* Expressions for substitution
* Expressions for translation
* Using special characters and other elements

General Notions

Regular expressions allow you to find, extract, and modify text that matches predefined patterns. As developed in Perl, programmers often call regular expressions *regexes*. Regexes often depend on the use of the *binding operator*, which consists of an equal sign preceded by a tilde (~=). You can also use a negative form of the binding operator, which consists of an exclamation mark or negation operator preceding a tilde (! ~).

The binding operator associates the regex with the string it operates on. When associated with a string, it returns either a modified string or a Boolean value from an expression that evaluates the string.

You employ regular expressions extensively on isolated strings, but it remains that regexes often enter the picture as you work in broader contexts, such as when you use the `split()` or other functions to translate strings into arrays or hashes or hashes and arrays into strings.

There are three fundamental aspects of regular expressions: matching, substituting, and translating. Technically, a translation does not constitute a regular expression, but it is traditional to discuss it as a regular expression.

Overview

Matching takes the following form:

```
$TestString ~= m/<Regular Expression>/
```

In this expression, `m/  /` constitutes the *matching function*. The matching function matches the string, `$TestString`, against the expression between the slashes. The binding operator effects the comparison. If the expression finds a match, it returns true.

Substitution takes the following form:

```
$TestString ~= s/TermToSub/TermReplaced/
```

In this expression, `s/  /  /` is the *substitution function*. The expression looks roughly the same as the matching function, but it results in a different outcome. The function operates on the string to the left of the binding operator according to the expression given on the right. Rather than returning a Boolean value, it modifies the string on the left. The function returns the string to itself, modified. The string you place in the a position is substituted for the item in the b position.

In addition to matching and substitution functions, Perl offers *translation functions*. Translation takes the following form:

```
$TestString ~= tr/A-Z/a-z/
```

This example is more specific than the previous examples. This is an actual example of the use of the translation function to search `$TestString` and change all the capital letters to lowercase letters.

Statement Formulations and Matches

The expression `m/  /` constitutes the basic form of the regular expression you use for matching. The expression matches a string in a string. Here is a starting string that you can use in the exercises in this and the next few sections. For the complete program, see Listing15_01.

```
$NL = "\n"
$TestString = 'It is winter and snow lies on the roof.';
print "String is '$TestString $NL";
```

Using the binding operator =~, you can explore whether a given term matches the literal string and the binding operator. When you use the binding operator to create regexes, it is common to set up a form of if selection statement that Perl accommodates and that often proves easier to use than the standard form. Consider, for example, testing whether snow matches a term in $TestString:

```
print("Found 'snow' $NL ") if($TestString =~ m/snow/);
```

The if statement follows the call to the print() function, and you do not use a block involving curly braces. Since the if selection statement evaluates the expression and finds the match, it returns true, and the print() function executes. Here is the output:

```
Found 'snow'
```

In standard form, the statement appears as follows:

```
if ($TestString =~ m/snow/){
    print("Found 'snow' $NL ");
}
```

Here is the output:

```
Found 'snow'
```

Identifiers

Regular expressions accommodate identifiers without problems. As shown in Listing15_01, consider a situation in which you assign a literal string to an identifier ($Pattern) to create a matching operation:

```
#Listing15_01
$NL = "\n"
$TestString = 'It is winter and snow lies on the roof.';
$Pattern = 'and';
print "Found literal string \'and\'"
    if ($TestString =~ m/$Pattern/);
```

The matching function evaluates the literal string the identifier stores and returns true. The return result is as follows:

```
Found literal string 'and'
```

To set up a negative test, your expression takes the following form. Note the change in the binding operator:

```
if($TestString !~ m/"nowhere"/){
    print("Did prove false. $NL");
}else{
    print("Did not prove false. $NL")
}
```

The expression test determines whether nowhere is part of the tested string. The match returns nowhere Did prove false. since the expression confirms the absence of nowhere.

You can insert a string into the regex without using quotation marks. You can also combine strings with an identifier through concatenation operations. Consider a situation in which you combine the identifier $Pattern (which is defined with snow) and the literal term snow. The concatenation is implicit. A space separates the two words:

```
$Pattern = "and";
if($TestString =~m/$Pattern snow /){
    print("$NL\'$Pattern snow\' found. $NL");
}
```

The output is as follows:

```
'and snow' found.
```

The line prints because the function reads all the arguments presented to it as one continuous string, regardless of whether it is a literal or defined in an identifier.

In the following lines, you create a string that generates a false evaluation. The operation involves the use of an identifier and a literal string.

```
if($TestString =~ m/$Pattern snowz/){
    print "Found variable and literal\n";
}else{
 print "Did not find variable and literal\n";
}
```

In this case, since you have corrupted the matching string by adding a z to snow, the result match does not occur, so you see the statement in the else block.

Match Variations

You can use a number of variations in the forms of matching you employ. The slashes are the most common delimiters, but you can change the delimiters in many ways. Consider, for example, a few basic alternatives involving matches:

```
if ($TestString =~ m!roof!){
    print("Match delimited with !! $NL");
}
if ($TestString =~ m{roof}){
    print("Match delimited with {} $NL");
}
```

In these two expressions, you substitute exclamation marks and curly braces for slashes. The output is as follows:

```
Match delimited with !!
Match delimited with {}
```

When you evaluate expressions that contain special characters, you must identify the special characters using escape sequences:

```
$EscapeTerms = "\"\@\$";
if ($EscapeTerms =~ m"\@"){
    print "Match with escape \@ $NL";
}
```

Exactness

When you create a pattern, you can match almost any series of letters. In other words, the letters can be separated by spaces, other letters, or words, but the match requires (in most cases) that you match the sequence.

```
if ($TestString =~ m/ on the r/){
    print "An exact pattern works. $NL";
 }
```

If you include spaces to indicate that a given word lacks completion, the match remains inexact. Consider the following matches:

```
if($TestString =~ m/ on the r /){
    print "Found on the r (space after r)$NL ";
}elsif($TestString =~ m/ on the r/){
```

```
        print " Found on the r (no space after r)$NL";
   }
```

The selection produces the following result:

```
    Found on the r (no space after r)
```

The first expression allows a space to occur after the r. The original expression contains no such space. The elsif expression evaluates true because it allows no extra space.

Along the same lines, as long as you do not imply that any spaces exist, you can match part of a word. Consider a match with a literal expression:

```
    if ("Snow fell every day in February" =~ m/bru/){
      print "Found part of \'February\'.$NL" ;
    }
```

You see the following result:

```
    Found part of 'February'.
```

Matching with Arrays or Lists

You can use the matching function in any number of ways with lists or arrays. Consider this use of the list function combined with the foreach selection statement:

```
foreach $Word ("howie", "howa", "howda", "howdy")
{
    if(m/howdy/){
        print("$NL $Word IS the right word.$NL ");
    }else{
        print("$NL $Word is not right.");
    }
}
```

The foreach statement traverses the list, retrieving each term to $Word. The selection statement then evaluates each term against howdy.

```
howie is not right.
howa is not right.
howda is not right.
howdy IS the right word.
```

Substituting

The substitution function allows you to replace a given expression with another expression. The most elementary approach to using the substitution function involves substituting one word for another. The basic substitution function replaces the first occurrence of a term you identify. As the example in Listing15_02 shows, you name the expression you want to replace in the first part of the expression. You name the replacement term in the second. Here is the example:

```
#Listing15_02
$TestStringA = "Say hello to the world.";
$ResultString = $TestStringA;
$ResultString =~ s/hello/your greetings/;
print("Result: $ResultString $NL");
```

The output appears as follows:

```
Result: Say your greetings to the world.
```

You can use the substitution statement as you traverse a string with a repetition control statement. As Example 2 in Listing15_02 shows, you can employ a repetition statement to traverse a string and sequentially alter words in the string.

```
$ResultString = "Tell me about the world as a world in the world";
$Count = 1;
do{
    print("$ResultString $NL");
    $ResultString =~ s/world/planet/;
    $Count++;
}while($Count < 5);
```

The output of Example 2 shows you how the substitution function alters a new term with each repetition of the block:

```
Tell me about the world as a world in the world
Tell me about the planet as a world in the world
Tell me about the planet as a planet in the world
Tell me about the planet as a planet in the planet
```

Global Changes

The g (global) argument provides an alternative to using a repetition control structure. It detects all instances of the terms you have designated for substitution and changes them. Example 3 in Listing15_02 explores both how to use global substitution and how to obtain the number of substitutions the function performs:

```
$ResultString = "Tell me about the world as a world in the world";
$NumOfMatches = $ResultString =~ s/world/planet/g; #use g for global
print("$NL Word occurred $NumOfMatches times");
print("$NL $ResultString");
```

As Example 3 shows, to obtain the number of substitutions the substitution function performs, you use the assignment operator (=) along with the binding operator (=~). You can see from this operation that the entire expression returns the number of substitutions.

Exactness

Successful substitution depends on providing the right criteria for substitutions. As with matching operations, substitution operations require that you be conscious of how you use white spaces.

```
$ResultString = "Tell me about the world as a world in the world";
$ResultString =~ s/w/W/g;
print("$NL Revised: $ResultString $NL");
$ResultString =~ s/a / A /g;
print("$NL Revised: $ResultString $NL");
$ResultString =~ (s/a/A/g);
print("$NL Revised: $ResultString $NL");
```

The results of the operation are as follows:

```
Revised: Tell me about the World as a World in the World
Revised: Tell me about the World as A World in the World
Revised: Tell me About the World As A World in the World
```

The substitution changes the first line because no spaces appear before or after the w argument that you insert into the substitution function. You succeed in making only one change in the second line because in the substitution function you insert white spaces before and after the w. Only one article occurs in the sentence, so the expression changes only one letter. With the third line, you see that the expression capitalizes all the As. In this instance, you have, as before, not included white space before or after the letter you want to alter.

Fundamental Ranges

You can select items for substitution using the range operator. The range operator consists of a set of open and close square brackets ([ ]). Inside the brackets, you can designate two or more characters you want to change. To separate the items, you employ commas. Example 5 of Listing15_02 examines making changes to a range of letters:

```
$ResultString =
"Tell me about the planet as a planet in the planet.";
# Change P and T to -
print("Use [] to set a range");
$ResultString =~ (s/[p,t]/-/g);
print("\nRevised: " . $ResultString);
```

The output appears as follows:

```
Revised: Tell me abou- -he -lane- as a -lane- in -he -lane-.
```

Numbers and Identifiers

You can use alpha numeric substitutions, and you can also define identifiers. Examples 6 and 7 in Listing15_02 shows substitutions involving both of these situations. In Example 6, you replace a letter (small "o") with a number (a zero):

```
$ResultString =~ (s/[o]/0/g);
```

The output reveals the numbers have replaced the letters:

```
Revised: Tell me ab0ut the w0rld as a w0rld in the w0rld.
```

Example 7 experiments with assigning a capital "W" to an identifier, $Replacement and then supplying the identifier as the second argument to the substitution function to replace occurrences of lowercase "w."

```
$Replacement = "W";
$ResultString =$SourceStringA;
$ResultString =~ (s/[w]/$Replacement/g);
```

The output shows that the substitution easily accommodated the identifier:

```
Revised: Tell me about the World as a World in the World.
```

Substitution and Matching with the System Variable

Perl programmers often make use of the system variable. The system variable consists of a dollar sign followed by an underscore ($_). Use of such shortcuts to programming make Perl a powerful programming language. At the same time, when you use the system variable, it can be hard for programmers who lack extensive experience with Perl to understand your code. In situations in which you can easily infer the flow of the program from the position and use of the system variable, using it can reduce the clutter of needless identifiers. Example 1 of Listing15_03 examines the use of the system variable to change world to place.

```
    $ResultString = "Tell me about the world as a world in the world";
    $_ = $ResultString;
$_ = s/world/place/g;
    print "$NL Revised: $_";
```

As the output indicates, the substitution of `place` for `world` occurs even though you see no binding operator. The set of statements depends on the reader's understanding that the system variable works along the lines of the argument array and return values of functions. It receives a value. The selection statement implicitly receives its target from the system variable. Because the substitution statement returns the transformed string, you are able to retrieve this value from the system variable to form the interpolated string for the `print()` function. Here is the output from the `print()` function:

```
    Revised: Tell me about the place as a place in the place.
```

Because the system variable allows you to capture the result of a previous statement, you can alter a `foreach` operation using the list function so that it appears in an abbreviated form:

```
foreach ( "canada", "mexico", "peru", "brazil"){
    print "Not " . ucfirst($_) . " $NL";
    if($_ =~ m/brazil/){
        print "But " . ucfirst($_) . " $NL";
    }
}
```

The result of Example 2 in Listing15_3 shows you that the repetition statement traverses the list using the system variable.

Translation

Translation offers you a way to effect operations that in many ways resemble those you accomplish using substitutions. When you translate a string, you can operate on existing characters. When you substitute, you can completely alter the length and content of a string. Listing15_04 provides a few examples that combine substitution and translation. In a few instances, such as reversing strings, you enjoy great advantages by using the translation function.

Reversing Strings

The translation function allows you to reorder the characters in strings according to a range and an order you provide in the translation argument. Example 1in Listing15_04 reverses a string of numbers.

```
$Numbers = "9876543210";
$Numbers =~ tr/[0-9]/ 9876543210 /;
```

The result of this operation is that you rearrange the order of the numbers based on the order of the integers in the range you create. The result of this operation is as follows:

```
Reversed (sub): 012345678
```

The translation function also acts on letters. You employ the same strategy you use with numbers. You set the order to the reverse of what you want to achieve.

```
$Letters = "gfedcba";
$Letters =~ tr/[a-g]/ gfedcba /;
```

The result is that the function reverses the order of the letters:

```
Reversed (sub): abcdefg
```

Translating a Range

As the use of the reversal capability of the translation function shows, you can work with a range when you deal with translations. As Example 2 in Listing15_04 reveals, if you set a range of letters for translation, you can selectively capitalize letters in a string:

```
$Letters = 'BNNDISIksisnBsB';
$Letters =~ tr/A-E/a-e/;
```

As a result of this translation, you see the following output:

```
Original: BNNDISIksisnBsB
Changed (sub): bNNdISIksisnbsb
```

The expression affects only the letters in the range from A to E, translating them into lowercase.

Substitution and Translation

When you combine substitution and translation, you can clean up data in a selective way. In Example 3 of Listing15_04, you begin with a set of alphanumeric codes. You then use substitution and translation to select from them and translate them into a different form.

```
#Create an array
@AlphaNumSet = ('b2', 'b2', 'c2', 'b3', 'c3');

    #Change b to ben using substitution
    #Add a space
    foreach(@AlphaNumSet){
```

```
            s/b/ben/;
    }
    #Change the lowercase to the uppercase for the range
    foreach(@AlphaNumSet){
        $_ =~ tr/[a-b]/[A-B]/;
    }
```

The results of the substitution and translation actions are as follows:

```
Original:
b2 b2 c2 b3 c3
Changed (sub):
ben 2 ben 2 c2 ben 3 c3
Changed (tr):
Ben 2 Ben 2 c2 Ben 3 c3
```

Substitution and Encryption

You can use the translation function to shift letters to numbers or numbers to letters to achieve a rudimentary form of encryption.

```
@AlphaNumSet = ('111', '222', '333', '444', '555');
#Create code for whatever reason
foreach(@AlphaNumSet){
  $_ =~ tr/[1-5]/[s-x]/;
}
```

In Listing15_04, when you print the original and the translated forms, you achieve the following results:

```
Original:
111 222 333 444 555
Changed (tr):
sss ttt uuu vvv www
```

Escape Sequences and Limiters

Regular expressions offer a number of special characters you can use to shape expressions in interesting, effective ways. Table 15.1 provides a discussion of characters you commonly use in regex expressions. Subsequent sections discuss these characters in detail.

Table 15.1 Regex Special Characters

Character	Discussion
{ }	Curly braces serve as a multiplier. You can indicate you are looking for two or more of a given character.
[ ]	Square braces establish classes. A class consists of subgroups of characters or expressions that you can search for.
^	You can use the caret to signal to exclude a character. You negate the character. At the start of a pattern, the caret indicates the start of a line.
$	You can use the dollar sign only at the end of a line of a pattern as a special character; otherwise, it is read as a scalar identifier. When you use it at the end of a line, it indicates that no more characters should follow in the pattern you are searching for.
,	You can use commas to establish a range. A comma between 2 and 6 signals the range from 2 to 6.
|	The separator (or pipe) serves to indicate options.
*	Use an asterisk to indicate "any character." It matches zero or more instances of characters, so you can indicate "Coronado" with "C*do."
+	Use the plus sign to indicate one or more instances of a given character.
?	Use the question mark to indicate zero or more occurrences of letters.
\	The escape character allows you to indicate that the character that follows it is to be read as a literal character rather than a metacharacter.
.	The period serves as a substitute for characters. It indicates one occurrence of any character. Use two periods to stand for a series of characters.

Listing15_05 provides examples of the use of special characters and escape sequences. As a starting observation, if you want to match special characters as literal characters, you must precede them with a backslash. Here is an example involving a plus sign:

```
print "found 6+2\n" if ("6+2=8" =~ /6+2/);
```

This expression results in no match because it attempts to match the plus sign (+) without compensating for the fact that the plus sign constitutes a special character. To correct the expression, you employ a backslash:

```
print "found 6+2\n" if ("6+2=8" =~ /6\+2/);
```

Now the expression prints because it recognizes the plus sign as a plus sign. Here is the output of the expression, which you find as Example 1 in Listing15_02:

```
found 6+2
```

ASCII Characters

ASCII characters often do not have representations on your keyboard. To deal with such characters, you can use hex values. If you use hex values, you prefix an "x" and a backslash to the number to designate it as a hex value. In the following example, you search for the word `lack` using the hex values of its letters:

```
print "lack (\\x6C\\x61\\x63\\x6B) found\n"
    if ("The cat is black" =~ m/\x6C\x61\x63\x6B/);
```

Here is the output of the expression, which is Example 2 in Listing15_05:

```
lack (\x6C\x61\x63\x6B) found
```

The Caret (^)

You use a caret to indicate that no character precedes the expression you are looking for. Since it often represents word boundaries, the caret is often referred to as an *anchor* or *word marker*. The following lines illustrates that if the caret precedes the characters for which you are searching and you are searching for a character that does not start a word or expression, the result is false.

```
# Example 3 The Caret (^)
if("Peace" =~ m/^ace/){
    print "ace found\n";
}else{
    print "ace not found \n";
}
```

Because the caret establishes that you are beginning a line, when you try to match the three characters preceded by others, the expression returns false. Here is the output of the expression, which is Example 3 in Listing15_05:

```
ace not found
```

The Dollar Sign ($)

You employ the dollar sign to indicate that no character follows the character or string you are searching for. The dollar sign is referred to as a *line marker* or *anchor*. The following lines render a true result because the e in Peace marks the end of a line.

```
if("Peace" =~ m/ace$/)
{
    print "ace found\n";
}else{
```

```
    print "ace not found \n";
}
```

Here is the output of the expression, which is Example 4 in Listing15_05:

```
ace found
```

Using a Sequence of Items

The list function when combined with a `foreach` repetition statement allows you to traverse a sequence of strings and effect any number of regex operations. For example, in Example 5 of Listing15_05, the match operation compares each item in a list. You use the `foreach` statement to traverse the list:

```
foreach ( "not here", "not there", "not yet", "but at last found"){
    print "Not yet.\n";
    print "last found\n" if m/last/;
}
```

The matching expression evaluates each term in the list to determine whether it corresponds to `last`. The terms it evaluates are enclosed in quotation marks. For this reason, you see four messages as the output of Example 5 in Listing15_05:

```
Not yet.
Not yet.
Not yet.
Not yet.
```

Use of the Braces (Multiplier) and the Period

You can employ curly braces to indicate a range, such as a number of characters to be skipped. A period indicates any character except the newline. In Example 6 of Listing15_05, you use the curly braces to indicate that two letters lie between the letters m and `t`. The period indicates that any characters are acceptable:

```
@WordList = qw(mast mart mort moot must muck mist mope);
print "\nTest for words.\n";
foreach $Word(@WordList){
    print "\nMatch 1: $Word" if($Word =~ m/m.{2}t/);
}
```

Given that the expression allows that the word can start with m, consist of any two characters, and then end in `t`, you see every word in the list except `muck` and `mope`. Here is the output of Example 6 in Listing15_05:

```
Test for words.
Match 1: mast
Match 1: mart
Match 1: mort
Match 1: moot
Match 1: must
Match 1: mist
```

The Comma (Multiplier) as a Range Setting

You can use the comma with the curly braces to multiply a given character. In Example 7 of Listing15_05, the words in the list starting with de and ending with te are all candidates. Between these characters, you allow an acceptable number of occurrences that match the pattern.

```
@WordList = qw(deracinate designate demote denigrate demonstrate);
print "\nTest for words.\n";
foreach $Word (@WordList){
    print "\nMatch 2: $Word" if ($Word =~ m/de.{2,6}te/);
}
```

In the set given, the expression finds only demonstrate because seven characters lie between the selected groups. This is the only word long enough to exceed the range. Here is the output of this part of Example 7 in Listing15_05:

```
Test for words.
Match 2: deracinate
Match 2: designate
Match 2: demote
Match 2: denigrate
```

If you drop the second number and the comma, you abolish the range, so the expression allows for only words that have two characters between the named characters. This reduces the field considerably. The only word that meets this narrow stipulation is demote. Here is the output of this part of Example 7 in Listing15_05:

```
Test for words.
Match 3: demote
```

The Asterisk (*)

When you employ an asterisk you achieve a result similar to using braces or periods. Asterisks indicate that you are allowing any number of characters. In the following example, a is followed by any number of characters, followed by a c, followed by any number of characters, followed by a d. The asterisk in this instance works as a multiplier.

```
$TestString = " a xxx c xxxxxxxx c xxx d";
print "\nMatched: $TestString \n" if ($TestString =~ m/a*c*d/);
```

Since the string contains three xs, eight xs, and then three xs, when you use the asterisk between the a and the c and the c and the d, you make it possible for the expression to return true. The asterisk following what is in effect the first c encompasses the second c along with the xs. Here is the output of Example 8 in Listing15_05:

```
Matched: a xxx c xxxxxxxx c xxx d
```

❈ Use of the wildcard (*) can lead to problems. Use the wildcard sparingly. As a general rule, use regular expressions as restrictively as possible, especially if you use patterns that involve multiple lines. Regular expressions select the largest match that they can. Consider the following string:

```
I came. I saw. I conquered.
```

If you use the expression m/ I .*\./ and expect to match I came., you get a surprise. You get instead the whole string:

```
I came. I saw. I conquered.
```

Given the choice of the shortest string that can match the pattern (I came.) and the longest (the whole thing), the regular expression returns the largest.

The Plus Sign (+)

You employ the plus sign following a given letter to indicate one or more instances of the letter. The following lines match any word that begins with any letter, has two os, and ends with a t:

```
@WordList = qw(moat soot root boat toot cold foot);
print "\nTest for words.\n";
foreach $Word (@WordList){
    print "\nMatch 4: $Word" if ($Word =~ m/[a-z]o+t/);
}
```

Only two words fail to meet the match. Here is the output of Example 9 in Listing15_05:

```
Test for words.
Match 4: soot
Match 4: root
```

```
Match 4: toot
Match 4: foot
```

The Question Mark (?)

You use the question mark to indicate zero or one previous letter. These characters can be optional. In Example 10 of Listing15_05, the question mark allows c to be optional. Given the optional c, the expression renders true.

```
@WordList = qw(snide ride hide confide inside);
foreach $Word (@WordList){
    print "\nMatch A : $Word" if ($Word=~ m/c?.*ide/);
    print "\nMatch B:  $Word" if ($Word=~ m/c.*ide/);
}
```

Option A allows all the words on the list because it makes the c optional. Option B allows only one word, confide, because it lacks the question mark to make the c optional. Here is the output of Example 10 in Listing15_05:

```
Match A : snide
Match A : ride
Match A : hide
Match A : confide
Match B: confide
Match A : inside
```

Ways of Extending Expressions

A number of operations you perform with regular expressions involve using brackets and other elements to create complex queries. Many of these operations involve the elements named in Table 15.1, but a few additional items come into play as you go. The following sections explore a number of different directions your regular expressions can take. Listing15_06 provides the program samples.

Using Character Classes—Square Braces []

You use character classes to indicate a range of characters or digits you want to match. You can employ several approaches to creating a class of characters. One is to use a group of characters between square brackets []. The following sequence of matches shows different ways of setting ranges for searches.

```
print "1 Match cat found\n" if ("The cat is black" =~ m/cat/);
print "2 Match cat found\n" if ("The cat is black" =~ m/[cba]at/);
print "3 Match cat found\n" if ("The cat is black" =~ m/[cba]a[tab]/);
```

Here is the output of Example 1 in Listing15_06:

```
1 Match cat found
2 Match cat found
3 Match cat found
```

A Series in a Class

From another angle, you can designate a series of character classes. In the following example, you search for any combination of lower- or uppercase letters that might be used to compose the word yes.

```
print "Match of yEs found $NL"
if ("yES" =~ m/[yY][eE][sS]/);
```

Here is the output of Example 2 in Listing15_06:

```
Match of yEs found
```

Use of Multiple Periods

You employ a period to represent a letter. You can use two or more periods to represent multiple letters. The characters allow for characters of any type. In Example 3 of Listing15_06, you use periods following p. In this way, you allow for any two characters of any type.

```
$TestString = "Colorado is complemented by its capitol".
              "building and Denver, a capital city much complimented.";
if ($TestString =~ m/(c[a-z]p..ol)/){
    print "\nFound: $1";
}
```

Here is the output of Example 3 in Listing15_06:

```
Found: capitol
```

Overcoming Case Problems

You can use a lowercase "i" following a match to indicate that the match is not to consider the case of the letters. Example 4 in Listing15_06 returns true even though the search term is lowercase and the searched term is uppercase;

```
print "5 Match YES found\n"
if ("YES" =~ m/yes/i);
```

Here is the output of Example 4 in Listing15_06:

```
Yes okay.
```

Searching for Numbers

You can search a term for a digit by using a range. When you create a range, you use two numbers to designate the range. You place a dash between them to indicate that you are establishing a range. In Example 5 in Listing15_06, you create an expression that establishes a range from 0 to 9.

```
print "Topic0 matched $NL"if ("topic0" =~ m/[0-9]/);
print "Topic7 matched $NL"if ("topic7" =~ m/[0-9]/);
print "Topic8 matched $NL"if ("topic8" =~ m/[0-9]/);
print "Topic08 matched $NL"if ("topic08" =~ m/0[1-9]/);
```

In the last example, the 0 precedes the brackets, so the search renders true only if a 0 precedes the digit searched for. Here is the output of Example 5 in Listing15_06:

```
Topic0 matched
Topic7 matched
Topic8 matched
Topic08 matched
```

Using the Caret for Negation

The caret (^) operator in class ranges has a special meaning. It works to negate the letter that immediately follows it. For example, ^c means "not c." Example 6 in Listing15_06 traverses an array and searches for any word that does not begin with a c.

```
@ThreeLetters = qw(mat cat bet sat rat fat net);
foreach $Word (@ThreeLetters){
print "Matched $Word \n"if ($Word =~ m/[^c]at/);
}
```

The expression matches all the terms that end in at except cat. Here is the output of Example 6 in Listing15_06:

```
Matched mat
Matched sat
Matched rat
Matched fat
```

Excluding a Range of Characters

As a variation on Example 6, assume that the search involves excluding a *range* of characters. The caret can be used to accomplish this operation. In Example 7 in Listing15_06, the match iterates through an array and excludes items that include numbers in the range from 2 to 4.

```
@NumWords = qw(rat1 rat2 rat3 rat4 rat5);
foreach $Word (@NumWords){
print "Match $Word found\n"if ($Word =~ m/rat[^2-4]/);
}
```

Here is the output of Example 7 in Listing15_06:

```
    Match rat1 found
    Match rat4 found
    Match rat5 found
```

Special Characters and Other Operations

You can employ a number of special characters to increase the power of regular expressions. Table 15.2 lists several of these characters. The sections that follow provide a few examples of their use.

Table 15.2   Special Characters

Character	Discussion
\d	This matches any digit.
\D	This matches any character that is not a digit.
\w	This matches a character of a word.
\W	This matches any non-word character.
\s	Any white space character – \t \n \f \r (space, tab, return, feed, return).
\S	Any non-white space character.
.	The period matches any character except a newline (\n).
\n	A newline character.
\t	A tab character.
\z	Matches at the end of a string.

Matching Digits

You can use the special character \d to match a digit. In the example that follows, a match occurs for any string that contains any digit. In other words, the match involves the evaluation of all the characters in the string.

```
$TestString = "This is 3 shades of gray.";
    if ($TestString =~ /\d/){
        print "$NL String has a number.";
    }
```

To extend the discussion a little, consider also that the use of \d equates to another, more involved expression: [0-9]+. In other words, you are checking for any digit in the given range. Here is the output of Example 1 in Listing15_07:

```
String has a number.
```

Matching Non-Digits

You can exclude digits using \D. The digits excluded are 0–9. In the following example, the expression culls the string for characters that are not numbers. This might be used if input of a numerical value were being verified:

```
$TestString = "345678";
if ($TestString =~ /\D/){
    #won't be true
print "$NL String is okay.";
}else{
    #so
    print "$NL String should not be a number.";
}
```

Here is the output of Example 2 in Listing15_07:

```
String should not be a number.
```

Using Groups ()

Group parentheses () allow you to establish alternative patterns to use in your matches. The statement created is similar to an OR statement:

```
$TestString = "This is with shades of gray.";

if ($TestString =~ m/(alive|with) shades/)
{
    print"$NL Match of (alive | with) shades";
}
```

Here is the output of Example 3 in Listing15_07:

```
Match of (alive | with) shades
```

Sentences Containing Specific Terms

An array of strings can be searched for sentences that contain given words. This code sample prints two of the sentences:

```
$TestArray[0] = "The earth is alive with care.";
$TestArray[1] = "The earth is teeming with care.";
$TestArray[2] = "The earth is pulsating with care.";


for($iv = 0; $iv < 3; $iv++){
  if($TestArray[$iv] =~ m/(alive|pulsating)/){
    print "$NL Found $TestArray[$iv] $NL";
  }
}
```

Here is the output of Example 4 in Listing15_07:

```
Found The earth is alive with care.
Found The earth is pulsating with care.
```

Note that with the use of the group, the match is returned as soon as the first match occurs. In the following, the match is with c, not with the whole word:

```
$Word = "cats";
print "$NL $Word (cat) found." if($Word =~ m/(c|ca|cat|cats)/);
```

Here is the output of Example 5 in Listing15_07:

```
cats (cat) found.
```

Conclusion

This chapter provided what should be regarded as an introduction to regular expressions. Since every operating system and many programming languages (Java, JavaScript, and C#, to name a few) offer some form of regular expression capability, your work with Perl regular expressions can prove useful regardless of what direction you take as a programmer. Likewise, regular expressions prove essential to working with Unix/Linux systems.

Generally, this chapter has emphasized the basics of working with matching and substitution as they might be applied to standard programming activities restricted to making selection statements or controlling repetition statements. You can easily extend this beginning in many directions, including the creation of files that help you work with file IO.

Index

A

abs() function, 102
abstraction, functions, 297–300
accumulators, 170–173
ActivePerl interpreter, 4
ActiveState, 6–7, 11–14
Alcott, Amos, 235
anonymous arrays, 352–355
anonymous hashes, 356–358
Apache Server, 3, 6–7
Apache Software Foundation, 6
applications, control structures, 255–296
    blocks, 282–285
    continue operator, 257, 285–288
    control values, 257
    do…until statements, 256, 277–280
    do…while statements, 256, 273–275
    for statements, 257–260
    foreach statements, 280–282
    handlers, 269
    incremental expressions, 257
    infinite loops, 262–270
    last operator, 257, 260–261, 282–288
    limits, 257
    loop controls, 257, 262–270
    next statements, 257, 285–288
    redo operator, 257, 282–285
    repetition, 255–260
    system() function, 268
    until statements, 256, 275–277
    while statements, 256, 270–273, 285–296
argument arrays, 309–313
arguments, functions, 301
    accepting, 309–313
    none, 303–306
arithmetic operators, 101
arrays, 8–9, 127–178
    adding elements, 128–131
    accessing elements, 138–139
    anonymous, 352–355
    concatenation, 135–137
    data containers, 153–178
      accumulators, 170–173
      adding elements, 166–168
      dynamic arrays, 168–169
      extracting elements, 160–162
      inserting elements, 162–164
      joining elements, 159–160
      numbers, sorting, 157
      queues, 174–178
      removing elements, 164–166
      reverse elements, 153–154
      shuttles, 169–170
      sorting elements, 155–156
      splitting strings, 158–159
      stacks, 169–173
    implicit assignment, 140
    initialization problems, 132–135
    iteration, 135–137
    returning, 324–328
    passing, 313–316, 347–349
    populating, 143–144
    qw() function, 143–144
    slicing, 141–142
    splicing, 144–152
      basic, 144–146
      end elements, removing, 149–150
      insertions, 150–152
      ranges, 146–148
      ranges, removing, 148–149
      selected set, 146–148
    swapping, 142–143
    values, assigning, 129–130
    values, printing, 130–131
    values, retrieving, 131
ASCII conversions, 119–121
ASCII text, 5
ASCII characters, 408
assignment operator, 40, 102
associative containers, 179
associativity, 100–101
asterisk (*), 410–411
at (@) sign, 8
atan2() function, 102
Auden, W. H., 93
augmentation operators, 102

B

basics, 1–9
    community, 4–5
    complexity, 5
    derivations, 5–6
    identifiers, 8–9
    power, 2–4

binding operator, 395
blocks, 55–56, 231
    control structures, 282–285
    functions, 301
    print functions, 91–93
Boolean operators, 237–239
braces, 409–410
built-in functions, 102–103

C
call and return operations, 59–62
calling functions, 307
caret (^), 408, 414
case of strings, 62–64
CGI programs, 3
characters, eliminating, 68–72
chomp() function, 68–71
Choose Setup Option dialog, 15
chop() function, 71–72
Christiansen, Tom, 9
code composition, scalars, 32–35
comma, 410
command line interactions, 72–74
command prompt, 16
community, 4–5
complexity, 5
concatenation, arrays, 135–137
concatenation and printing, scalars, 45–47
conditional statements, 229
containers, 168
ConTEXT, 21
contextually typed language, 8
continue operator, 257, 285–288
control statements, 8, 229
control structures, 227–296
    applications, 255–296
        blocks, 282–285
        continue operator, 257, 285–288
        control values, 257
        do…until statements, 256, 277–280
        do…while statements, 256, 273–275
        for statements, 257–260
        foreach statements, 280–282
        handlers, 269
        incremental expressions, 257
        infinite loops, 262–270
        last operator, 257, 260–261, 282–288
        limits, 257
        loop controls, 257, 262–270
        next statements, 257, 285–288
        redo operator, 257, 282–285

        repetition, 255–260
        system() function, 268
        until statements, 256, 275–277
        while statements, 256, 270–273, 285–296
    Boolean operators, 237–239
    conditional statements, 229
    control statements, 229
    expressions, 227–229
    logical operators, 237–239
    program flow, 229–230
    relational operators, 237–239
    repetition, 230
    selection, 230, 240–252
        if statements, 240–244
        if…else statements, 246–248
        if…elsif…else statements, 248–252
        unless statements, 244–246
    sequence, 229–237
        functional ordering, 233–235
        goto operator, 231–233
        incremental operations, 235–237
    statements, 227–229
control values, 257
conversion specifiers, 110–115
cos() function, 103
CPAN, 7
Crane, Hart, 93
currency sign ($), 39

D
data categories, 5, 8–9, 39
data containers, 153–178
    accumulators, 170–173
    adding elements, 166–168
    dynamic arrays, 168–169
    extracting elements, 160–162
    inserting elements, 162–164
    joining elements, 159–160
    numbers, sorting, 157
    queues, 174–178
    references, 352–358
    removing elements, 164–166
    reverse elements, 153–154
    shuttles, 169–170
    sorting elements, 155–156
    splitting strings, 158–159
    stacks, 169–173
data streams, 364
data structures, 168
decomposition, functions, 297–300
defined() function, 97–100, 208–211
defining functions, 307

Deitel, H. M., 9
Deitel, P. J., 9
delete() function, 218–220
delimiters, 86
dependencies, 299
dereferencing references, 338–339
derivations, 5–6
diamond operator, 8, 364
documentation, 8
dollar sign ($), 8, 39–40, 408–409
do...until statements, 256, 277–280
do...while statements, 256, 273–275
downloading program, 11–14
dynamic arrays, 168–169
DzSoft, 7, 16, 20–29, 73–74
    DOS window, 73–74
    first view, 25–26
    HTML output, 26–27
    installing, 22–25
    saving files, 28
    text output, 27–29

E
each() function, 187, 200–202
Eclipse, 21
editors, 7, 20–29
    code composition, 32–34
    ConTEXT, 21
    DzSoft Perl, 20–29
        first view, 25–26
        HTML output, 26–27
        installing, 22–25
        saving files, 28
        text output, 27–29
    Eclipse, 21
    Komodo, 20–21
    Notepad, 20
    vi, 20
efficiency measures, functions, 313–316
elements
    accessing, 138–139
    adding 128–131, 166–168
    deleting, 218–220
    extracting, 160–162
    inserting, 162–164
    joining, 159–160
    removing, 164–166
    reverse, 153–154
    sorting, 155–156
elsif statement, 240
encapsulation, 299

eq operator, 49
equality operators, 102
equal sign (=), 40
escape sequences, 406–407
evaluating relationships, 49–50
exists() function, 205–208
exp() function, 103
expressions, control structures, 227–229
extending regular expressions, 412–415
    case problems, 413–414
    character classes, 412–413
    negation, 414
    numbers, searching, 414
    periods, 413
    series, classes, 413

F
File Download dialog, 13
file handle operator, 364
file type associations, 20
File Types tab, 20
files, 18–20
first-time installation, 14–15
fixed-length records, 390–392
flags, printing, 114
flashing files, 19–20
floating decimals, 40
formatting data, 369–372
formatting scalars, 95–126
    ASCII conversions, 119–121
    built-in functions, numbers, 102–103
    conversion specifiers, 110–115
    defined() function, 97–100
    flags for printing, 114
    int() function, 105–107
    math functions, 102–103
    numbers, 95–97
    numerical operators, 101–102
    operations, numbers, 100–102
    operation variations, 117–121
    precision, 113–115
    print() function, 103–105
    printf() function, 109–117
    rand() function, 105–107
    random numbers and integers, 105–107
    rational operations, 107–109
    sprint() function, 121–126
    strings and space, conversion, 113
    tables, 115–117, 122–126
    undefined() function, 97–100
for statements, 257–260

foreach statements, 280–282
function blocks, 307
functions, 297–329
  abstraction, 297–300
  argument arrays, 309–313
  arguments, accepting, 309–313
  arguments, none, 303–306
  arrays, returning, 324–328
  arrays, passing, 313–316
  calling, 307
  decomposition, 297–300
  defining, 307
  efficiency measures, 313–316
  hashes, passing, 316–318
  hashes, returning, 324–328
  input/output, 374–389
    close() function, 364–368, 374
    die() function, 372–374
    eof() function, 374
    flock() function, 374
    getc() function, 374, 378–382
    open(), 364–368, 374–375
    pack() function, 374, 386–389
    print() function, 364–368, 374
    read() function, 374, 383–385
    seek() function, 374, 378–382
    tell() function, 374–378
    truncate() function, 374
    warn() function, 372–373, 375
  organization, programs, 302–303
  print() function, 309
  references, 349–352
  return keyword, 319–324
  subroutines, 301
  system() function, 308
  values, returning, 319–324
  viewMenu() function, 308
  viewOpening() function, 307
fun programming, 1–2

G
global arguments, 401–402
goto operator, 231
grouping operators, 101
groups and lists, 8

H
handles, 8–9, 364
handlers, 269
hashes, 8–9, 179–203
  accessing, 185–188, 342–344

  anonymous, 356–358
  associative containers, 179
  converting to strings, 220–222
  converting strings, 216–218
  defined() function, 208–211
  delete() function, 218–220
  each() function, 187, 200–202
  exists() function, 205–208
  identifying, 181–182
  implicit context, 181–182
  initializing, 183–185
  join() function, 220–222
  key() function, 187–190
  keys() function, 211–213
  key-value pairs, 179, 211–213
  pop() function, 192–195
  passing, 316–318, 344–346
  returning, 324–328
  reverse() function, 195–198, 223–225
  scalar context, 181–182
  scalar() function, 211–213
  sequential containers, 179
  shift() function, 198–200
  slicing, 213–216
  split() function, 216–218
  sprintf() function, 220–222
  values() function, 187, 190–192
hex() function, 103
hidden characters/strings, 65–67

I
identifiers, 8–9, 40, 98, 397–398, 403
if statements, 49–50, 240
if ... else statements, 240
if ... elsif ... else statement, 240
implicit assignment, arrays, 140
implicit context, hashes, 181–182
incremental approach, 33
incremental expressions, 257
increment operations, 53
increment operator (++), 53
index() function, 74–79
indexes, 74–79, 127
  algorithm implementation, 76–77
  searching algorithms, 75–77
  searching, from end, 78–79
indirect references, 334
infinite loops, 262–270
initialization problems, arrays, 132–135
input/output, 363–393
  data streams, 364

diamond operator, 364
file handle operator, 364
fixed-length records, 390–392
formatting data, 369–372
functions, 374–389
  close() function, 364–368, 374
  die() function, 372–374
  eof() function, 374
  flock() function, 374
  getc() function, 374, 378–382
  open(), 364–368, 374–375
  pack() function, 374, 386–389
  print() function, 364–368, 374
  read() function, 374, 383–385
  seek() function, 374, 378–382
  tell() function, 374–378
  truncate() function, 374
  warn() function, 372–373, 375
  handles, 364
  interactions, 364
  reading data, 368–373
  streams, 363–364
installing program, 11–20
  downloading, 11–14
  files, 18–20
  file type associations, 20
  first-time installation, 14–15
  flashing files, 19–20
  registering, 12–13
  testing, 16
int() function, 103, 105–107
integers, 40
interactions, 364
interpolated strings, 32, 40, 44–45
iteration, arrays, 135–137
iterative approach, 33

J
Java, 4
join() function, 86–91, 159–160, 220–222, 233–235
joining strings, 84–91
  concatenation, manual, 85–86
  join() function, concatenation, 86–87
  join() function, notification, 87–89
  operations, varrying, 89–91

K
keys() function, 187–190, 211–213, 342–344
key-value pairs, 179, 211–213
Komodo, 20–21

L
last operator, 257, 260–261, 282–288
lc() function, 63–64
lcfirst() function, 62–63
length() function, 64–67
limiters, 406–407
limits, 257
list() function, 409
list functions, 128
literal strings, 40, 44–45
log() function, 103
logical operators, 237–239
loop controls, 257, 262–270

M
matches, 396–400
  arrays, 400
  digits, 415–416
  exactness, 399–400
  functions, 396
  group parentheses, 416
  lists, 400–401
  non-digits, 416
  words, 417
math functions, 102–103
McPhie, D. C., 9
Mendeleev, Dmitri, 205
Miller, Perry, 253
modules, 2–4
multiplication operator (×), 47–48
My SQL, 3, 7

N
Newlands, John, 205
next statements, 257, 285–288
Nieto, T. R., 9
Notepad, 18–20
numbers, formatting, 95–97
  built-in functions, 102–103
  math functions, 102–103
  numerical operators, 101–102
  operations, 100–102
  random numbers and integers, 105–107
  regular expressions, 403
numbers, sorting, 157
numerical operators, 101–102

O

oct() function, 103
offsets, 74–75
operator precedence, 230
operators, 48
ord() function, 103
O'Reilly, 6–7
organization, program, 301–303

P

parentheses, 231
percent sign, 8
perl.org web site, 6–7
Pearl Package Manager (PPM), 15
period (.), 45, 409–410
plus sign (+), 411–412
pop() function, 164–166, 169, 192–195
populating arrays, 143–144
portability, 4
pound sign (#), 34–35
power, 2–4
precedence, 100–101
precision, formatting, 113–115
Prevalence, 7
print() function, scalars, 31–34, 37, 44–45, 60,
        103–105, 187, 309
print functions, 59–93
    blocks, 91–93
    call and return operations, 59–62
    case of strings, 62–64
    command line interactions, 72–74
    eliminating characters, 68–72
    extracting strings, 79–84
        simplifying, 82–84
        substr() function, 79–82
    hidden characters/strings, 65–67
    indexes, 74–79
        algorithm implementation, 76–77
        searching algorithms, 75–77
        searching, from end, 78–79
    joining strings, 84–91
        concatenation, manual, 85–86
        join() function, concatenation, 86–87
        join() function, notification, 87–89
        operations, varrying, 89–91
    length of strings, 64–65
    replacing strings, 79–84
printf() function, 109–117, 187
program flow, 229–230
programming syntax, scalars, 34–39
    comments, 34–35

escape sequences, 37–39
interpreter errors, 36
multiple statements, single lines, 36–37
statements, 35–36
program organization, 301
Prompt window, customizing, 17
push() function, 166–169, 174

Q

q() and qq() functions, 54–55
question mark (?), 412
queues, 168, 174–178
qw() function, 143–144

R

rand() function, 103, 105–107
random numbers and integers, 105–107
ranges, 402–403, 405, 415
range setting, 410
rational operations, 107–109
reading data, 368–373
redo operator, 257, 282–285
references, 9, 331–363
    anonymous arrays, 352–355
    anonymous hashes, 356–358
    arrays, passing, 347–349
    creating, 334–336
    data containers, 352–358
    dereferencing, 338–339
    functions, 349–352
    hash keys, accessing, 342–344
    hashes, passing, 344–346
    indirect, 334
    keys() function, 342–344
    ref() function, 336–337
    returning, 358–361
    symbolic, 334
    values, accessing, 340–344
ref() function, 336–337
regexes, *see* regular expressions.
registering program, 12–13
regular expressions, 9, 395–417
    ASCII characters, 408
    asterisk (*), 410–411
    binding operator, 395
    braces, 409–410
    caret (^), 408, 414
    comma, 410
    dollar sign ($), 408–409
    escape sequences, 406–407

extending, 412–415
  case problems, 413–414
  character classes, 412–413
  negation, 414
  numbers, searching, 414
  periods, 413
  series, classes, 413
global arguments, 401–402
identifiers, 397–398, 403
limiters, 406–407
list() function, 409
matches, 396–400
  arrays, 400
  digits, 415–416
  exactness, 399–400
  functions, 396
  group parentheses, 416
  lists, 400–401
  non-digits, 416
  words, 417
numbers, 403
period (.), 409–410
plus sign (+), 411–412
question mark (?), 412
ranges, 402–403, 405, 415
range setting, 410
sequences, 409
special characters, 407, 415
substitution functions, 396, 401–402
  encryption, 406
  translation, 405–406
system variables, 403–404
translation functions, 396, 404–407
  ranges, 405
  reversing strings, 404–405
  substitution, 405–406
wildcards, 411
relational operators, 48–55, 101, 237–239
repetition, control structures, 230, 255–260
returning references, 358–361
return keyword, 301, 319–324
reverse() function, 153–154, 195–198, 223–225
rindex() function, 78–79
Run Installation Program dialog, 14

S
scalar context, hashes, 181–182
scalar() function, 211–213
scalar identifiers, 40, 45
scalars, 8–9, 31–56, 95–126
  code composition, 32–35
  concatenation and printing, 45–47

formatting, 95–126
  ASCII conversions, 119–121
  built-in functions, numbers, 102–103
  conversion specifiers, 110–115
  defined() function, 97–100
  flags for printing, 114
  int() function, 105–107
  math functions, 102–103
  numbers, 95–97
  numerical operators, 101–102
  operations, numbers, 100–102
  operation variations, 117–121
  precision, 113–115
  print() function, 103–105
  printf() function, 109–117
  rand() function, 105–107
  random numbers and integers, 105–107
  rational operations, 107–109
  sprint() function, 121–126
  strings and space, conversion, 113
  tables, 115–117, 122–126
  undefined() function, 97–100
print() function, 31–34, 37, 44–45
programming syntax, 34–39
  comments, 34–35
  escape sequences, 37–39
  interpreter errors, 36
  multiple statements, single lines, 36–37
  statements, 35–36
stored and printed, 43–44
strings, 39–56
  blocks, 55–56
  creating, 40–43
  eq operator, 49
  evaluating relationships, 49–50
  if statements, 49–50
  increment operations, 53
  multiplication operator, 47–48
  operators, 48
  q() and qq() functions, 54–55
  relational operators, 48–55
  scalar variables, 41–43
  selection and equality, 49–50
  testing, 50–53
scalar variables, 41–43
Schwartz, Randal L., 9
selection, control structures, 230, 240–252
  if statements, 240–244
  if...else statements, 246–248
  if...elsif...else statements, 248–252
  unless statements, 244–246
semicolon (;), 35–36, 230

sequences, control structures, 229–237, 409
functional ordering, 233–235
goto operator, 231–233
incremental operations, 235–237
sequential containers, 179
shift() function, 160–162, 174, 198–200
shuttles, 169–170
sin() function, 103
slicing arrays, 141–142
slicing hashes, 213–216
sort() function, 155–157
special characters, regular expressions, 407, 415
specifiers, 8
splicing arrays, 144–152
basic, 144–146
end elements, removing, 149–150
insertions, 150–152
ranges, 146–148
ranges, removing, 148–149
selected set, 146–148
split() function, 158–159, 216–218, 235–237
sprint() function, 121–126, 220–222
sqr() function, 103
square() function, 103
srand() function, 103
stacks, 168–173
accumulators, 170–173
shuttles, controlling, 169–170
statements, control structures, 32, 227–229
storing and printing, scalars, 43–44
streams, input/output, 363–364
strings
converting hashes to, 220–222
converting to hashes, 216–218
extracting, 79–84
simplifying, 82–84
substr() function, 79–82
length, 64–65
replacing, 79–84
scalars, 39–56
blocks, 55–56
creating, 40–43
eq operator, 49
evaluating relationships, 49–50
if statements, 49–50
increment operations, 53
multiplication operator, 47–48
operators, 48
q() and qq() functions, 54–55
relational operators, 48–55
scalar variables, 41–43
selection and equality, 49–50

testing, 50–53
space conversion, 113
splitting, 158–159
sub keywords, 301
subroutines, 231, 297, 301
substitution functions, 396, 401–402
encryption, 406
translation, 405–406
swapping arrays, 142–143
symbolic references, 334
system() function, 268, 308
system variables, 403–404

T
tables, 115–117, 122–126
testing program, 16
text specifiers, see specifiers.
Thoreau, Henry David, 253
time() function, 103
Torkington, Nathan, 9
translation functions, 396, 404–407
ranges, 405
reversing strings, 404–405
substitution, 405–406
type identifiers, 40
type promotion, 107–109

U
uc() function, 62–64
ucfirst() function, 62–63
unary increment operator, 53
unary operators, 101
undefined() function, 97–100
unless statement, 241
unshift() function, 162–164
until statements, 256, 275–277

V
values, arrays
accessing, 340–344
assigning, 129–130
printing, 130–131
returning, 319–324
retrieving, 131
values() function, 187, 190–192
viewMenu() function, 308
viewOpening() function, 307
vi, 20

W–X
Wall, Larry, 1, 6–7, 9
while statements, 256, 270–273
  continue operator, 285–288
  each() function, 294–296
  selection statements, 288–294

wildcards, 411
Wordsworth, William, 93

Y–Z
Yeats, W. B., 93